GUSTAV

KLIMT

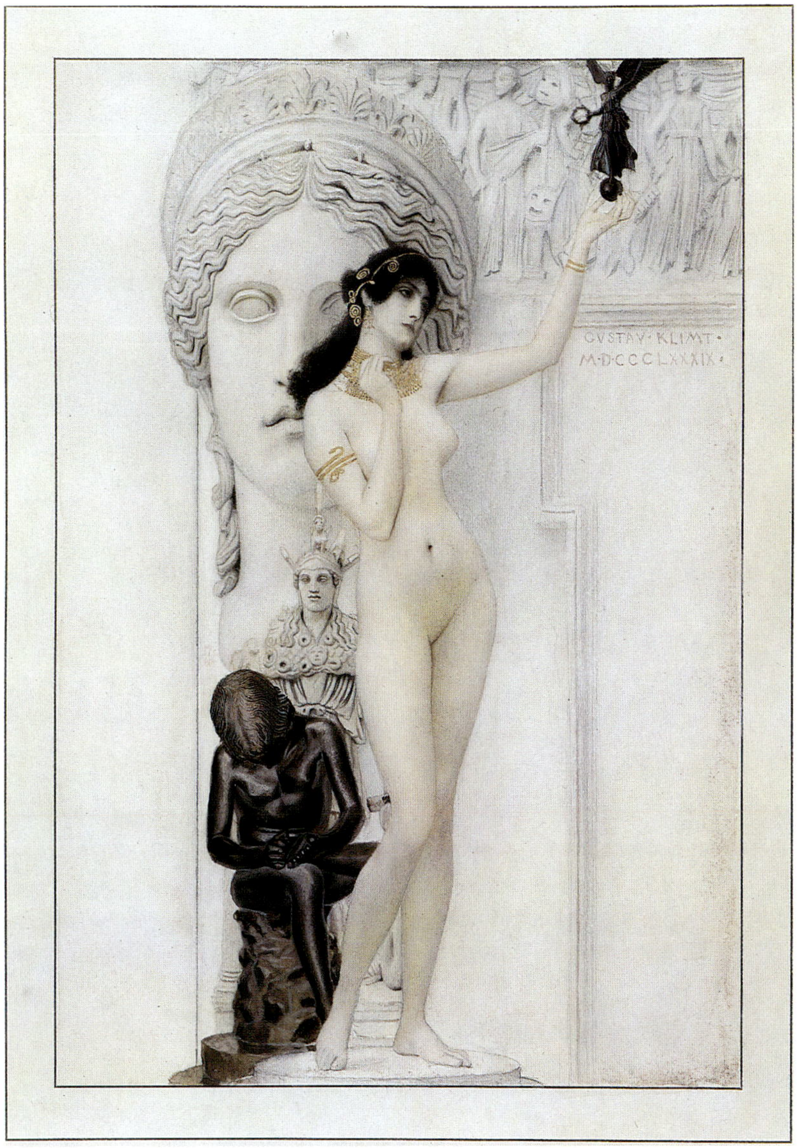

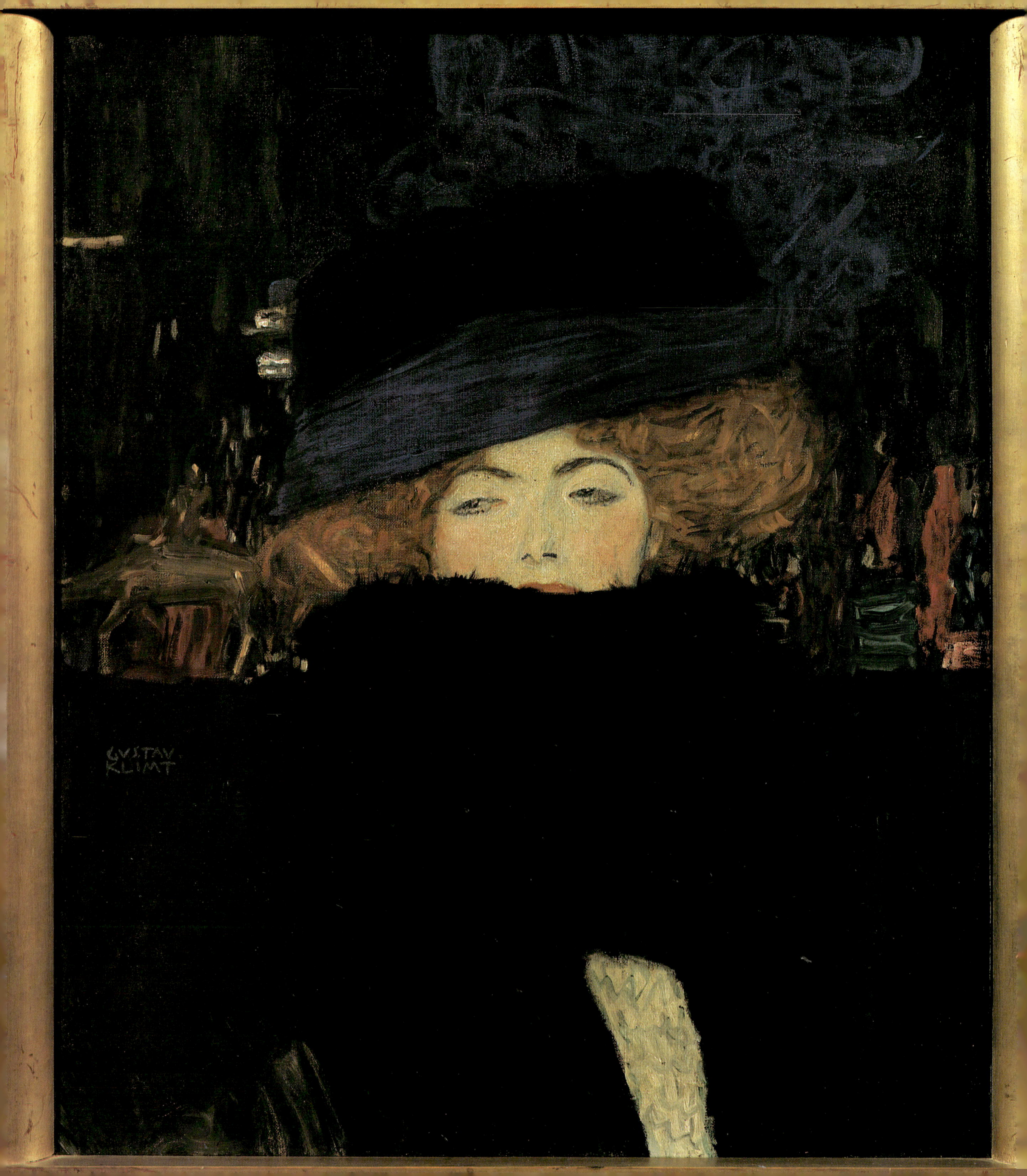
GUSTAV
KLIMT

KLIMT

Life and Work

by Susanna Partsch

with 96 colour plates and
35 drawings in black-and-white

Grange
BOOKS

Reproductions on pages 1 and 2:

1 Allegory of Sculpture, 1889
Mixed media, water colour with gold
on pencil drawing, 25.2 × 17.8

Vienna City Museums

2 Woman with Hat and Feather Boa, 1909
Oil on canvas, 69 × 55 cm

Austrian Gallery, Vienna

Published in 1999 by Grange Books
An Imprint of Grange Books Plc
The Grange
Kingsnorth Industrial Estate, Hoo,
Nr. Rochester, Kent ME3 9ND

ISBN-1840133139
Printed an bound by Graspo
Reprographics by Fotolitho Longo AG, Frangart
Typeset by Satz & Repro Grieb, Munich

Translated by Charity Scott Stokes

Contents

7 Vienna at the turn of the century
A 'total' work of art

8 The structure of Viennese society
11 The Emperor's Silver Wedding Jubilee and the Makart pageant
14 The Ring, and Vienna as a 'total' work of art
17 Cultural life in Vienna

24 Jugendstil – art nouveau –
an international movement

24 Antecedents
25 England on the way to 'Arts and Crafts'
28 The development of French painting from Impressionism
to art nouveau
36 One unifying concept in 'Jugendstil' painting – symbolism
37 The 'total' work of art

43 Klimt's early years

43 Background and training
48 Hans Makart – Vienna's prince of painters
50 The 'Company of Artists'
61 The Burg Theatre ceilings
72 The murals in the stairway of the Art History Museum
79 From the Ring to the Secession
82 The Palais Dumba

86 Founder-member and president of the
'Vienna Secession'

86 Conflict among artists
94 The 'heroic years' of the Secession
97 Ver Sacrum
105 The departure of the artists of the new style

108 Klimt offends public taste

108 The ceiling pictures in the great hall of the new university
108 Chronology of events
128 Designs and completed paintings – a comparison

141 The Beethoven Frieze

142 The XIVth exhibition of the Vienna Secession
Max Klinger's Beethoven
151 Gustav Klimt's Frieze

163 Emilie Flöge – couturier and companion

163 The Flöge Sisters' Fashion House
183 Gustav Klimt and Emilie Flöge

193 The Vienna Workshops

193 From foundation to liquidation
204 Commissions and challenges
208 The Art Exhibition of 1908
218 The Palais Stoclet and Gustav Klimt's Frieze

229 'Woman'

230 The Portraits
246 The 'Femme fatale'
254 'Hope I'
258 The drawings

267 'The Kiss' – theme and variations

279 Landscape painter

291 Draughtsman

299 Epilogue – Death and Tribute

309 Appendix

Vienna at the turn of the century – a 'total' work of art

Gustav Klimt died on 6 February 1918. He did not see the end of the First World War, a turning-point for the whole of Europe. Great European monarchies were replaced by republics, while the Russian revolution gave rise to the world's first communist state. The end of the Austro-Hungarian Empire meant the end of a central European state which had comprised many nations. The Emperor had died in 1916 after a reign of 68 years. When Klimt was born in Vienna in 1862 Emperor Franz Joseph I had already been head of state for 14 years.

As a child Klimt experienced the great expansion of Vienna, centre and capital of the dual empire. In 1857 the city walls were pulled down to be replaced by the Ring. This enormous project, with residences and public buildings on either side, was begun the next year and continued for decades. It was to be a key element in the concept of Vienna as 'a total work of art'. A miraculous harvest, all the more significant because crops failed in the rest of Europe, led to peak prosperity in 1867. The building of the Ring made rapid progress, and Vienna chose to host the World Exhibition of 1873. This decision was taken in 1870 and it intensified the fever of building and speculation. People counted on a new flow of riches from the many visitors to the exhibition, but by the time of the opening ceremony on 1 May 1873 it was already clear that the optimistic financial forecasts were not going to be fulfilled. The overpriced hotels acted rather as a deterrent to visitors. A week later came the great crash, recorded as 'Black Friday'. A cholera epidemic and a poor harvest caused the situation to deteriorate even further. The resulting stagnation in the economy increased the gap between Vienna and other European centres of industry, while at the same time creating favourable conditions for the setting up of new industries in the 1880s.

The structure of Viennese society

Vienna, at the turn of the century, calls to mind the coffee houses, the men of letters, the artists, but also the artisans, the shoemakers' apprentices and laundry-maids. The 'other Vienna' excluded from these idylls is less known. Since the end of the eighteenth century industries had been moved from the inner city out to what had been romantic market towns on the outskirts, for fear of the growing proletariat. These places rapidly became large industrial centres, in which the workers, who had often fled from the countryside, led wretched lives. New housing was put up in haste, and there was an enormous influx of unskilled labour from all parts of the empire. High rents and low wages meant that a family of ten might have to live in just one room. Shift workers' beds were often let two or three times over, so that they were in use all round the clock. Life in these barracks for the exploited led to a high rate of child mortality, and tuberculosis came to be known as 'the Viennese illness'. The upper and middle classes were not safe from it, but they at least had the means to procure help, and often a cure. A famous example of this is the later heir to the throne, Franz Ferdinand, who devoted years to his delicate health and even travelled to Egypt for the sake of the dry desert air, which did indeed cure him.

Nothing was done officially to combat the social misery in the suburbs. The church made some attempt to help, but such efforts only took the form of dispensing charity. The citizen of Vienna could satisfy his conscience on the subject of the poor by making a donation or taking part in some charitable event, but such activities glossed over the wretchedness without changing anything. People were not willing to see the need to improve the living conditions of the workers. Nobody except the social democrats was willing to tackle the root of the problem, and the social democrats did not have the necessary power or funds. They were, however, at least in a position to raise the political awareness of the workers, which expressed itself in the increasingly large rallies organised on May 1st from 1890 onwards, and finally resulted, after World War I, in 'Red Vienna'.

Since the dismantling of the city walls Vienna had been split up into nine districts, but the outlying areas were still cut off from the centre by a line dividing the rich from the poor; at every entrance to the city a so-called 'victuals tax' was levied on all food and drink that was brought in. This levy continued until 1899. Three years later the suburbs became part of the city and Vienna's population rose to more than a million overnight.

At the turn of the century there were distinct social classes in Vienna; some people lived in affluence, particularly apparent on the Ring, some in extreme poverty, which was consistently ignored by the more privileged.

The imperial residence was the centre of the city and the state, where Emperor Franz Joseph I, a legend in his own time, went about his duty. He worked for sixteen hours a day, receiving 300–400 documents, granting audiences and fulfilling a representative function. Strict attention to routine duties was all-important to this monarch who was entirely lacking in imagination, and his officials were of the same mind. The writer Joseph Roth (1894–1939) gives a masterly description of this lack of imagination and blind fulfilment of obligations and the resulting problems between father and son in his novel 'Radetzky March' (1932); the Radetzky family was linked by chance to the imperial house.

The emperor was surrounded by aristocrats, some wealthy, some impoverished, whose lives were devoted above all to pleasure. There were of course notable exceptions, people who did not spend their money on luxuries and extravagant entertaining, but rather on humanitarian projects or in support of the arts, but they were few compared with those whose way of life provided scandal for gossip. One archduke appeared stark naked in the Sacher Hotel. The townsman could follow in the press the affairs and marital disputes of the nobility. The aristocracy and the court provided an unfailing supply of topics for chit-chat. Hunting was the only pleasure the emperor allowed himself, and noblemen hunted on a grand scale, if only to demonstrate their closeness to the monarch. Just as the aristocracy was strictly divided into upper and lower ranks, so was the bourgeoisie.

The upper middle class included the industrialists, the men of finance and business, traditionally a domain of the liberals, in which the assimilated Jews had also established a footing, so that liberalism and Judaism became interchangeable. The lower middle class, on the other hand, was conservative and likely to be anti-semitic. Dr. Karl Lueger, Mayor of Vienna from 1897, drew his support from this third estate. His achievements should not be underestimated. He initiated a second water supply line which was urgently needed, and it was in his time of office that the gas and electricity works were built; he succeeded in taking over and unifying the city transport system, which had previously been in private hands, but he was also a strong proponent of anti-semitism. One of his great admirers was the young Adolf Hitler, who lived in Vienna from 1907 to 1913.

The Jews made up a large part of the population, and it is important to distinguish between the assimilated Jews and the 'Ghetto Jews'. Those who belonged largely to the liberal bourgeoisie were accepted members of their own class. They thought of themselves as Austrians – which indeed they were – and played an important part in Vienna's cultural life. The others lived apart, with fixed beliefs and traditions, and were at pains to maintain their cultural identity, so that it is not surprising that the idea of a Jewish state should have arisen in Vienna. 'The Jewish State: Suggestion for a Modern Solution to the Jewish Problem' by Theodor Herzl (1860–1904) appeared in 1896, and Herzl continued his campaign for a homeland in Palestine, unassailably secured by acknowledged legal process, until his death in 1904.

The 'Ghetto Jews' were not the only isolated minority in Vienna. The multiplicity of nationalities in the empire was reflected in the population in the capital. Alongside Germans there were Bohemians, Czechs, Ruthenians, Serbs, Italians, even Greeks, often living in ethnic groups in different districts. In this way Vienna at the turn of the century was similar to Manhattan today, though not on the same scale, with different national groups trying to preserve their cultural identity in a foreign country by living apart.

The Emperor's silver wedding jubilee and the Makart pageant

The real social structure of the dual monarchy was obscured by the festive pageant which wound through the streets of Vienna in 1879 in honour of the Emperor's silver wedding jubilee. The speech made when planning began demonstrated the intention: "On 24 April next year our royal sovereigns celebrate their silver wedding. This day will be a day of rejoicing and celebration for our royal house and for all peoples of the empire, but especially for Vienna, the capital of the empire and the royal seat. Since the royal wedding 25 years ago the capital city of Austria has risen to undreamt-of splendour, and the most significant achievements of this era, which serve to adorn, to honour and to strengthen Vienna, are linked with the names of our imperial majesties... The pious hope in everybody's hearts when cries of joy and exultation rang out 25 years ago has been fulfilled. Our beloved sovereign who performs his high office in full health is now in the prime of life, active always in untiring devotion to the fatherland, at his side his dear companion, the mother of his children! A young prince full of promise, whose excellent gifts make him the darling of the empire, compounds the good fortune of his imperial parents, so that immediate present and distant future seem to merge in a coronal of light."[1]

After this laudation the address became more direct. The pageant was to express "the homage of sciences and arts, of husbandry, mining, industry, business and transport, historically and symbolically, but not in principle excluding groups from corporations or associations in modern festive attire or in their usual costume."[2]

The arrangements for the pageant, which was to move along the Ring, still dominated by builders' scaffolding, were entrusted to Vienna's artists. In the painter Hans Makart (1840–84) Vienna had an artist who was a dedicated historicist, not only in his painting but also in his own dress on festive occasions; frequently he would choose to dress up, and to fit his behaviour to his clothes. He was put in charge of the pageant. He did not make sketches, but produced instead a rapid series of paintings in which the different groups were presented in clothes of Dürer's time. "It was the beginning of the sixteenth century, a stirring time in all areas of German cultural life, breaking with the traditions of the Middle Ages, compelled towards novelty of all kinds, even in people's outer appearance. The bizarre details of mediaeval dress were rejected and designs became simpler and more natural, while materials of unaccustomed spendour and rare combinations of colours were favoured."[3]

14,000 people were dressed in historic costume for the pageant, which began with flags and standard-bearers and continued with occupational groups and their products. On the floats the craftsmen displayed their wares, and some production processes could be observed. On one float 'Gutenberg' at a press was printing a chronicle which was handed out to the spectators. As well as artisans there were representations of trade, shipping, the railway, mining and engineering. The aristocracy were presented, engaged in a historic hunt which demonstrated their closeness to the imperial court. Makart deliberately placed the artists at the end of the procession and he increased the gap between them and the other participants by having them appear in costumes of Rubens' time. In this way Makart succeeded in celebrating not only the sovereign but also those responsible for the pageant. He had delegated the responsibility for individual floats to other artists, who turned to their own students for help. This gave Gustav Klimt, just seventeen years old, the honour of being involved with the preparations.

With the Ring as its backcloth, and with the splendidly adorned floats demonstrating the work of so many different trades and callings, the pageant became a total Viennese work of art. The empire was a great power, the old order was stable. Yet this was the beginning of morbidity, of decadence. The splendid decorations, designed to show crafts flourishing as heretofore, and the homage paid to an apparently harmonious imperial house, with all members present, seemed to embody only the wish for, and not the substance of, reality.

It was the last public appearance of the shy and retiring Empress Elisabeth. She came to prefer long journeys through Europe, separated from the monarch. The marriage was not happy. Emperor Franz Joseph I's marriage for love had turned out to be a failure. The

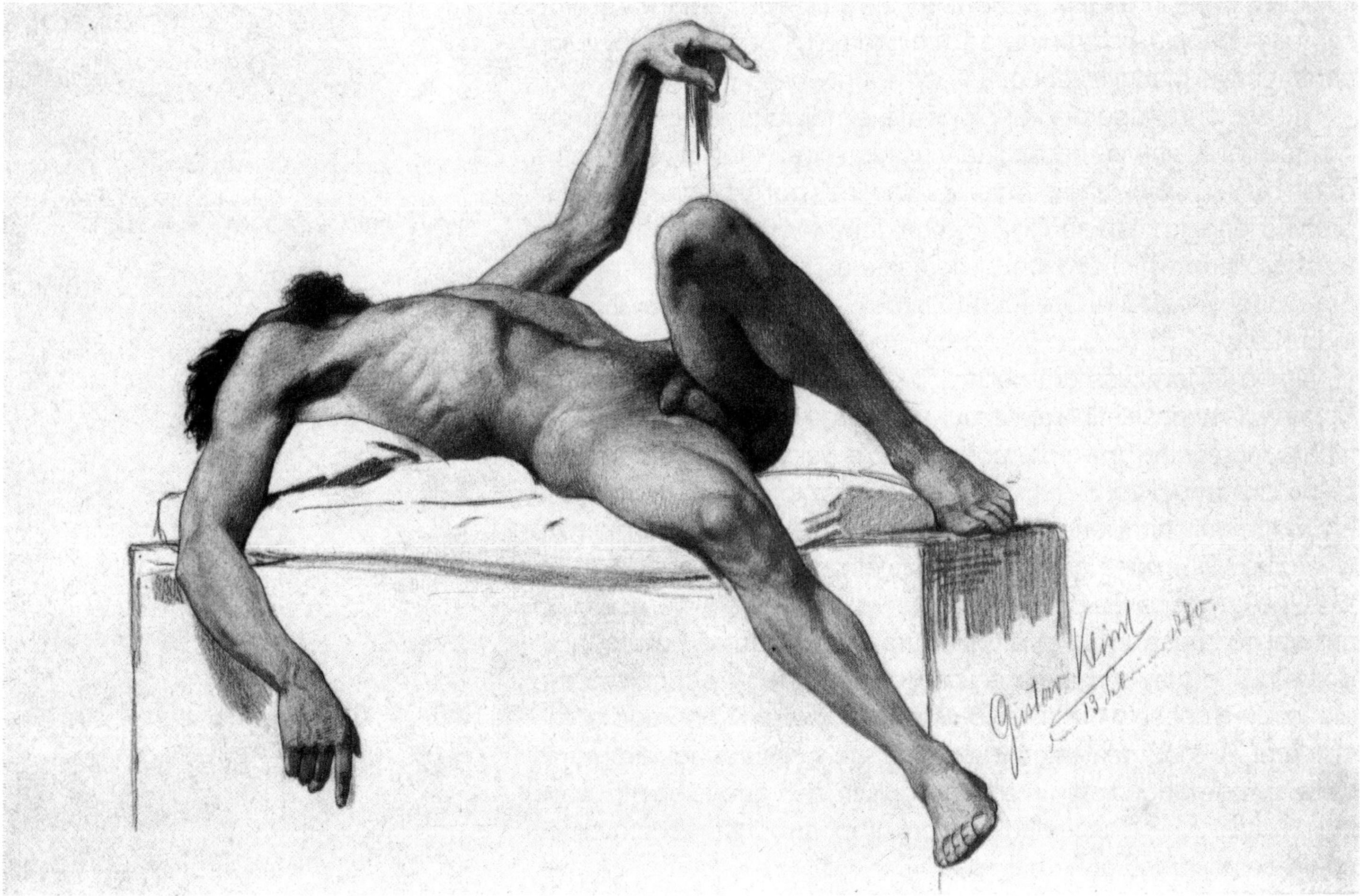

Recumbent male figure, 1880
Pencil, 28.9 × 43.2 cm

empress did not share his cares nor did she return his love. Ten years later she was the victim of an assassination in Geneva. The emperor's only son, Crown Prince Rudolf, had much more liberal views than his father, and avoided joint public appearances. He finally committed suicide with his mistress. It was only for the emperor that showing himself to the people who honoured him and paid homage to him in the pageant was the fulfilment of a positive duty.

The rich and elaborate trappings of the individual floats, which the guilds or associations had to finance themselves, drew a veil over the crash of 1873 which had put many small firms out of business. Craftsmen no longer prospered as they had done, threatened as they were by mass production, which of course was not represented in the pageant any more than the suburban proletariat employed by the new industries.

Vienna's glory was crumbling. The grim attempt to cling to old norms was unmistakably apparent in the pageant. The aristocracy still tried to repress the upwardly mobile bourgeoisie, and the new proletariat was overlooked, but it was not possible to go on ignoring the altered social conditions. The contradictions became evident in 1918 when the old empire of the Danube finally collapsed.

In the last decades before that time Vienna had developed into a cultural hothouse, in which architecture, theatre, music, painting, literature, philosophy and science fertilised each other and contributed to the total Viennese work of art, forever ready to pay homage to the emperor. It is of great significance that new cultural achievements were acknowledged only by a few people in Vienna, and had to prove their worth by being accepted in other European countries before they could be accepted at home.

The Ring, and Vienna as a 'total' work of art

The idea of the total work of art is best demonstrated by the Ring. It had been the emperor's wish that the city wall should be pulled down and replaced by this splendid street. The street was to be lined by both public buildings and private residences. Building began at a time when there was no sign of a decline, and there arose in historicist style a new parliament, the town hall, the university, the opera house and the Burg Theatre, museums and baroque residences. The most

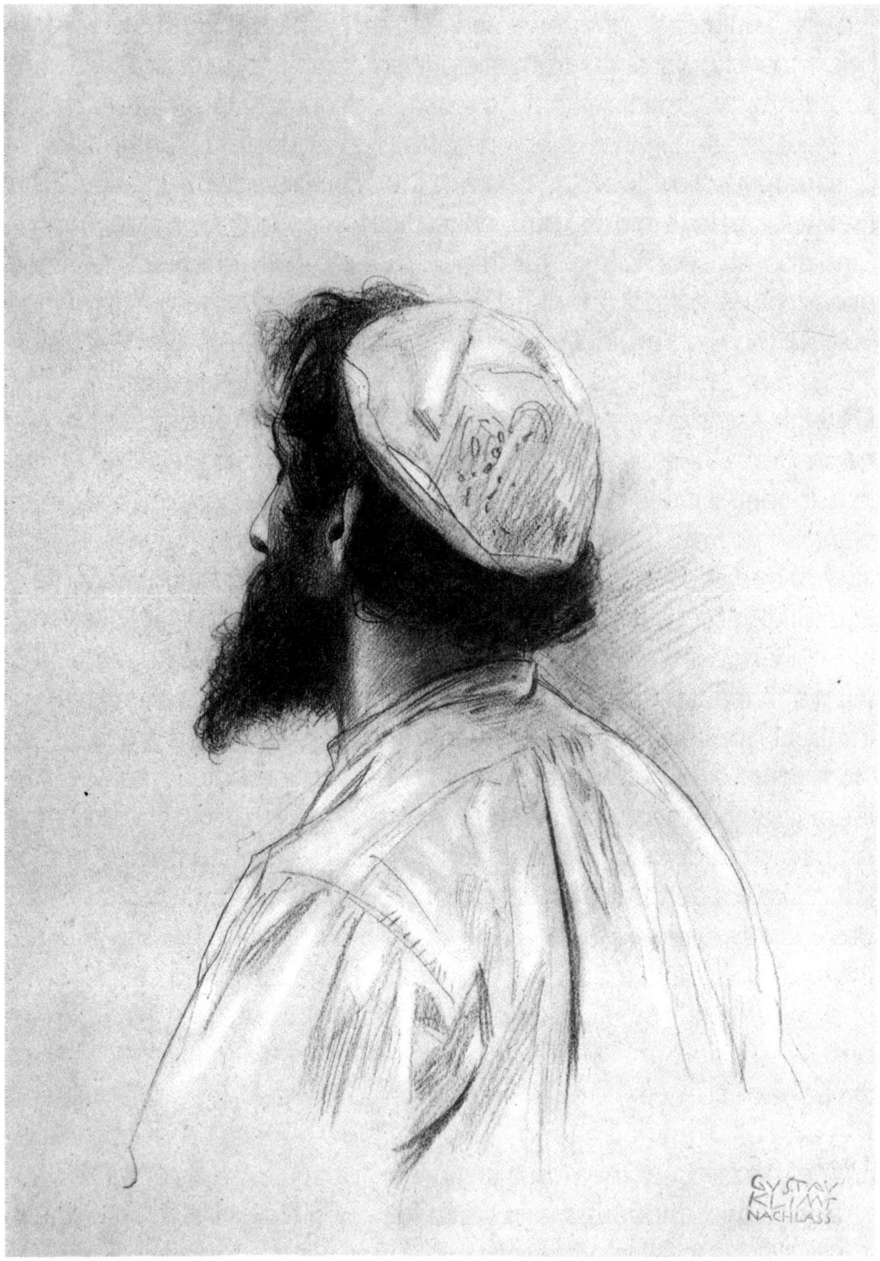

Bearded young man with cap, turned to the left, 1886/88
Black crayon, highlighted in white,
45.1 × 31.7 cm

famous architects of the time were employed, but also sculptors and painters. The young Gustav Klimt was involved in painting for three of these public buildings: the Burg Theatre, the Art History Museum and the university. The last of these three projects, the faculty paintings for the great hall of the new university, caused a scandal. By this time Klimt had moved right away from historicism, and his paintings aroused such massive criticism that he was forced to buy them back.

Erected at a time of change, but with the possibility within itself of gradual evolution, the Ring became the symbol of a dying society. The desire for art was intense during the second half of the nineteenth century, and architects and artists did what they could to express their notion of the total work of art. Yet very soon, adverse criticism was voiced: the Ring project was already out of date. The writer Hermann Bahr (1863–1934) was a polemicist: "Yesterday's styles do not please today; these palaces decorated in renaissance or baroque style are no longer in tune with the times. We demand to live in a manner suited to our needs, just as we dress according to our needs. We no longer want fancy dress, nor do our houses. When we walk across to the Ring we encounter a cheap carnival. Everything is hidden, disguised, masked. But life has become too serious for that. We want to look life in the face". Bahr went on to demand 'realistic architecture' and explained what he meant by it: "We mean that a building must fulfil a purpose, not conceal it but express it openly. The artist we want is the one with the strength to provide his shapes with constructive solutions, not hide them in a stupid and ugly way behind strange forms. People used to require a building to 'look like something'. We require it to be something. We are ashamed when working people of today live like yesterday's princes and patricians". He called it a fraud, and demanded that the appearance of a building "should indicate the occupant's calling and way of life". Finally he declared with some pathos: "We are not baroque people and we are not living in the Renaissance; why should we behave as if we were? Life has changed, every thought, every feeling, and all of art has changed. So people's houses must change, to give expression to their new tastes and deeds".[4]

Bahr's demands were met by modern architects like Otto Wagner (1841–1918), Josef Hoffmann (1870–1956) and Adolf Loos (1870–1933), though in very different ways. The wide disparities between conservatism and modern thought impressed themselves on the Ring. In buildings put up relatively late, like Otto Wagner's Post Office Savings Bank (1904–06), 'form followed function' as required, but also in some of the public buildings erected in the historical spirit, cultural events took place which were not at all in keeping with the conservative ethos.

The Artists' House, erected on the Ring between 1865 and 1868, was built for the Vienna Artists' Association, which included the architects responsible for the buildings which lined the Ring, as well as the artists who painted portraits of the members of the great families who lived there. Young up-and-coming artists caused disagreements, which resulted in 1897 in a breakaway movement – the Secession – led by Gustav Klimt. A year later the new association of artists presented their first exhibition in a house on the Ring belonging to the Horticultural Society. The Secession became increasingly important in the years that followed: in it were those artists who later pledged their allegiance to Jugendstil – the style of youth; from among their number came the founders of the Vienna Workshops, which from 1903 made important contributions to interior design and decorating.

Cultural life in Vienna

From 1897 to 1907 Gustav Mahler (1860–1911) was artistic director of the Royal Opera House. He was the first to put into practice the idea of the modern music theatre. With the help of the painter and graphic artist Alfred Roller (1864–1935), a member of the Secession employed by Mahler as chief designer at the Opera from 1903, a new symbiosis of music and design was achieved. Through all his experiments with lighting, materials and colour, Roller attempted not to obscure the work being performed but to assist it. This co-operation enabled Mahler to realise his idea of opera as total work of art. To the same end he concerned himself with all the people involved, that is to say, with orchestra, soloists, choir, scene-shifters, costume makers, painters, lighting men. The general public responded enthusiastically to Mahler's new concept. On 31 March the 'Neues Wiener Tagblatt' carried a review of the première of 'The Marriage of Figaro': "Mozart's immortal masterpiece... was performed to perfection... Gustav Mahler, Max

Kalbeck and Alfred Roller must be acclaimed as the creators of yesterday's new production, which was the harmonious result of the intensive complementary planning and thinking of three intelligent men with great knowledge of the theatre . . .".

Yet although Mahler was celebrated as conductor, the public rejected his compositions. Success as a composer was granted him in other countries. He travelled widely in the Netherlands and in Germany in order to be allowed to conduct his own works. Intrigues arose during his increasingly frequent periods of absence, and caused him to leave Vienna in 1907, after which time he worked mostly in America.

Arnold Schönberg (1874–1951) and his pupils Anton von Webern (1883–1945) and Alban Berg (1885–1935) found no more success than Mahler with their compositions in Vienna. Twelve-tone music was born in Vienna and was rejected there. These modern musicians were in close contact with the Secession. Mahler worked not only with Roller but also with other Secessionists. In 1902 he conducted Beethoven's Ninth Symphony in the Secession's rooms, on the occasion of the exhibition devoted to Beethoven, and Gustav Klimt was indebted to him for some of the ideas used in the Beethoven Frieze.

Schönberg was a close friend of one of the other painters, Richard Gerstl (1883–1908). After Gerstl's death he painted some impressive portraits himself, and above all 'Visions', which harmonised with his music.

There was a close network of relationships in the arts. The man of letters Hermann Bahr, who gathered together a circle of poets and writers, including Hugo von Hofmannsthal (1874–1929), Arthur Schnitzler (1862–1831) and Felix Salten (1869–1947), in the celebrated Café Griensteidl, was a supporter of the Secession, and played a decisive part in the launching of their journal Ver Sacrum, although he never became editor.

The philosopher Ludwig Wittgenstein (1889–1957), whose Tractatus Logico-Philosophicus of 1921 became one of the most important philosophical works of this century, was also active as an architect. He built a house for the sister whose portrait Gustav Klimt painted in 1905 at her parents' request.

The cross-fertilisation of architects, painters, master craftsmen,

3 The Fable, 1883
Oil on canvas, 84.5 × 117 cm
Vienna City Museums

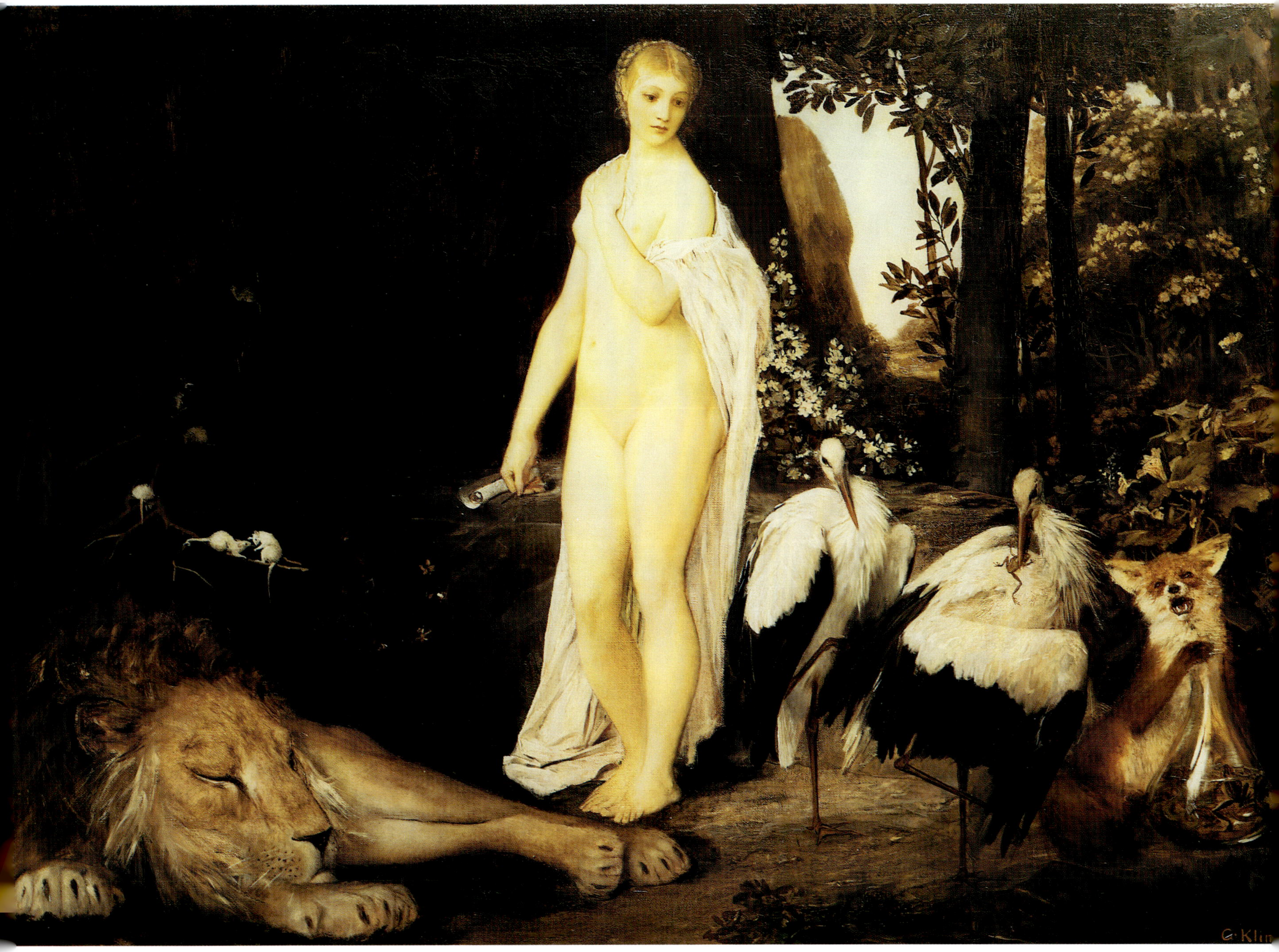

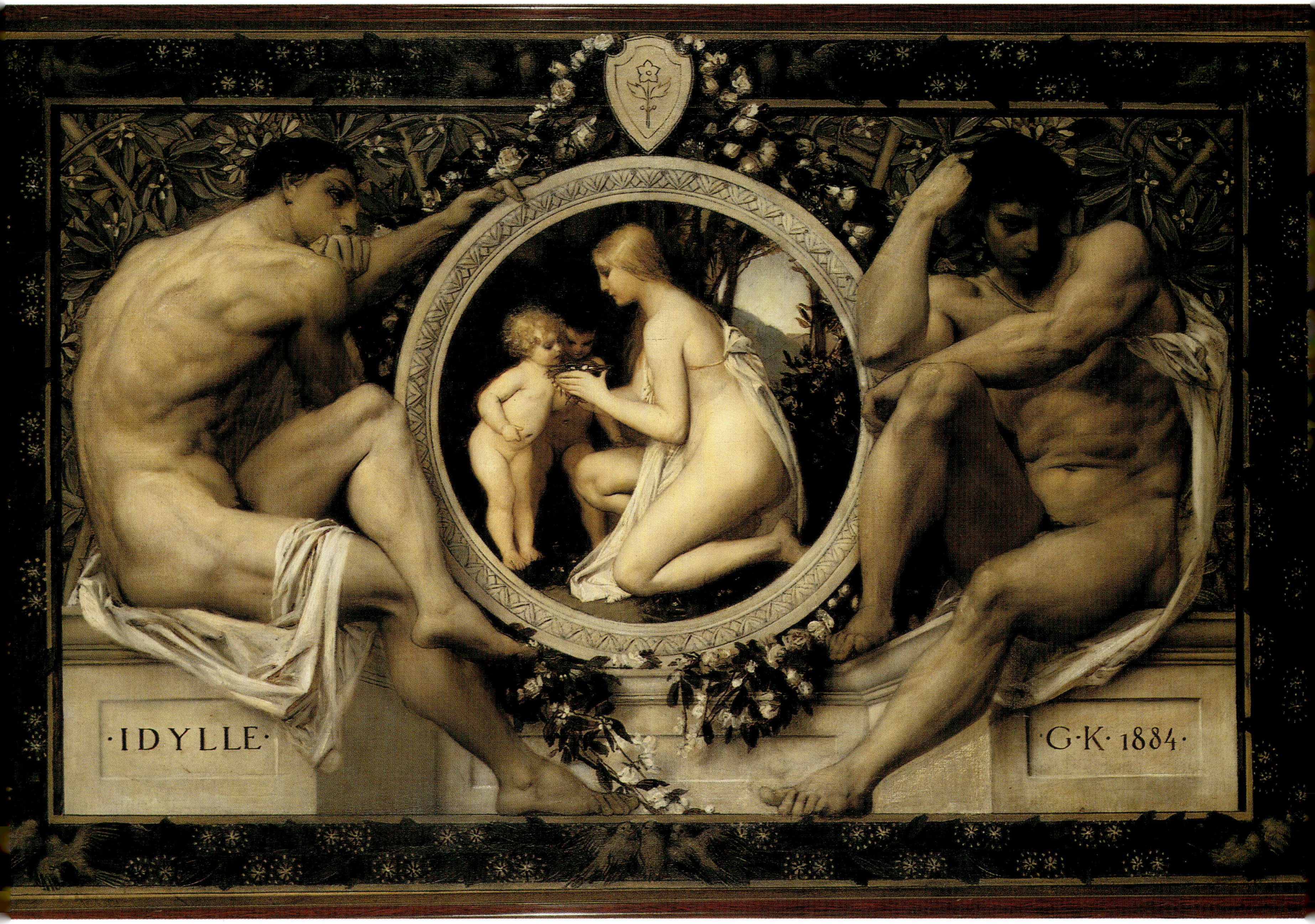
·IDYLLE·
·G·K· 1884·

musicians and writers led to the hothouse climate so often cited. But there were two people above all others who kept their distance and never tired of criticising Viennese culture at the turn of the century: the architect Adolf Loos and the journalist and writer Karl Kraus (1874–1936).

Adolf Loos settled his account with the Jugendstil artists in a public lecture given in 1908 under the title 'Ornament and Crime'. The lecture was repeated in Vienna in 1910 and 1913. The stylized ornamentation which Klimt and his associates saw as progress, was for Loos a step backwards. For him the ornamental was an instrument of aesthetic spoon-feeding and political incapacitation: "The urge to adorn one's face and everything within reach is the earliest gropings of pictorial art. It is the infantile babble of painting ... Evolution means the removal of ornament from the utilitarian ... Mankind is once again to be enslaved to ornamentation ... and the state, whose responsibility it is to maintain the momentum of mankind's cultural development, takes upon itself the revival and development of the ornament. Woe to the state whose revolutions are taken care of by court officials ... Well, the decorative pestilence is recognised by the state and receives assistance from the Treasury. But I see this as regression. I refuse to acknowledge the argument that ornament enhances the pleasure of a cultured individual, and will not listen to such words as: 'but what if the ornament be beautiful ... !' No ornament enhances life's pleasure for me or for any civilised person ... It would be possible to put up with the terrible ravages caused by the revival of ornamentation in the nation's aesthetic development, because no-one, and no state power, can halt the evolution of mankind. Evolution can only be delayed. We can wait. But it is a crime against economic progress that men's work, money and materials should be brought to nothing in this way. This damage cannot be made good by the passage of time ... ornamentation is not only generated by criminals, it commits a crime itself by damaging people's health, the nation's wealth and its cultural development ... ornament is a waste of work, power and therefore of health. That has always been the case. But today it means waste of material as well, and both together mean waste of capital. Absence of ornament is a sign of mental strength."[5]

4 The Idyll, 1884
Oil on canvas, 49.5 × 73.5 cm
Vienna City Museums

Karl Kraus, a friend of Loos, pursued the same line of thought, although his criticisms were aimed mostly at writers rather than artists. He spoke of the coffee house decadence of modern thought. When Café Griensteidl had to close in 1897 because the building was about to be demolished, Kraus took the opportunity to write his essay 'Demolished Literature', criticising Hermann Bahr and his circle. His biting censure and his verbal wit are revealed in the listing of the characteristics attributed to the members of the 'Griensteidl Group': "Lack of talent, premature mellowing, posturing, megalomania, working class girls, cravats, mannerisms, grammatical errors, monocles and undisclosed convulsions".[6]

Yet in spite of Karl Kraus's polemics, published mostly in the journal he founded in 1899, the literature of so-called 'Young Vienna' had substance; the most important works were written after the turn of the century, at a time when Café Griensteidl had long since ceased to exist.

It is not unfitting that it was in Vienna, with its conflicting trends, its decadence, that the first scientific description of neurosis was attempted. In 1900 Sigmund Freud (1856–1939) published his first book, 'The Interpretation of Dreams'. The Austrian psychiatrist Erwin Ringel (*1921) tellingly described the favourable conditions for the birth of psychoanalysis prevailing in Vienna at the time: "It remained for the secular genius Sigmund Freud to write the first scientific description of neurosis, to discover the unconscious and therefore to enrich human existence with an enduring new dimension ... It can hardly be by chance that an Austrian succeeded in doing this; in no other country is this form of illness so much 'at home' as it is here with us. Where else other than here could it have been discovered? It is tragic beyond belief that people in Austria continue to live as if Freud (and Adler) had never lived, and that his teachings have resulted in next to nothing: people are just as neurotic, children become innocent victims, neurosis is still not recognised as an illness, prophylactic and therapeutic considerations are suppressed as if the whole subject had nothing to do with us. We are, and remain, masters of repression and self-deception ..."[7]

Art historians began to rediscover the Vienna of the turn of the century a few years ago. Large-scale exhibitions in Vienna, Paris and New

York were accompanied by a wealth of written material. Of central importance is the distinctive Viennese Jugendstil protest movement, which was called 'The Art of Style'. The idea of the total work of art, which was operative first of all on the Ring, in the historical style of the 1879 pageant, was still to be found at that later period, despite different appearances. Yet this new attempt to create Vienna's 'total work of art' was also destined to fail and its end could be foreseen.

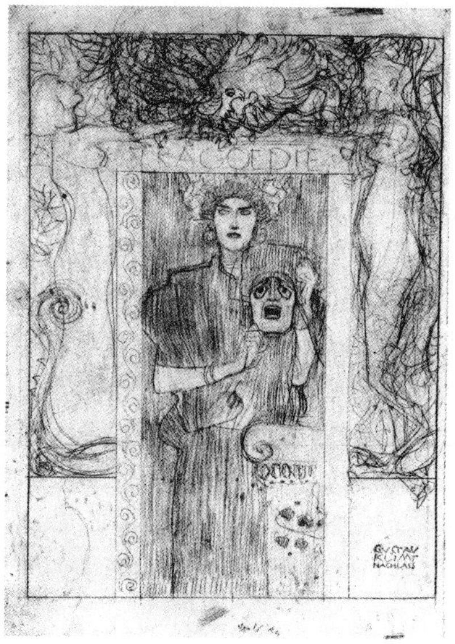

Sketch for 'Tragedy', 1897
Pencil, 45.7 × 31.5 cm

Jugendstil – art nouveau – an international movement

Antecedents

Describing, comparing and classifying the art of different eras has always been one of the art historian's tasks. The great eras of Romanesque, Gothic, Renaissance, Baroque art are clearly distinguishable and form a logical sequence in which historical relationships, philosophical concepts and art forms are interconnected.

In the nineteenth century, however, there were radical upheavals in society, and corresponding changes in art. It was the time of bourgeois revolutions, immediately followed by the so-called industrial revolution. New discoveries led to rapid development. The invention of the railway and the steamship revolutionised transport; telephone and telegraph brought drastic change to communications. The effect on art was to cause an increasingly rapid proliferation of new forms and subjects, and rejection of the old, to such an extent that totally different styles might be favoured at one and the same time.

The invention of photography in 1839 was of great significance for the development of painting. At a relatively early time portrait and landscape painters found photographs a useful aid. Long sittings for portraits, previously unavoidable, could now be reduced to a minimum; with photographs the landscape artist could do much of his work at home. Gradually photographers came to be employed in preference to portrait painters, if only because the costs were so much less, but the fears that the new medium would in time entirely replace the old turned out to be unfounded.

The artists' search for new forms and means of expression led in time to abstract painting. New modes of looking at things developed at breathtaking speed, leading in different countries to varying results, all of which then influenced and were enriched by one another in turn. It was a creative time.

New thoughts and new ideas were reflected not only in visual art but also in literature and music.

Critics disdainfully called this era the time of 'isms', and were quick to itemise them: realism, naturalism, historicism, impressionism, cubism, constructivism ... One style did not appear on the list. It was not one of the 'isms' and in fact critics often preferred not to mention it until the 1960s. At first glance it did not seem directly comparable to the other styles, and there was even some doubt as to whether it really was 'art'. Critical opinion has changed, and today Jugendstil, the style of youth, which spans the turn of the century, receives widespread recognition.

Jugendstil spread over most of Europe, and therefore appears in a variety of forms. Conditions varied from one country to another. The artists had been trained in different schools so that the new style drew on various influences. Its origins lay in England and France. Conditions were very different in these two countries, yet very similar forms and ideas were developed which in England found their truest expression in arts and crafts, whereas in France their more significant manifestation was in painting.

England on the way to 'Arts and Crafts'

In England the first beginnings of the development that led to the 'Modern Style' can be traced in the mid-nineteenth century. The industrial revolution had caused an increasing gap between handicraft and mechanical processes. Mass-produced objects began to replace those made by hand. The discrepancy between handicraft and machine, and the living and working conditions of the industrial proletariat, gave rise to discussion of the decreasing possibilities of self-realisation through work. The philosopher Max Stirner (1806–1856) had contended that labour organisation should only affect the average man, whereas the one who counted, the 'individual', for instance the artist, must be free from such organisation. Karl Marx (1818–1883) opposed this view. He argued that the exclusive concentration of artistic talent in the individual and his resulting suppression in the mass was the consequence of the division of labour. In a communist society a painter would not exist, only a man who painted.[7]

Marx also demanded that man should be served by the machine, not serve it. But he expressly did not oppose the machine as a means of finding self-realisation in the process of work, as did, some years later, the writer, social reformer and art historian John Ruskin (1819–1900). Ruskin hoped for a return to mediaeval crafts which would enable the artist-craftsman to realise himself in his work. Both the realistic and the romantic viewpoints gained new impetus for debate at the Great Exhibition in London in 1851. The conflict between handicraft and industrial production was openly displayed.

After the exhibition the architect and theoretician Gottfried Semper (1803–1879) demanded that the arts should be industrialised. He opposed the academies which trained artists in isolation from reality. A small section of society could be surrounded by beautiful objects while the rest of the population lived amidst ugliness. But the realistic theoreticians did not succeed in harnessing industry to art, whereas John Ruskin's ideas were taken up by William Morris (1834–1896) who developed them further and put them into practice.

In 1857, when he had completed his training, Morris moved into a studio in London, but when he came to furnish it he found that none of the furniture on the market was to his taste. Since the right atmosphere was important to him if he was to paint, he decided that he and his friends would make the furniture. They used massive mediaeval pieces as models. Not long afterwards he furnished a house for himself and his wife in the same style. Then in 1861 he and his friends set up an arts and crafts business. The range of this enterprise included painting, carving, furniture-making, metalwork, floor-coverings, wall-coverings, textiles and tiles. Later various other firms modelled on this one were set up.

There was an inherent contradiction between Morris's ideas and their realisation. As a socialist he had radical aims. He did not want art for the few, any more than he wanted education or freedom for the few.[8]

On the other hand he rejected all post-mediaeval methods of

production. There was no escape from this dilemma. He refused to acknowledge the idea of inspiration in art which had prevailed since the Renaissance. What mattered to him was man's work done with his own hands.[9]

His notion of art, which he tried to put into practice, required that it should not appeal only to a small élite; but the radical rejection of modern means of production made the creation of his pieces so expensive that only this élite could afford them. Morris spoke resignedly of the need to work for the rich, since all art cost time, trouble and thought.[10]

In spite of these contradictions it would be a mistake to belittle his achievements. His desire to do away with specialisation in art, and to focus co-operative artistic endeavour on people's domestic living-space and humdrum surroundings, provided a new conception of the total work of art, and his aims were handed on by his followers in the Arts and Crafts Movement. It was here that the foundations for the Modern Style were laid. The most important of these artists were Walter Crane (1845–1915), Charles Robert Ashbee (1863–1942) and, pre-eminently as book-illustrator, Aubrey Beardsley (1872–1898).

More radical than the Arts and Crafts Movement was a Scottish group that became known as the School of Glasgow; their work was first shown in London at the Arts and Crafts Exhibition of 1896. This group systematically conceived of living space as a total work of art, extending from architecture to interior decoration down to the last detail of cutlery. The unity of the whole became an explicit principle.

Margaret Macdonald (1865–1933), one of the principal members of this group, also executed watercolours and drawings which, by their lineation between colours, are reminiscent of cellular enamelling. She transferred this technique to other materials. With embossing of precious metal, cloisonné and inlaid woods she united picture and ornament in a style that exerted a strong influence on Jugendstil in Munich and Vienna.

The development of French painting from Impressionism to art nouveau

In France in the 1880s voices critical of Impressionism were heard, not only those of the conservatives who wanted to maintain the old style of the academy, but also those of young artists who upbraided the Impressionists for their scientific, rational attitudes and argued that their pictures had reached the ultimate exemplification of naturalism.

The declared aim of the Impressionists was to paint something other than the object as such: the object was only of momentary importance; in the foreground was the painting of light in colours. Claude Monet (1840–1926) painted Rouen Cathedral several times during the year, at different times of day, in order to capture the varying 'impressions'. The object was merely a means to an end. People, animals, landscapes, but also the new manifestations of technology such as factories, railways and their stations were all accorded the same treatment and painted for their impressions. The achievements of this group of painters, which led ultimately to abstract painting, were scarcely recognized by the critics, who saw in Impressionism an aesthetic exercise irresponsible towards the object, towards nature, towards life itself.

It was enthusiasm for the Impressionists that led the former sailor, then bank clerk, Paul Gauguin (1848–1903) to teach himself to paint. He began painting in 1872, and from 1879 he showed his pictures at various Impressionist exhibitions, but a turn towards mysticism led him away from the group. At a time when his style of painting was still close to that of the Impressionists (1885), he described in a letter to a friend his own way of seeing. He spoke of the powerful feeling for the supernatural, and of the feelings that people have when they look at a spider, a tree-stump or a rat.[11]

He was already able to say what means were necessary in order to transpose these feelings into painting:

'he distinguished between noble lines, leading to eternity, and false lines which impose limits. He spoke of the power of colours, again noble, or vulgar. People's character could be read in their handwriting.

5 Sappho, c. 1888/90
Oil on canvas, 39 × 31.6 cm
Vienna City Museums

6 Poster Design, right half, for International Exhibition of Music and Theatre, 1892
Oil on canvas, 84 × 56 cm
Vienna City Museums

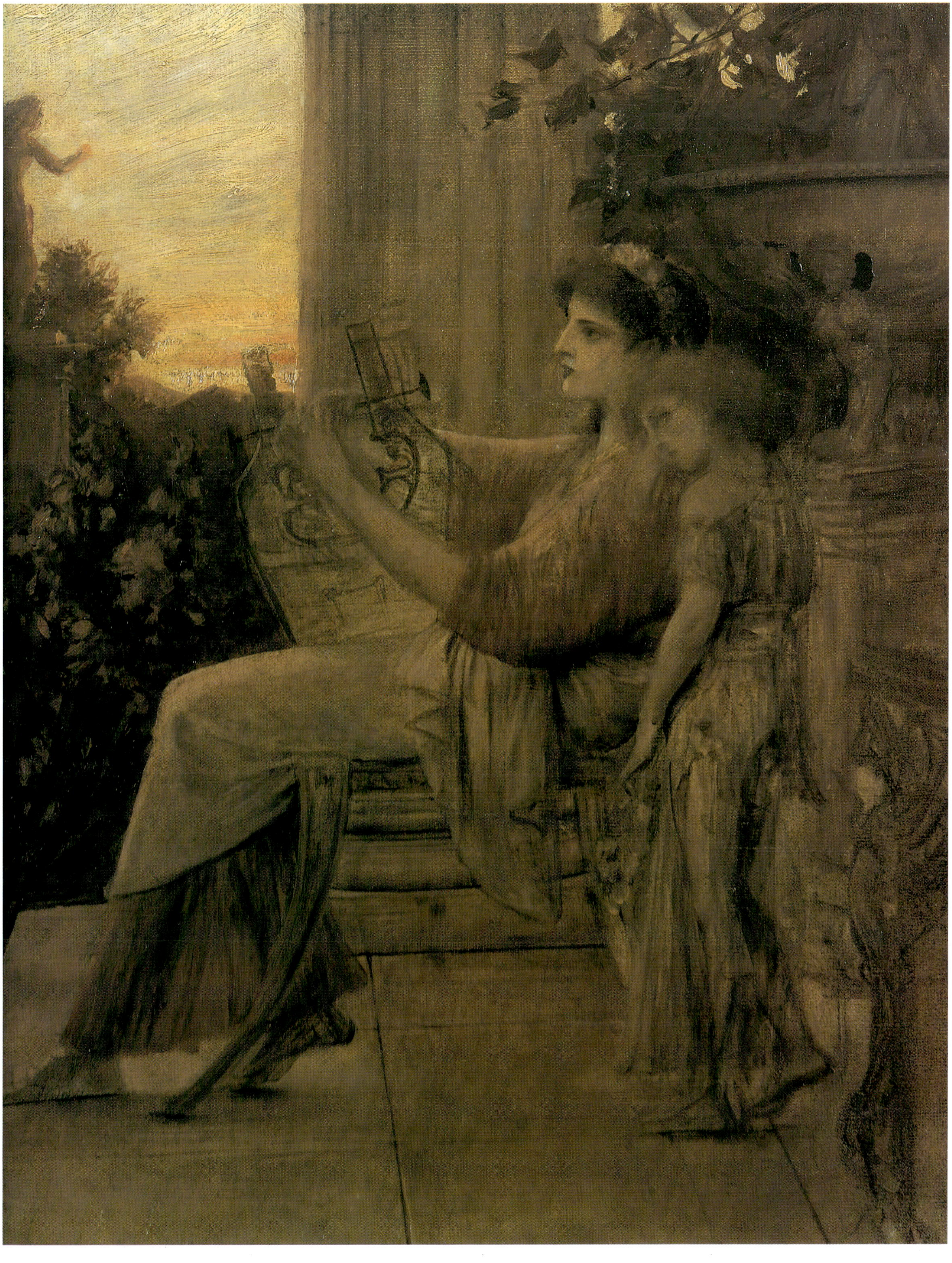

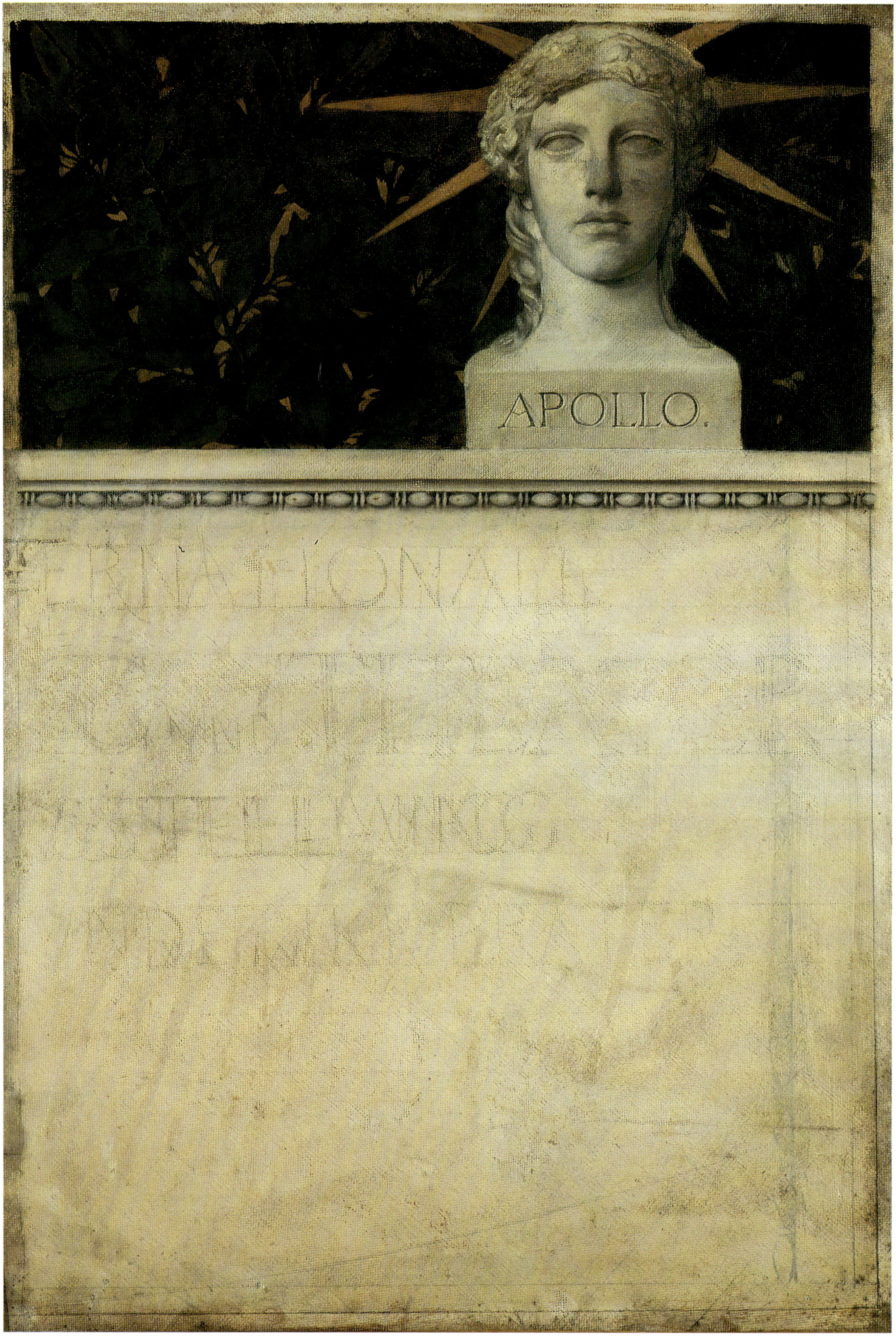
APOLLO.

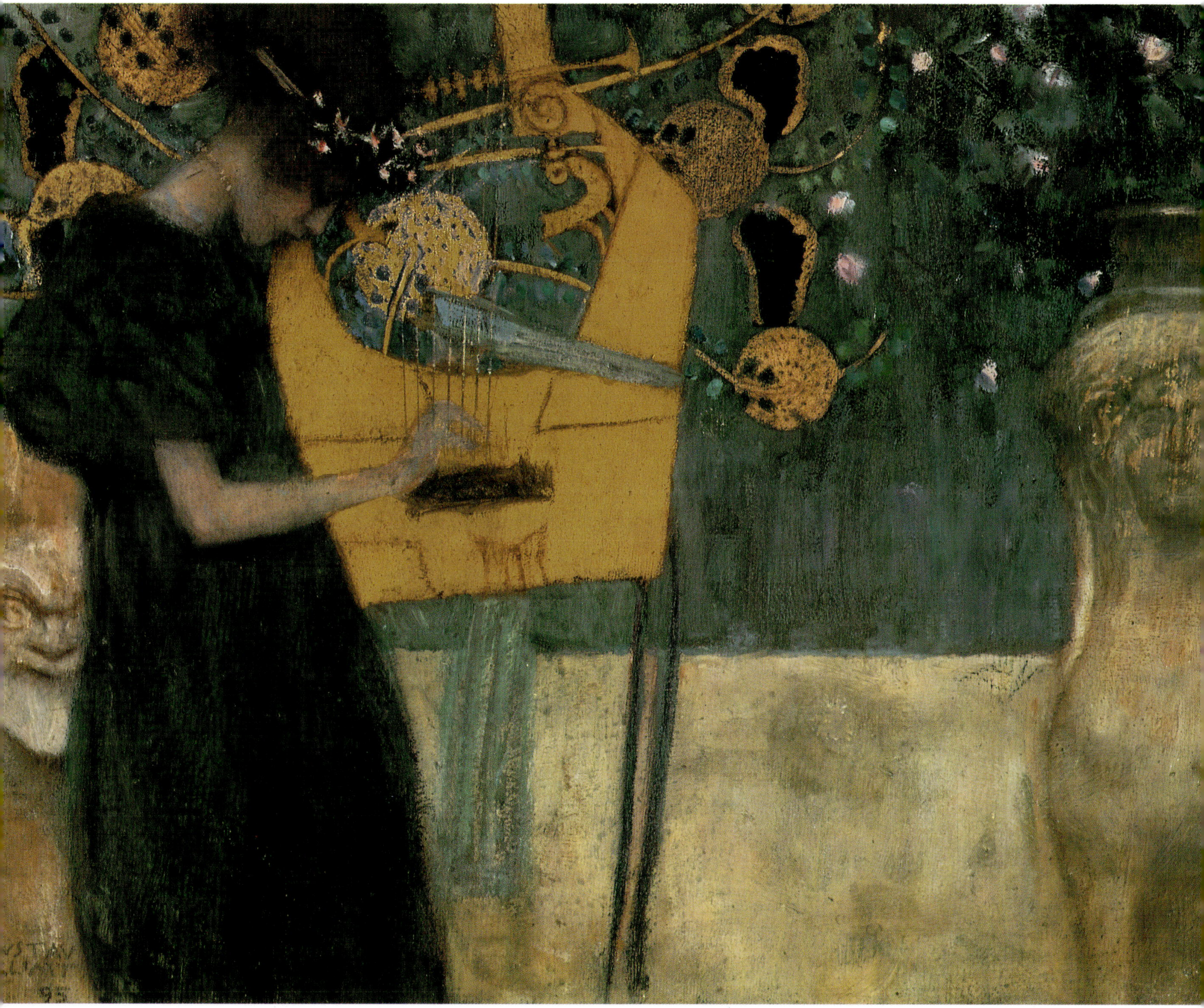

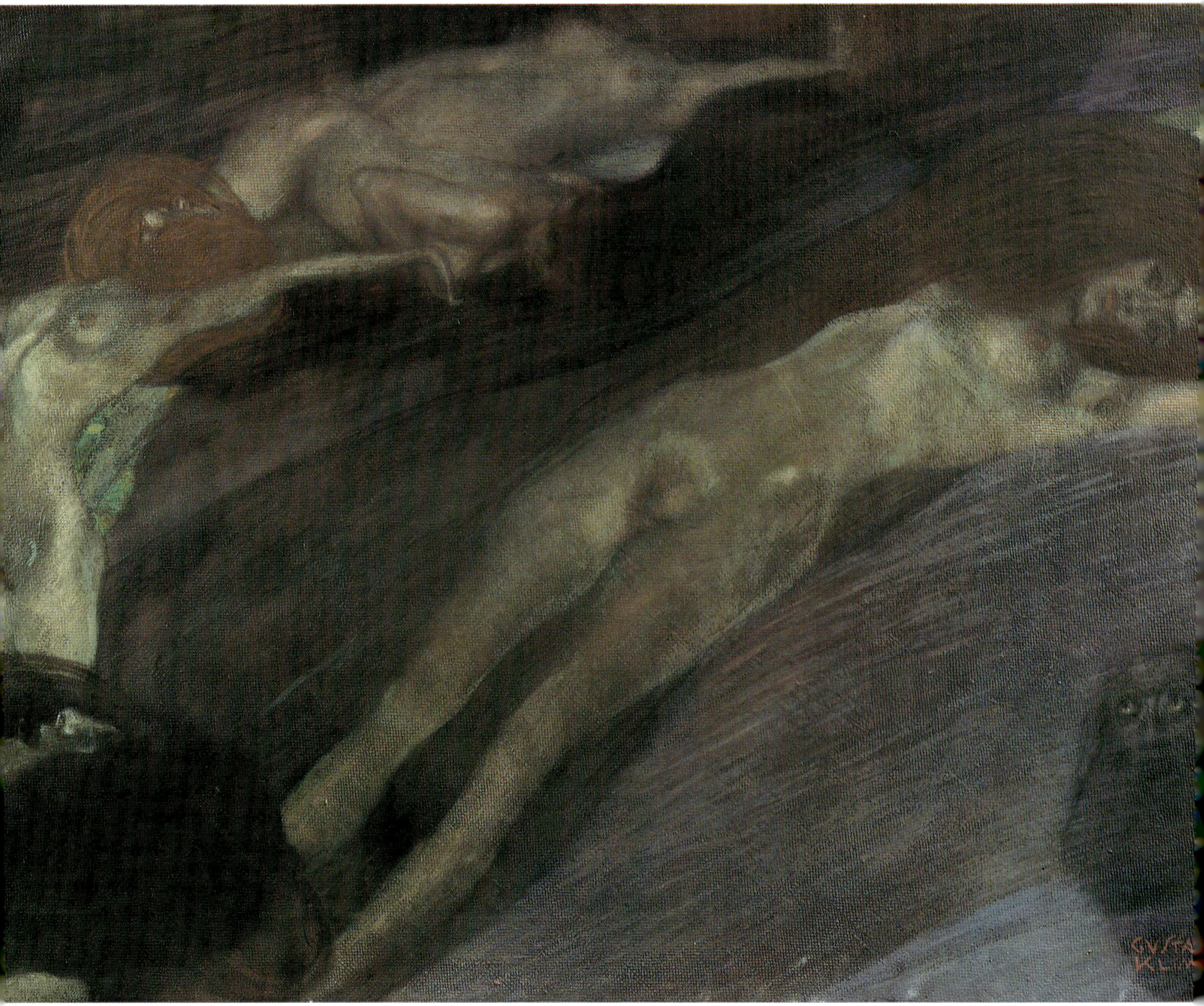

7 Music I, 1895
Oil on canvas, 37 × 44.5 cm
Neue Pinakothek, Munich

8 Moving Water, 1898
Oil on canvas, 52 × 65 cm
By kind permission of Galerie St Etienne, New York

Why should not an artist's more or less noble character be revealed by his lines and colours?'[12]

The much younger Emile Bernard (1868–1945), who had similar ideas and was able to implement them much earlier in his paintings, spent the summer months, as did Paul Gauguin, in the village of Pont-Aven in Brittany, which had become an artists' village in the 1880s. The two painters became acquainted and soon they were in close contact with one another. Before long they were surrounded by a group of young artists, and what had started with informal discussions of new pictures became a coherent group of painters, whose activities culminated in a first exhibition of their work in the Café Volpini in Paris during the Great Exhibition of 1889.

In Brittany these painters found the right setting for their own style. They went so far as to say that in this landscape it was impossible to paint in any other way. Armand Séguin (1869–1903) spoke for these artists and their feelings for the Breton countryside and its people, and the place of their own art in it, in his lyrical account of their time in Pont-Aven. He wrote that the Breton landscape facilitated most wonderfully the study of synthesis and the technique of 'cloisonné': trees stood out black against the sky, the pine drew a straight line, the branches of the oak suggested a fabulous creature, the rock was shaped by the unceasing friction of the waves into the form of an unknown monster. All of nature seemed to speak to the artist of beauty and majesty, and to claim the strong men and resolute women of Brittany as her own. The artist completed the picture, balancing the curve of the working peasant's silhouette with the straightness of his line. The blue of the skirt was attuned to the orange of the sand just as the green of the artist's trees was attuned to the red of his earth, all yielding the eternal book in which man must read.[13]

What was new about these pictures? The painters worked with clear, pure colours. In one picture there were only a few prevailing colours. The line became much more important. Above all the artists rejected the notion that the painter should work with his object in front of him. The recently formulated principle that the landscape painter should work outside, painting directly from nature, was discarded again. Emile Bernard reminded his colleagues repeatedly that they should not paint with the object in front of them. Rather the object must be newly created and seen with the inner eye. The object must be reduced to the archetype. Only what was recollected was essential, only in this way could the special characterisation be recalled. In formulating these ideas Bernard was strongly influenced by Arthur Schopenhauer: "Neither a single individual nor a single act can be the meaning: in all, and through all, the idea of mankind evolves . . . The inner significance of an act is quite different from the outer significance, and often the two have quite separate paths, though close to one another . . . In art only the inner significance counts, whereas the outer significance counts in history. Each is independent of the other; they may arise together but may also appear separately."[14]

The painting of the Pont-Aven group, which moved to the nearby village of Pouldu in 1890, is often labelled by art historians as 'Early Expressionist'. It is true that Gauguin's pictures influenced the early development of the Expressionist style from 1905, although he himself left for Tahiti in 1891. But Emile Bernard, who did not accompany the group to Pouldu, and who dissociated himself from Gauguin, as well as from the group as a whole, went to increasing lengths to suppress the 'expressive' traits found in his paintings of the 1880s. By emphasizing the line he developed the principles quoted above to achieve a decorative style of painting, one of the basic principles of Jugendstil. In the pictures he painted in the nineties, arabesques and decorative lines prevail, linking individual objects so that everything becomes part of one two-dimensional composition. These features of style were taken up by other artists and used in a wide variety of ways.

The new style from France influenced painters in Switzerland, Holland, Belgium, Germany, in the countries of eastern Europe, and also in Vienna. But it spread back to England also, declaring itself most particularly in book illustration.

Conditions in different countries varied very much, so that the new style took effect in a corresponding variety of ways, and the name given to it also varied from one country to another: Jugendstil, Modern Style, Art Nouveau, Secession style. But the painters had one thing in common – a leaning towards symbolism.

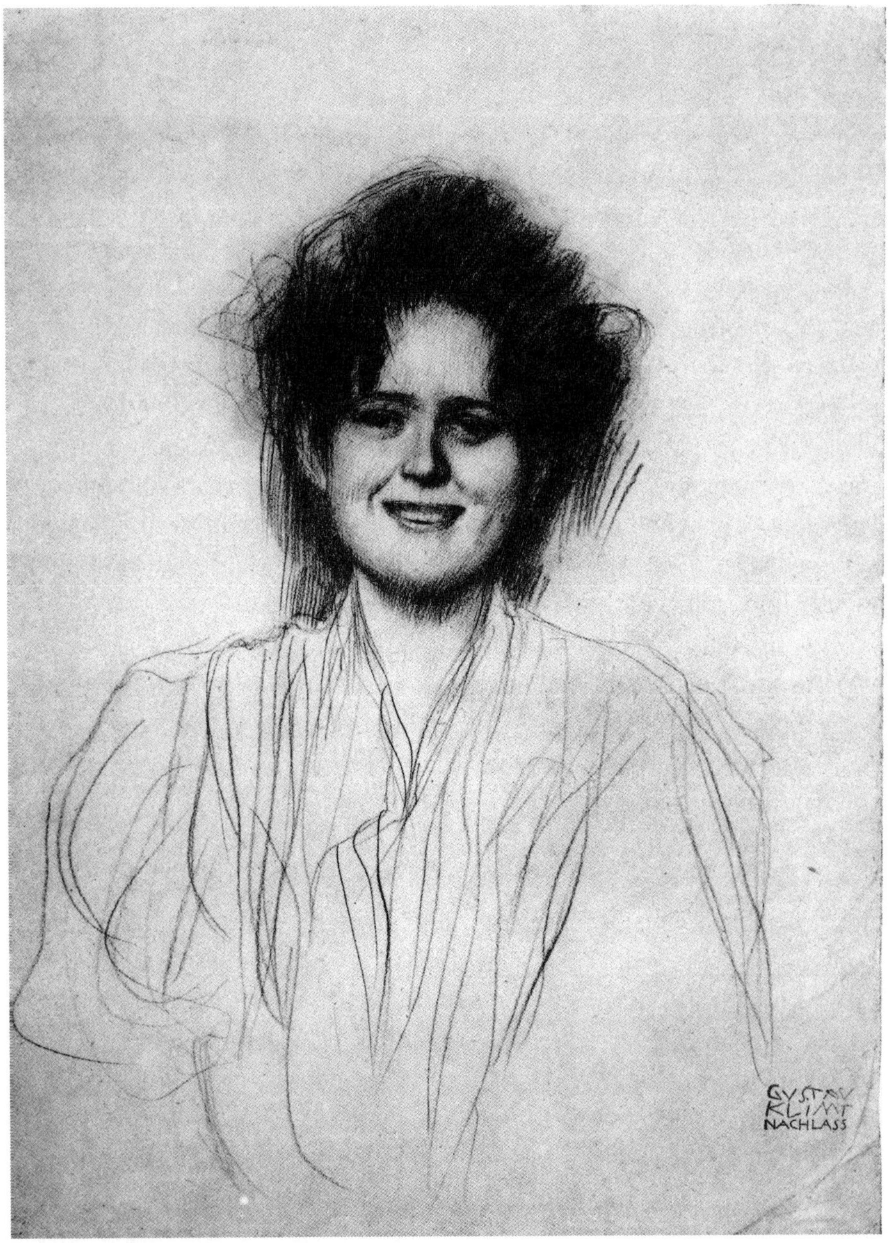

Half-length sketch of laughing girl,
front view, 1895/96
Black crayon, 44.8 × 31.7 cm

One unifying concept in 'Jugendstil' paintings – symbolism

Since the end of the eighteenth and beginning of the nineteenth century there had always been rebels against the Enlightenment, against positivism, against rationalism, who had given their pictures symbolic meaning.

Such painters objected to the notion, common to Realists, Naturalists and Impressionists, that visual art should be restricted to the portrayal of visible reality. They were more interested in penetrating to the deeper meaning beneath the surface. Dreams, fantasy and visions were very important to them. There was a return to old tales and sagas, and also to ancient mythology, though the use made of the old themes was often puzzling. Love and death were all-important, and one went with the other. Woman was either glorified or labelled 'femme fatale', as so often in the nineteenth century.

The sense that the visible world is penetrated by the invisible world and that the invisible can be perceived in dreams and in altered states of consciousness, is impressively described by Alfred Kubin (1877–1959), himself both painter and writer. His words convey this sense better than any explanation:

"With a full heart I roamed the town, and in the evening I entered a music hall; I wanted to find indifferent and yet noisy surroundings to counterbalance the ever more violent inner pressure. There I underwent a remarkable and decisive spiritual experience that I still cannot fully comprehend, although I have thought about it a great deal. Just as the little orchestra began to play I suddenly became aware of everything around me being clear and sharp, as if in a different light. The faces of those sitting around me I saw as strangely part-human, part-animal; every noise sounded unfamiliar, detached from its origin; I seemed to hear a mocking, deafening composite language that I could not understand, but which clearly had some eerie inner sense ... And suddenly there was a whole torrent of black and white pictures – it is impossible to describe the thousandfold wealth that my imagination held out for me ... I sat quite passive the whole time, and what I could remember of those images that succeeded one another with amazing ease, I sketched with a few marks and lines in a notebook".[15]

Reading these lines makes it easy to understand the 'modern' appeal of symbolism and Jugendstil, in a time when people have sought to attain such levels of consciousness with the aid of hashish, LSD and other drugs. A comparative analysis of social structures at the turn of the century and in the 1960s might well show similar feelings among young people in both periods.

Although art historians today find symbolist tendencies as far back as the eighteenth century, in Goya (1746–1828) and Runge (1777–1812), the term 'Symbolism' was not coined until the late nineteenth century, the 1889 exhibition in Café Volpini being regarded as the first exhibition of the Symbolist group. The Symbolists' criticism of the basic tenets of Impressionism coincides to a degree with objections levelled at concepts of form and style from which Jugendstil grew.

The 'total' work of art

The Jugendstil artists were great innovators in the synthesis of architecture, interior decorating and painting. Each part must be subordinated to the whole. Pictures, like furniture and tableware, were designed for specific rooms. The Belgian Henry van de Velde (1863–1957) united the different influences coming from England and France, and as architect, painter, craftsman and pedagogue he in turn was enormously influential, particularly in Germany, where most of his work was done. Today only fragments of van de Velde's rooms remain, but there is sufficient documentation to create a sense of the whole.

The journalist and art critic Karl Scheffler (1869–1951), a friend of the artist's, tried to put into words the feeling these rooms gave him: "Nowhere else in modern interiors is there such a strong and lasting sense of atmosphere. Being in one of these rooms is a unique experience, unlike anything else. To enjoy for any length of time the special character of this type of interior would not be to everybody's taste. The atmosphere in van de Velde's rooms is heavy, even gloomy, no easy cheerfulness anywhere. Although the overall atmosphere commands attention and serious and thorough reflection, it is slightly oppressive; while it evokes lofty emotion, it excludes spontaneity. Life in these rooms requires people in the right clothing; only when ladies in decorative attire sweep through these interiors will they really come to life."[16]

The total work of art needed people, more particularly women, who unlike men fulfil a decorative function. Fashions, like everything else, became a component of the total work of art, elevated to the level of art. Gustav Klimt, a painter of some standing, did not hesitate to design clothes; his relationship with the proprietress of a fashion house certainly heightened his interest.

Yet Klimt was no exception. In the German journal KUNST UND KÜNSTLER fashion shows were reviewed. The position of the woman as object was made very clear in such descriptions:

"These female figures, who are all more or less of the Ionic-Attic type, with sweeping shoulders and narrow hips, look themselves like works of art. These shapes, forms and colours as we see them have all been designed, thought out, created by an artist. This human material – I can find no other expression for it – has been selected with the realisation of an idea in mind, in such a way that the result does not divide into two parts – into clothing and woman – but offers itself to our eye as a unity. We accept it, as if the two belonged together".[17]

The idea of the total work of art was not restricted to the surroundings in which people lived, it extended to the production of books, and the effects of Jugendstil on book production can still be seen today. Beginning in England with the ideas and designs of William Morris, a wholly new art developed, which included the binding in the artist's design.

Another innovation was the dustjacket, designed to advertise the book with a blend of lettering and illustration. This new development owed much to the poster art of Henri de Toulouse-Lautrec (1864–1901). Then the flyleaf, which before that time had only fulfilled a technical function, was given meaning. It provided the link between cover and contents. Moreover, decorative 'Ex Libris' spaces were often provided, in which the owner only had to inscribe his name. In other

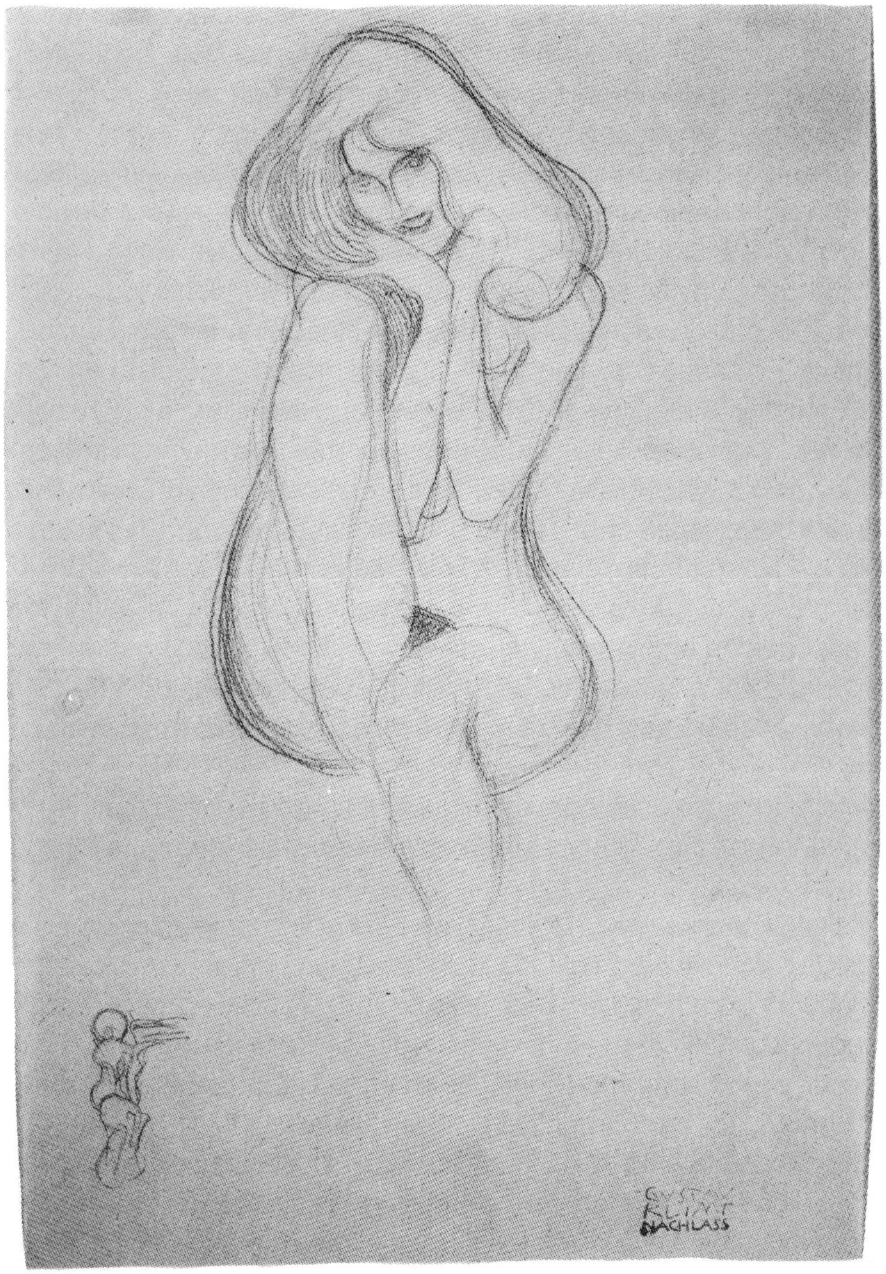

Seated woman, front view,
Composition sketch, 1901
Black crayon, 44.5 × 29.8 cm

books spaces were left for the personalised 'Ex Libris' plates which could be commissioned from well-known artists. New book faces were developed. Illustrations did not simply reproduce the text in picture form any more, they offered interpretations.

The new function of text illustrations was described in detail in 1898, in the Viennese journal VER SACRUM: "I am indeed grateful to the artist who is able by means of his art – no other art can achieve it – to make me consciously aware of the dark stirrings of the unconscious which are set in motion as I read. He makes well-tuned strings sound in resonance. He causes no interruption, no constraint; the effect of his work is liberating. Tied notes are released. That is the ultimate purpose of this art... which has most scope when it comes to symbols, to arabesques, to vignettes. It is itself a tendril, an ornament and yet at the same time a deeply meaningful allegory in lines and colours, that enwraps the work and shuts out everything else around it... The artist-decorator follows the writer as the harp follows the song. He can strike the right opening chord, major or minor, with a well chosen headpiece; then accompany him, lifting and falling, weaving back and forth, with arabesques up and down the scale of feeling, sometimes reaching right in, at other times drawing back, to end with a full, clear cadence, or to fade with a quiet questioning or yearning. That is the essence of book illustration in a modern sense, or rather at all times, if the illustrator is an artist."[18]

VER SACRUM was the last in a series of new bibliophile journals in the 1890s. Others were PAN, INSEL, SIMPLICISSIMUS and above all JUGEND (Youth), which was started in Munich in 1896. In Germany at least JUGEND gave its name to the new style. All these journals strove for good artistic typography, which in turn affected book production. Woodcuts and lithographs introduced the artists to the public. The original prints, widely circulated with these popular journals, caused the artists to become better known, so that the journals made a great contribution to the rapid spread of the new style, at the same time as documenting its enormous variety.

9 Portrait of the pianist and piano teacher Josef Pembaur, 1890
Oil on canvas, 69 × 55 cm
Tyrolean Museum, Innsbruck

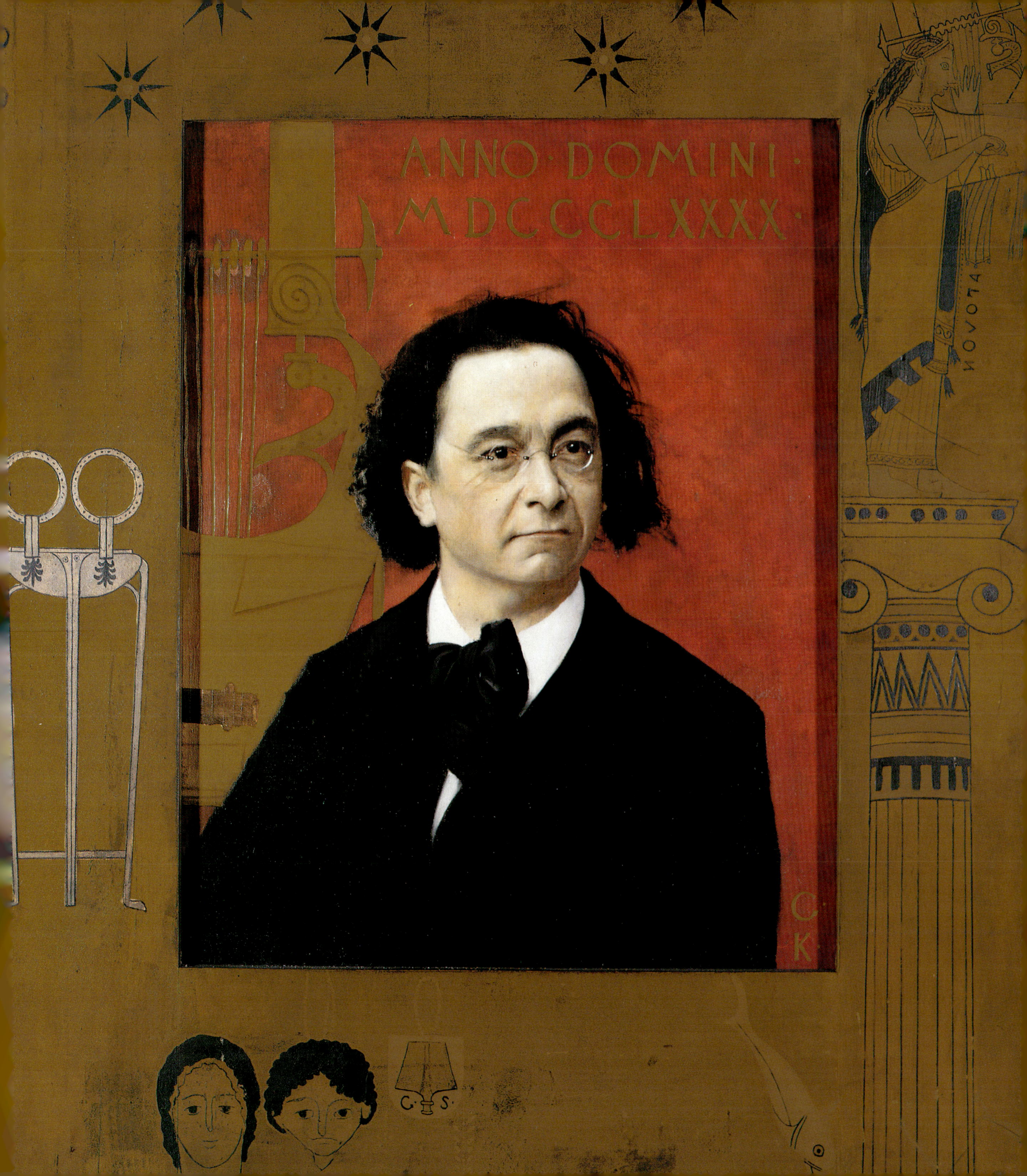
ANNO·DOMINI·
MDCCCLXXXX·

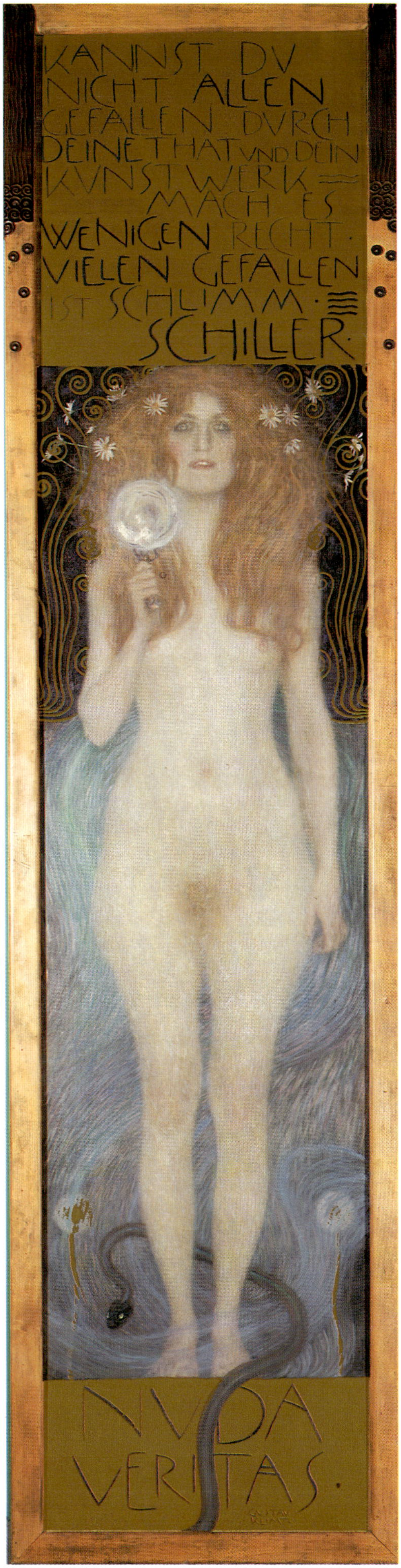
KANNST DV
NICHT ALLEN
GEFALLEN DVRCH
DEINE THAT VND DEIN
KVNSTWERK =
MACH ES
WENIGEN RECHT.
VIELEN GEFALLEN
IST SCHLIMM.
SCHILLER.
NVDA
VERITAS.

Klimt's early years

10 Nude Veritas, 1899
Oil on canvas, 25.2 × 56.2 cm
National Library Vienna, Theatre Collection

Background and training

Gustav Klimt was born on 14 July 1862 in Baumgarten, just outside Vienna; when the boundaries were redrawn in 1892 Baumgarten became the XIVth district of the city. Klimt's paternal forefathers were peasants or soldiers in Bohemia. Ernst Klimt (1834–1892), father of Gustav, moved to Vienna with his parents at the age of eight, from Drabschitz near Leitmoritz, in the Elbe area of northern Bohemia. The grandfather had advanced to the position of lifeguard in the household troops of Emperor Ferdinand I (1793–1875; Emperor 1835–48).

Ernst Klimt became an engraver and married Anna Finster (1836–1915) of Vienna, who in her youth had dreamt of becoming an opera singer; instead she became the mother of seven children.

The family lived in modest circumstances, often in one room. There were frequent moves, whenever the rent could not be paid. The crash of 1873 reduced them to such poverty that Gustav's younger sister, Hermine, later recalled: "There wasn't even bread for Christmas, let alone presents".[20] Gustav Klimt was the eldest son. His sister Klara was two years older, his brother Ernst, born in 1864, two years younger. Hermine was born in 1865, the brother Georg two years later. Anna, who only lived to the age of five, and Johanna, came last.

Gustav spent eight years at the Vienna city school. At the age of fourteen he obtained his leaving certificate. The teachers recognised his gift for drawing and advised his parents to let him sit the entrance examination for the School of Arts and Crafts.

This School had been in existence for little more than a decade. In 1864 Emperor Franz Joseph founded the Austrian Museum of Art and Industry. At the suggestion of the art historian and archaeologist Rudolf Eitelberger von Edelberg (1817–1885) the School of Arts and Crafts was set up as an extension of the Museum. The model for this joint institution was the South Kensington Museum, now the Victoria and Albert Museum. The school was also organised on English lines.

Klimt was set the task of drawing an antique female head. Next to him sat Franz Matsch (1861–1942), with whom he subsequently worked very closely for many years. Both young men passed the examination and had the prospect of a three-year training which would qualify them for the position of drawing teacher in a secondary school. Klimt's brother Ernst passed the examination a year later. Since the brothers received a scholarship, and had to pay nothing for their training, the family's position soon improved. Moreover they were soon commissioned to undertake small pieces of work for their teacher.

Professor Reiser was one of those responsible for designing stained glass windows for the Votive Church which was erected as a memorial of thanksgiving for the safety of the monarch after the attempted assassination. The Klimt brothers and Franz Matsch were commissioned to produce large-scale drawings of the designs. "We were very happy to do it, particularly because he always paid us well. After that time things looked up for us – for the Klimts it was a real blessing".[21]

Franz Matsch recalls this time in his autobiographical writings. Apart from tasks of this sort, the main area of study was classical antiquity. Students were instructed to draw plaster casts in order to learn how a sculpture is transposed to two dimensions. At the same time classical antiquity was supposed to impart a feeling for true proportion. Klimt profited from this basic training for the rest of his life. The creative principles of classical art were always important to him.

In their third year all three had passed the qualifying examinations and wanted to sit the state examination for drawing teachers in secondary schools. "Then it happened that Eitelberger, a man of high rank in Vienna . . . once more visited the School . . . Professor Rieser probably drew Eitelberger's attention to us. He had a thorough look at our work. 'Drawing teachers?' – and shook his head in disagreement . . . 'You must become painters!'. Each of us received a scholarship of twenty guilders a month, and we studied under Professor Ferdinand Laufberger in the Department of Painting and Decorative Art".[22]

Laufberger (1829–1881) had been professor of figure drawing at the School since 1868. He was one of the successful painters commissioned to decorate the public buildings on the Ring. His first task, the creation of the second curtain in the Vienna Opera House, was completed in 1869. After that he was involved with the wall paintings for the stairway of the Austrian Museum of Art and Industry and was responsible for the medallions on the façade of the School of Arts and Crafts when the new building was put up between 1873 and 1879. His paintings were always attuned to the architecture he was decorating. He was of the opinion that the paintings were subservient to the architecture and he did not accord them an independent, let alone a dominating, rôle. There was no danger of his work seeming empty or rigid – his forms and figures were charming. Laufberger's ability as a decorative painter was highly rated in Vienna. His principles, and above all the integration of decorative painting in architectonics, were handed on successfully to his pupils.

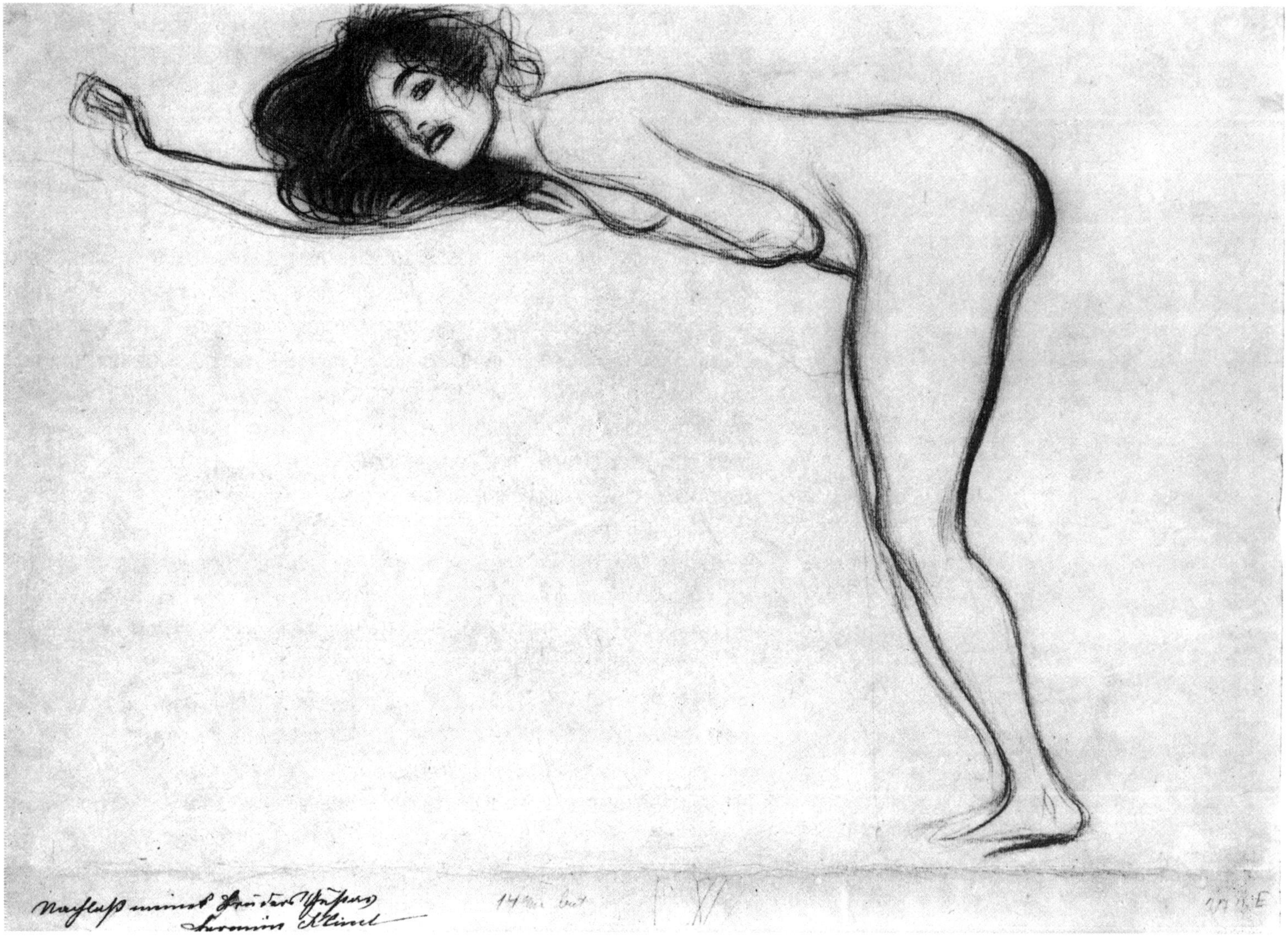

Girl standing with body inclined to the left, 1898
Black crayon, 30.7 × 43 cm

Franz Matsch spoke highly of Laufberger's gifts as artist and teacher: "Not only did Laufberger's own art benefit from his stay in Italy, and the Italian influence; he also brought back to Vienna old formulas and diverse techniques, such as sgrafitto, the old art of fresco painting, the painting of terra cotta, and so on. He mastered these various techniques in practice as well as in theory. That made Laufberger the ideal teacher for the new School of Arts and Crafts that Eitelberger had just founded".[23]

Laufberger was quick to recognise the talent of his three pupils. In them he saw those who would one day continue his own work, so he soon employed them in the public building programme.For the Klimt brothers this meant enormous financial progress. Since joining the painting class they had been augmenting the scholarship money by doing technical drawings for the well-known ear specialist Adam Pollitzer. They also painted portraits from photographs, for which they charged six guilders.

In 1879 their teacher commissioned them to execute his designs for the festoons with allegorical sgrafitto paintings in the courtyards of the Art History Museum in Vienna. He also arranged for them to participate in the preparation of Makart's pageant. Whether they came into contact with Makart himself at that time is not known. A year later their teacher, who had already procured a separate studio for them, recommended the young men to the theatre architects Fellner and Helmer. Between 1872 and 1915 this architect's office built eighty-four new theatres in the Austro-Hungarian countries, in Germany and in the Balkans. Apart from building the theatre they were also responsible for the interior decoration. For this purpose they always had an eye open for capable decorative painters. It was from them that the Klimt brothers and Franz Matsch received their most important commissions during the next few years.

Ferdinand Laufberger died in 1881. His successor, Julius Victor Berger (1850–1902), was another of the Ring painters. He was deeply appreciative of Makart's style, and this probably accounts for the fact that the Klimt brothers and Franz Matsch visited the prince of painter's studio several times. In their painting at this time they were already beginning to take issue with Makart's principles of style.

Although they did not leave the School of Arts and Crafts until 1883, they had set up a studio together in 1881. From that time on they were always sure of public work. Gustav Klimt was just nineteen years old.

Hans Makart – Vienna's prince of painters

Hans Makart (1840–1884), the most favoured of painters, was one of the most striking personalities in Vienna. He began his studies in Vienna and Salzburg in 1858 but moved the next year to Munich, where he studied until 1865, mostly under the great historical painter Karl Theodor von Piloty (1826–1886). It is astonishing that in spite of his long training under Piloty he never mastered the basic principles of historical painting. His paintings had no direct message, and often received a title only after they were finished. It could happen that a personage clad in sixteenth-century costume appeared in a picture on a fifteenth-century subject. For Makart the purpose of painting did not lie in the subject matter but in the magic of shapes and colours.

In 1868, while still in Munich, Makart achieved sudden fame with two of his pictures. The 'Modern Amoretti' and the 'Pestilence in Florence' were considered sensational in every sense. Not only in Munich but also in other German cities, wherever they were shown, they attracted surprising numbers of viewers. The pictures were also shown in Vienna, and it was decided that the painter, who came from Salzburg, should be appointed to an official position in Vienna. The Ring project was in urgent need of good artists; Makart was an Austrian and he had spent a year studying at the Vienna Academy before going to Munich, the artists' capital at the time.

Makart's condition of acceptance – that a studio should be provided for him at state expense – was agreed upon. In 1869 he moved to Vienna and first of all set up his studio according to his wishes. This magnificent studio – in itself a consummate work of art – became so famous that visitors were constantly trying to get in, both in and out of visiting times. Sumptuous fancy dress feasts took place here, to which Makart often succeeded in inviting famous people, for instance Richard Wagner (1813–1883). He lived the life of a wealthy prince.

According to art critic Ludwig Hevesi (1842–1910), about whom more will be said, Makart spent his whole life in costume. This view of the painter's behaviour referred not only to his clothing, but also to his bearing. He made the costume of a prince or a Maecenas his own. "He was not, like Titian, a clever businessman, who wrote wretched letters to Charles V about his financial embarrassment in order to obtain lucrative privileges in connection with his woodland property in the Ampezzo valley. He was a nobleman wallowing in gold, a Lorenzo de' Medici, and like him he designed legendary processions. His whole life was decked out as a fairy tale, with Vienna as his Baghdad; the year had to have 365 days and 1001 nights."[24]

Although he had been officially appointed in Vienna, public commissions were not forthcoming. Makart's activities were limited at first to setting up his studio and his own apartments. Then he designed interiors for private residences on the Ring and painted society portraits. His pictures were sold by private dealers for enormous sums. After the crash of 1873, however, his main source of income, namely the commissions for interior decorating, dwindled to almost nothing.

In 1879 he was granted a chair at the Vienna Academy, and in the same year he was given his first official task: he was to be in charge of the 1879 pageant. His penchant for historical costume made him the ideal person (see p. 11–14). The first thing he did was to prepare sketches – typically, for him, not drawings but oil on canvas. Within a few weeks he produced a cycle of paintings consisting of 35 individual studies. Afterwards he was to reproduce the whole cycle in large pictures for the new Town Hall so that there would be a permanent record of the glorious pageant, but this project came to nothing because of his exorbitant honorarium requests.

In 1887 he was commissioned to decorate the staircases of the Art History Museum. At his death in 1884 the lunettes were almost finished, but he had not been able to paint the ceilings, the spandrels or the intercolumnar spaces. He had received commissions for two further pieces of work: the decorating of the stairways in the Burg Theatre and the painting of Empress Elisabeth's rooms in the Villa Hermes situated in Lainz, outside Vienna. For these he had completed the designs but not begun on the actual painting. This meant that the lunettes were the only official evidence of this prince among painters who had been a leading figure in Vienna in his time, but whose fame quickly faded after his death.

The 'Company of Artists'

Franz Matsch and the Klimt brothers owed the setting up of the studio they shared to the initiative of their teacher, Laufberger. It was his support that won them their first commissions. The great success of this 'Company of Artists', as they called themselves from 1881 onwards, lay in the fact that they could work more quickly than one painter alone, and yet could guarantee unity of style. This was partly because they had trained together under the same teacher, partly because they saw themselves as painter-decorators and set no store by establishing individual artistic identities.

This phenomenon was not destined to last; there came a time when Gustav Klimt in particular began to change, and the end of the Company of Artists was clearly to be foreseen. But for a good ten years the studio was a flourishing concern, with various styles learnt under Laufberger at its command.

Franz Matsch was the unacknowledged head of the enterprise. He did the paperwork, kept the accounts and in general organised things. Moreover he had a special gift for ferreting out commissions.

The three artists worked according to clear plans. Only in two cases – in the Villa Hermes in Lainz and the theatre in Karlsbad, when they were decorating the curtain – did they work, as Franz Matsch termed it, 'all at once and higgledy-piggledy'. As a rule there was a clear division of work. As soon as they received a request for sketches to be submitted for a project, each one of them produced a complete set, giving the client the opportunity to choose one of three alternatives, or a combination of two or three. When the sketches were returned, the artists drew lots to decide which of them would paint which picture, so that it was quite possible that Gustav Klimt might paint from one of Franz Matsch's designs, or Matsch from one of Ernst Klimt's designs.

But the distribution was perhaps not quite so fair as Franz Matsch suggests in his memoirs. The youngest member of the group, Ernst Klimt, seems to have played a subordinate rôle. On several occasions his signature is found only on borders or background painting. Nevertheless it is important to keep in mind that design and execution did not have to be the responsibility of one and the same person. The

11/12 Love, 1895
Oil on canvas, 60 × 44 cm
Vienna City Museums

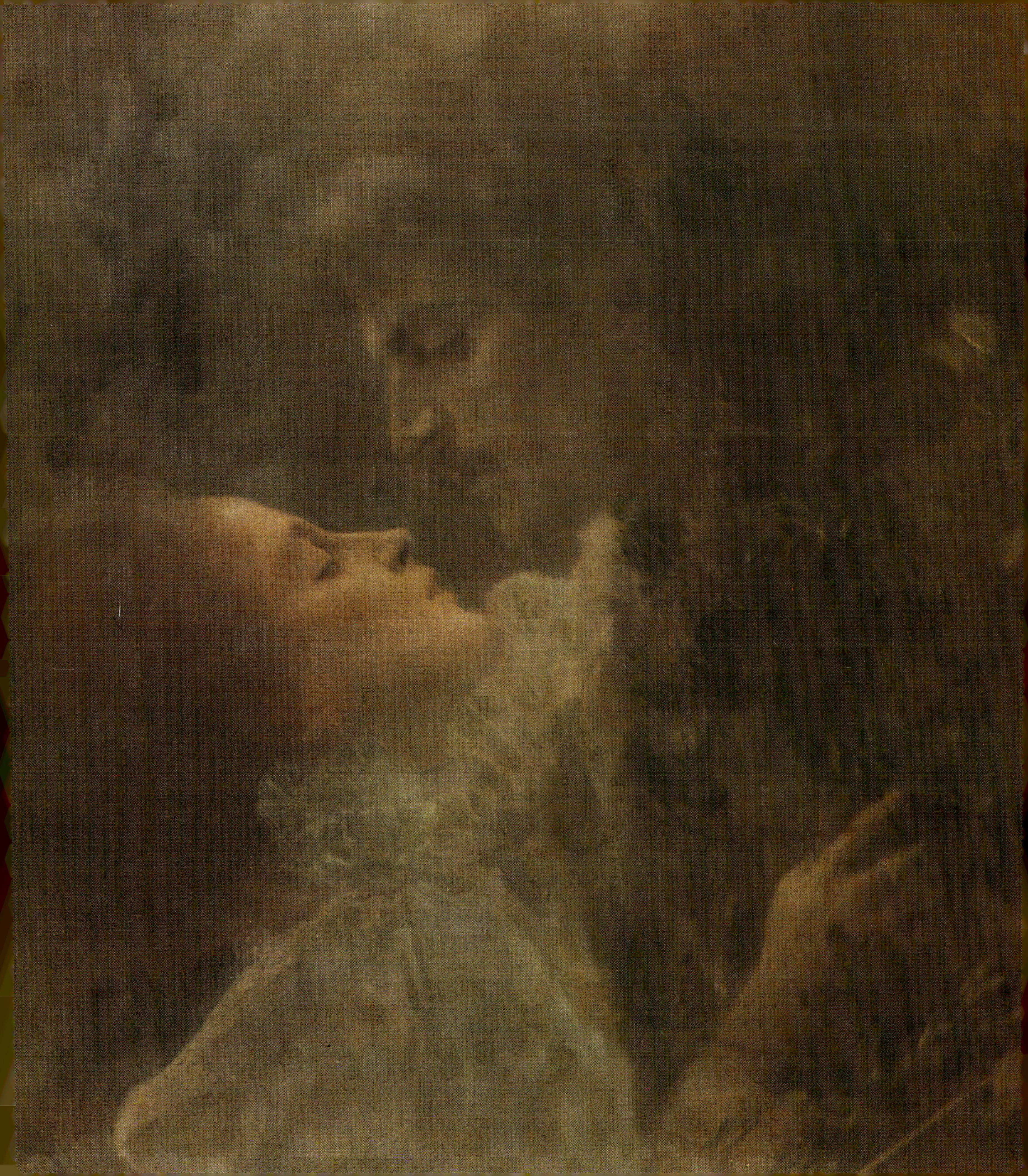

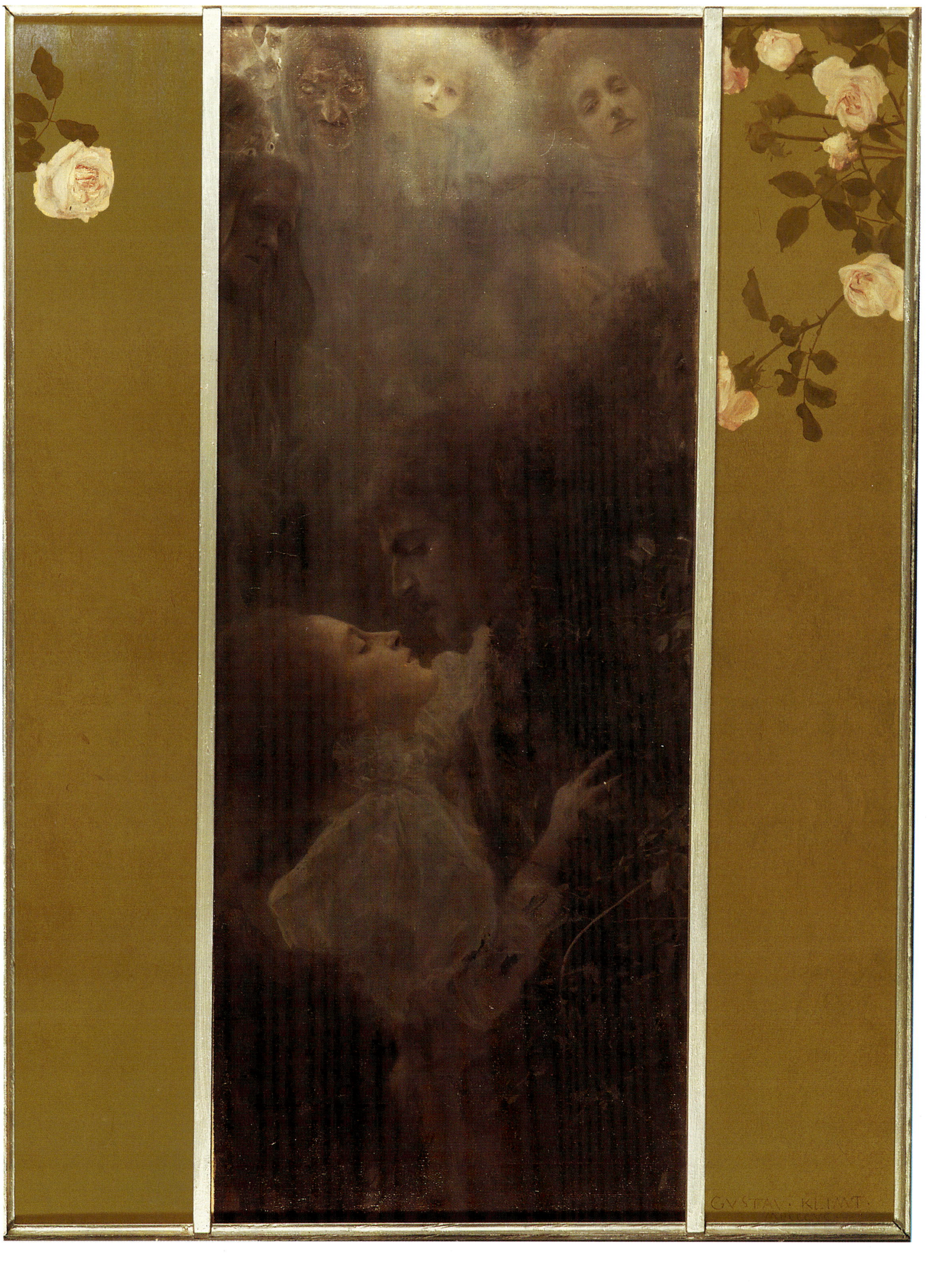
GVSTAV · KLIMT ·

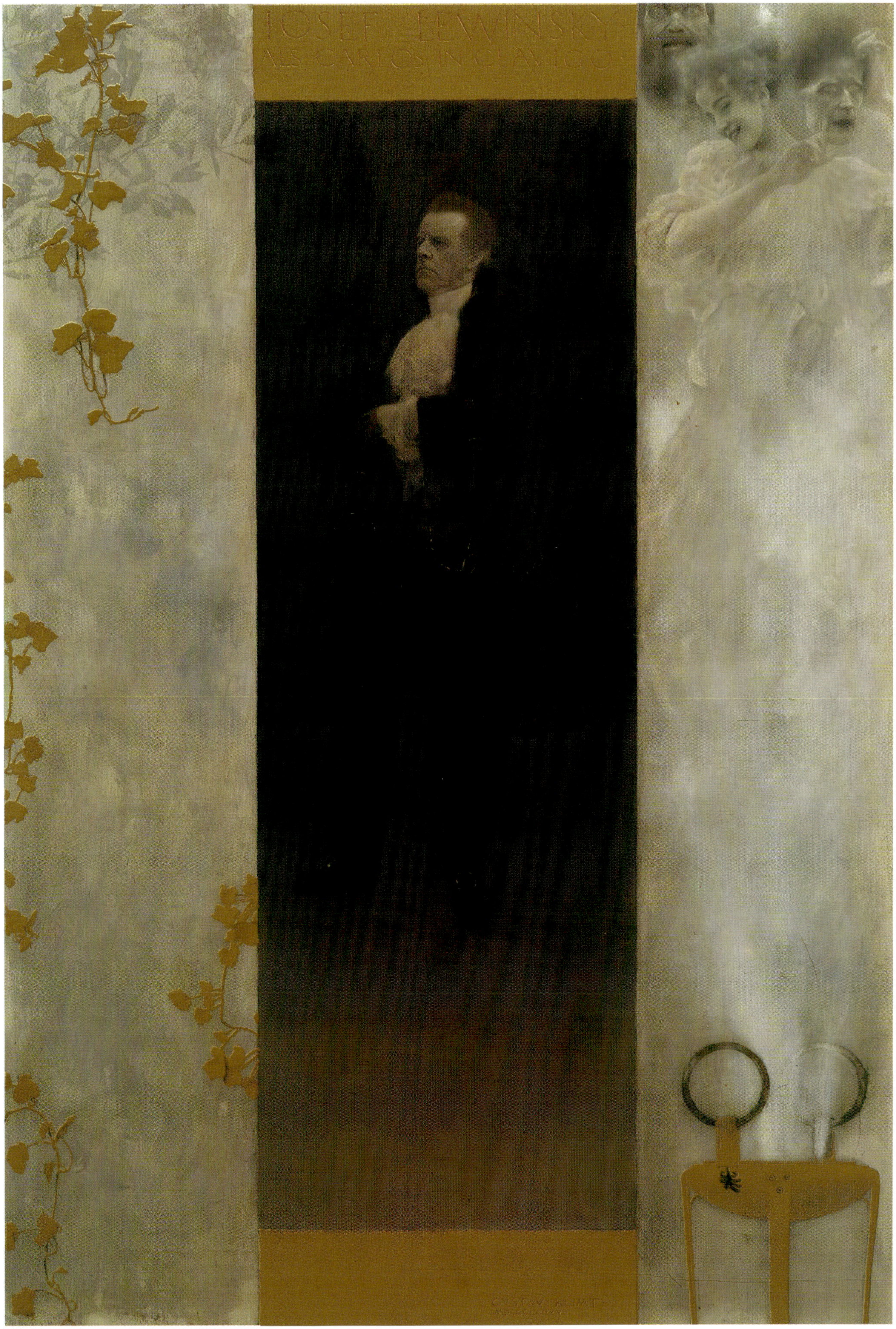
IOSEF LEWINSKY
ALS CARLOS IN CLAVIGO

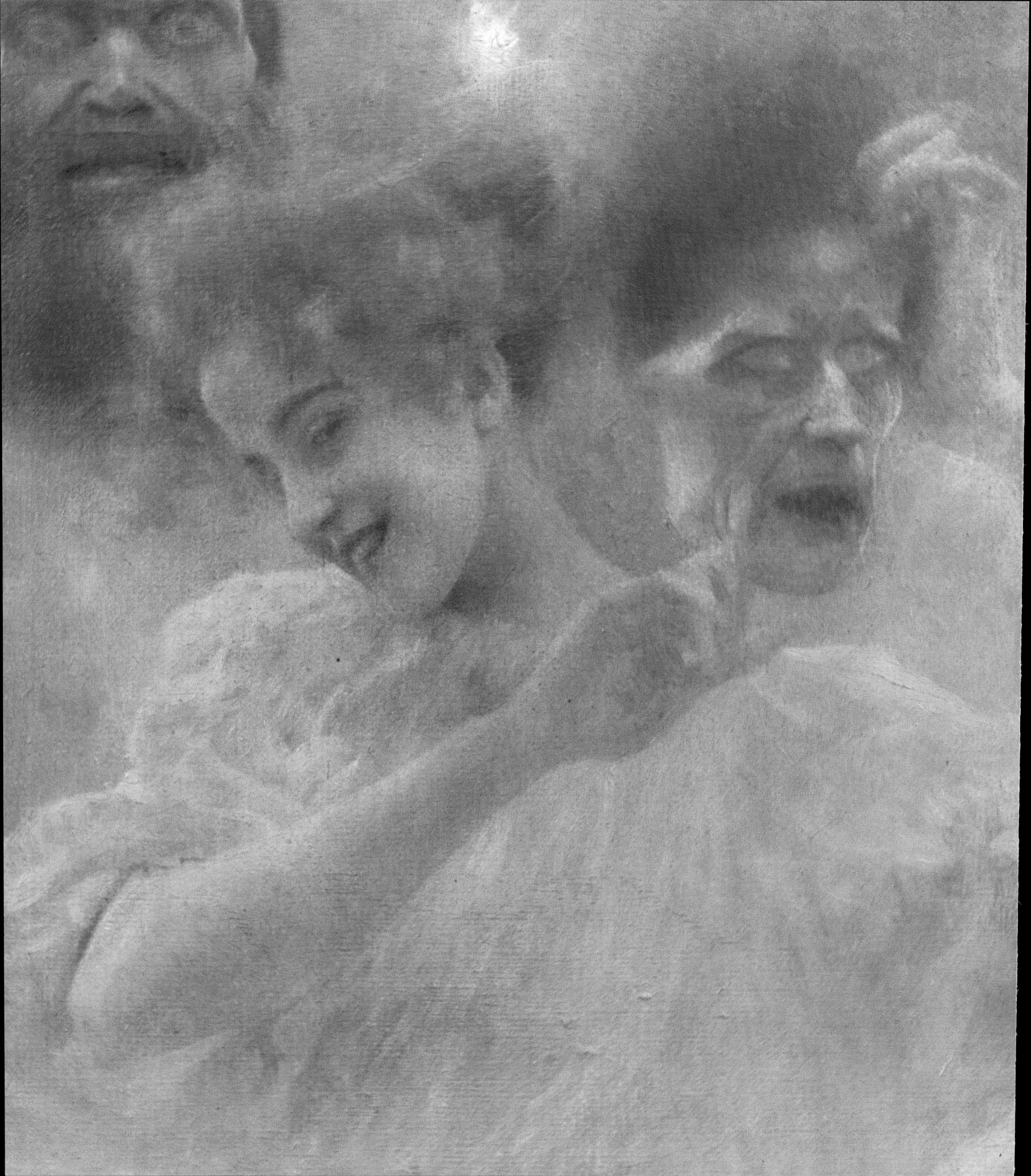

artists did not see themselves as individual 'creators', rather they maintained that they were interchangeable.

In 1880, before the Company had actually been set up, the studio received its first independent commission. For the meeting-room in the house of a master builder they produced four oil paintings which were fitted into the corners of the ceiling and given stucco frames. Franz Matsch recorded that Gustav Klimt painted 'Music', his brother Ernst 'Dance' and he himself 'Poetry' and 'Drama'. The paintings depict four female figures 'swaying in the air', with their distinctive attributes. 'Drama' carries a mask in her hand, 'Music' blows two wind instruments, and so on.

These pictures are strongly influenced by Laufberger, as are the first drawings for the compendium, 'Allegory and Emblem', a work which occupied them from time to time over a period of many years. It was a good source of income, again procured for them by their old teacher.

The three-volume work comprised 'Original designs by the most outstanding modern artists, and reproductions of ancient guild emblems, with modern heraldic figures in renaissance style', as advertised by the subtitle. This was no exaggeration, since such important contemporary painters as Max Klinger and Franz von Stuck (1863–1920) agreed to participate. Albert Ilg (1847–1895), a director of the Imperial Art History Collections, wrote the accompanying text. The first two volumes, 'Allegory' and 'Emblems and Heraldic Figures', appeared in instalments between 1882 and 1884; the third volume, 'Allegory. New Series', followed more than ten years later, between 1895 and 1900.

This extensive compendium was conceived in the historicist spirit. The aim was a revival of the allegory so frequently used in Renaissance, Baroque and Rococo art. New figures were introduced beside the 'old' allegorical ones. The introduction told the reader that the work aimed to 'illustrate the most important notions of the ideal and the real'. Not only times of day and seasons, and emotions such as love, and realities such as death, but also forms of government, trade, the different estates, and even the modern achievements of technology were presented as allegorical figures. These last in particular met with relentless criticism, which questioned the use of allegory in any form in

13/14 Burg Theatre actor Joseph Lewinsky as Carlos, 1895
Oil on canvas, 64 × 44 cm
Austrian Gallery, Vienna

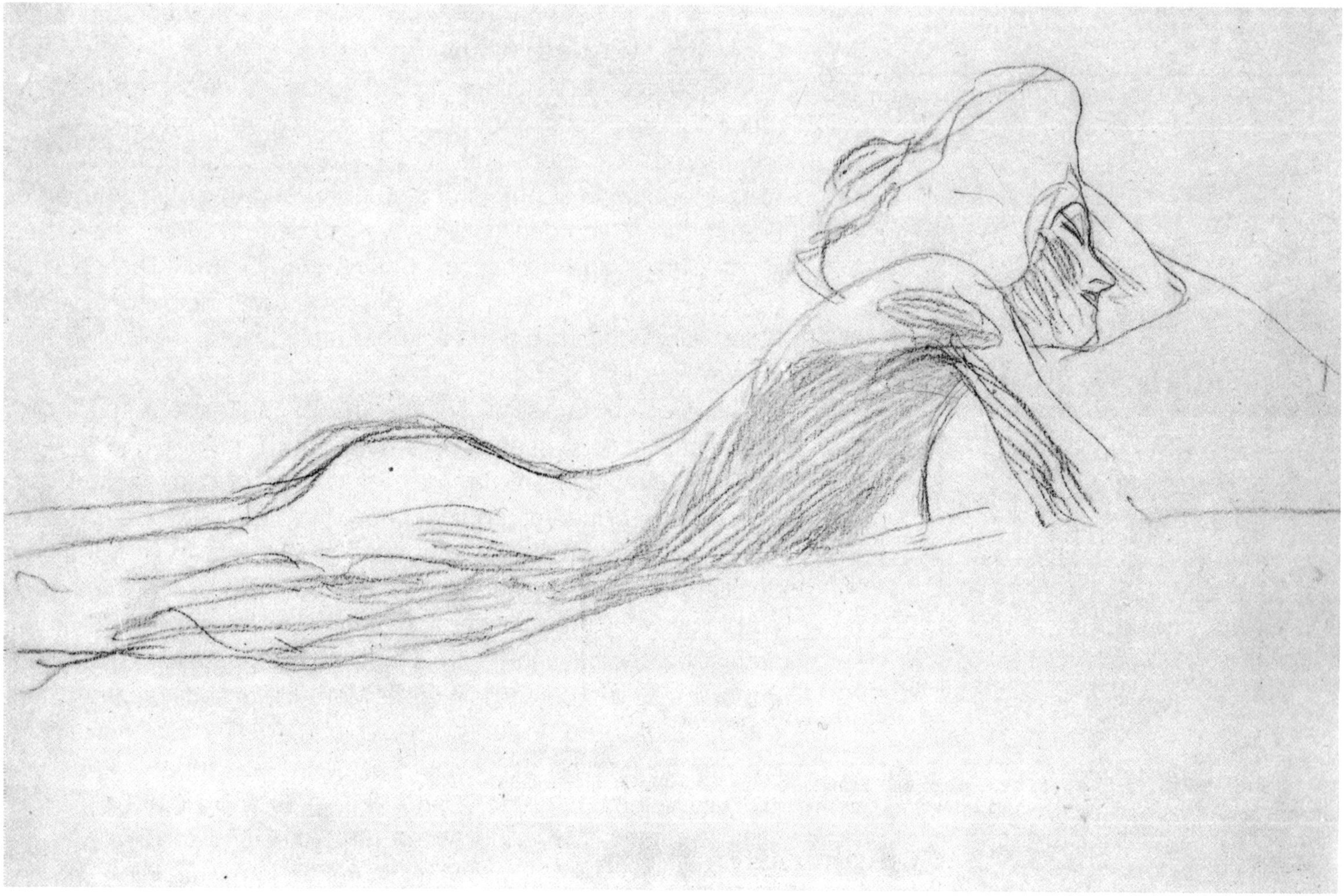

the industrial age, and was particularly scathing about such allegorical figures as magnetism and electricity. Nevertheless the work was very popular, and effective across a wide spectrum.

For the development of Gustav Klimt's drawing this work was of great significance. The first sketches, such as 'The Four Seasons' (1887) and 'Youth' (1882) still show the strong influence of his teacher, Laufberger. In the later pieces, 'The Realms of Nature' (1882), 'Opera', 'Fable' (1883) and 'Idyll' (1884) the influence of Makart is discernible, which is to be accounted for partly by Klimt's last teacher at the School of Arts and Crafts, Julius Berger, and partly by Klimt's own grappling

Prone figure turned to the right, 1901
Black crayon, 30.5 × 44.8 cm

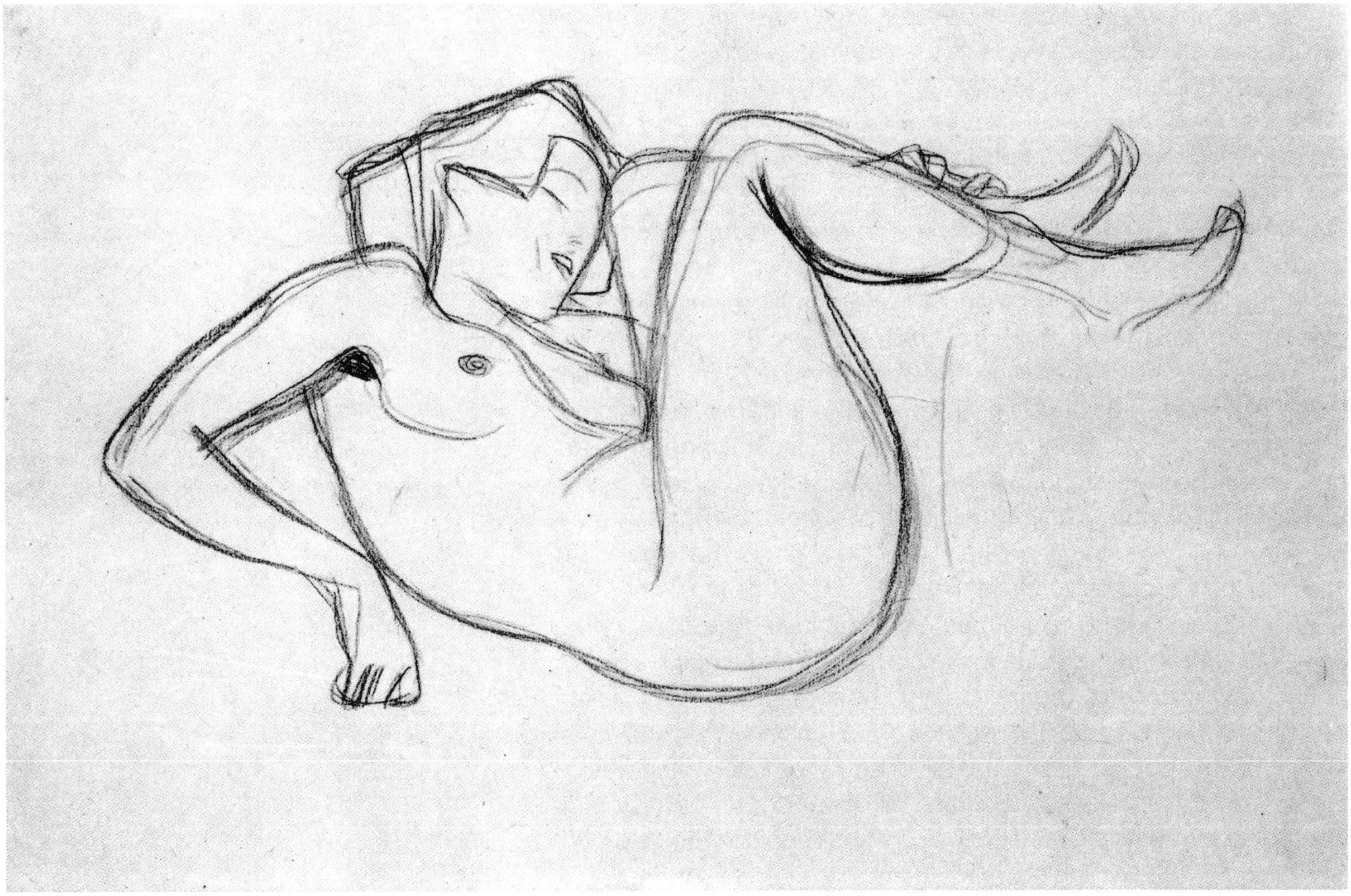

Crouching girl, 1903
Blue pencil, 30.6 × 44.6 cm

with Makart's work. Although Klimt attempted to approach Makart's style more closely, he was not able, even at that time, to free himself from a certain constraint of aloofness which is always evident in his work. He could paint in the style of the older artist but he was not personally involved in the mood of the picture. Makart succeeded in drawing together the mood of the picture and the public response to it.

In 1882 the Company of Artists received their first commission from Fellner and Helmer for the decorating of a theatre. In 1880 they had already worked for the architects' firm on the ceiling of the Kursalon, the spa hall at Karlsbad (Karlovy Vary). Now they were given the much greater task of decorating the town theatre at Reichenberg (Liberec). The work continued through 1883. The execution of the four ceiling paintings was shared equally between Gustav Klimt and Franz Matsch. Ernst Klimt did the painting above the curtain. The curtain itself they painted jointly.

During work on the theatre the three painters made the acquaintance of a rich silver manufacturer in Vienna, who put a large room in his factory at their disposal as a studio. In the meantime they had completed their training at the School of Arts and Crafts. The common studio was necessary for the setting up of their company. Since they had to pay no rent, they designed silver jewellery for the firm, and painted small pieces of ivory which were then set in silver and sold as brooches. They worked in this studio, No. 8 Sandwirthgasse, in the VIth district of Vienna, until 1892. A picture of a cherub blowing a trumpet can still be seen today on the wall of the factory's main stairway, attesting the Company of Artists' nine-year presence in this house.

After the paintings in Reichenberg were completed the artists worked for the king of Rumania. He wished to make a stairway in his castle at Peles into an ancestral portrait gallery. The portraits were to be painted from poor engravings and pictures of old masters. Gustav Klimt is known to have copied Titian's portrait of Isabella d'Este, which was in the Imperial Gallery. During the course of this work the artists had great difficulties with canvas; here too the king wanted them to keep close to the original. Franz Matsch describes Klimt's long search for a suitably patterned damask for the Titian copy. The Klimt brothers also worked on the frescos in the castle, and designed tapestries, but there is little documentation about this.

As well as undertaking these large commissions Gustav Klimt painted other pictures, usually of a personal nature. At the time when he was copying Titian's picture he was also painting his elder sister, Klara. A great many drawings and life paintings in oil have also survived. These pictures reflect the academic style of the times, as do the commissioned works. The last contributions in the two first volumes of 'Allegory and Emblem' are particularly notable, compared with the preceding ones. Klimt was gradually becoming aware of his own capabilities and inclinations. These last inclusions are not drawings as the others were, but oil paintings.

'Fable' (1883, pl. 3) presents a wood which gives an immense sense of depth. In the mid-foreground stands 'Fable', a nude female figure with the drapery that should veil her slipping down from one shoulder. The scientifically designed posture – weight on the standing leg, free leg bent, arms extended straight out from the body and vertical upper trunk – makes the whole figure seem wooden, indeed 'lifeless'. No more dynamic are the sleeping lion on her right and the two storks standing on her left. Even the wriggling frog in the beak of the stork on the right seems suspended in his movements. Only the mice playing on the branch over the head of the sleeping lion bring a little life into the picture.

In 'Idyll' (pl. 4), painted one year later, Klimt succeeded in making his figures more convincing by turning them into stone. Before a background of intertwining branches, leaves and flowers, two nude male figures sit on a marble base, in which the title of the picture, the artist's initials and the year are cut; the secular bodies and their posture are reminiscent of Michelangelo's sculptures. Apart from dark hair, eyes and mouth, the figures are uniformly painted in a yellowish tone. This gives the impression of living heads on stone bodies. Between them the background opens up to reveal – again in a wood – 'Idyll' kneeling in front of her children and giving them a drink.

This picture has a round frame of decorated stucco, and its plasticity is emphasized by the hand of the nude figure on the left which reaches out to grasp it. Because of the frame the tondo seems like a picture within a picture.

In this composition Klimt succeeded in making static lifelessness appear 'natural', no longer irksome as in 'Fable'. The decorative background which was later to become such a distinctive characteristic of Klimt's oeuvre, appears here for the first time. Even though the figures are well defined as bodies, Klimt clearly became aware of his own unwillingness to make them seem life-like. His solution was to present them as sculptures. Only with the heads was he inconsistent. Interestingly enough, providing the examples required for 'Allegory and Emblem' repeatedly gave impetus to his own creative development.

In the years that followed, the firm of architects, Fellner and Helmer, gave the Company of Artists further opportunities to decorate theatre interiors. In 1885 they worked for the National Theatre in Bucharest and for the town theatre in Fiume (Rijeka). A year later they received a commission for the ceiling paintings and curtain for the theatre in Karlsbad (Karlovy Vary). At the same time they tried to establish themselves on a firm footing in Vienna. In 1884 Franz Matsch penned a letter to Eitelberger which all three painters signed. He reminded the influential professor of Art History that it was he who had diverted them from their plans to become drawing teachers, and who had smoothed the way for them to continue their studies. At the same time he wrote of the founding of the studio and listed the commissions executed to date. Finally, he requested Eitelberger to use his influence on their behalf.

The letter reached its addressee at exactly the right moment. Makart had died before his official commissions could be carried out. Only the lunettes in the stairways of the Art History Museum were nearing completion. The apartments of the empress in Villa Hermes in Lainz, outside Vienna, were still bare. Only the designs were there. For the large ceiling and wall paintings artists were being engaged who had worked closely with Makart, in the hope that the prince of painter's style might be maintained. For the cavetti in the bedchamber Makart had planned scenes from Shakespeare's 'A Midsummer Night's Dream'. This cycle was entrusted to the Company, but they did not – as has been assumed until recently – work directly from Makart's designs. Franz Matsch's memoirs make it certain that the painters received sketches from their teacher, Julius Berger, who did indeed base his sketches on Makart's designs. It is remarkable that the artists departed at this point from Makart's 'baroque' style of painting and turned to much stricter forms, closer to the classicist tendencies of the German painter, Anselm Feuerbach (1829–1880).

When work on 'A Midsummer Night's Dream' was completed they were asked to take over complete responsibility for the ceiling painting in the empress's salon. They painted 'Spring' direct onto the ten-meter-long ceiling from Franz Matsch's sketch. The goddesses Flora and Diana float in the vault of heaven, genii hold ribbons and bouquets. The relatively sparsely painted ceiling appealed to the empress far more than the luxuriance of the bedchamber in the spirit of Hans Makart.

At the time the Company was said to be a thoroughly capable group of painter-decorators, concerned to continue work in Makart's luxuriant style. Through Eitelberger the artists had come into contact with the architect of Villa Hermes, Karl Freiherr von Hasenauer (1833–1894). He was the best known architect in Vienna at the time, entirely committed to historicism. His official state buildings were erected in High Renaissance Roman Style or in High Baroque. In 1871 Hasenauer was appointed chief architect of the Great Exhibition of 1873 in Vienna. Important buildings in this connection are the Art History Museum (1872–81) and the Burg Theatre (1874–88). The plans for the theatre were designed jointly by Hasenauer and Gottfried Semper (1803–1879), but Hasenauer alone was responsible for the building after Semper's departure from Vienna in 1876.

The Company owed their most important large-scale commission in Vienna to Hasenauer. It is an irony of fate that they were chosen to continue the tasks which the prince of painters had begun to work on at the very moment when they were turning away from his principles. It had taken twelve years for Makart to receive a public contract, after he had first been appointed in Vienna. At the time, in 1881, he was 41 years old. The Company had just set themselves up, having completed their studies three years earlier.

Gustav Klimt was 24 when he was asked to do the paintings for the Burg Theatre stairway.

The Burg Theatre ceilings

In 1885 Eitelberger and Hasenauer appeared in the Company's studio in order to look at the ceiling paintings for the theatre in Fiume (Rijeka), now nearing completion. These paintings found approval and not long after that Hasenauer gave the artists verbal assurance that they could count on the contract for the ten paintings in the two main stairways of the Burg Theatre. The official contract was issued on 20 October 1886 by the buildings committee responsible.

Adolf von Willbrand (1837–1911), the theatre director, had determined that the pictures should present a world history of theatre. For each stairway four ceiling paintings were planned, and a fifth picture in the tympanum over the entrance. In the stairway on the right Gustav Klimt executed the ceiling paintings 'Thespian Cart' and 'Shakespeare's Theatre' ('Romeo and Juliet'), and 'Dionysos' Altar' in the tympanum. The 'Greek Theatre Scene' ('Antigone') was done by Franz Matsch, 'Molière's Theatre' ('Le Misanthrope') by Ernst Klimt. In the northern stairway on the left, Gustav Klimt painted only the 'Taormina Theatre', whereas Franz Matsch executed the 'Classical Improvisation', the 'Mediaeval Mystery Stage', and in the tympanum 'Apollo's Altar'.

This last picture has in the past been attributed to Gustav Klimt, but since the publication of Franz Matsch's memoirs and the discovery during the 1976 restoration work of his signature, there can be no doubt about the matter. In the northern stairway Ernst Klimt again painted only one picture, namely 'Buffoon on the Impromptu Stage in Rothenburg'. It often used to be said that Gustav Klimt completed this picture after 1892, and comments made by his sister, Hermine, were cited. In the meantime, however, it has been shown that shortly before his death Ernst Klimt took up this subject once again and made an easel painting of it, which Gustav Klimt completed between 1893 and 1894. The painting in the Burg Theatre is entirely Ernst Klimt's work.

In subject matter the pictures in the two stairways form two distinct groups. The artists themselves could determine the subjects for the tympanum paintings. They drew their ideas from the ceiling paintings and chose to portray the two Greek gods from that series.

'The Altar of Dionysos' in the southern stairway signifies the very beginnings of the theatre. It was from the rituals enacted in honour of the Greek god that the classical theatre took its origins. As the number of onlookers increased, so the circular space, where they had gathered in order to watch the players in the middle, gave way to the amphitheatre, with stage in the middle and raised seating for the audience. An integral part of this ritual performance was the appearance of

15/16 Sonja Knips, 1898
Oil on canvas, 145 × 145 cm
Austrian Gallery, Vienna

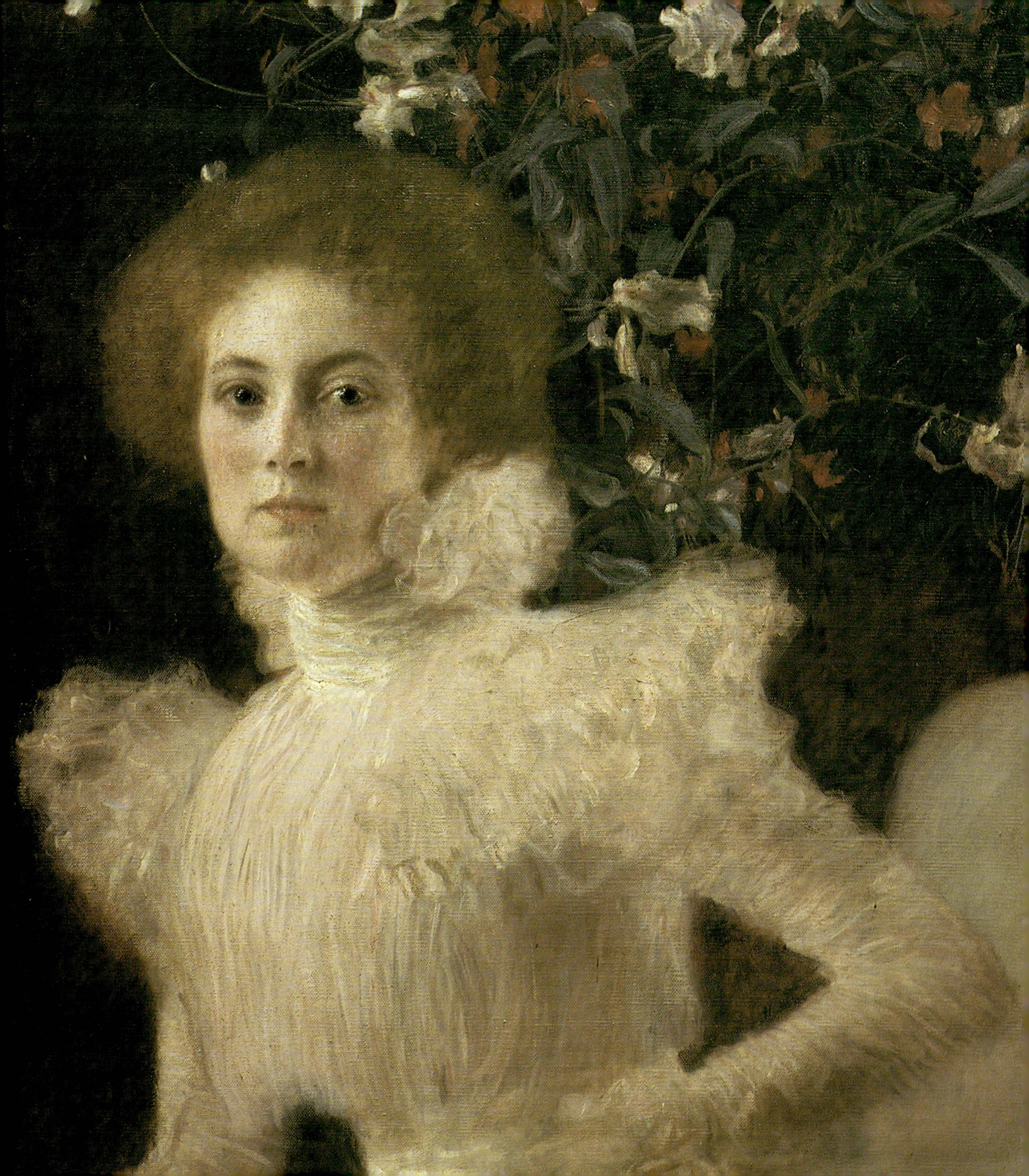

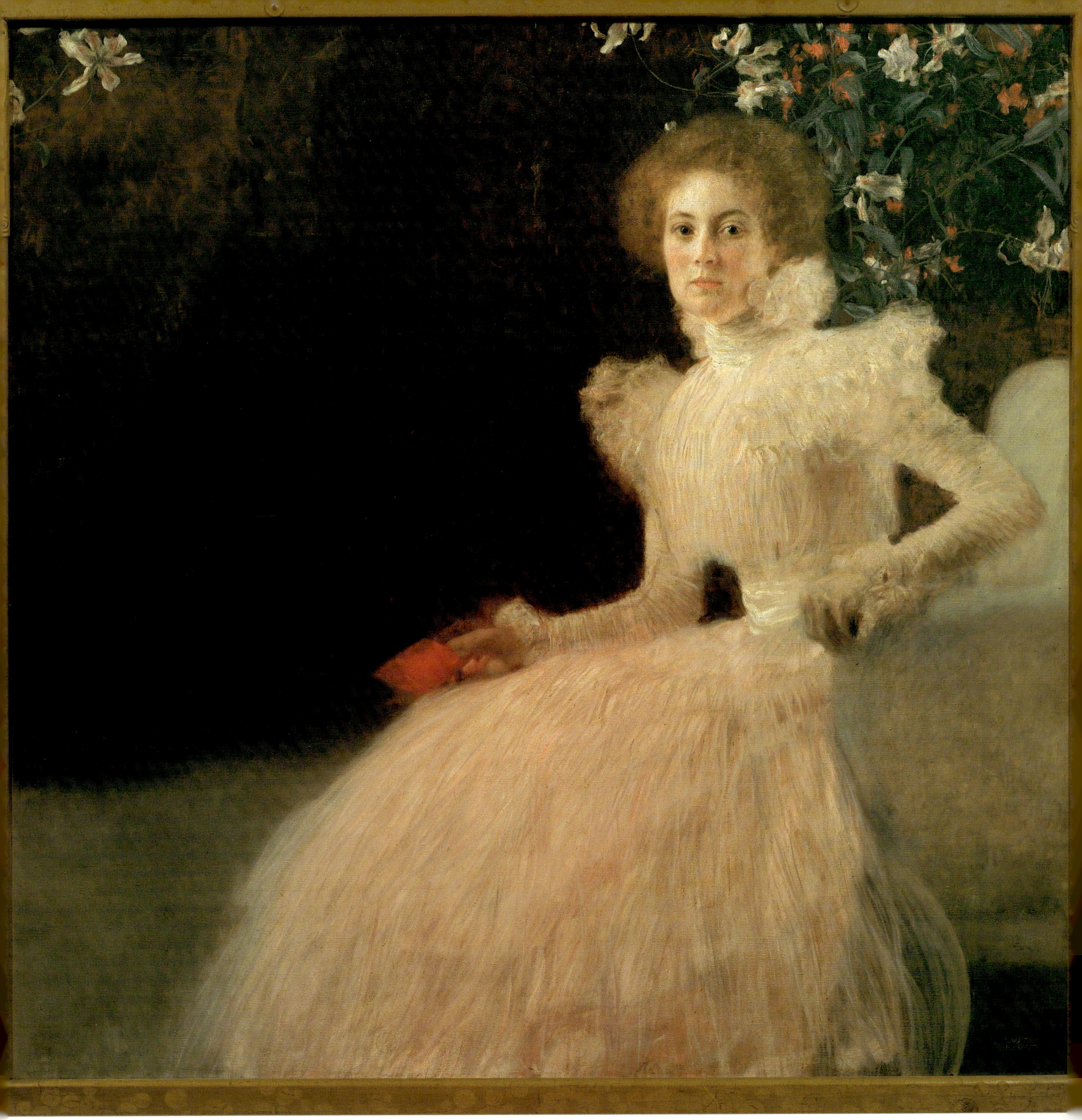

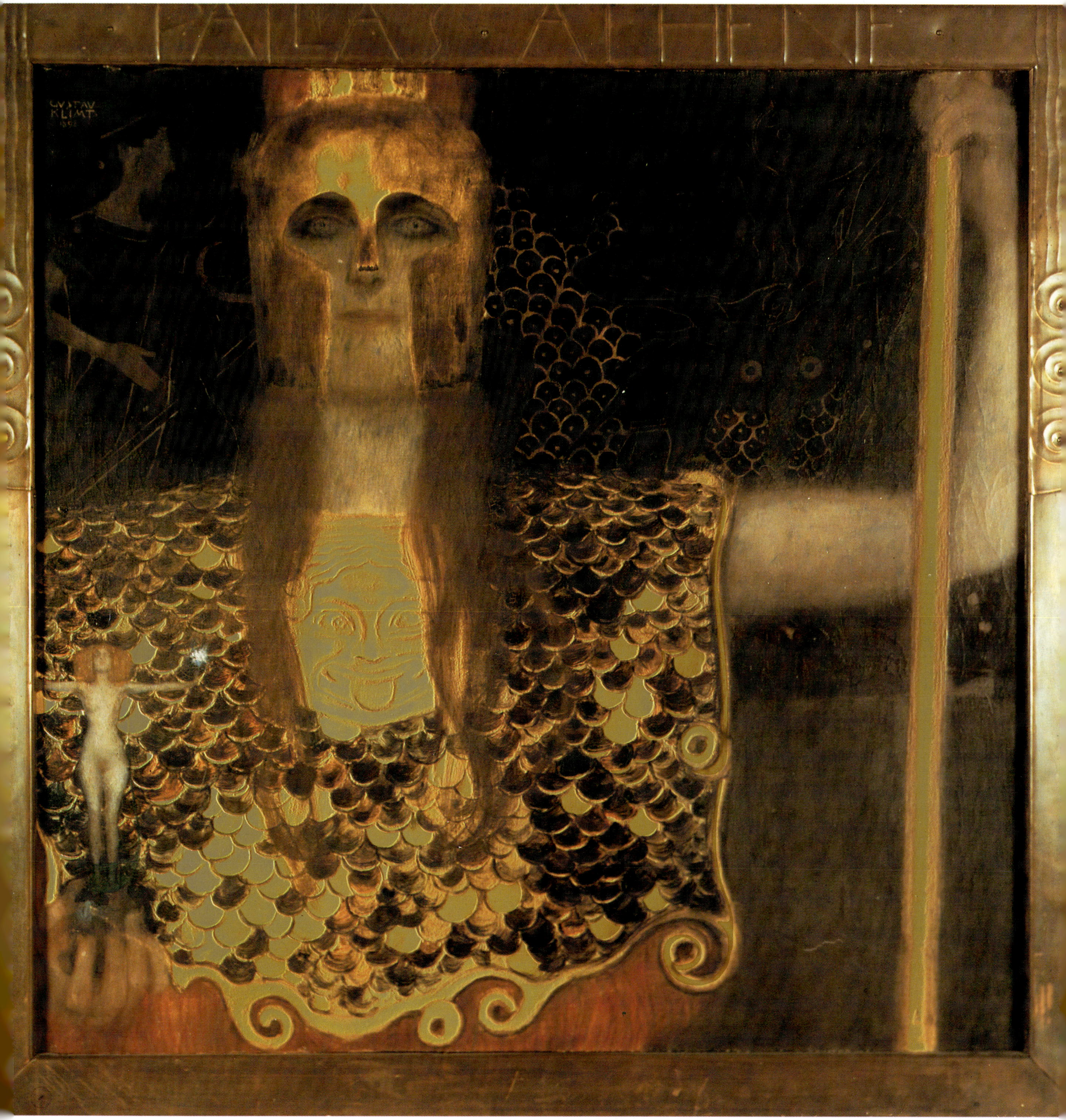
PALLAS ATHENE

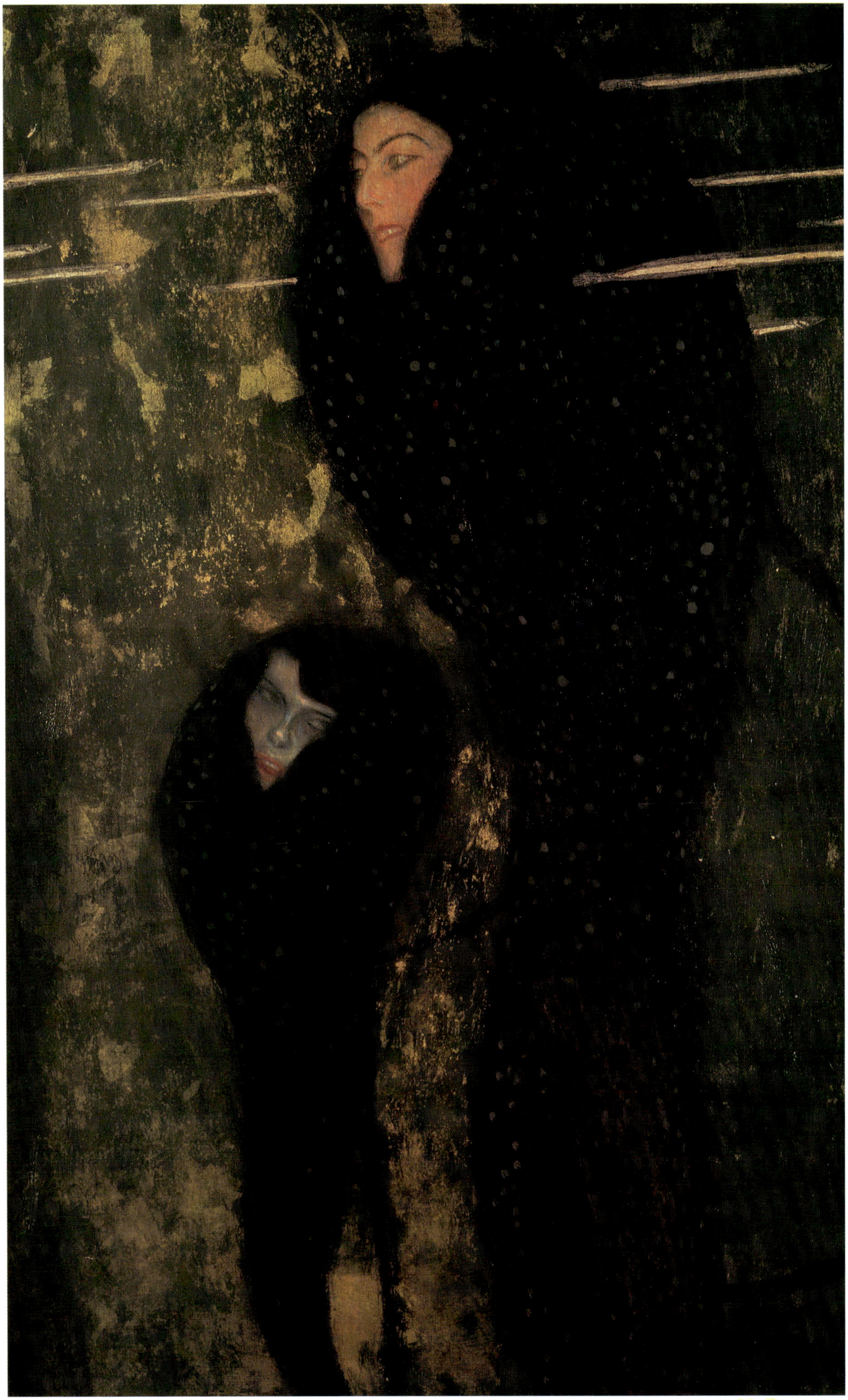

17 Pallas Athene, 1898
Oil on canvas, 75 × 75 cm
Vienna City Museums

18 Water Sprites, c. 1899
Oil on canvas, 82 × 52 cm
Zentralsparkasse, Vienna

Dionysos' followers. Dressed in goatskins the sileni and satyrs danced round the altar and sang songs drawn from myth. The 'goat songs' were called 'tragodia'. After them came the satyr players, out of which the 'komodia' developed.

On the occasion of one of the great Dionysos festivals in Athens in 534 BC, a man named Thespis was represented on one of the carts in the procession. Later on this 'Thespis cart' became the symbol of the travelling theatre, so two of the five pictures are devoted to the beginning of the theatre. The remaining three show scenes from the most famous plays of three great dramatists who had a decisive influence on the theatre.

In the northern stairway it is music, dance and the impromptu stage that are represented rather than classical drama. The tympanum is devoted to the god Apollo because one of his functions is to watch over music and the arts, as lord of the muses. Again, there are two ceiling paintings with classical themes, namely, an improvisation, and music and dance in the ancient theatre at Taormina in Sicily. The Middle Ages are represented by a mystery play, and finally there is the buffoon, a traditional favourite with Viennese audiences since the time of Josef Anton Stanitzky (1676–1726).

In these pictures the painters conformed to the scholarly spirit of historicism, trying to recreate the style, costumes and architecture of each era. Since they could not afford so many models, the Klimt brothers and sisters and other friends and relations had to sit for them, and on occasion they sat for each other. It is known that Gustav Klimt worked from posed photographs, and a picture of his brother Georg posing as Romeo for 'Shakespeare's Theatre' has survived. In this picture Klimt also painted the Company of Artists: Ernst Klimt is standing beneath the box leaning against the wall, with Gustav in front, wearing a large ruff, and Franz Matsch in between them. It is the only self-portrait of Klimt in existence.

When the paintings were completed in 1888 and the scaffolding was taken away, the artists were horrified, at least according to Franz Matsch's account in his memoirs. They had to be forced to remain there when Hasenauer arrived with the court official, Prince Hohenlohe, and the building commissioners to inspect the results of their endeavours. The official verdict was more than favourable and the artists' minds were put at rest. The veracity of this anecdote is doubtful. Most probably it was intended to emphasize the modesty of the painters and their critical faculties. They received the highest praise from the emperor in the form of the Gold Order of Merit, so it is very likely that the story was told as proof of their readiness to criticize their own works.

Whatever the truth of the matter may be, the Klimt brothers and Franz Matsch prospered after the completion of these paintings. The contract had secured their position not only financially but also socially. Franz Matsch remarks that until that time they had all three lived a fairly quiet life, but that now a sociable and cheerful time began. In this connection he mentions the portrait of the musician Josef Pembaur (1848–1923) which Klimt painted in 1890. The picture will be of interest later on, since the two years between 1888 and 1890 brought further developments in Klimt's painting.

It is possible to make connections between the classical scenes painted for the Burg Theatre and Klimt's later work. The decorative female figures with their gold jewellery, above all the maenad lying before Dionysos' altar, and the empty background indicate the beginning of a development which came to determine his later work. More evidence of this has come to light, but before more detailed comment on that subject it is necessary to consider another contract which was given to Franz Matsch and Gustav Klimt only, and from which other characteristic traits emerge, namely the pictures of the old Burg Theatre before it was demolished.

In 1887 the Company was commissioned to portray the interior of the old theatre with as much precision as possible. Klimt and Matsch asked to be allowed to postpone the task until they had finished the paintings for the stairways. This was approved and in 1882 they started on the works which were finished the next year. At that time it was not yet possible to take accurate photographs of such large spaces, so the view of the stage, and of the auditorium from the stage, had to be carefully studied.

Lots were drawn and Gustav Klimt was assigned the more pleasant task of portraying the auditorium, but the work was more troublesome than they had expected since the plans they were given were not accurate enough. The result was that they had to measure out the whole theatre again, a thankless task as it was about to be demolished. The great advantage was that they were given two season tickets for the stalls. Their interest in theatre led them to see every play, but they also had to observe the audience since the contract further stipulated that they should include portraits of some 250 prominent theatre-goers. Regular ticket holders were to appear in the picture, but also well-known people in Vienna: first and foremost the emperor and his court in the royal box, then the popular noblemen and officers, representatives of the arts, of finance and business as well as famous people in the private theatres and some of Vienna's most beautiful women.

When the news spread round Vienna that Klimt and Matsch were painting these two pictures they were inundated by models, since everybody wanted to be immortalised in these pictures. They could easily have painted 500 instead of the required 250. In order to give life to his picture Klimt added several women standing or sitting, who are not mentioned in the printed guide leaflets that have survived. Once again he was painting his sisters and their friends. The picture gave Klimt the reputation of being a painter of beautiful Viennese women, which, at a later date, he really did become. With these pictures Matsch and Klimt won the 'Emperor's Prize' in 1890, worth 400 guilders.

In the course of the two years between the completion of the Burg Theatre ceilings (1888) and the next large contract, the spandrel and intercolumnar pictures in the Art History Museum (1890), Gustav Klimt painted a picture of decisive significance which has only recently come to light. In the library of the Austrian Museum for Applied Art is a magnificent volume with the title Homage to Archduke Rainer. On the occasion of the 25th anniversary of the founding of the School of Arts and Crafts, teachers and former students wrote a history of the school, with original illustrations, for presentation to their patron Archduke Rainer.

The work displays every nuance of historicism that the various Arts and Crafts teachers could pass on to their students. The allegorical representation of the three highest arts, architecture, painting and sculpture, was entrusted to the former students Frans Matsch, Ernst and Gustav Klimt. This distinction shows how highly their artistic capabilities were esteemed.

Gustav Klimt's illustration is interesting chiefly because it gives a first suggestion of the use of form which was to attain its full development much later, but which already distinguished his work from that of his fellow painters. The 'Allegory of Sculpture' is a pencil drawing with water colouring heightened with gold, which precedes the section 'School of Sculpture'.

In the middle of the upright rectangular drawing is a nude female figure facing three-quarters towards the front like a turning statue on a pedestal. In her raised left hand she holds a small bronze sculpture of Victoria, the goddess of Victory. Wrist, upper arm, neck and hair are decorated with sumptuous gold jewellery. To the left of her are famous classical sculptures, ranged one above the other to form a kind of pillar. Above the bronze boy with a thorn Athena Parthenos is enthroned, and above her can be seen the head of Juno Ludovisi. The masonry in the background is crowned by an antique relief, for which Klimt chose to follow the pattern on the Sarcophagus of the Muses which had been acquired for the classical collection of the Art History Museum in Vienna. Beneath it the artist's signature and the date 1889 in Roman figures – as in 'Idyll' – are chiselled into the stone.

Klimt created a very similar picture for the third volume of 'Allegory and Emblem' in 1896. It is closely related in composition, although the earlier picture has several antique sculptures and in the later picture 'Victoria' is replaced by 'Eve'. In this picture the sculptures shaped into a pillar have moved into the centre of the picture, with the female figure, Eve, holding the apple (pl. 1) in front. The relief above the masonry has been replaced by an assortment of antique heads. This drawing has in the past been regarded as a turning point in Klimt's oeuvre. The discovery of the earlier picture makes it possible to recognise the new direction leading to Jugendstil seven years earlier, even though Klimt held back in the pictures that immediately followed it; in spite of this restraint there are intermittent signs of the attempt to break away from historicism in the works that post-date the 'Allegory of Sculpture'.

Another picture painted during these years has to do with the Company's social progress. The three artists were present when the

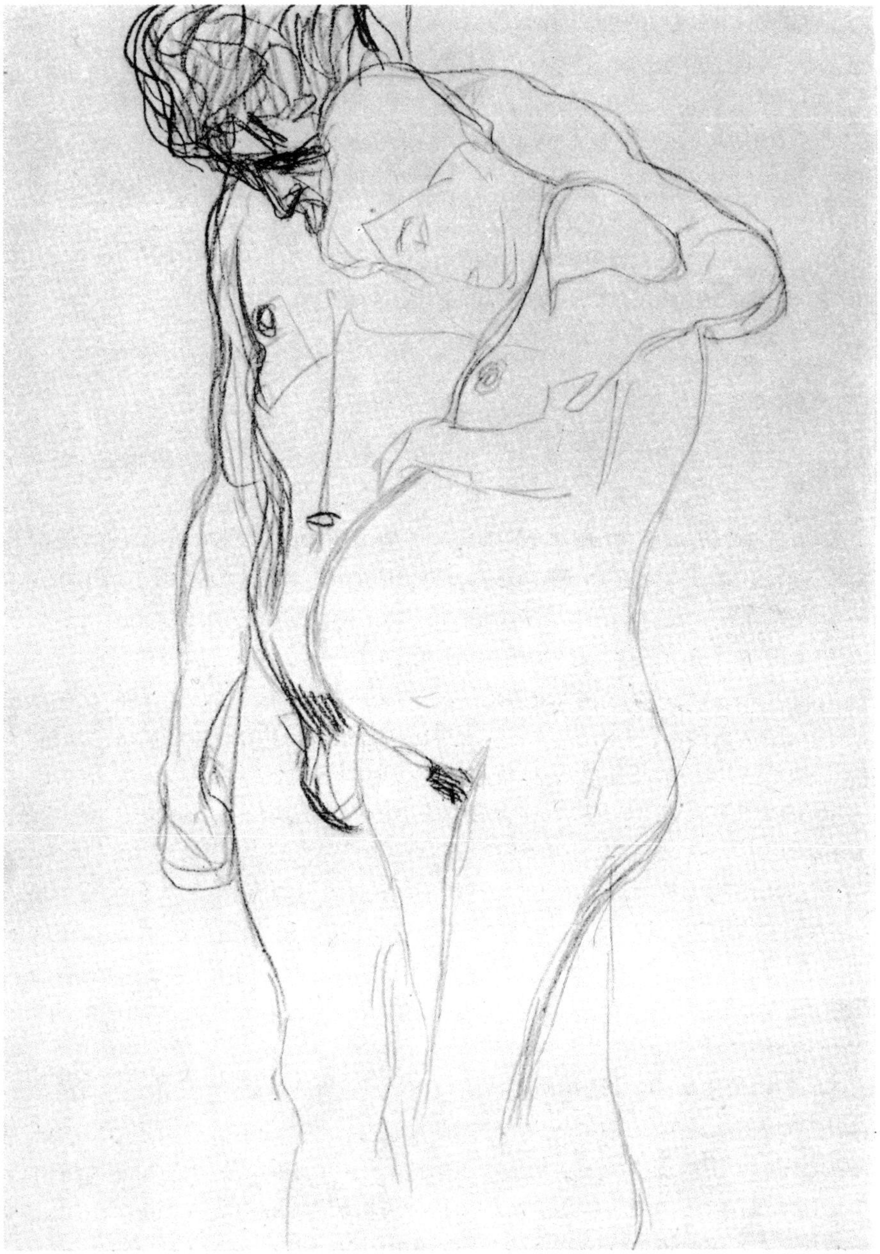

Pregnant woman with man, 1902
Blue and orange crayon, 44.8 × 30.5 cm

memorial to Walther von der Vogelweide was unveiled in Bolzano. On this occasion a friend of theirs, Georg Reimers, spoke in honour of the pianist, composer and keyboard teacher Josef Pembaur, one of those responsible for organising the ceremony. This speech gave rise to the idea of founding a Pembaur Society in Vienna. The members – artists and actors – met every Thursday in the Löwenbräu tavern, and in 1890 Klimt painted a picture of the musician for the room where they met. The picture is set in a painted wooden frame, probably also designed by Klimt. It is a likeness of photographic precision, with a golden lyre in the background indicating Pembaur's consuming passion. The decoration on the frame is a clear sign that Klimt in the meantime was acquainted with English book illustrations.

The murals in the stairway of the Art History Museum

On 28 February 1890 the Company was commissioned to paint the spandrel and intercolumnar decoration in the stairway of the Art History Museum in Vienna. Initially they were also supposed to execute Makart's design for the ceiling, but Princess Marie Hohenlohe-Schillingfürst had intervened for this on behalf of Mihály von Munkacsy (1844–1909); his picture, the 'Apotheosis of the Italian Renaissance', had been in place since 1889.

It had been agreed with Makart that the forty remaining pictures should be painted on a gold ground. The artist had plans for decorative grotesquerie. This was then changed: the director of the Arts and Crafts collection in the Museum, Albert Ilg, author of the commentaries in 'Allegory and Emblem', conceived a series of pictures illustrating the history of fine art and handicrafts from the beginnings up to modern times.

Makart devoted the lunettes to the most famous painters. This did not do justice to the scope of the museum's holdings in sculpture and arts and crafts. Balance was restored in an historicist spirit; the objective of comprehensive representation was achieved in the remaining sequence of pictures, the last, and indeed the lowest. Up aloft the ceiling painting shone resplendent – as it still does today. Just below are the lunettes, let into the cavetti. The main cornice beneath separates the ceiling from the walls, into which are built arcades with pilasters.

It was the wall space between the arches of the arcades and the cornice (the spandrels) and the intercolumnar space between the pilasters that the Company was commissioned to decorate. For this task lengthy studies in the history of art were necessary, but the result was impressive. Even more than in the Burg Theatre pictures, each separate style was faithfully reproduced in the paintings. It is doubtful whether the three painters still drew lots to decide who should paint which picture, since Klimt in particular seems to have assumed responsibility for styles most suited to his own way of painting. The three artists were no longer interchangeable. Gustav Klimt and also Franz Matsch were developing individual styles.

Although the gold ground that Makart had planned was not in the event used, much of the background painting was done in gold and some of the figures were decorated with gold. In the intercolumnar pictures styles were represented by works of art of the relevant time. Klimt created a picture of Egyptian art bringing together several sculptures. In the spandrel picture on the same theme a nude female figure appears in the foreground with works of art in the background.

In the case of classical antiquity the process was reversed: the spandrel picture shows Athena, though in human form; the intercolumnar picture has in the background a vase and a figurine. The 'Girl from Tanagra', intended to symbolise classical antiquity, is a mismatch. She is not placed in the centre of the picture, nor does she look particularly 'antique'. Rather she glances into the picture from the left, as if she was just about to hide behind a pillar again. She resembles more one of Klimt's contemporaries than a classical figure. This marks a stylistic incongruity which points in the direction of Klimt's subsequent development as a painter. In the other pictures he kept closely to the programme agreed. Early Italian was represented by eight different pictures in all, of which he painted one in the style of Sandro Botticelli (c. 1444/45–1510), another in the style of Giovanni Bellini (c. 1430–1506). Overall it can be said that Klimt's pictures are most rigorously composed. The blocked figures are set off against the ornamented wall space.

In this the 'Girl from Tanagra' is no exception. Three-dimensionality is least heeded in this figure. Figure and background create the effect of two layers, one on top of the other. Ernst Klimt, by contrast, developed a much more painterly style, which may, however, be regarded more as imitation of various other trends in style than as his own. Only Matsch continued to display the stylistic multiplicity that kept him in such demand as an historicist painter; in this he had develooped great virtuosity.

Of the total of forty pictures each Klimt brother painted thirteen, Franz Matsch fourteen. Gustav Klimt kept to Egyptian art, ancient Greece and Italian Renaissance. All these styles display the rigorous formal manner which dominated his later work.

In the stairway pictures the differences between the three members of the Company became apparent, but they remained together nevertheless. In 1891 they completed the murals for the Art History Museum and joined the Artists' House association. They were now numbered among the recognised painters of the Vienna Ring.

In 1892 they moved into a new studio in the Josefstädterstraße that Franz Matsch, who lived next door to it, had found. It was a pavilion in an overgrown garden, and later on it became Gustav Klimt's. Egon Schiele (1890–1918) described it in 1907 after his first visit to Klimt: "... in a garden – one of those old concealed gardens which the Josefstadt district have in such abundance – and at the end of the garden in the shade of tall tress, stood a low building with several windows. The path was edged with flowers and ivy. That was where Klimt worked for many years".[25]

Shortly after the move, on 9 December 1892, Ernst Klimt died. Gustav Klimt and Franz Matsch shared the studio for two years, and then parted, but in that time they were given the important commission to decorate the great hall of the university. While there developed a growing separation between Gustav Klimt and Franz Matsch as artists, their social paths also diverged. In his memoirs Franz Matsch noted that after the completion of the ceiling paintings in the Burg Theatre they entered Viennese society. This was true of Matsch much more than of the Klimt brothers, and it was important to him. For the ceiling paintings the brothers had used family and friends as models almost entirely, but in his picture 'The Greek Theatre Scene' ('Antigone') Matsch deliberately gave the female figure standing at the feet of the Sophocles statue the features of the well known Burg Theatre actress

19 Judith I, 1901
Oil on canvas, 84 × 42 cm
Austrian Gallery, Vienna

20 Goldfish, 1901/02
Oil on canvas, 181 × 66.5 cm
Art Museum, Solothurn

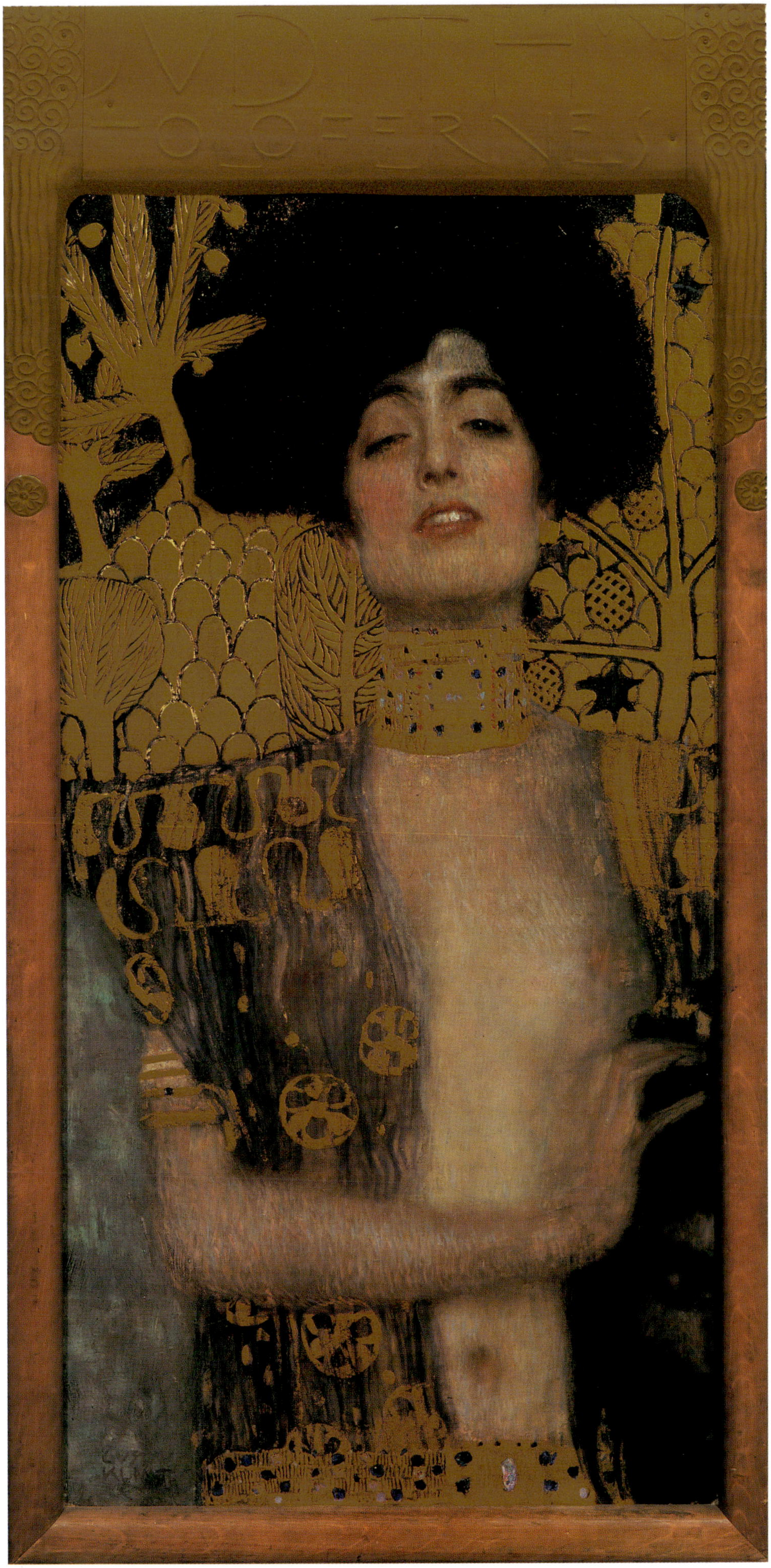

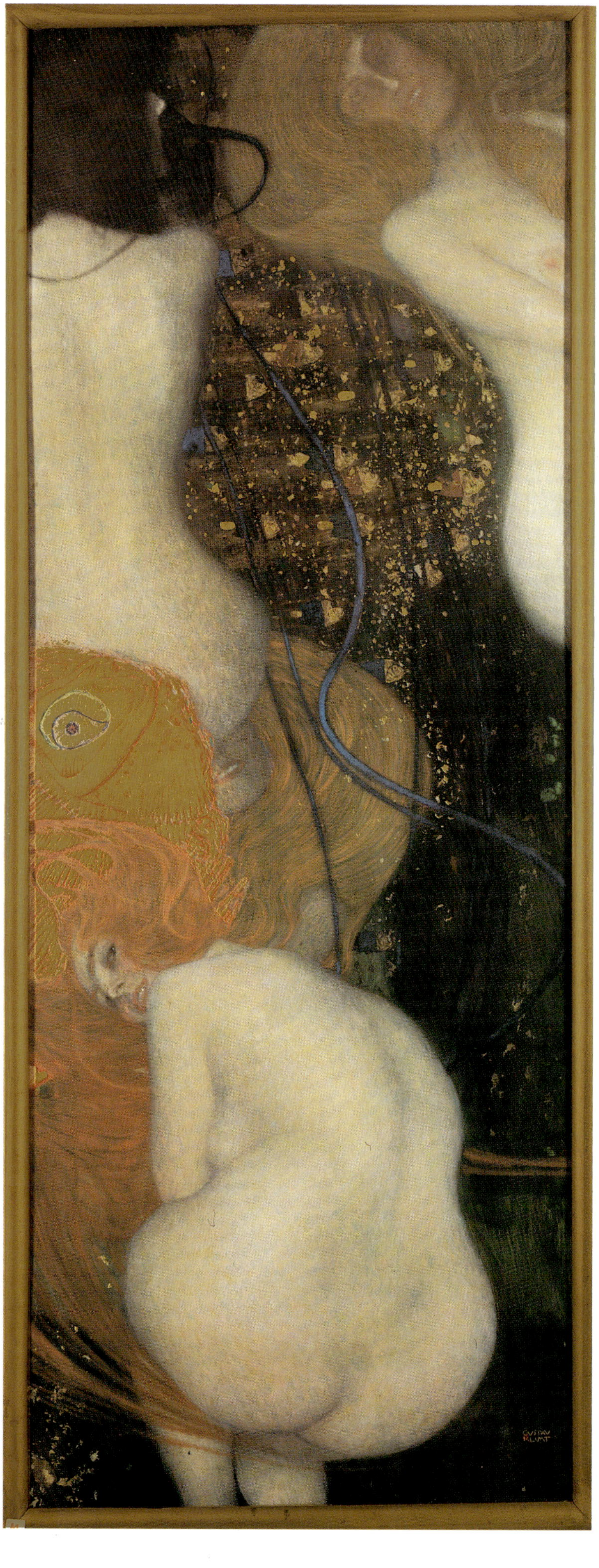
GUSTAV
KLIMT

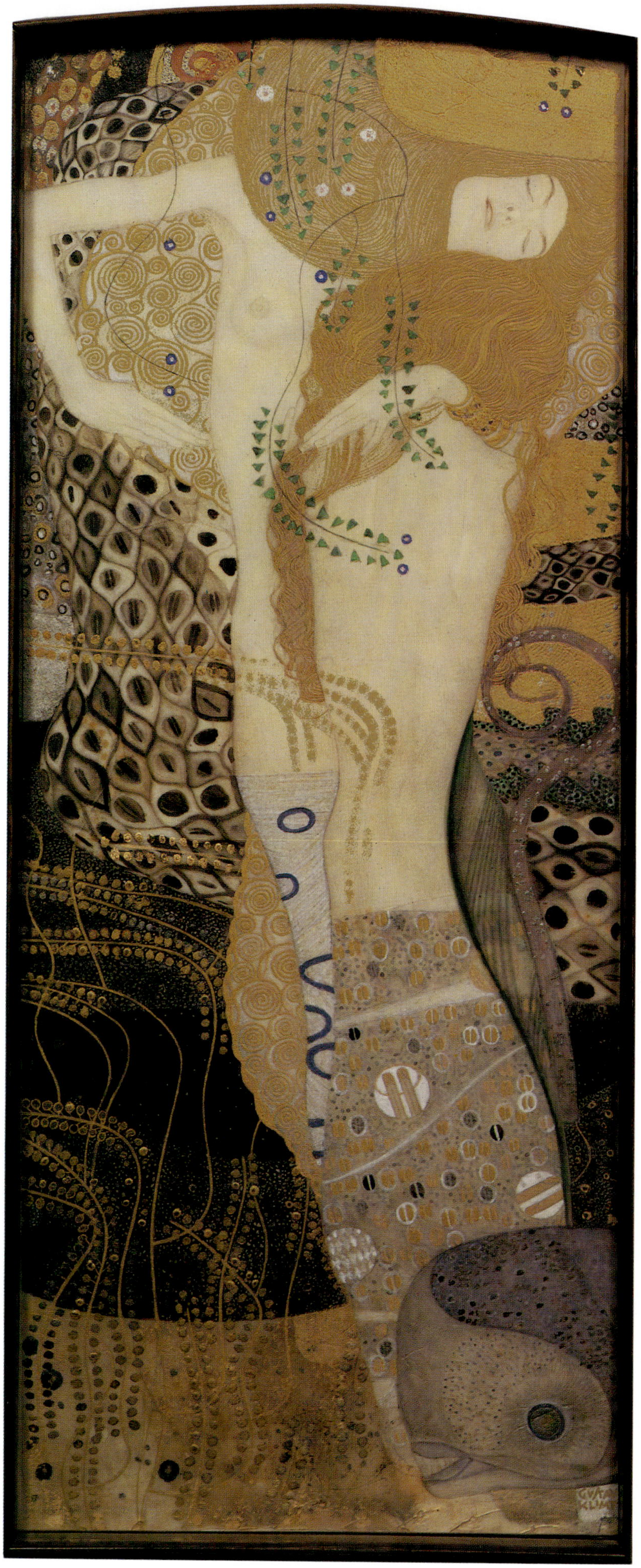

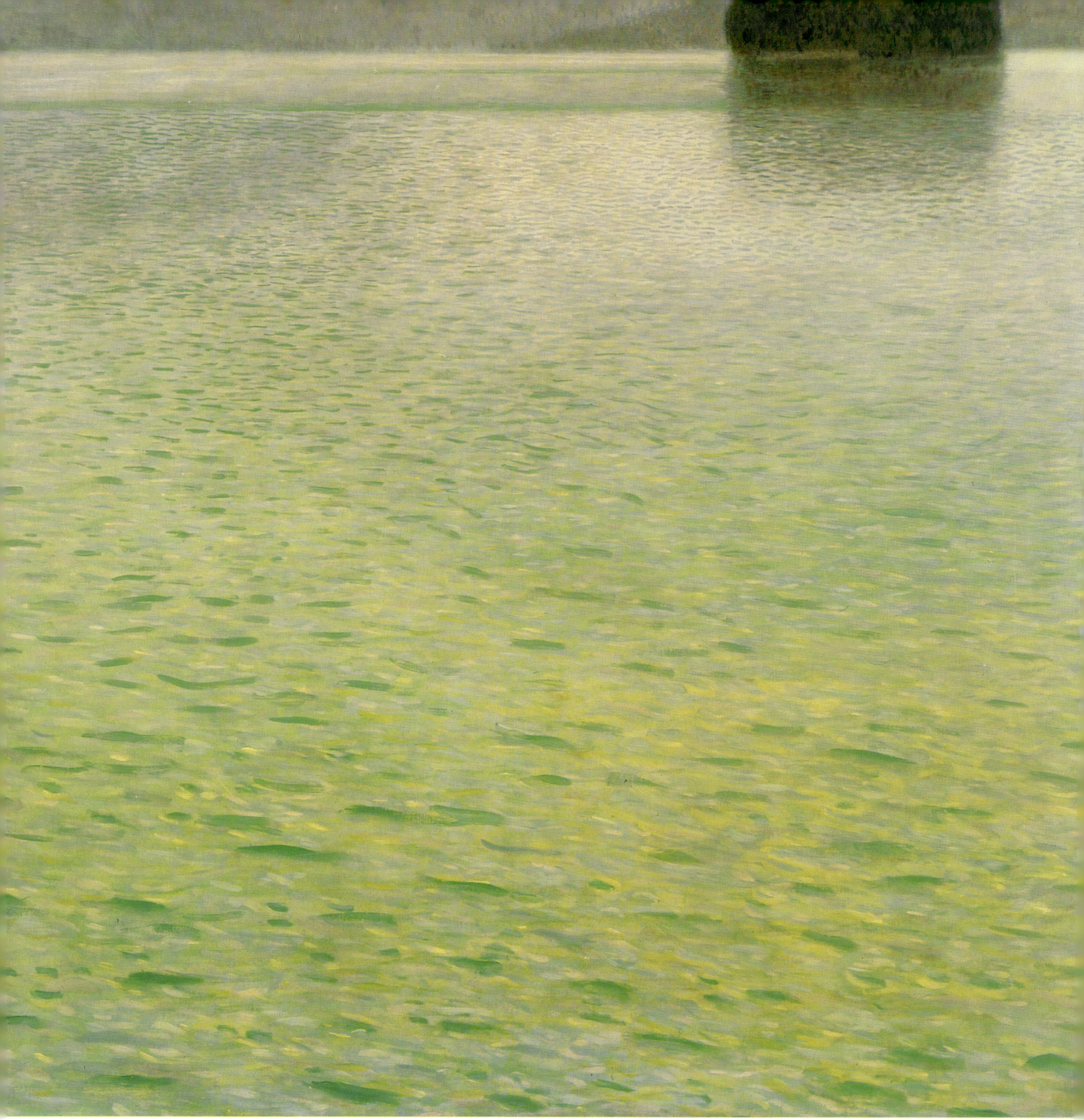

Charlotte Wolter. As a result the actress not only sought his advice on artistic matters but also introduced him to prominent people in Viennese society, giving him in effect an entrée. In this way Matsch achieved social prestige.

In 1893 he was put in charge of the advanced painting class at the School of Arts and Crafts. He gained access to the court, painted a triumphant Achilles for Empress Elisabeth's Castle Achilleion on the island of Corfu and became a sought-after society portrait painter. In 1912 he was elevated to the hereditary aristocracy.

He was not willing to jeopardise this career in any way. Although he joined Klimt in quitting the Artists' House in 1897, he did not follow the call to become a member of the Secession, "for the building of my house, the teaching and the overwhelming burden of commissions obliged me to devote all my time to my work. Moreover, I wished to retain my freedom in this period of conflict . . .".[26]

This decision led to a clear parting of the ways for the two painters, who had worked in close co-operation from 1876 until 1894. In the 1880s they had achieved renown and their subsequent path seemed to be mapped out. Matsch resolutely followed this path.

From the Ring to the Secession

Until recently art historians placed Klimt's turn to Symbolism and Jugendstil around 1900. For the unequivocal stamp of his personal style this is no doubt correct, but there are plenty of earlier signs of the 'break' in style. Some of the earliest signs can be observed during the time of the Company, especially in the spandrel and intercolumnar pictures in the stairway of the Art History Museum.

In 1890/91 Klimt undertook several short journeys, made possible by the money awarded with the Emperor's Prize. He travelled to Munich, and it is very possible that he saw the second annual exhibition in Munich's Crystal Palace, in which case he would have encountered there for the first time the exhibited works of Fernand Khnopff (1858–1921).

21 Water Serpents (Female friends) I, 1904/07
Oil on canvas, 50 × 20 cm
Austrian Gallery, Vienna

22 Island in the Attersee, c. 1901
Oil on canvas, 100 × 100 cm
By kind permission of
Galerie St Etienne, New York

This Belgian of Austro-German origins broke off his studies of Jurisprudence in 1877 in order to study painting at the Brussels Academy. During the years that followed he was often in Paris, where he was influenced above all by the Pre-Raphaelites. Back in Brussels his style moved from Naturalism and Impressionism towards Symbolism. Holland and Belgium came in contact with the new trends in England and France very early on, partly because of their geographical situation. The new style had established itself there by the beginning of the 1880s.

Khnopff was one of the founder members of 'Les Vingt', a group set up in 1884 with the aim of exchanging ideas between artists at home and abroad by inviting foreign artists to annual exhibitions. Invitations were issued in return by groups established in other countries, especially the self-styled Secession groups in Germany.

Khnopff worked under the aegis of such mythical beings as sphinx and chimaera. One of his friends was the Symbolist writer Maurice Maeterlinck (1862–1949), whose mystical pantheism affected him greatly, and whose work he sometimes illustrated.

Either in Munich, or by way of illustrations in art journals which he saw shortly after his visit there, Klimt was alerted to Khnopff's work, and it exerted a lasting influence on him. The Symbolist tendencies first hinted at in the stairway pictures developed fully in four pictures painted in 1895/8.

In 1895 Klimt was commissioned by the Society for Reprographic Art to paint a portrait of an actor at the old Burg Theatre. He was to portray him in a rôle which did not remove him too far from reality. Klimt decided on Josef Lewinsky (1835–1907), and chose to portray him as Carlos in Goethe's 'Clavigo'. The actor stands life-size against a dark background; the whole is a tall narrow rectangle with a light border, crowned with the title 'Josef Lewinsky as Carlos in Clavigo'. The light, cloudy-looking border surrounding the figure of the actor is decorated on the left with delicate tendrils. From a wooden vat at the bottom on the right, vapour ascends and envelops three people at the top of the picture so that only their heads and the upper body of one woman can be seen. Perhaps these are the other main characters from 'Clavigo', but they are probably not portraits; the vapour gives them a ghostly appearance.

During the same year Klimt resumed work on the third volume of 'Allegory and Emblem'. Quite different artists collaborated on this 'New Series' who later joined Klimt in founding the Secession. Klimt himself executed three drawings and an oil painting on canvas. This painting, 'Love', displays for the first time motifs which are to recur in his work many times. Again an upright, dark rectangle has a light edging, though only to left and right, so that the height of the panel is emphasised. Sprays of roses reach into the light 'frame'. In the middle of the picture a pair of lovers embrace, but without the consummation of the kiss which later pictures show. Behind the lovers rises smoke – or perhaps mist – which, however, does not obscure the view of heads poised at the upper edge of the picture to look down on the lovers. Here we meet for the first time the three ages: childhood, youth, old age – and with them death. Klimt returned to them time and time again.

In painting the female figure Klimt is known to have drawn on one of Khnopff's drawings. The roses were probably suggested by Munich Jugendstil pictures. Contemporary poets used them as symbols of poetry, of music, of life's mystery, of virginity. It is interesting that in this first picture to be painted with overtly Symbolist motifs, demonstrating the move towards Jugendstil, Klimt chooses the two motifs which are the guiding force in his oeuvre: the kiss and the three ages.

One year later he drew the plate 'Sculpture' for 'Allegory and Emblem' described above (see p. 72). At this point it is necessary only to recall the head at the upper edge of the picture. These antique busts are closely related to the poised heads in the last two pictures. Links can also be made between the central structure of antique sculpture with the allegorical figure in the foreground and the dark rectangular picture sections. The wall surface has been represented by the light surround of canvas.

After this Klimt submitted to the publisher the design for the allegory of the month of June. 'Junius' is reminiscent of contemporary book illustrations, showing the linear style so characteristic of the later Klimt far more strongly than do the paintings of the time. This applies less to the head of the allegorical figure drawn in black crayon than to the two female figures surrounding it, which, in their long flowing robes drawn with fine parallel lines, appear incorporeal. The foliage in the background looks back to the painting 'Idyll', and at the same time looks forward to the purely decorative backgrounds of the later work.

In these four pictures the radical change in Klimt's style is tangible. It is symptomatic that during the crucial years 1893 to 1897 he created scarcely anything apart from these four pictures, other than trivial portraits and a few studies of heads. It has commonly been assumed that Klimt's output was so small during these years because of his grief at his brother's death, but he himself spoke of much work. Probably he meant the design for the decorating of the music room in the Palais Dumba.

However much work this project may have involved, it seems that he simply needed time in order to adapt to the new style. In 1897, even before he had worked out the details sufficiently to be able to reproduce the new style with his own distinctive mark, he turned away from the conservative Artists' House association and, with a few like-minded fellow artists, established the Secession. In this manner of proceeding there are echoes of Paul Gauguin, who could put into words what he wanted to achieve as a painter before he was able to achieve his aims in painting (see p. 33). Having reached the zenith of success by the time he was thirty, Klimt turned to new forms and ideas, which initially aroused much hostility, but later brought him, once again, success.

The Palais Dumba

In 1893 Franz Matsch and Gustav Klimt were commissioned by the industrialist Nikolaus Dumba (1830–1900) to take over the decoration of the music room and the dining room in his residence on the park section of the Ring. Twenty years earlier, Hans Makart had decorated the study which had created something of a stir. Not until 1897 did Klimt submit the sketches for the music room, which had been allotted to him, but there are two oil studies of 1895 for the supraportal picture, probably executed in order to secure the contract.

Klimt was not only responsible for the decorating of the salon, but for all its appointments, and he used the most precious materials: the doors were framed in Carrara marble with two dark green marble pilasters crowned by masked capitals. The grilles of the stoves were adorned with flame motifs and musical notes. Mahogany was the wood chosen. The flat white ceiling was painted with coronals of stars and interlocking sinuous lines, while the sprays, blossom and circles in the corners were of bronze-gilt. Klimt's brother Georg was responsible for the embossed ornamental metalwork and bronze casts. The furniture will probably have been provided according to the owner's wishes. Nothing remains of it all except an old photograph since the entire contents were sold in 1937, after the death of Dumba's widow. The supraportal pictures above both doors were burnt in 1945.

The photographs which exist show the two pictures, 'Music' and 'Schubert at the Piano'. Until recently it was assumed that the oil study for 'Music' was a picture painted in its own right, which was then used to procure the contract. The study for 'Schubert at the Piano' was thought to have been done at the same time as the painting. The contract was said to have been given in 1896. New documents have shown that these assumptions were mistaken.

The studies have little to do with the pictures that were subsequently painted. The presentation of 'Music I' is reminiscent of the personification in the Art History Museum. The sketch of 'Schubert at the Piano' is one of the few pictures in which Klimt attempted an Impressionist style. In 'Music II' the composition is accented very differently and the Symbolist element is given stronger emphasis. The personification and the sphinx are juxtaposed as equals, even though the sphinx is of stone. Both direct their gaze out of the picture without meeting the eye of the viewer. The playing of the lyre has become an incidental aside, the ornamental background takes up much more of the space than in the first picture.

The difference between the two versions of 'Schubert at the Piano' is even more marked. Neither in the sketch nor in other studies which preceded the picture is the pianist recognisable as Schubert. It is probable that the version with the portrait of the composer was made in response to a request by Dumba, who was a great admirer of Schubert. In his youth he had himself sung Schubert Lieder and he owned a considerable collection of his original manuscripts. For the portrait Klimt was provided with the 1821 watercolour 'Schubertian Society Pastimes in Atzbrugg' by Leopold Kupelwieser (1796–1862), which was in Dumba's possession.

In Klimt's picture the composer sits at the piano surrounded by singing women.The candlelight on the piano no longer lights up the whole room as it does in the sketch, it is less realistic and makes the whole scene unreal. In contrast to the photographic precision with which Schubert's face is painted, the women are a little indistinct, their long flowing gowns reminiscent of Neo-Impressionist paintings.

In order to paint the picture Klimt not only bought a piano, which he never leant to play, but also borrowed from the wife of his patron, August Lederer, the clothes in which he dressed his models. Serena Lederer, whose portrait he later painted, was reputed to be one of the best-dressed women in Vienna.

Before the picture was hung in the place for which it was destined, Klimt showed it at the IVth exhibition of the Secession in 1899. It achieved instant fame. The Munich publisher Hanfstaengl made a collotype reproduction which meant that it reached a wide public. Hermann Bahr was full of praises: "I said not long ago that Klimt's Schubert is in my estimation the most beautiful picture ever painted by an Austrian . . . No other modern painting strikes me as so pure and so great".[27] Similar hymns of praise were heard on all sides.

But there was another voice which in short sharp sentences heaped scorn on Dumba as well as on Klimt. The mocker was Karl Kraus who wrote scathingly in the journal 'Fackel' at the beginning of April 1899: "He (Dumba) had commissioned Klimt to paint these pictures for his music room when Klimt was still working in the worthy manner of the Laufberger school and only occasionally allowed himself an extravaganza à la Makart. But in the meantime the painter discovered Khnopff (German 'Knopf' = 'button', trans.) and lest the tale seem pointless, he has become a Pointillist. And the client of course had to keep up with him. So Herr von Dumba became one of the Moderns."[28]

The pictures in Palais Dumba are of such interest because they were commissioned at a time when Klimt's first success was at its height, but they were not executed until after the Secession,when the artist was seeking his own individual style. Only with this in mind is it possible to explain the trace of Impressionism which emerged, only to be dropped again almost at once. It took Klimt a long time to find the way from his first tentative attempts to the style of painting which made him famous. The Secession took place while he was engaged in this process.

Founder-member and president of the Vienna Secession

Conflict in the Artists' House

The Vienna Society of Visual Artists, with its headquarters in the Artists' House on the Ring, was the only association representing artists in the capital in the early 1890s. Its exhibitions enabled artists to show their work to a wide public, but if an artist did not receive the approval of the committee or the jury there was vey little chance of his making a name for himself at all. This being the case, the situation was inevitably explosive when it happened that 'old' members still held the reins while many young artists were joining with different ideas. Moreover the old historicist painters organised the exhibitions with an eye to commercial profit; they were less interested in the presentation of new departures in art, and not at all interested in introducing foreign artists to the public.

The first disagreement came at the beginning of the 1890s. Theodor von Hoermann (1840–1895) had achieved great success in Paris with his plein-air painting, but when he submitted the same pictures to the Vienna jury three years later in 1891, they were rejected. After he had lodged an unsuccessful complaint, he accused those responsible of being interested only in sales. He said that his purpose in painting was to find his own individuality. His criticism and the misapprobation with which he was confronted made him popular with the young artists who proposed that he be awarded the gold medal of the Artists' House association. But this was turned down.

Only after his death in 1895 was it possible for an exhibition of his works to be organised as a tribute to his memory, and it had considerable success. Hoermann was regarded as a pioneer in the ensuing

23/24 Hermine Gallia, 1903/04
Oil on canvas, 170 × 96 cm
National Gallery, London

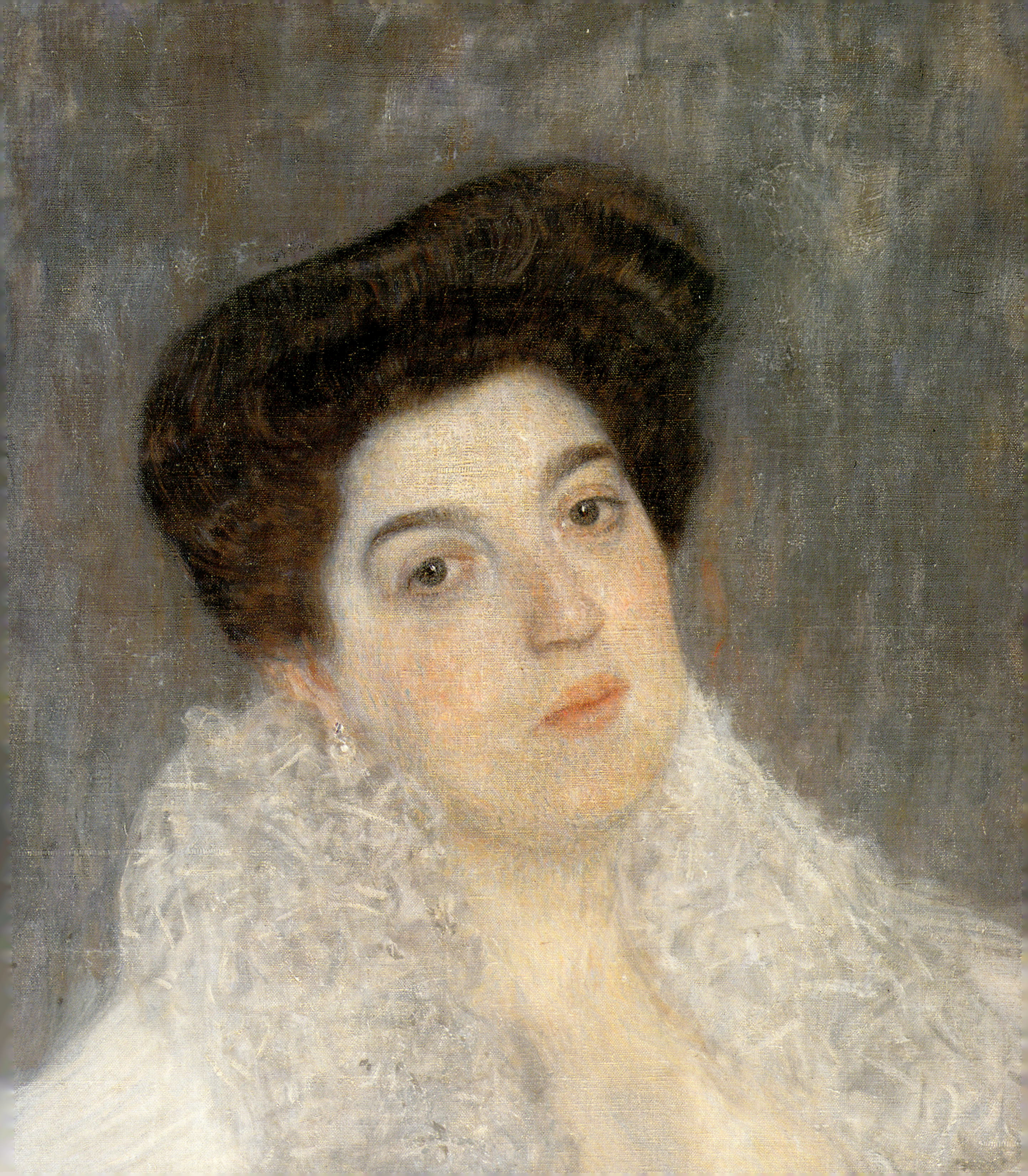

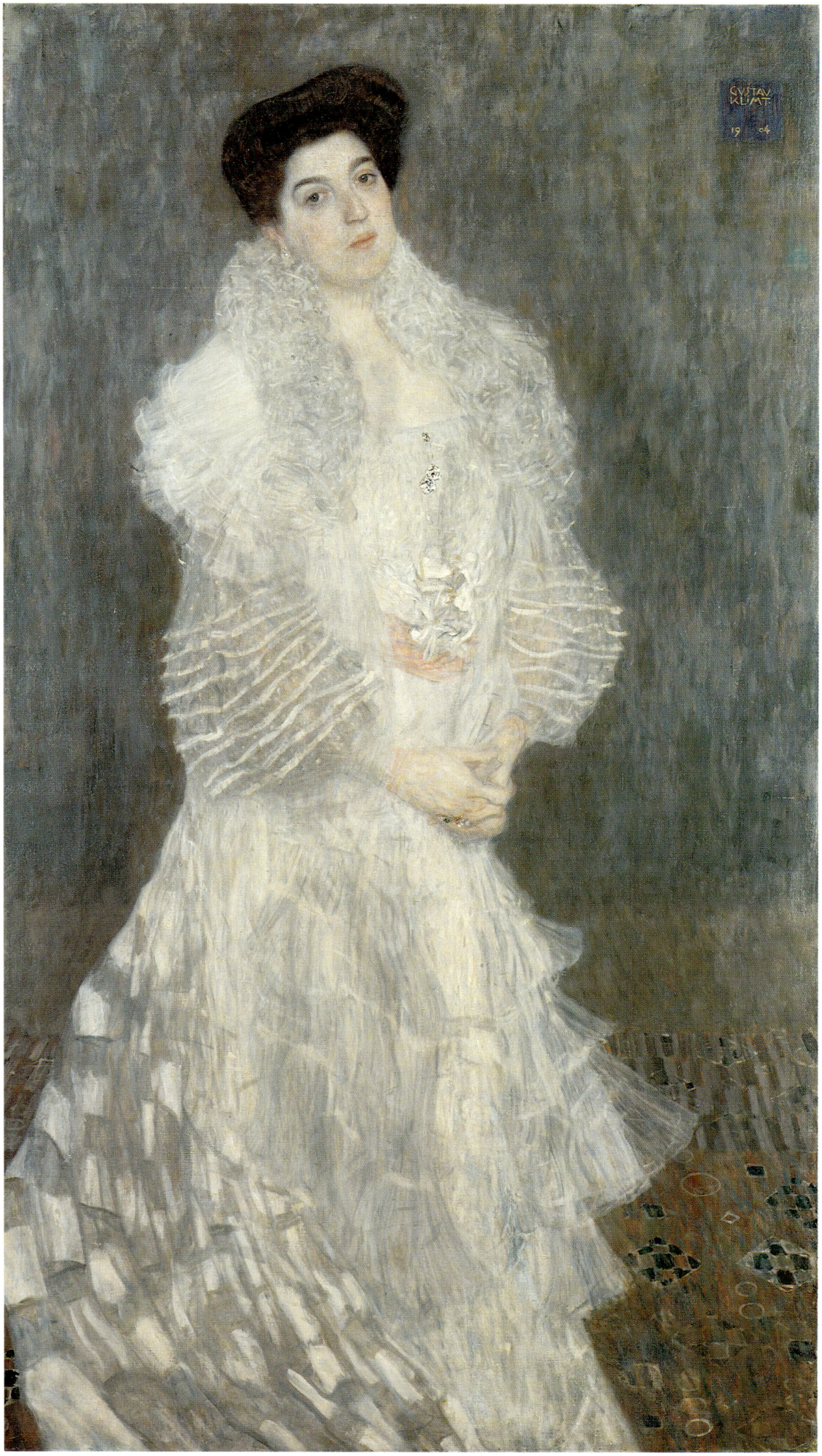
GUSTAV
KLIMT
19 04

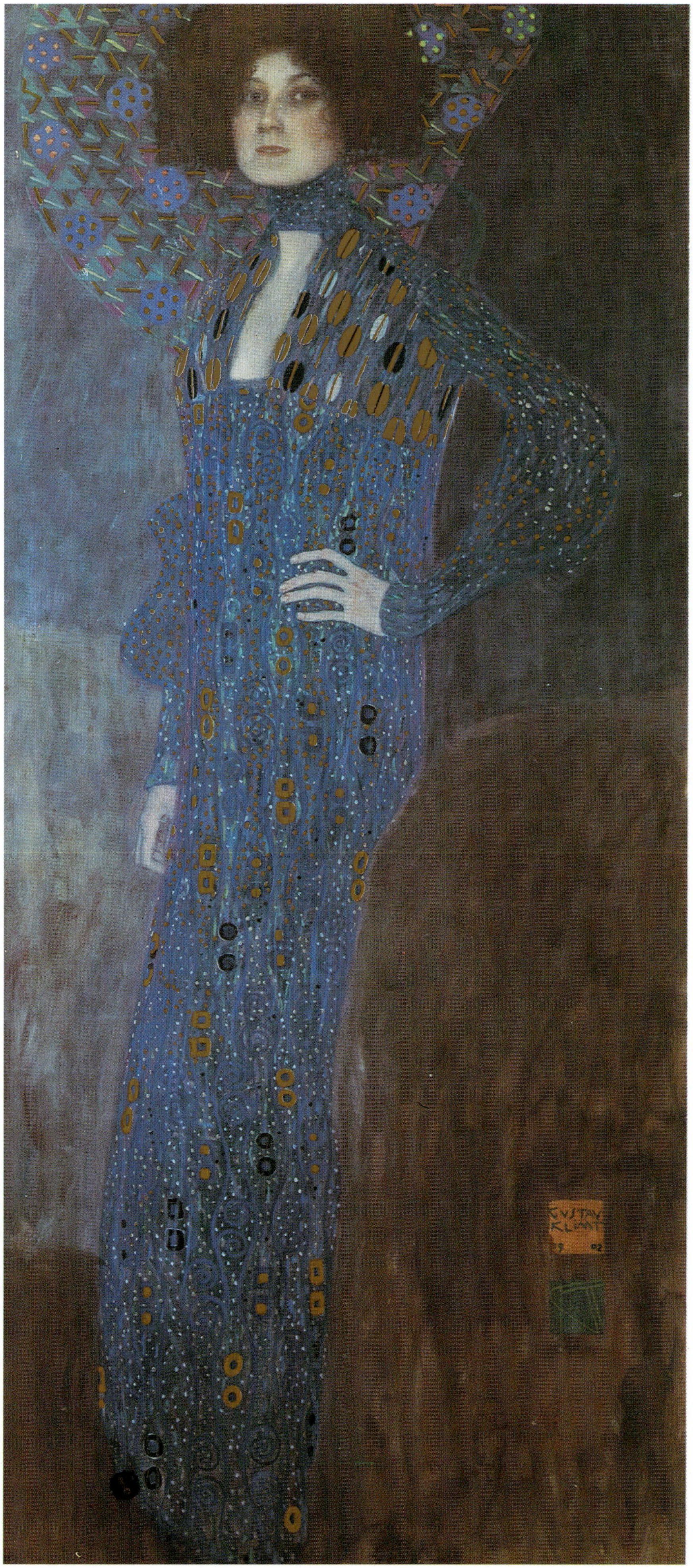

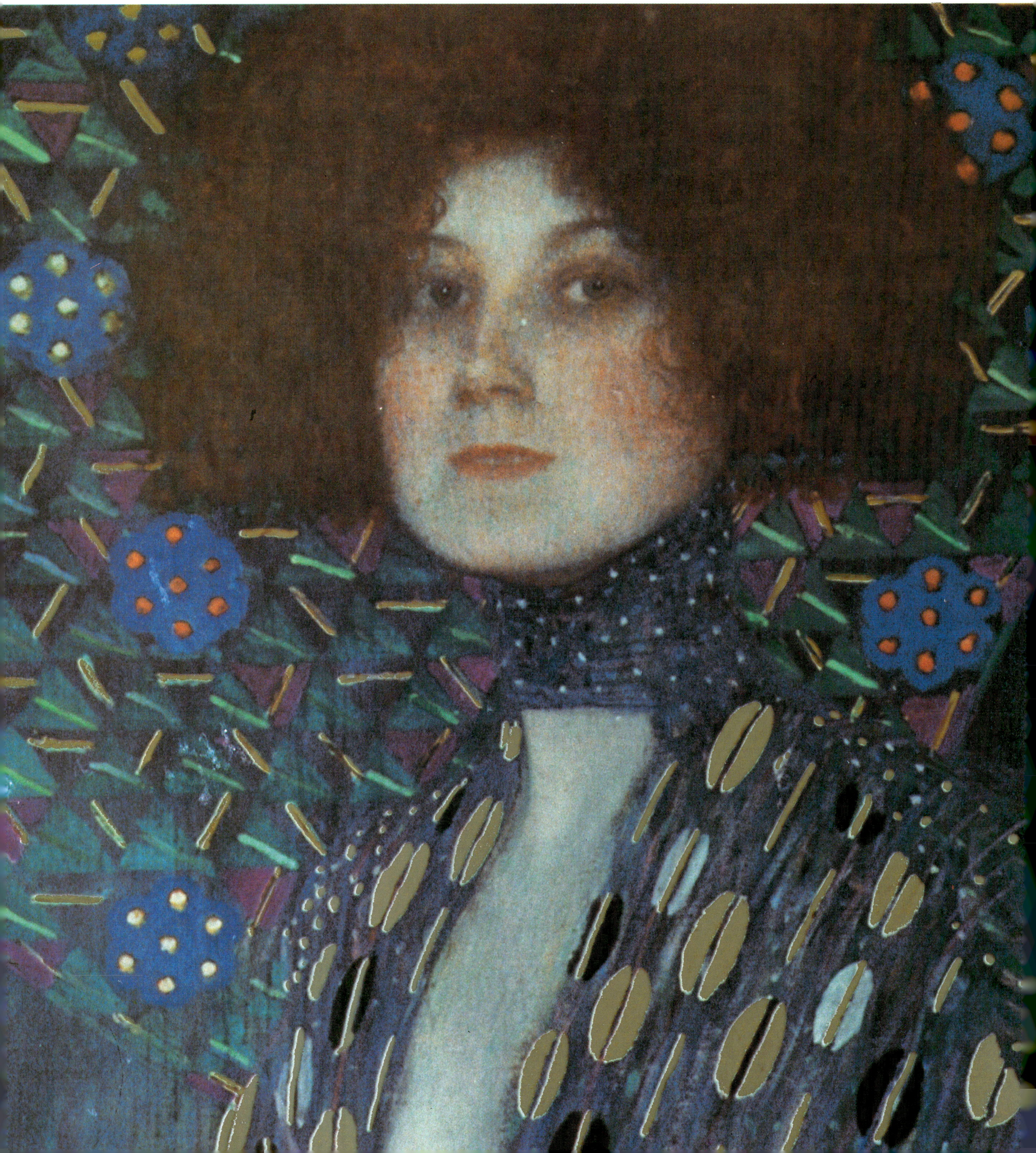

battles. The members of the Secession met on the first anniversary of their foundation at his grave, made speeches and laid wreaths. In 1899 there was an auction of his pictures in the Secessions's rooms; his widow used half the proceeds to set up the Theodor Hoermann Foundation in aid of needy artists among the Secessionists.

A second case played a decisive part in precipitating the break. Josef Engelhart (1864–1941) had encountered the Impressionists in Paris with important consequences for the development of his style of painting. In 1893 he returned from Paris to Vienna. On the occasion of the next watercolour exhibition at the Artists' House he tried to show his picture 'Girl Picking Cherries', which portrayed a nude girl beneath the trees in changing sunlight. The jury rejected the picture, not because of artistic reservations, but because it was not considered proper to inflict the picture on the ladies of the society, who made up a large section of the viewing public. Engelhart did not let this opportunity for polemics pass him by. Moreover he demanded a general reform of the association.

In the same year Gustav Klimt's name was put forward for a professorship at the Academy of Visual Arts, to teach a master class in history painting. Nevertheless someone else was appointed, presumably because of intervention by the imperial court.

Apart from these internal conflicts there were impulses from abroad which urged the discontented young artists to take action. In the European art centres more and more artists' associations were being formed in opposition to the official style of the academies. The 'Société des Independants', founded by the Impressionists in Paris in 1884, was of decisive importance for the Viennese, as was in all probability the setting up of the Munich Secession in 1892. The name 'Secession', derived from the Latin, was intended further to suggest the 'secessio plebis' of 493 BC when the people of Rome 'seceded' to a position outside the city walls in order to win acceptance for their demands.

In 1895 the Munich Secession showed their work in Vienna at the invitation of the Artists' House. This provided moral support, enabling vague ideas to take more concrete shape. It is known that Josef Engelhart, Gustav Klimt and Carl Moll (1861–1945) first contemplated a split in 1896. The general assembly of the Artists' Association in the same

25/26 Emilie Flöge, 1902
Oil on canvas, 181 × 66.5 cm
Vienna City Museums

year provided provocation for an outburst. Both parties in the Artists' House presented a candidate for president. With three hundred votes recorded, the conservative painter Eugen Felix (1837–1906), known for his commercial bias, beat his opponent by a majority of only sixteen. This result showed clearly that the two factions had about equal support. The conservatives responded to the malcontents' call for immediate resignation by filling all the offices with their own nominees, and the jury was then entirely in their hands. The conservatives precipitated the founding of the 'Austrian Association of Visual Artists – Vienna Secession', though still with the idea of remaining in membership of the Artists' House. This seemed to be feasible. There were already two sub-sections in the Artists' House which met regularly to discuss matters of common interest. One was the Haagen Society founded in 1876, the other the 'Club of Seven', established as recently as 1895. Both groups met once a week in a coffee house, but they were not concerned to pursue exhibition policies of their own. Many of them joined the Secession, whereupon the 'Club of Seven' was soon dissolved.

On 27 March 1897 Ludwig Hevesi (1842–1910), chronicler of the Secession, wrote that the new foundation was imminent. A few days later on 3 April, Gustav Klimt, as president of the new association, wrote a letter to the committee of the Society of Visual Artists to inform them of the Secession and to present the reasons for the new grouping: he mentioned first the efforts of a group of artists within the Society to find acceptance for their ideas on art; this group had seen the need to bring Viennese art face to face with the art of other countries; moreover it was important to them that exhibitions should be organised according to artistic criteria only, and that the market place values which prevailed should be rejected; in addition, the members intended to awaken an interest in modern art among wide sections of the population. None of their ideas, it said, had met with understanding from the committee. For all these reasons and because the organisation of the Society favoured activities not directly concerned with art, making free artistic movement impossible, they had decided to form the 'Austrian Association of Visual Artists'. They expressed the hope that they would be able to remain in membership of the Society. To the

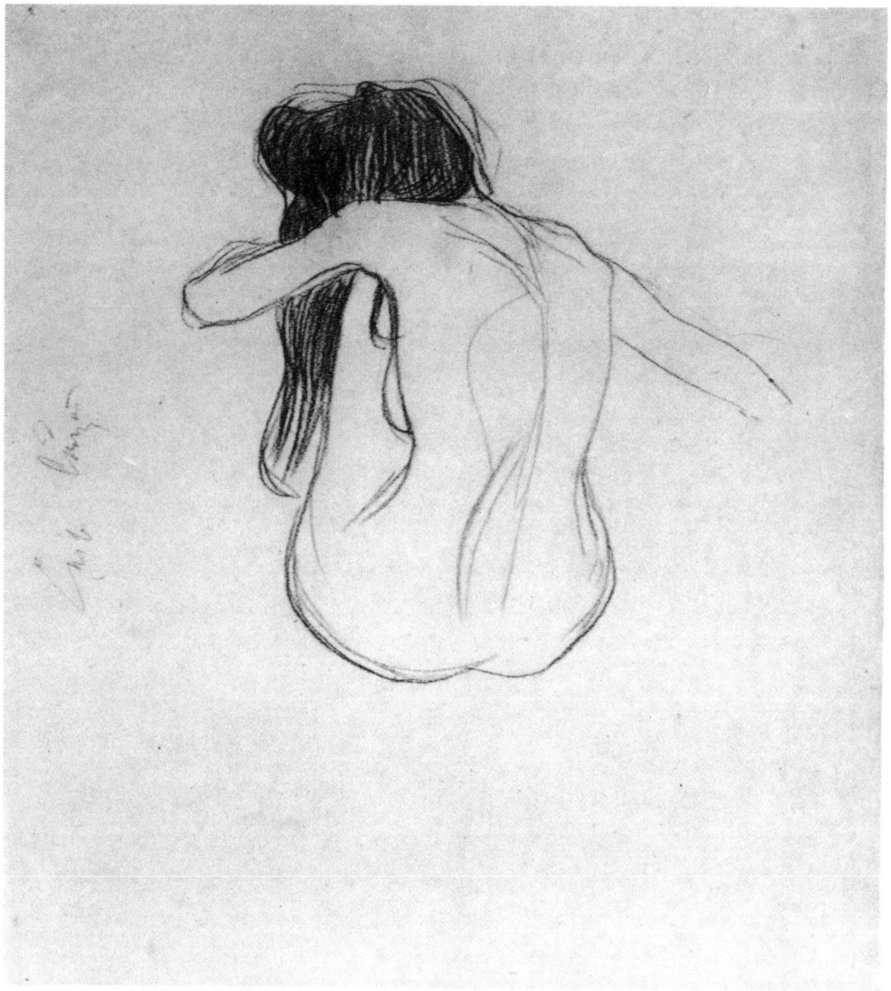

Seated female figure from behind, right arm outstretched, 1901
Black crayon, 45.1 × 31.8 cm

letter was appended a list of members, revealing that of the forty founder members twenty-three came from the Artists' House. There were twelve from other groups and five who had previously been unaffiliated.

As a result of the letter the Secessionists received invitations to participate in foreign exhibitions too late, whereupon they sent their pictures to Munich without submitting them to the jury. That led to a rebuke at the general assembly on 22 May, which they refused to accept. They declared their resignation. On 27 June 1897 the first general meeting of the Secession took place, at which they agreed on a constitution, decided to build exhibition rooms and founded an art journal.

The immediate conflict which precipitated the break was not in itself of great importance, but positions on both sides were so entrenched that diplomacy was impossible. Any other provocation could have caused the same reactions. It is worth noting that of the many who had voted against the new president only twenty-three actually had the courage to leave. A few more were to follow, but most remained in the Artists' House.

The 'heroic years' of the Secession

The fight of the new art against the old had been the vital force behind the secessions in Paris, Munich and Berlin, but in Vienna there was no argument for or against a tradition, because, as Hermann Bahr rightly observed, there was none. It was a matter of art itself, of whether art or commerce should be the prime concern. This was made clear in the statutes put forward at the first general meeting.

In the statutes the members formulated the ideas which were behind everything they had tried so often to achieve in the Artists' House. The Secession was to restrict its activities to the promotion of purely artistic concerns and the awareness of art among the general public. The exhibitions should not be influenced by the values of the marketplace. Contact with foreign artists should be aimed for, as should the showing of Austrian art abroad. A few members should be given responsibility for each exhibition. The first such group to be set up consisted of the president, Gustav Klimt, Josef Hoffmann and Carl Moll.

In order to be able to exhibit, the Secession first of all needed suitable rooms. Patrons were very soon found who were ready to finance a new building for the purpose. In spite of opposition to the new Artists' Society among city councillors, the support of the Mayor, Dr. Karl Lueger, among others, moved the city of Vienna to give them a site. It was at the end of the Naschmarkt, central and very close to the Academy of Visual Arts, that the Secessionists were able to build their house. At their first general meeting they chose one of their members, Josef Maria Olbrich (1867–1908) as architect.

After his training at the State School of Arts and Crafts in Vienna, Olbrich had studied architecture from 1890 to 1893 at a school of architecture directed by Hasenauer. He was then employed by the architect Otto Wagner (1841–1918), who exerted a strong influence on him. The Secession House was his first large contract. Later he achieved fame principally through the plans for the Darmstadt Artists' Colony on the Mathildenhöhe.

His exhibition house came to typify Vienna Jugendstil architecture. The construction was derived from the basic geometrical forms, cube, square and sphere. On top of the outer cube of white rough-cast walls he placed a cupola of pierced metal that rested sphere-like on the roof. The ornament was restrained and did not conceal the underlying form. Above the portal Ludwig Hevesi's slogan for their work shone resplendent in large letters: "To each age its art – to art its freedom".

In Vienna this building – like novelty in general – was not immediately acclaimed with enthusiasm. It was named the 'Mahdi's Tomb'. Two preliminary sketches show that not only Wagner but also Klimt had a great influence on Olbrich, and that the architect took the painter's suggestions so seriously as to incorporate them in the final design.

Although building progressed very rapidly – the foundation stone was laid on 28 April 1898 and the first exhibition in the new rooms opened on 12 November – the Secessionists wanted to present their work to the public before that. They succeeded in renting the premises of theHorticultural Society on the Ring, and on 15 March 1898 their first exhibition opened, with work by members but also with many works by foreign artists. The invitation to participate had been accepted by Böcklin, Crane, Khnopff, Klinger, Liebermann, Puvis de Chavannes, Rodin, Segantini, Stuck, Thoma, Uhde and many others. Arts and Crafts were well represented. The exhibition was enormously successful in spite of gloomy prognostications, and even made a profit which could be put towards their own building.

Klimt created the poster for this first exhibition. It was intended to convey the triumphant battle of the new art against the old. Klimt chose a theme from Greek antiquity: the triumphant fight of Theseus against the Minotaur under the aegis of Pallas Athene, who was not only the goddess of the arts and sciences, but more particularly the patron goddess of the Secession. Theseus personified the Secession, the Minotaur the Artists' House. The first version of the poster could not be printed because the censors would not accept the nude Theseus. They demanded a bush. Klimt designed two trees which covered the offending part but which gave a suggestion of its presence.

The poster is strictly geometrical in layout. At the top is the battle, to the left is written VER SACRUM and 'Theseus and the Minotaur'. The right edge is filled with the figure of Athene, in profile, her spear flung across into the fight, demonstrating her participation in the victorious outcome. Her face shows the influence of one of Khnopff's illustrations. The lower part of the poster contained information about locality and duration of the exhibition, the remaining space was void. The same composition was used for a prospectus of the Secession journal and printed again in one of its numbers, naturally in the censored version.

In the same year a picture of the warrior goddess was painted. It was first shown at the Secession's second exhibition on the occasion of the opening of their new house.

The square picture is set in a metal frame made by Georg Klimt. The canvas is filled with head and upper body of Pallas Athene clad in golden armour. At her neck is hung the head of Medusa which was thought to represent a public admonishment and achieved its effect. The small figurine of Nike, goddess of victory, which Athene offers the beholder, symbolises the victory of true art. Pallas Athene threateningly takes up her stand against those forces in society which stand in the way of true art. Her belligerence is reinforced by the combat between Heracles and the sea creature Triton which is being fought out in the background beside her head.

The painting, inspired by one of Franz von Stuck's posters of 1897, became the trademark of the Secession and was used several times as a poster and also as the title page for one number of VER SACRUM.

Ludwig Hevesi defended it vehemently against public attacks and interpreted it in the spirit of the Secession: "Nor does the wearer of the armour meet with approval. The public is used to Pallases which clearly show that they are actually painted marble statues. But Klimt has portrayed her as a present-day Secessionist, or at least as a goddess or demon of the Secession ... This is no statue hewn out of the earth and no woman drawn from life, it is a phenomenon, the incarnation of a mood of defiant creativity and inspired craftsmanship".[29]

In the following eight years the Secession succeeded in organising twenty-three exhibitions. Apart from bringing together art from abroad and Viennese art at every opportunity, they soon began to mount exhibitions of a specialised nature. The last show of 1899 was devoted to graphic art. The next exhibition showed Japanese works, documenting the influence of Japanese art on the new style. In 1900 they also presented the most important European exponents of Arts and Crafts. English and French artists were represented and also the married couple Charles Rennie Mackintosh and Margaret Macdonald from the Glasgow School (see p. 26). In 1903 the Viennese public had the opportunity to see a comprehensive exhibition of French Impressionist works in the Secession House. Up to that time only a few isolated Impressionist works had found their way to Vienna.

Naturally the members had regular opportunities to show their work, and Gustav Klimt as 'King of the Secession' was given ample space. Usually his works provoked polemical comments in the press.

Some of the profits from the exhibitions were spent on purchasing contemporary pictures by foreign artists, which were then presented to the Austrian Gallery so that modern art might be introduced to Vienna. These gifts included such famous paintings as Van Gogh's 'Plain at Auvers' and 'The Unnatural Mothers' by Segantini.

They honoured their undertaking to widen the public appeal of art by introducing 'Workers' Tours' on Sunday mornings. For these guided tours the normal catalogue was offered gratis. It is not possible to say whether this activity achieved the desired effect.

Ver Sacrum

At their first general meeting the members of the Secession had resolved not only to build their own premises, but also to launch an art journal, comparable to THE STUDIO, London (from 1893), PAN in Berlin (from 1895) and JUGEND (= Youth) in Munich (from 1896).

The name VER SACRUM ('Sacred Spring') referred to a Roman story: at a time of great peril to the fatherland, the people dedicated all living things of the following spring to the gods. This was then the 'sacred spring'. When those who were born during the sacred spring grew up, they strove to establish a new polity. Ludwig Hevesi surmised that the direct source was a poem with the same title by Ludwig Uhland, which ends with the following lines:

'You have heard what is pleasing to the god./Go forth, prepare yourselves, then listen!/You are the cornseed of a new order./That is the sacred spring the god desires.'[30]

In the first number the Secessionists declared the function and purpose of their journal: "VER SACRUM is the official organ of the Austrian Society of Visual Artists ... offering a challenge to people's artistic sensibility so that the life and independence of art may be stimulated, encouraged and extended. Highly qualified experts in the literary field have agreed to contribute to the text..."[31]

The last sentence was no exaggeration. As literary adviser the Secessionists had succeeded in engaging Hermann Bahr, and even after he relinquished this office he continued to procure literary contributions. In the early numbers there appeared theoretical treatises by Bahr himself, by Giovanni Segantini and Fernand Khnopff and others, including Adolf Loos who was ready to acclaim the Secession in its early days. However, the functionalist ideas which he put forward in VER SACRUM and elsewhere could not be reconciled with the art of style, as was only too apparent in his later lectures such as 'Ornament and Crime' (see p. 21).

More important than the treatises were the poems: even Rainer Maria Rilke, Hugo von Hofmannsthal and Maurice Maeterlinck were persuaded to contribute. The poems sparked off discussions about the presentation of pictures and texts; it was important to achieve harmony between the contents of a poem and the artistic design. Different artists found very different solutions. There were drawings which included recognisable figures in the ornamentation, but there were also abstract forms. Koloman Moser (1868–1918) did away with

27 After the Rain, 1899
Oil on canvas, 80 × 40 cm
Austrian Gallery, Vienna

28 Farmhouse with Birch Trees, 1900
Oil on canvas, 80 × 80 cm
Austrian Gallery, Vienna

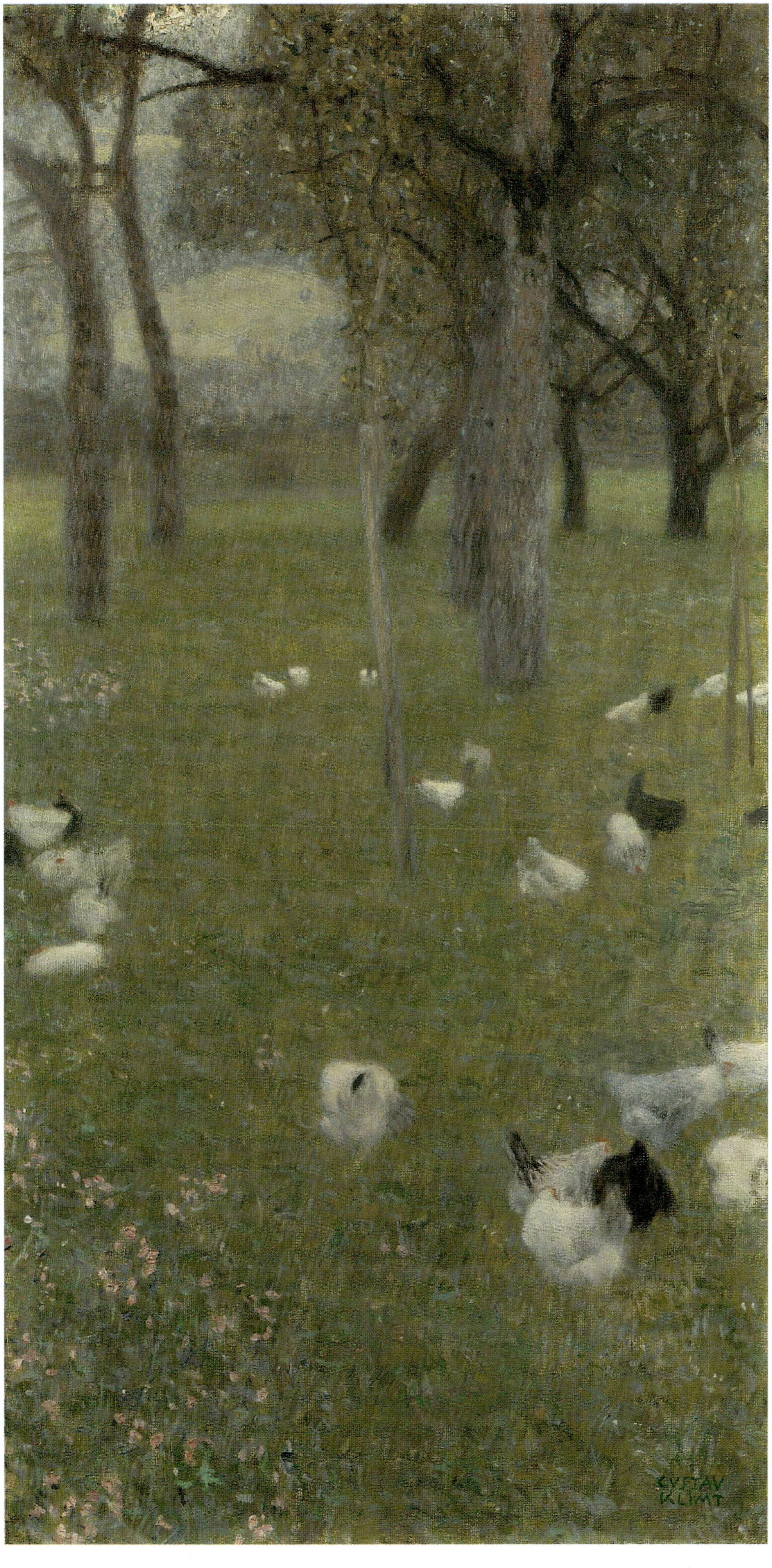
GUSTAV
KLIMT

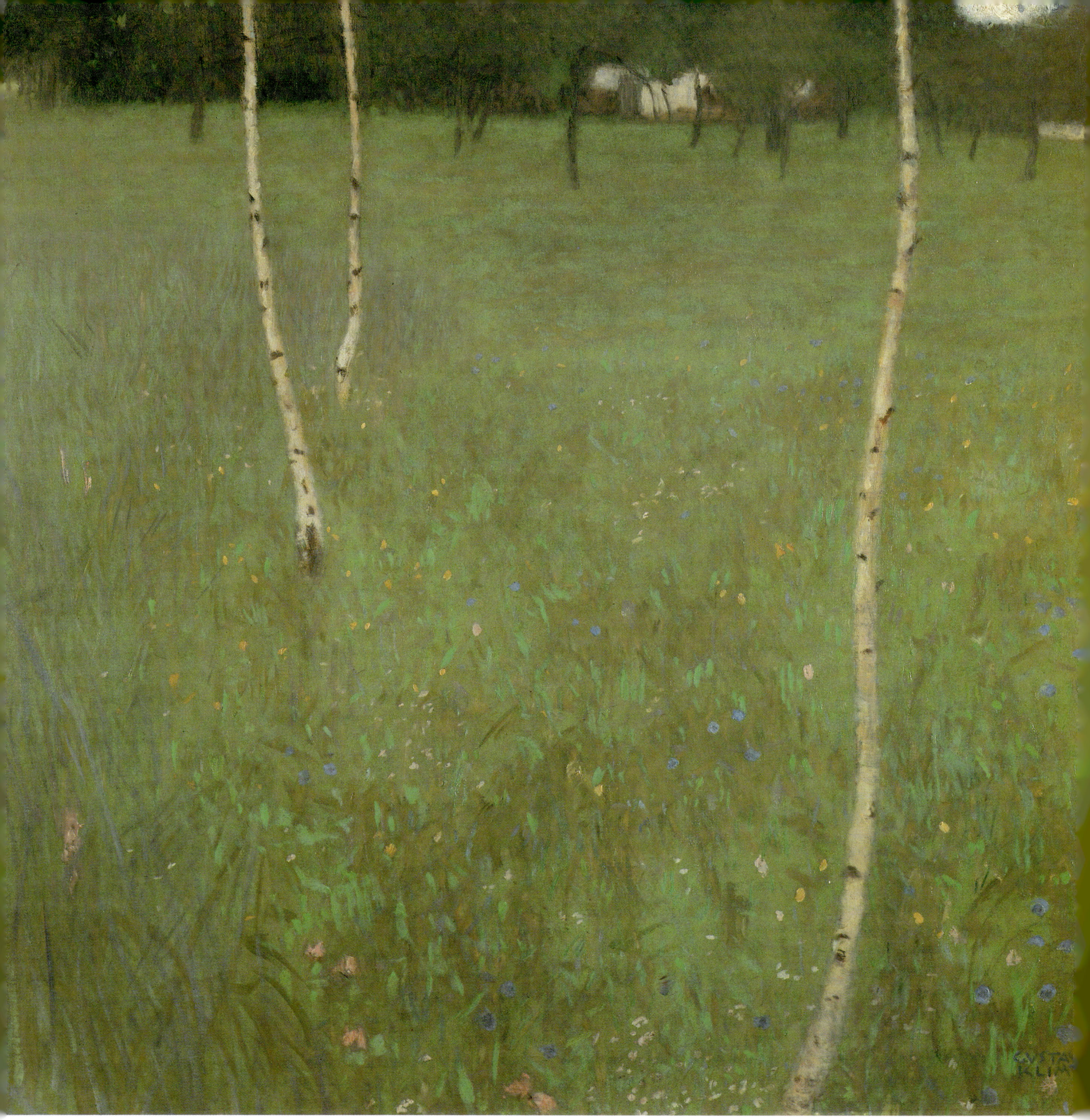

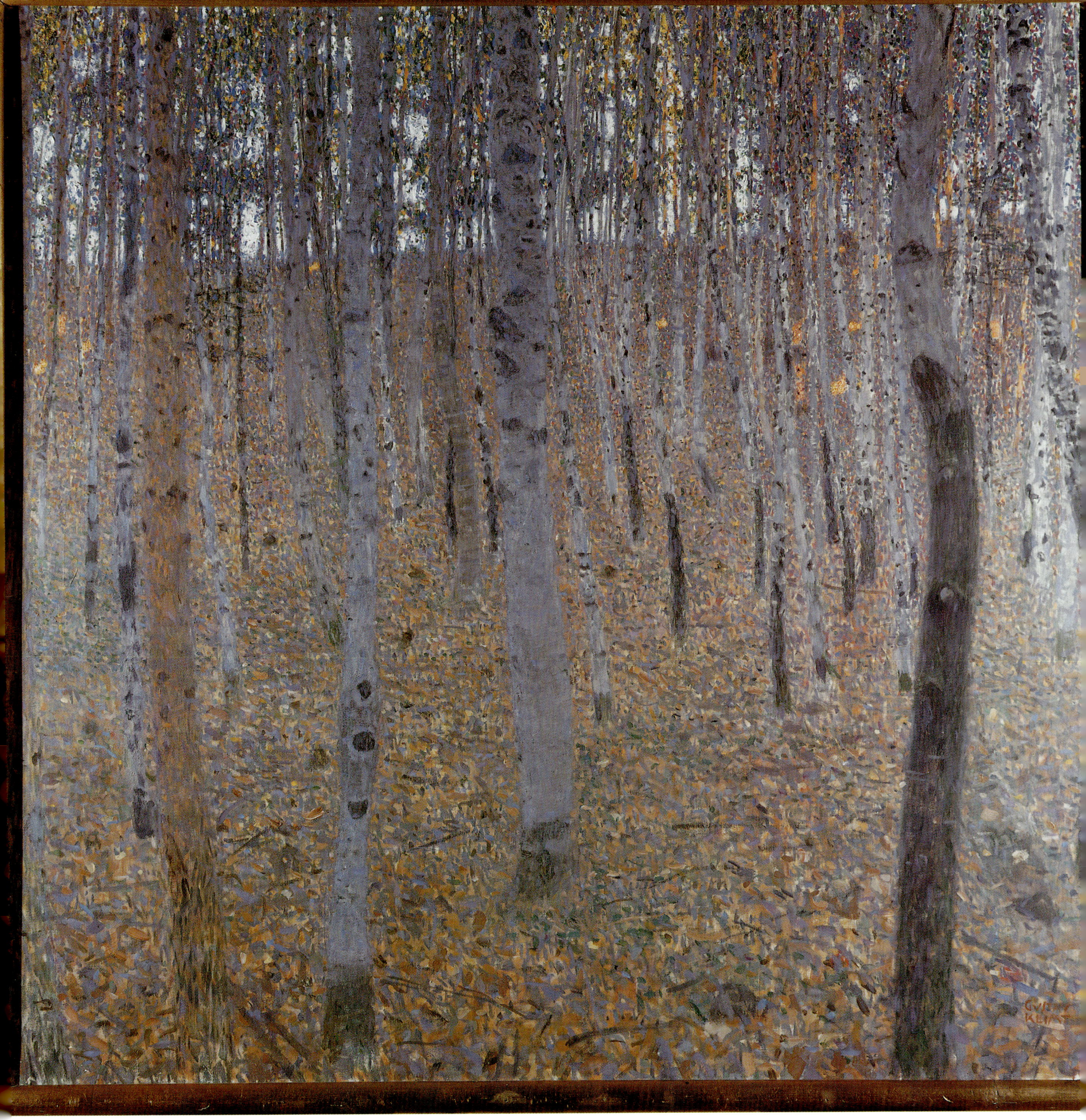

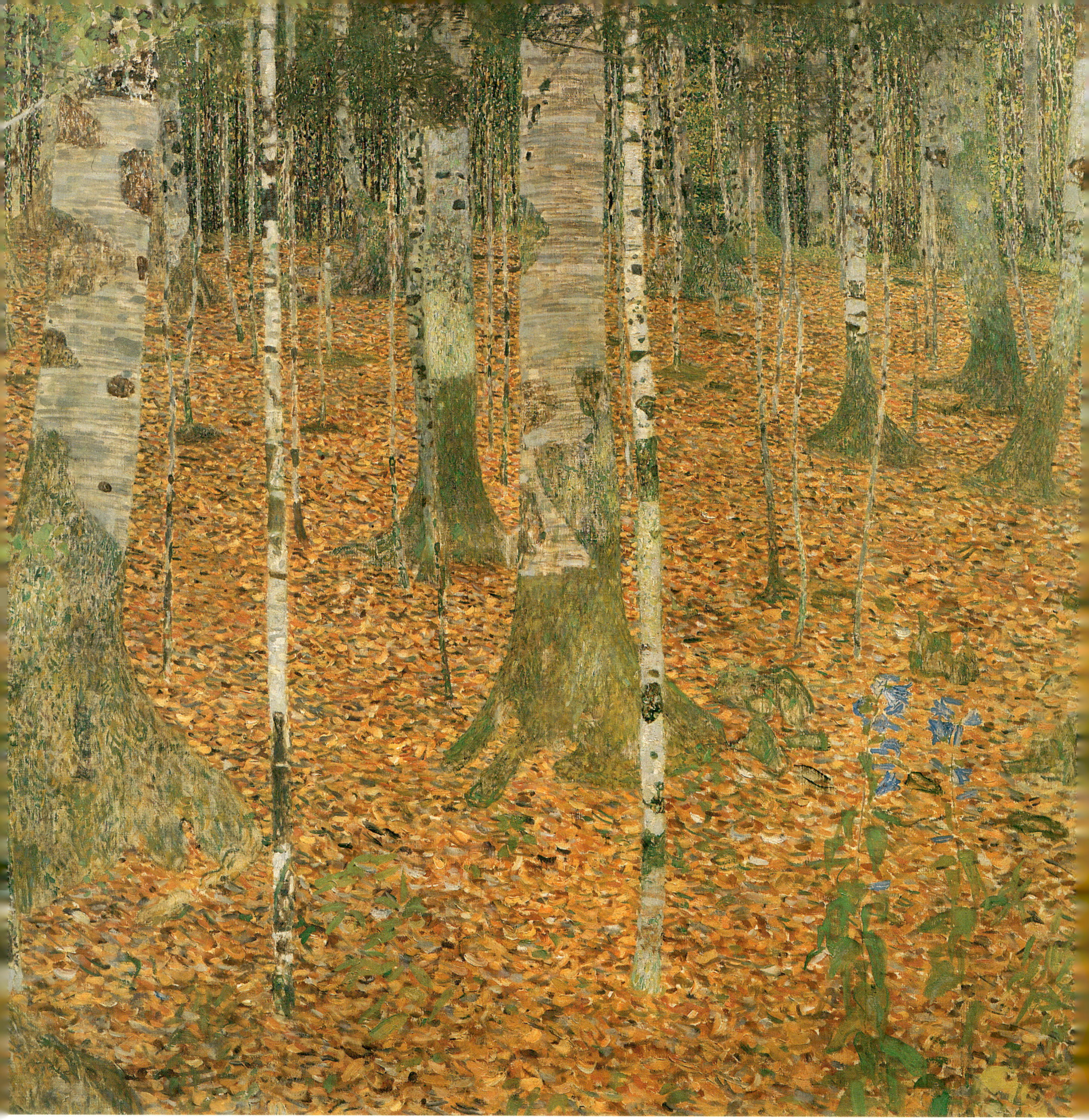

29 Beech Forest I, 1902
Oil on canvas, 100 × 100 cm
Modern Gallery, Dresden

30 Birch Forest, 1903
Oil on canvas, 110 × 110 cm
Austrian Gallery, Vienna

the dividing line between blocked text and decoration, which led to an abstract design covering the whole page. These 'book illustrations' became a field of experiment in which organically curved lines coexisted with geometrical shapes. In fact, abstract possibilities were being tried out, though without the slightest idea of painting abstract pictures. Viennese art remained representational even when, at a rather later time, abstract art began to spread all over Europe. Yet it was now possible for experiment to be undertaken in two dimensions which could lead to a constructivist streak even in Jugendstil artists like Koloman Moser.

There was always a small group of artists, with a constant turnover of membership, responsible for the artistic design of the journal. Naturally the result varied and presented a cross section of the Secessionists' creative work. For this reason VER SACRUM is an unparalleled artistic legacy of the Vienna Secession. Only the technical arrangements remained constant, and in this area every detail was significant. Great importance was attached to the quality of paper and dye, of lettering and picture, of cover and endpaper. The more or less square shape made it possible to print oblong and upright pictures in such a way that it was not necessary to turn the page round in order to look at them. Each issue formed a self-contained work of art and represented the current state of Secessionist ideas on art.

The individual numbers also contained notes on the exhibitions, with accompanying pictures and commentaries. Since the catalogues did not contain illustrations, VER SACRUM is still an invaluable source of information about the exhibitions.

During the six years of its publication — the last issue appeared in 1903 – 471 drawings, 55 lithographs and etchings and 216 woodcuts were specifically prepared for it. These numbers were given, not without pride, in the last issue.

With the exception of the contributions to 'Allegory and Emblem', it was only for VER SACRUM that Gustav Klimt worked as illustrator. Whether no other opportunity arose or whether he wanted to restrict his activities to painting and drawing for its own sake is not known.

Most of his illustrations are found in the third journal of the first year, which he designed. It contains among other things the drawing 'Nuda

Veritas' which he executed as a painting a year later. The high upright drawing shows the frontal view of a nude female figure who is looking out of the picture, holding a mirror in her hand with which she displays to everyone the 'naked truth'. She appears to be standing on a pedestal on which the title of the picture and the artist's signature can be seen. Flowers are growing out of the pedestal into the black background. On a level with her shoulders the pure black of the background becomes ornamental lattice work. Above the figure is written: "Truth is fire and telling the truth means shining and burning. L. Schefer". Opposite to this figure is another representing 'Envy'. The haggard female figure dressed in black has a crown of thistles, and a snake hanging round her neck. The thistles appear again as background. Above her head is poised a large 'N' (German 'Neid' = 'Envy') and her neck is framed with the letters of the word. The contraposition of two such female figures recurs in the Beethoven Frieze of 1902 (pl. 10), if not before.

Klimt painted 'Nuda Veritas' in oils, but not 'Envy'. The composition of the oil painting closely resembles that of the drawing. Only the text above the head of 'Truth' has altered: "If you cannot please everyone with your deeds and your art, then please a few. To please many is worthless. Schiller". This picture with its message has been linked with Klimt's function as president of the Secession, but he will certainly have quoted Schiller's lines in connection with the increasingly harsh criticisms which were being made of his work. Later, when the disputes over the faculty pictures were at their intensest, he repeated the message in his own words (see p. 117; 120).

With VER SACRUM the 'artists of style' among the Secessionists succeeded in creating an integral work of art in which text and picture became one. Shortly after publication of the journal ceased came the departure of the artists of the new style, and the so-called 'heroic years' of the Secession were over.

The departure of the artists of the new style

When people speak today of Vienna Jugendstil, the term 'Secession Art' is often used synonymously, but that is not quite correct because there had been, from the very beginning, two very different styles in the Secession, and it was not the artists of the new style who took over the inheritance.

From the outset it had been planned that the Secession should exist only for ten years, in which time art should have been rescued from commerce, but after the first two combative years difficulties of an artistic nature had arisen. On the one hand there were members who rejected not only academicism and historicism, but also Impressionism. Others, however, described as 'Naturalists', were particularly in favour of Impressionism, and it was they who had initiated the great Impressionist exhibition. For them the prime task was to create their own individual works of art. Today they would be classed as champions of autonomy.

The artists of the new style strove to achieve a union of all arts. Decorative or applied art was of paramount importance to them. This was evident in the layout and organisation of the exhibitions, but also in the increasing move towards arts and crafts in their own work. Their efforts were strengthened by unexpected success, not only in Vienna but also in foreign cities, for instance at the Great Paris Exhibition of 1900. One consequence of this was the Arts and Crafts Exhibition in the Secession's rooms, and a much more far-reaching one was the founding of the Vienna Workshops by Josef Hoffmann, Koloman Moser and Fritz Waerndorfer (1869–1939).

The foundation of the workshops in 1903 led to conflict within the Secession because it resulted in the formation of an exclusive circle from which numerous members felt excluded.

The conflict was exacerbated during the preparation for the exhibition in St Louis in 1904, ending in blatant hostility. The ministry hesitated for a long time before finally deciding to approve the despatch of works of art to St Louis. Hoffmann and Klimt restricted selection to the works of five artists only, including Klimt. The ministry refused this selection on the grounds that these five artists did not form a repre-

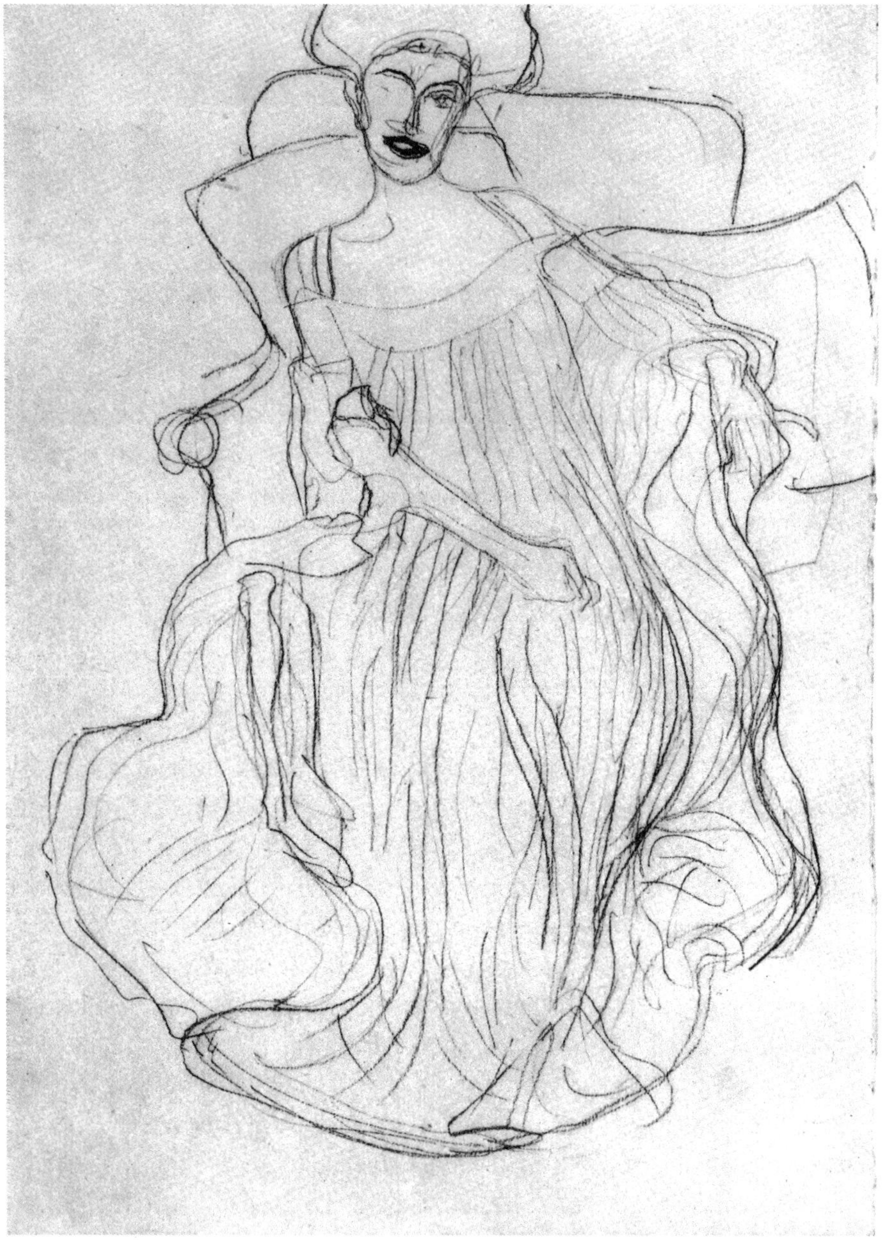

sentative sample. Because of these delays the negotiated display space was allotted to another country and the Secession failed to be represented at all in St Louis. The 'Naturalists' were enraged by Klimt and Hoffmann's high-handed decisions, which had in fact resulted in

Seated female figure, left arm on arm-rest (Adele Bloch-Bauer), 1903/04
Pencil, 45 × 31.5 cm

failure. Repeating the pattern of the Artists' House conflict, all that was needed now was a trifle to precipitate a split. This was provided by the death of the owner of the private Galerie Miethke, who had always been closely associated with the Secession. A jeweller declared himself willing to finance the gallery, on condition that Carl Moll should take over the artistic direction and manage it as a commercial gallery associated with the Secession. Moll had already organised exhibitions of Gauguin, Van Gogh and Goya's work there.

This link between the Secession and a commercial gallery was too much for Josef Engelhart and his circle, among others. He charged the artists of the new style with that same amalgamation of art with money that had led them to quit the Artists' House years before. In the course of the crucial meeting it came to a vote in which Klimt's group lost by one voice. Emotions had risen to a pitch which made agreement impossible. Eighteen members left the Secession, and they had for eight years been the most outstanding. The Secession continued; far from coming to an end after ten years it still exists today. The centre of Jugendstil shifted to the Vienna Workshops.

Klimt offends public taste

The ceiling paintings in the great hall of the new university

In retrospect the contract for three of the ceiling paintings in the great hall of the new university was the most important official contract Klimt ever received. It was also the last. After the first discussions about the contract (1892), fifteen years passed before the pictures were completed (1907). During this time Klimt progressed from history painter on the Ring to Secession artist, and the pictures testify to this development. They provoked criticism both from the public and from those who had commissioned them, and were the cause of Klimt's rejection of any further official contracts. The story of these pictures is therefore of great importance both for the biography and for the study of the development of his style. The problem in discussing them is that, except for one of the preliminary paintings, all have been burnt, and only black and white photographs of poor quality have survived (p. 314/315).

Chronology of events

In 1848 the university was forcibly ejected by the military from the building which had been erected under the Empress Maria Theresia. The professors regarded the new building on the Ring as a triumph since they regained appropriate surroundings for social and academic events. When the new university was opened in 1883 the ceiling in the great hall, symbol of the whole institution, was still bare. The expense had caused the decoration to be postponed, but all were agreed that, as in the old building, magnificent frescos representing the four faculties (Theology, Philosophy, Medicine and Jurisprudence) must form the crowning glory of the hall. The division of the ceiling into a large central section and four smaller ones adjoining each other on the narrow side, was already decided. The plans must keep to this.

In 1891 the Ministry of Education finally asked the rector of the university for suggestions and a calculation of costs. The university art commission, which was responsible for the decoration of the building, proceeded to formulate the following points: oil painting on canvas, to be stuck to the ceiling with glazier's putty, was preferable to fresco, and this technique had already been used successfully in the Burg Theatre, in the Court Museums and in other places; the paintings should be not historical but allegorical; the large central picture should depict the importance and function of the university in general; the four smaller ones would be reserved for the faculties; the sixteen spandrel pictures would present a general history, with illustrations of the oldest and most important universities. A scheme representing the different nations of the empire was also considered. The calculation of costs was followed by the suggestion that three different artists should be asked to submit sketches so that there could be a choice between various alternatives. The ministry rejected this last point, preferring to negotiate with one artist only. Various suggestions were made, resulting in the Company of Artists, still intact at that time, being selected. For functional details and preliminary sketches the ministry first singled out Franz Matsch and approached him alone. In 1893 his programme was presented, but the university art commission rejected it and renewed the suggestion that further artists should be asked to submit designs. The ministry chose rather to have Matsch produce a new design for the central picture in collaboration with Gustav Klimt (Ernst Klimt had died by this time). In the meantime the professors had suggested that the large ceiling painting should portray 'The Victory of Light over Darkness'.

The second plan worked out by Matsch and Klimt in collaboration was accepted without demur. In 1894 the artists, whose communal working arrangements were to end before the year was out, received a contract. One of the conditions was that they should have coloured sketches approved by the ministry before the paintings were executed. Another condition was that each had to guarantee to take over the work of the other in the event of one of them not continuing. This clause became important later on. The paintings were supposed to be delivered by the end of 1898.

Yet it was not until 1896 that a plan for the arrangement of the spandrel and ceiling paintings was submitted. The plan provided for 'Philosophy' and 'Theology' to be placed on one side of the ceiling, 'Medicine' and 'Jurisprudence' on the other side. Franz Matsch assumed responsibility for the central painting, 'Theology', and six of the spandrel pictures, while Klimt took over the remaining three faculties and ten spandrel pictures.

Not until 26 May 1898 could the art commissions of ministry and university arrange a meeting for the purpose of expressing their expert opinion on the five coloured designs for the ceiling paintings, which had at long last been completed. The pictures by Franz Matsch were approved without reservation, but Klimt's designs were criticized. The central figure 'Jurisprudence' must be more clearly characterized, and more light on 'Philosophy' would give the composition clarity. When they came to 'Medicine' the panel of experts found a nude female figure in the centre of the picture. Much later their discussion was reported in the press: "With regard to the picture 'Medicine' the wish was expressed that the bearing of the female figure characterizing 'suffering humanity' should be made more decent, less objectionable and less inclined to provoke obscene jokes; perhaps it should be replaced by the figure of a youth".[32]

Moreover the two artists should make their composition harmonise more with one another, so that the overall impression should not be one of disparate styles. If the artists were prepared to fulfil these conditions there would be no further objection to the contract being given.

Klimt is said to have been so embittered by this criticism that he wanted to withdraw from the contract at once. In an interview given in 1905 (see p. 122/127) he spoke of a divisional councillor Weckbecker whose mediation persuaded him to continue with the pictures, although he and Matsch declared themselves willing to take account

31/32 Margarethe Stonborough-Wittgenstein, 1905 Oil on canvas, 180 × 90 cm

Neue Pinakothek, Munich

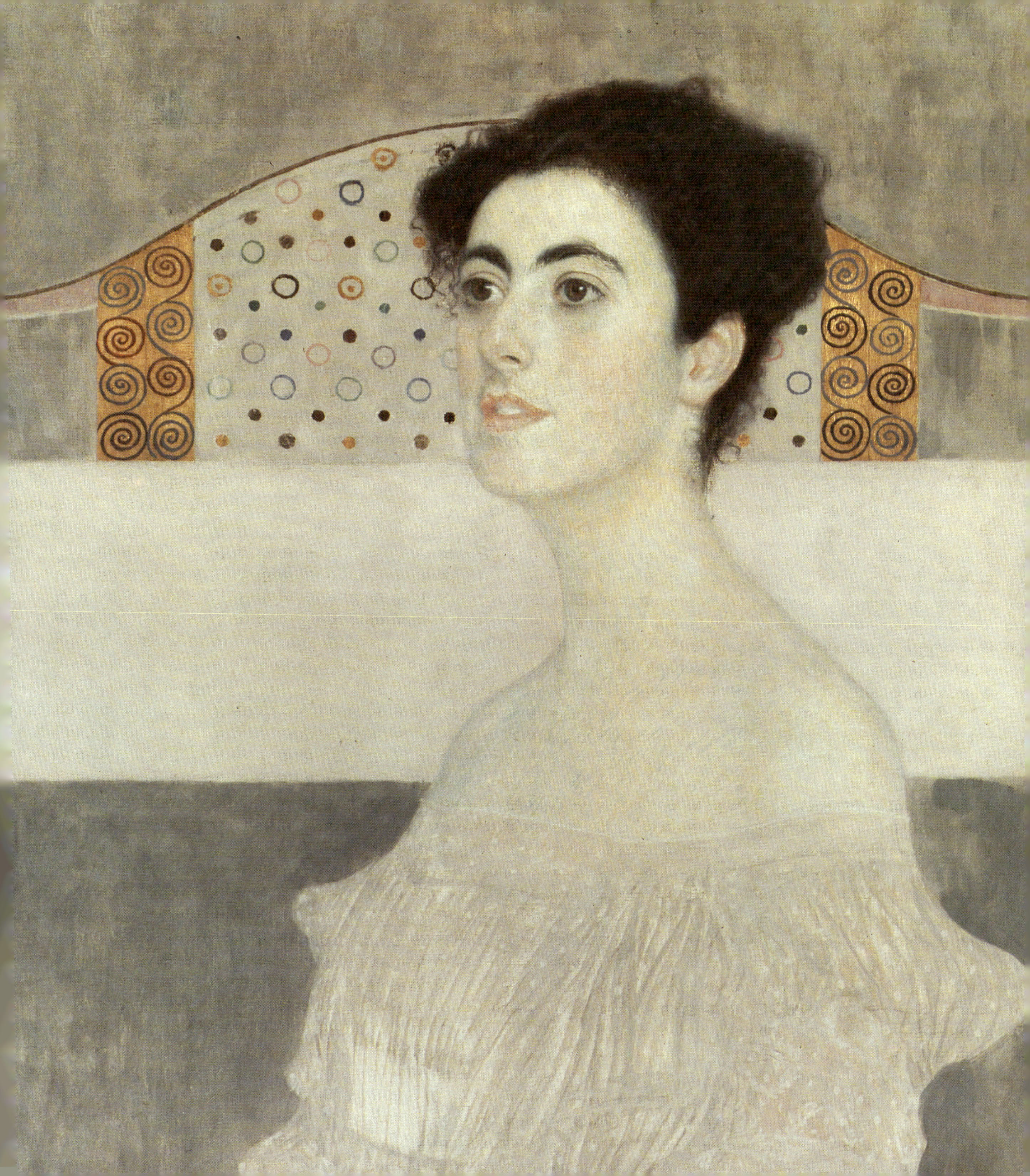

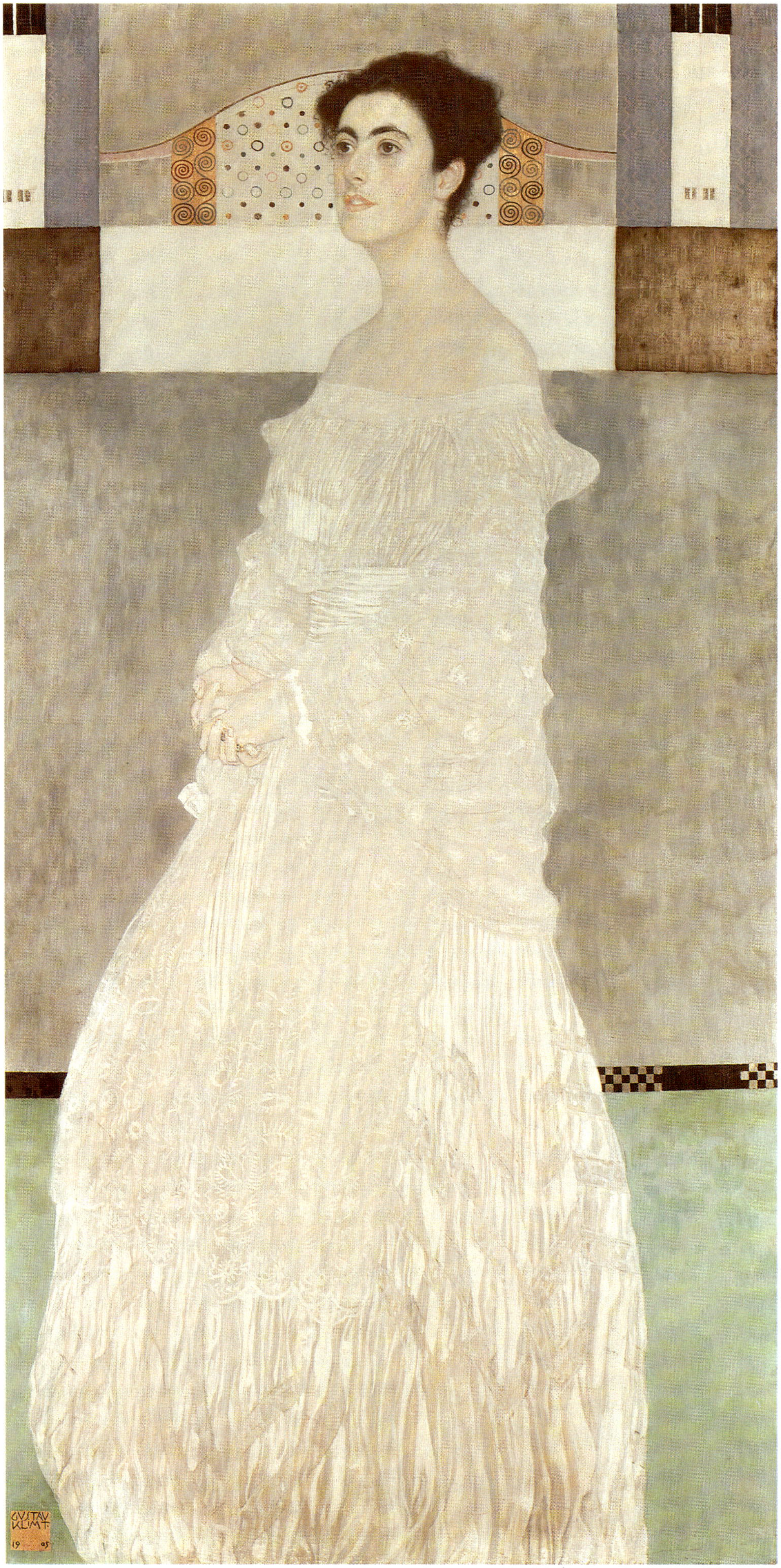
GVSTAV
KLIMT
19
05

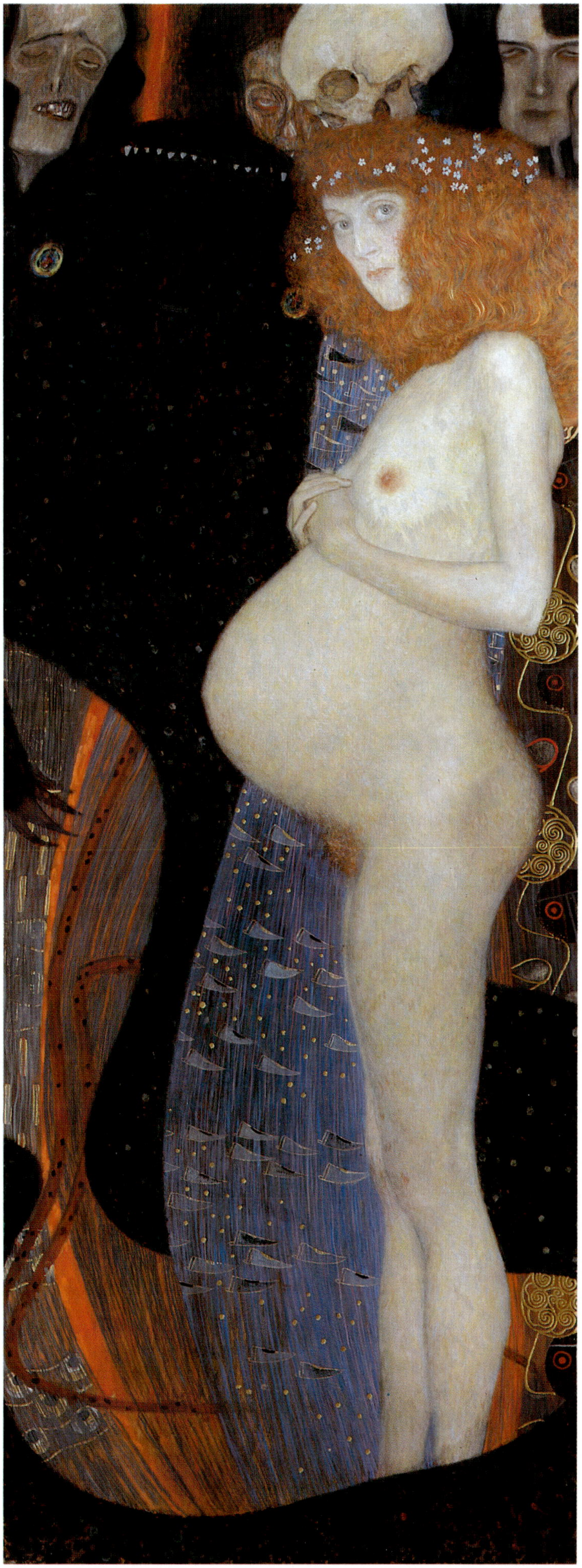

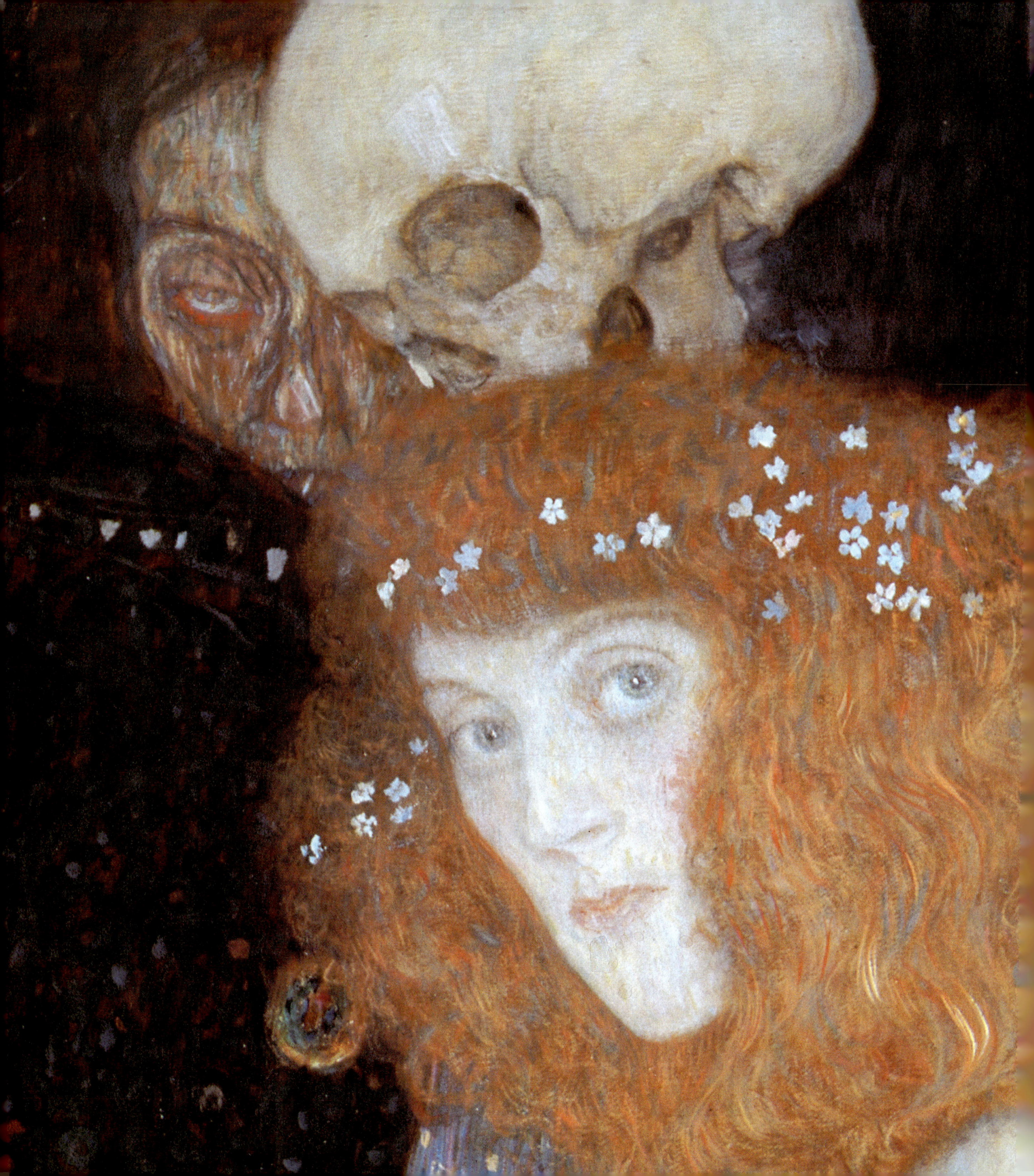

of the proposals only "within the limits necessary for the preservation of artistic freedom".[33]

In 1900 the first version of 'Philosophy' was finished and was shown to the public for the first time at the VIIth exhibition of the Secession from March to May; Klimt made subsequent alterations as he did with many of his pictures. In the catalogue an explanation was given: "Group of figures on the left: incipience, fertility, decay. Right: the globe, the mystery of the universe. Rising from below a figure of enlightenment: knowledge".[34]

A storm of indignation broke and was reflected in the press. Karl Kraus once more engaged in polemics: "Klimt's original design revealed, as I am given to understand, a naked boy deep in reverie . . . his long hair hung forward into his face, concealing the blushes which had suffused his child's cheeks at the sight of the two figures aloft entwined in a loving embrace . . . when the design was submitted to the commission the rector of the university is said to have commented 'that is not philosophy, that is a boy who is wondering at too early an age where children come from'. Mr. Klimt recognized that his allegory was not a success . . . and created the picture that may now be viewed in the Secession's little temple . . . Mr. Klimt was supposed to be painting philosophy, but unfortunately his notions of it are even hazier than his notions of jurisprudence, which he is also supposed to be painting . . . of what concern are Mr. Klimt's notions of philosophy to anyone? An unphilosophical painter can paint philosophy; he must make an allegory of the ideas painted inside the brains of his philosophical contemporaries."[35]

The humorist Eduard Pötzl (1851–1914) caricatured the picture: "We see . . . an aged naked man . . . Perhaps the sad want of garments is meant to suggest that this pitiful old fellow has been exposed to a cold sponge-down as a result of his persistent philosophising . . . A third unclothed girl, on the other hand, has arrived at a very understandable conclusion. She is arranging her hair with a glance in the direction of the mystery of the universe which frankly declares: 'get lost' "[36]

Attacks of this nature naturally summoned Klimt's supporters to the arena, resulting in a running battle in the press. Even more decisive was the massive protest of the professors. Eleven of them composed a

33/34 Hope I, 1903
Oil on canvas, 181 × 67 cm
National Gallery of Canada, Ottawa

petition which was submitted to the ministry with eighty-seven signatures, criticising principally the transfer of images:

"When the mystery of the universe is presented as a greenish gleaming mist, with vague suggestions of a sphinx-like shape in it, and knowledge is presented as a head lighted up inside... then simple metaphors, common enough in language, have been transposed into visual images, or rather into hieroglyphics, in such a manner that they cannot convey the sense of artistic insights, but only of parables or puzzles... we will not go into the blurred movements, the artificial forms or the numerous instances of misshapen human anatomy. It is possible that the painter had definite artistic ideas in mind, even if they are not recognisable to the public. But in general we can see no virtue in the reproduction of hazy ideas by means of hazy forms... We doubt very much... whether this visionary symphony of colour is really likely, as has been maintained, to inspire associations of ideas which will give the viewer an enlightened understanding of the intellectual content of this picture posing as philosophy."[37]

This criticism, which of course did, indirectly, attack Klimt's manner of painting as well, then took a prophetic turn: "Although we do not expect that posterity will grant this picture a place on any but the most crooked path of progress, we do believe that it will be of interest as a remarkable offshoot of the tree of modern art, testifying to the ferment of artistic endeavour in Vienna at the turn of the century. On the ceiling of the great hall of the university we would not like to see such a picture, which in its style and approach is inappropriate for that particular place..."[38]

One of the likely objections not mentioned in the petition is Klimt's understanding of philosophy. The professors, who favoured a decidedly positivist approach, could not accept a contrary opinion. In another place they expressed their view that at a time when philosophy was seeking its wellspring in science, it did not deserve to be interpreted as a nebulous figment of fantasy.

The petition was accompanied by a counter-protest written by professorial colleagues who took up the cudgels on Klimt's behalf. They charged the authors of the petition with incompetence and pointed out the misguidedness of judging the picture on its own, as it was part of a larger whole. At this point the petition had no further consequences.

At an official meeting at the ministry presided over by Minister von Hartel himself, a supporter of Klimt and of the Secession, it was noted that Klimt had acceded to the requests made after the earlier presentation of the preliminary sketches. The professorial protest could be ascribed to a certain taste in art and need not be further considered. It was not even felt necessary to send an answer to the petition.

'Philosophy' was shown at the Great Exhibition in Paris the same year, and was awarded the grand prix. The French press reacted favourably to the picture.

The protest was repeated the following year when Klimt showed 'Medicine' at the Secession's Xth exhibition. Favourable and unfavourable reviews followed one another in rapid succession, lectures were held on the subject. The public prosecutor demanded that the issue of VER SACRUM which contained the sketches for the painting should be sequestrated, but the Provincial Court did not agree: "... it is a matter of the submission of sketches ... for a publicly displayed work of art ... and their publication in a journal devoted to art, read by artists and by lay people interested in art and artistic endeavour (in a sense a professional journal), and cannot be described as improper, nor should it be forbidden ..."[39]

The dispute reached its height when it became the subject of parliamentary debate. On 20 March twenty-two parliamentarians submitted a question to Minister von Hartel: "1. Does His Excellency really intend to purchase the picture? 2. Does His Excellency intend, by purchasing Klimt's 'Medicine', to give material support and the official Austrian seal of approval to the style represented in this picture, which is offensive to the aesthetic sense of a majority of the population?"[40]

Von Hartel replied that there could be no question of a purchase since the picture was already in the possession of the state. He said that a state commission did not by any means give a style the 'official Austrian seal of approval' and that such a thing was not within the powers of his ministry.

Two days later Klimt put a brief announcement in the Vienna morning paper: "I have no time to become personally embroiled in these

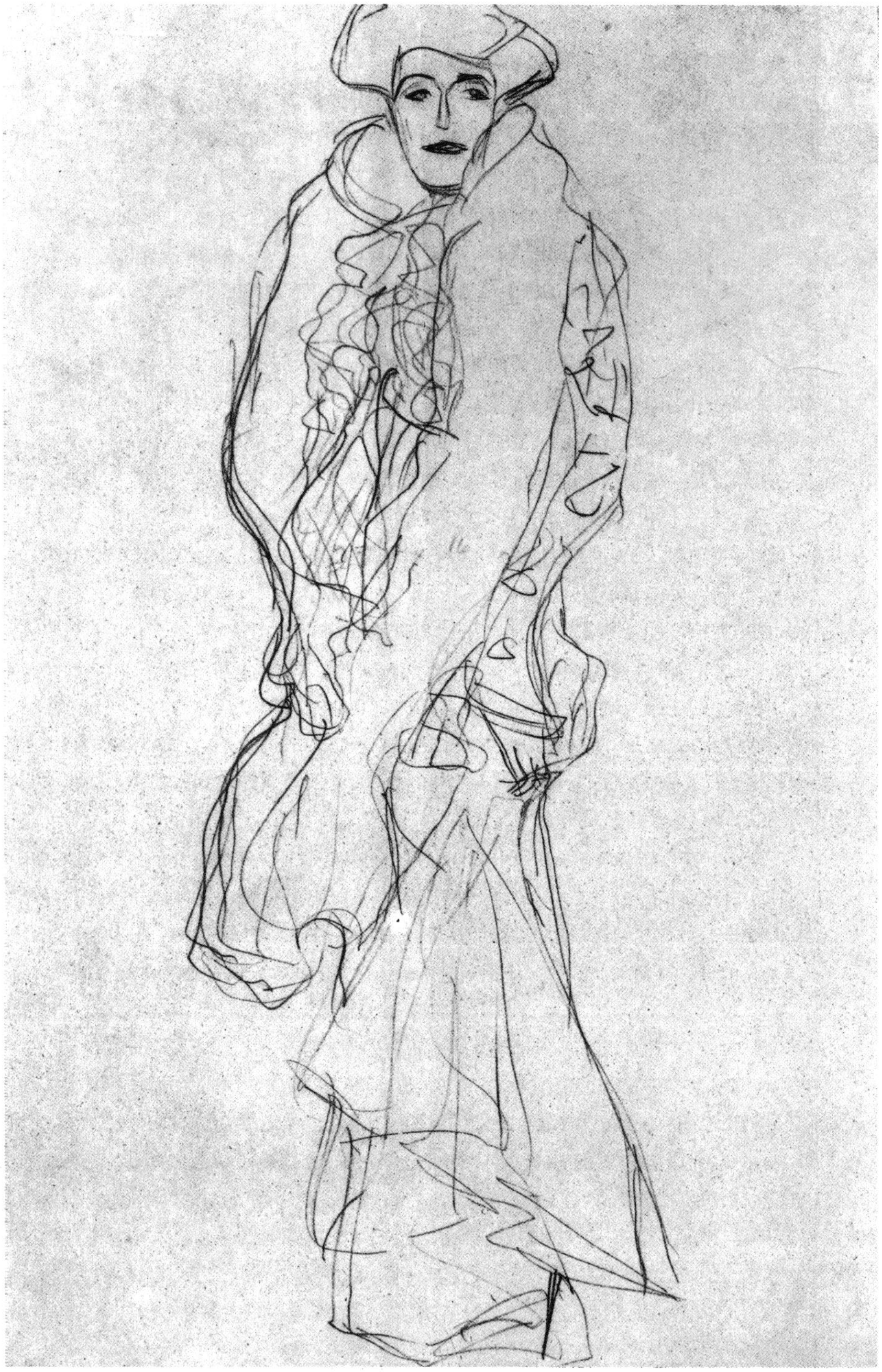

Female figure standing turned to the left, face towards the front (Adele Bloch-Bauer), 1904/05
Black crayon, 55 × 34.8 cm

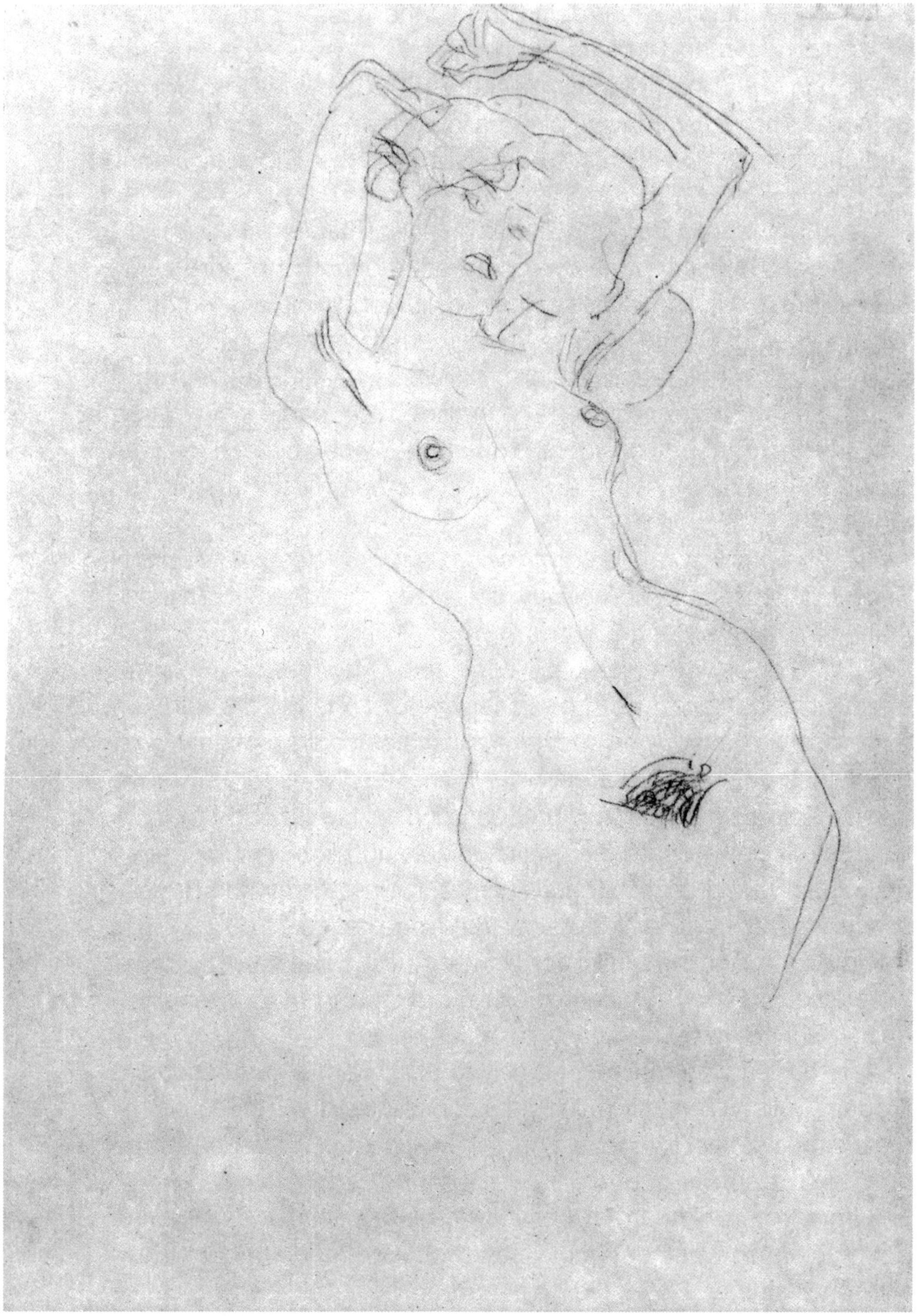

Girl holding her arms above her head,
1905/06
Pencil, 44.5 × 30.5 cm

don't want to spend months defending it to the masses. I'm not bothered about how many it pleases, but whom it pleases. Well, I've had don't want to spend months defending it to the masses. I'm not bothered about how many it pleases, but whom it pleases. Well, I've had enough . . ."[41] He seems to have kept out of the whole argument, more or less.

In 1903, when 'Jurisprudence' was at last finished and Matsch had completed 'Theology', Matsch was asked to bring his picture to the Secession's exhibition rooms so that the four faculty pictures could be viewed together. Klimt's pictures were already there, as they were to be shown as part of a large exhibition of his works. After the viewing on 11 November 1903 the ministry's art commission met, partly to assess the pictures and partly to consider the question of whether such different pictures as those of Matsch and Klimt could be brought together on the ceiling.

The composition of this commission, in which there were several Secessionists, led to a completely different set of opinions from those that had previously been voiced in public. Klimt's pictures were not discussed at all, while the quality of those by Matsch was not highly rated. In this matter the commissioners were of one mind. The much more difficult question of whether the pictures could reasonably be mounted together in the great hall was not resolved. Some were in favour of mounting Klimt's pictures only and having the gaps filled at a later date. One favoured the original plan, and his reasoning might have made good sense: in earlier times, for instance in the Renaissance, very different painters had worked together on a single project; in thirty years' time the similarities between these two contemporaries' works would probably seem much more striking than their differences. But he made no headway on his own.

A third idea was mooted, namely to hang Klimt's pictures in the Modern Gallery. The only result of the consultations was to record that the pictures did not fit together, but that Matsch must nevertheless be spared criticism.

Klimt must have heard of these discussions because he inquired, not much later, whether the pictures should be made to harmonize with one another. He would have had no objection to his pictures being mounted together with those by Matsch. He was, however, sceptical about them being used in any other way. When in 1904 the ministry declined to approve the showing of the faculty pictures at the St Louis exhibition (see p. 107), Klimt withdrew from the contract for the spandrel pictures.

Franz Matsch was obliged by contract to assume responsibility for them. In 1905 most of them were finished. He submitted a new plan for their exact positioning on the ceiling, in which he altered the positions of the four faculty pictures. Klimt had always wanted to place 'Philosophy' and 'Medicine' opposite one another; the opposition was expressed in the composition and in the colouring of the pictures. Matsch now acceded to this wish. He added to the revised plan an estimate from the scaffolding hire company for the cost of a trial mounting of the pictures.

The university art commission received the estimate from the ministry and decided against a trial mounting of the pictures, on the grounds that it would be disproportionately costly. Since such very different pictures could not be mounted together anyway, it was not worth the expense. Moreover they anticipated a re-opening of "the question that became so very unpleasant on the previous occasion, as to whether Klimt's pictures were suitable for the originally intended purpose."[42]

This reasoning shows that the professors, whose earlier petition had received scant attention, were still opposed to Klimt's faculty pictures although it was only the quality of Matsch's pictures that had been criticized at the meeting of November 1903, attended by the art commission. No more mention was made of that meeting: the three faculty pictures by Gustav Klimt should be hung in the Modern Gallery; Matsch's large central picture and the twelve spandrel pictures, now finished, should be mounted as originally intended. The four spaces should remain unfilled, or be decorated ornamentally. Matsch's faculty picture 'Theology' was consigned to the assembly room of the theological faculty; it still hangs in the dean's office.

In March Matsch was invited to a further meeting of the art commission. He pointed out that the construction of the ceiling required that the spaces be lined with pictures; if not, cracks would appear and damp would get in. It is impossible to know whether Matsch was simply angling for the contract for three further faculty pictures, or whether his point was valid. It is certain that during the autumn of the same year he made every effort to secure the contract. Even before that, Klimt had withdrawn his pictures.

On 3 April 1904, directly after the second meeting of the art commission, Klimt addressed the following letter to the ministry: "When I received the contract for the great hall of the university over ten years ago, and set to work, I was fired with enthusiasm. My long years of earnest endeavour have earned me many harsh words, which, considering the nature of their provenance, did not at first dampen my enthusiasm. But in time that changed... If I am to complete this task, which has consumed so many years of my life, I must first of all find pleasure in it again, which is quite impossible as long as I have to regard it as a state commission subject to present conditions. I am therefore faced by the impossibility of fulfilling the contract which has progressed so far... My withdrawal from the whole contract follows, and I am repaying in entirety the advances received over the years."[43]

The ministry responded at once by stating that the pictures were already state property, and instructed Klimt to deliver them. Then on 10 April it was announced in the paper that Klimt was taking back his pictures. This was followed two days later by a long interview in which Klimt explained this step. The 'Klimt Affair' was once again front-page news. In the interview Klimt emphasized that he wanted to withdraw the pictures not because of the attacks and criticism coming from various quarters, but because he had the feeling that the commission was not satisfied with his work. "For the artist there is... no more awkward situation than creating works of art for, and receiving payment from, an employer whose heart and mind are not entirely sympathetic to him. I cannot reconcile myself to that at all, and I tried for a long time to find a way of freeing myself from this dilemma which I regard as a total debasement of true creativity." He pointed out that he had wanted to withdraw eight years prior to this and recalled the mediation of Baron Weckbecker (see p. 110). Since the contract had been confirmed, Minister von Hartel had been held responsible for Klimt's work, to such an extent that he did actually come to feel

35/36 Fritza Riedler, 1906
Oil on canvas, 153 × 133 cm
Austrian Gallery, Vienna

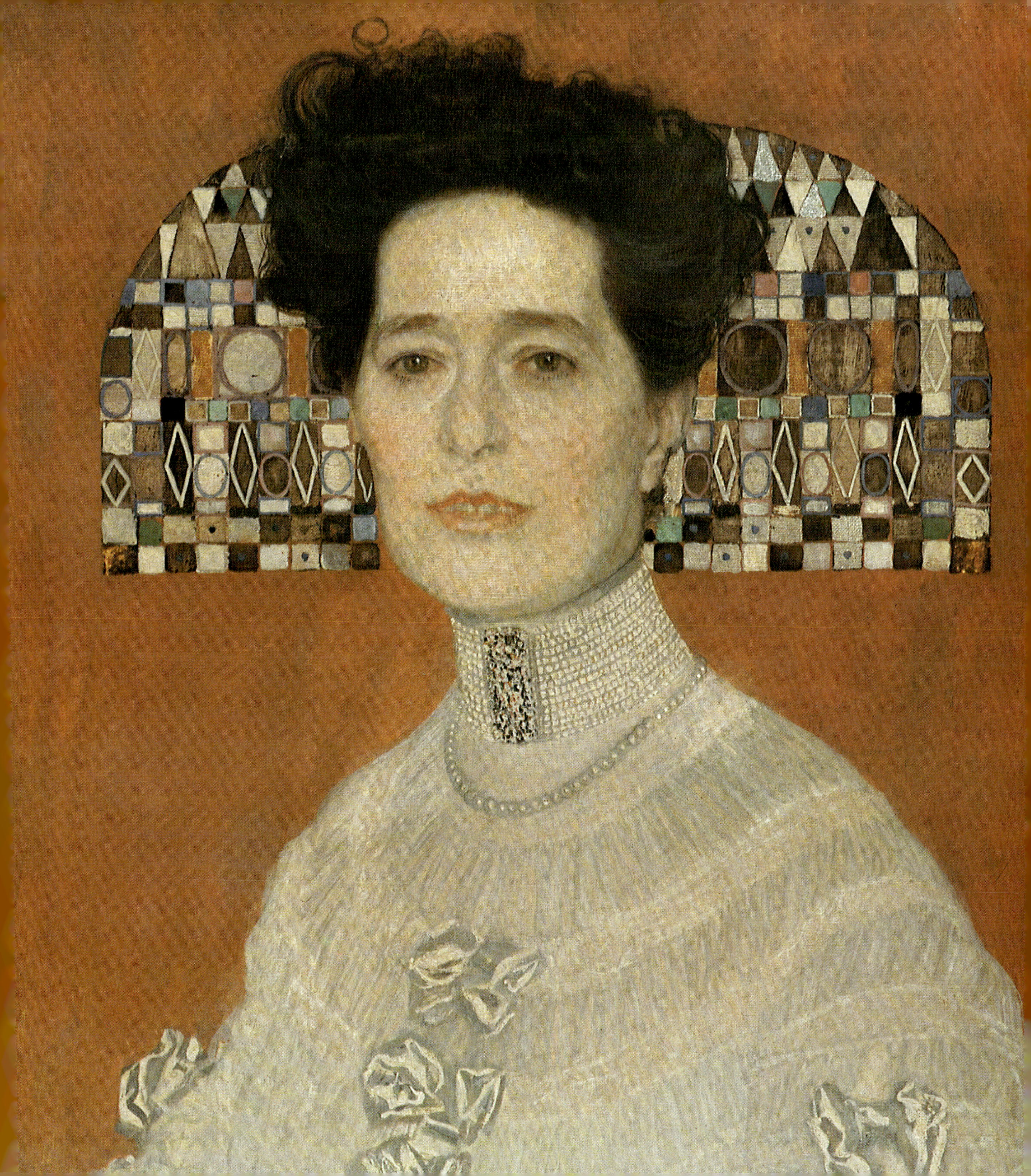

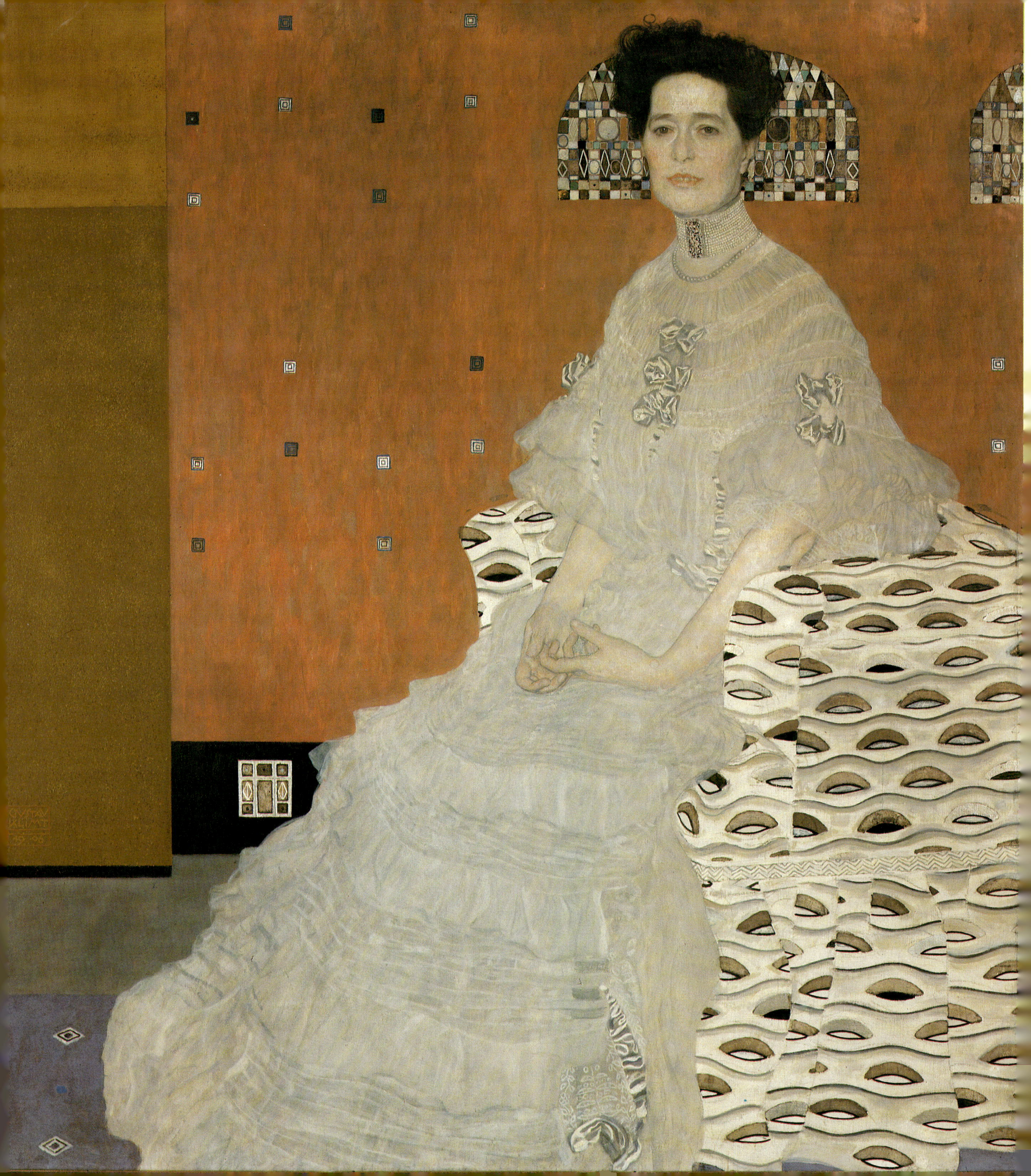
GUSTAV
KLIMT

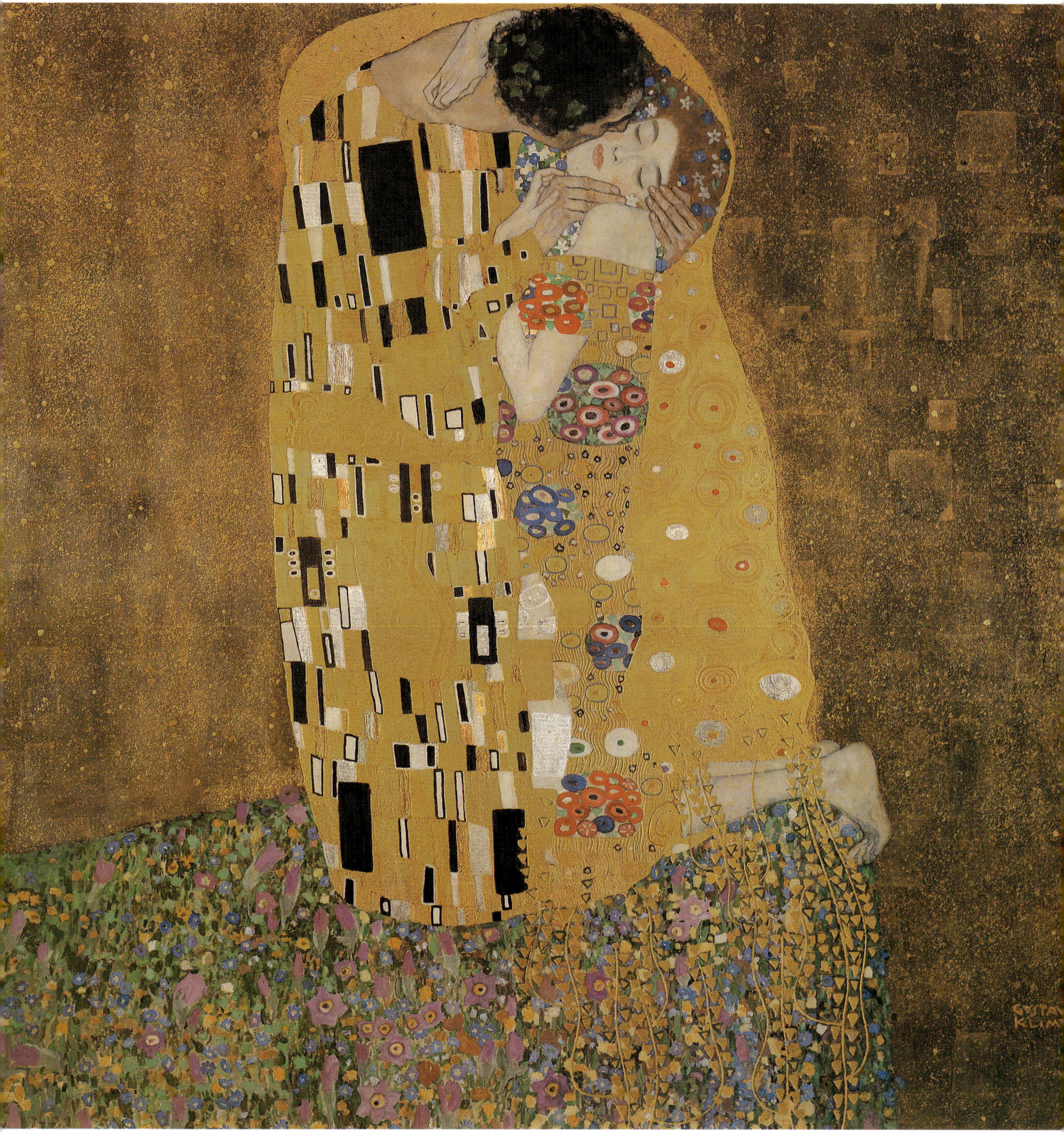

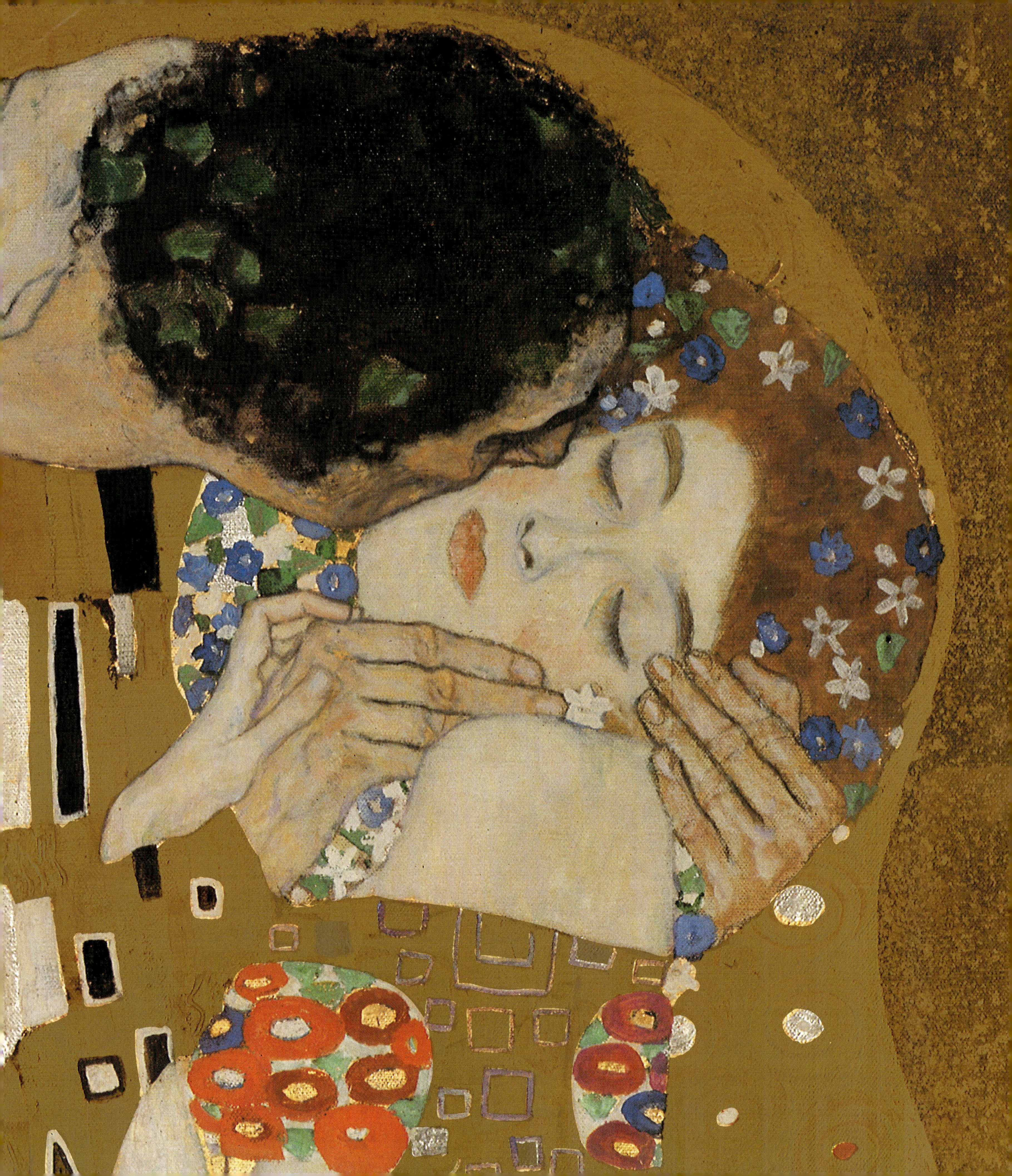

responsible. "No, I have been a terrible liability to the minister, and I intend by the step that I am now taking to relieve him permanently of this strange sponsorship that has hedged me in. Nor will I ever take part in an official exhibition, or certainly not under this ministry . . . This is self-help. I want to get out. I want to escape from all these ridiculous unpleasantnesses that hold up my work. I refuse any sort of state assistance, I lay no claim to anything." After this clear statement he spoke of his right to the pictures: they were not finished; the final adjustments could only have been carried out with the pictures in place on the ceiling. Then he quoted the clause from the contract stipulating that each artist must complete the work if the other should be prevented from completing his part: "This is now the case. I am not able to deliver pictures which do not match the expectations of the employer. I return the money and keep the pictures. I cannot be dependent on those I must fight."[44]

After this campaign in the press Klimt wrote a second letter to the ministry, in which he referred to the contract and substantiated his claim that the pictures legally belonged to him and not to the state. He repeated his request for a banking address to which the 30,000 crowns could be repaid. At this point the minister, for whom the publicity given to this affair was highly embarrassing, yielded.

It was of course not possible for Klimt to raise the enormous sum of 30,000 crowns, but his patron, the industrialist August Lederer, came to the rescue. In return he received 'Philosophy'. In 1907 the pictures were once more exhibited together in Galerie Miethke. Klimt's friend Koloman Moser purchased the other two pictures later, when he had made a rich marriage. After Moser's death in 1918 'Jurisprudence' also passed into Lederer's collection, while 'Medicine' went to the Austrian Gallery. In 1944 an enforced sale brought 'Philosophy' and 'Jurisprudence' to the Austrian Gallery. The three pictures were evacuated with many others to Schloss Immendorf because of air-raids on the capital. On 8 May 1945 retreating SS troops set fire to the castle in order to prevent the art treasures falling into Russian hands. This senseless action destroyed the three faculty pictures, two of the preliminary compositions and four further pictures by Klimt.

In September 1905 Franz Matsch made his final attempt to secure

37/38 The Kiss, 1907/08
Oil on canvas, 180 × 180 cm
Austrian Gallery, Vienna

the contract for the three faculty pictures. He succeeded in convincing the art commission of the necessity; but the sketches which he submitted in 1907 were turned down. His offer to prepare new sketches was not accepted. Matsch refused to withdraw from the contract. He insisted on his contractual right to execute the pictures. After long and tedious discussions an offer of compensation was made and accepted in 1910.

Designs and completed paintings – a comparison

As has already become apparent, Gustav Klimt did not paint the faculty pictures in quick succession but over a long period. The preliminary compositions, on the other hand, were all done in 1898. In the changes which Klimt made it is possible to trace his development as a painter. For 'Philosophy' and 'Medicine' transfer sketches give evidence of intermediate stages.

In the preliminary composition for 'Philosophy' the allegory of knowledge sits at the right lower edge of the picture. With her head in her hand she gazes downward. Above her is the bust of a three-headed sphinx. Klimt modelled this bust on an Egyptian four-headed sphinx in the Art History Museum. Its original significance is still uncertain, but for Klimt it symbolised the mystery of the universe. Beside this figure, at the upper left hand edge of the picture, a naked man and woman embrace, with a half-grown child at their side. They represent human procreation and continued existence. Below them shadowy figures of philosophers can be made out.

In the transfer sketch there is a marked shift of emphasis. The allegory of knowledge has moved to the centre of the lower edge of the picture, though she still looks down. The sphinx takes up more space, and is now entirely visible. Above her is the cosmos. The man and woman have a second child, which gives a stronger sense of family. Instead of philosophers there now appear below the family group a loving couple and two old people who shield their faces with their hands in despair. In this way Klimt gives more precision than in the first

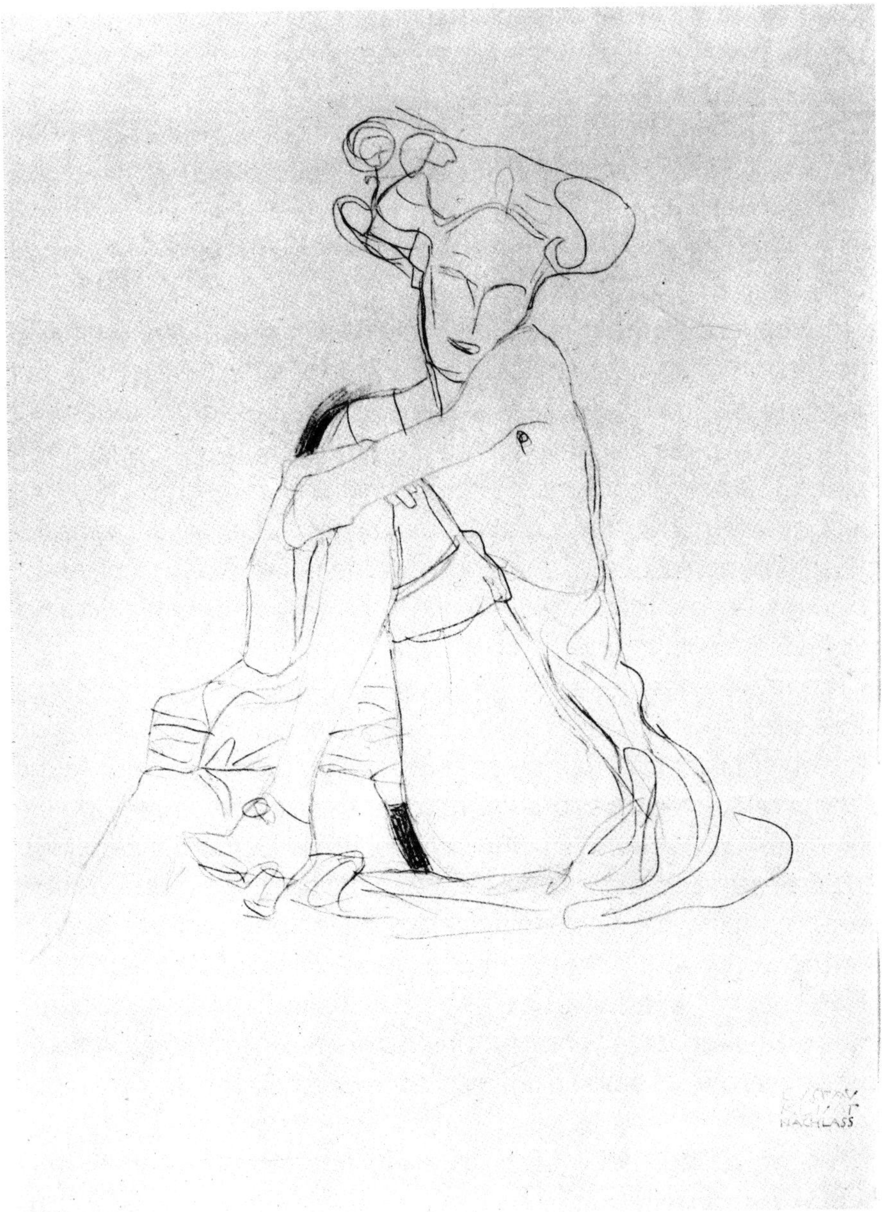

Seated figure, left leg drawn up, 1908
Blue pencil, 52.7 × 38.7 cm

version to the ideas of becoming, being and decaying. In the painting the scene is localised by the star-spangled sky most visible above the sphinx and between the entwined human bodies. The modifications of their embrace make their love less sensuous than before. A young woman tumbles into the lap of the old woman, above the allegory of knowledge crouches a male figure seen from behind, an embryo hovers in space.

But the most significant change is in the allegory of knowledge. She has lost all contact with the naked figures soaring over her, linked with one another by a black veil. Her head rises from the depths, she looks straight out of the picture to the front and her head seems illuminated from within.

Models for the individual figures in the painting have been identified first and foremost in the sculptures of Auguste Rodin (1840–1917), but for a long time nothing definite was known about literary sources. Not long ago a previously overlooked commentary by Ferdinand von Feldegg came to light, written in 1900, which links Gustav Klimt's 'Philosophy' with current theosophical ideas. "Klimt's picture presents not the schoolmen's idea of philosophy as the sum of individual 'exact' sciences, but a unified world science, not the doctrine of the tangible but that of the intangible."[45]

The most recent research replaces this relatively general view by more precise information, allowing speculation about Klimt's own reading. 'Philosophy' can be seen in relation to the works of Arthur Schopenhauer who was of such importance also for the development of the French Symbolists in the circle of Emile Bernard (see p. 36).

His pessimistic atheist metaphysics of salvation exerted a great influence in the late nineteenth century, on the philosopher Friedrich Nietzsche (1844–1900) and the composer Richard Wagner (1813–1883) among others. The general relationship between Schopenhauer's ideas and the contents of the picture having first been noted, it then became possible to identify actual 'quotations' from various writings.

The prevailing mood of the painting and the entwined human bodies clearly refer to the beginnings of the commentary on 'The World as Will and Idea': "Innumerable shining spheres in endless space, each surrounded by a dozen smaller ones that spin in the light, hot inside, covered outside with a cold hardened shell on which a mildewy coating has generated living, cognisant beings: that is empirical truth, reality, the world. Yet for a being given to reflection it is a misfortune to be standing on one of those spheres soaring in unbounded space, without knowing whence or whither, merely one of innumerable similar beings propelled painfully forwards, restlessly and rapidly growing and decaying in time without beginning or end . . ."[46]

The allegory of knowledge has another direct literary source, but the ultimate meaning is again derived from Schopenhauer: ". . . without doubt it is the knowledge of death, and then the contemplation of the suffering and hardship of life, that gives the strongest impulse to philosophic reflection and metaphysical exegesis of the world."[47]

This makes the black veils round the head of the figure rising from the depths more comprehensible, and the propinquity of the two old people close to death is given a deeper meaning. In another work, 'Parerga and Paralipomena', Schopenhauer equates all existence with the great sphinx, so that the remaining part of Klimt's picture can also be seen in its relation to the philosopher.

As has already been noted, a second literary source for the allegory of knowledge has been identified. In 'Rheingold', the prelude to Wagner's 'Ring', Erda, mother of the gods, appears to Wotan, their father. Wagner's stage directions for the moment of her appearance are a fitting description of the allegorical figure: "The stage . . . has darkened: from the gorge at the side a bluish light shines forth; in it Erda, rising from the depths to half the height of her body, suddenly appears to Wotan; she is of noble appearance, with flowing black hair . . ."[48]

This attribution is plausible partly because Klimt is known to have paid close attention to Wagner's writings in another connection, when he was working on the Beethoven Frieze. The question still remains, whether Klimt found these literary sources himself or whether one of his friends, for instance Hevesi or Bahr, pointed him in their direction.

Klimt always claimed to be a simple, relatively uneducated man. He never wrote about his pictures. Yet from accounts given by friends it is known that he not only had Goethe's 'Faust' and Dante's 'Divine Comedy' in his pocket very frequently, but also quoted from Dante and Petrarch while he was painting. He possessed an extensive library which was destroyed during World War II, of which unfortunately no records remain. It is also known that opened books were often seen lying around in his studio when he was working on a particular subject, and that he acquired from them the knowledge he needed. This makes it quite possible that the programme for 'Philosophy' was entirely his own. It is important to be aware that Klimt had the means to choose his own sources, and was not, as his detractors maintained, dependent on his 'advisers'.

In 'Medicine' the theme of growth, maturity and decay recurs. In the preliminary composition the right side of the picture reveals a mass of human bodies, among which 'Death' and 'Pain' alone are clearly recognisable. The left half is taken up with a nude female figure which was considered indecent at the time. She holds out her hand to a man in the tangle of bodies. The link between them suggests the everlasting renewal of mankind, and this becomes clearer in the actual painting. Below, comparable to the allegory of knowledge in 'Philosophy', appears Hygieia, goddess of health and daughter of Aesculapius. Not only is her head visible, but almost the whole figure, clad in a long antique robe.

In the transfer sketch the nude female figure is moved further towards the left edge of the picture, the human mass takes up much more space and figures of all ages can be recognised. In the actual painting this becomes even clearer. The position of the isolated female figure has not changed, her left arm is still extended away from the body, reaching into the mass at the level of 'Death' and 'Pain'. Her right hand is grasped by the hand of the man standing above Hygieia, which means that his arm too is extended and arms and bodies are at right angles. A newborn child swathed in black lies at the feet of the female figure, renewal of life being linked in this way to the threatening of young life by death. Among the children, women, men and old people, a pregnant woman is worth noting. The theme of the pregnant woman recurs in Klimt's later work. The figures of 'Death' and 'Pain' are set apart from the mass by the black ornamented veil that links them and partly covers them. Hygieia now rises from the depths exactly in the centre of the picture, clothed in a magnificent robe, with a vessel in one hand and the snake of Aesculapius wound round the other.

As in 'Philosophy', the separation between knowledge and mankind is emphasised. Klimt sees not science but human suffering in the foreground. It is important to note that he always intended 'Philosophy' and 'Medicine' to form a contrasting pair, with the human bodies on the inside, the sphinx and the hovering female figure on the outside.

A photomontage projection of the four faculty pictures onto the empty ceiling spaces shows how well these two pictures would have fitted. In both Klimt applied the principle of sotto in su (viewing from bottom to top), so that viewing the pictures from any other angle would have destroyed much of the effect. That was certainly one of the reasons for his obstinate refusal to have the pictures used for a different purpose.

In the case of 'Jurisprudence' preliminary composition and painting are very different. The preliminary design was done at the same time as the other two and displays an allegory of 'Justitia'. The great figure of 'Justice' clothed in a billowing white robe holds aloft the sword of judgement. The presentation of this faculty is the most traditional of the three, which may be one of the reasons why Klimt did not keep to the design.

'Philosophy' and 'Medicine' were painted in the period immediately following the acceptance of the design and the issuing of a firm contract, but Klimt did not hurry to complete 'Jurisprudence'. In the intervening period there were marked developments in his painting. The ornamental appeared more and more strikingly in the foreground, he emphasised the two-dimensionality and the 'lifelessness' of the figures. It was the time of the first female portraits in which the bodies were conceived entirely as ornament. The Beethoven Frieze (seep.168–181) marked an important stage in his development. Moreover the attacks on the other two faculty pictures altered his attitude to 'Jurisprudence'. By the time he came to paint it, it was already apparent that the pictures might never reach their appointed place, which may well explain why 'Jurisprudence' is not conceived sotto in su and some of the figures could not have been made out at all if the picture had actually been mounted on the ceiling.

At the bottom of the picture, again rising from the depths, there is this time no allegory or personification but the sinner, tried and found guilty. The naked man in bowed, penitential stance, his hands behind his back, is being gripped round the arms by a giant polyp with monstrous suckers. The three Erinyes who avenge every wrong accompany the polyp, the guilty conscience. The three naked female figures with snakes in their hair rise out of a black seething mass signifying hell. Smoke and vapour ascending from the black mass partially conceal a square stone building, recognisable through its occupants as the supreme court of law. Here, at the very top of the picture and so small that they almost seem to have passed into another region, rule 'Truth', 'Justice' and 'Law'. These three female figures appear entirely lifeless. 'Justice' resembles a statue, with closed eyes, geometrically sectioned and ornamented robe, and arms extended stiffly, bent upwards at the elbows. One hand is raised to take the oath, the other grasps the sword. Behind the women and below them the heads of the judges can be seen, small, with no bodies.

In this picture 'Justice' is no longer in the centre as in the preliminary composition; the central theme is the cruelty of the punishment. The three representative female figures have become powerless witnesses of the merciless punishment inflicted before their eyes.

It has recently been suggested that Klimt may have drawn on cantos from Dante's 'Inferno' for this picture. That is very probable, particularly as he is known to have recited passages from Dante by heart, as was mentioned above.

Just as in 'Philosophy', where several passages from Schopenhauer seem to have blended to form a whole, so here the polyp, the Erinyes and the heads looking down from a wall in hell seem to be drawn from several different cantos in the 'Inferno', (the polyp being derived from Dante's infernal judge Minos).

The different literary texts which seem to have provided source material for the pictures were all concerned, in different ways, with death. That is also the common theme that links the three faculty pictures with one another. Love and death, the three ages – these are the central themes of these pictures, and they became very important to Klimt after he had given up painting historicist pictures to order. In 'Philosophy' and 'Medicine' the three become one, and the pictures can be seen as variations on a single theme, but in 'Jurisprudence' death is the centre.

39 Farm Garden with Sunflowers, c. 1905/06
Oil on canvas, 110 × 110 cm
Austrian Gallery, Vienna

40 Cows in Stall, 1900/01
Oil on canvas, 75 × 75 cm
New Gallery, Linz

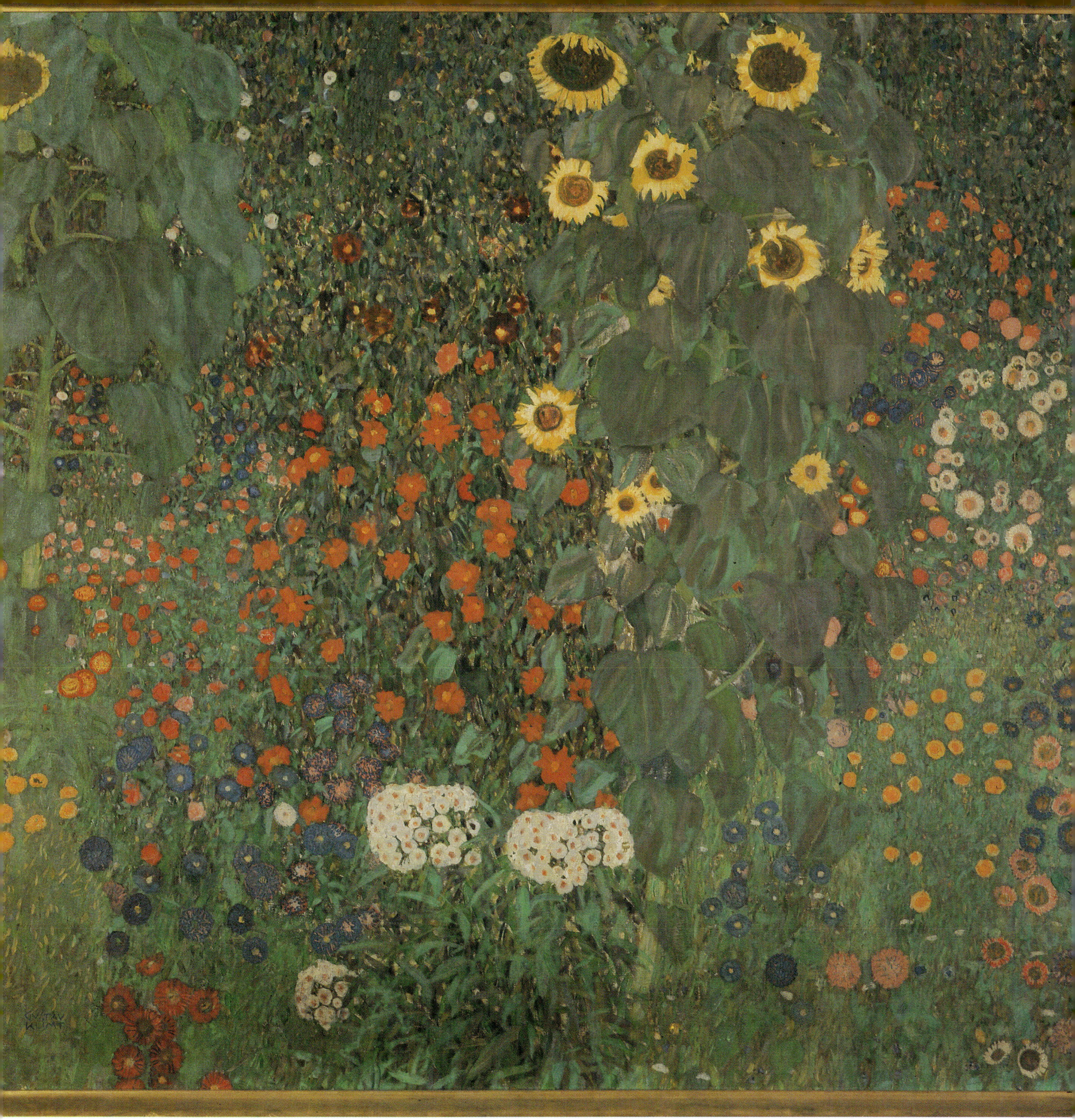

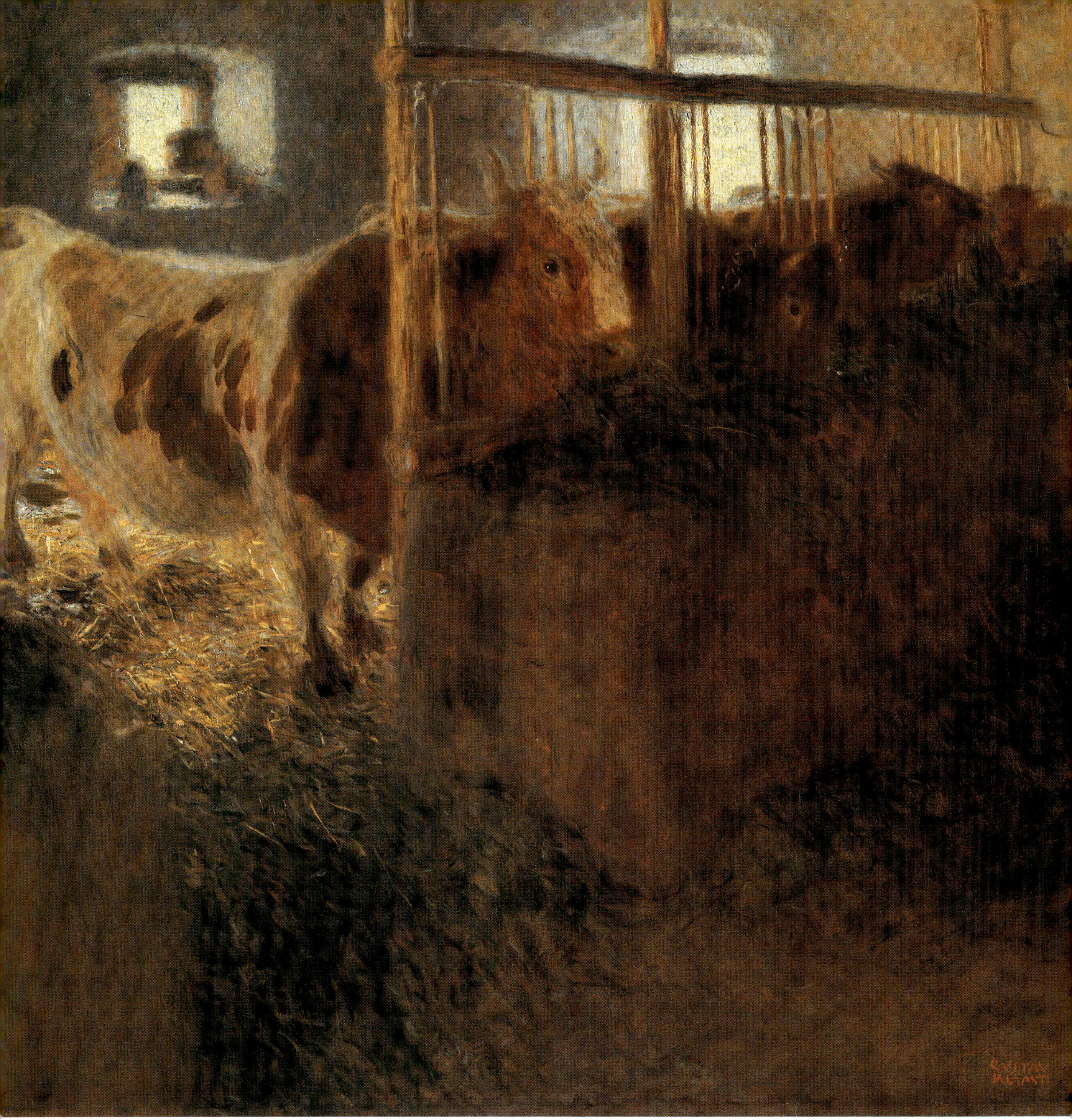
GUSTAV
KLIMT

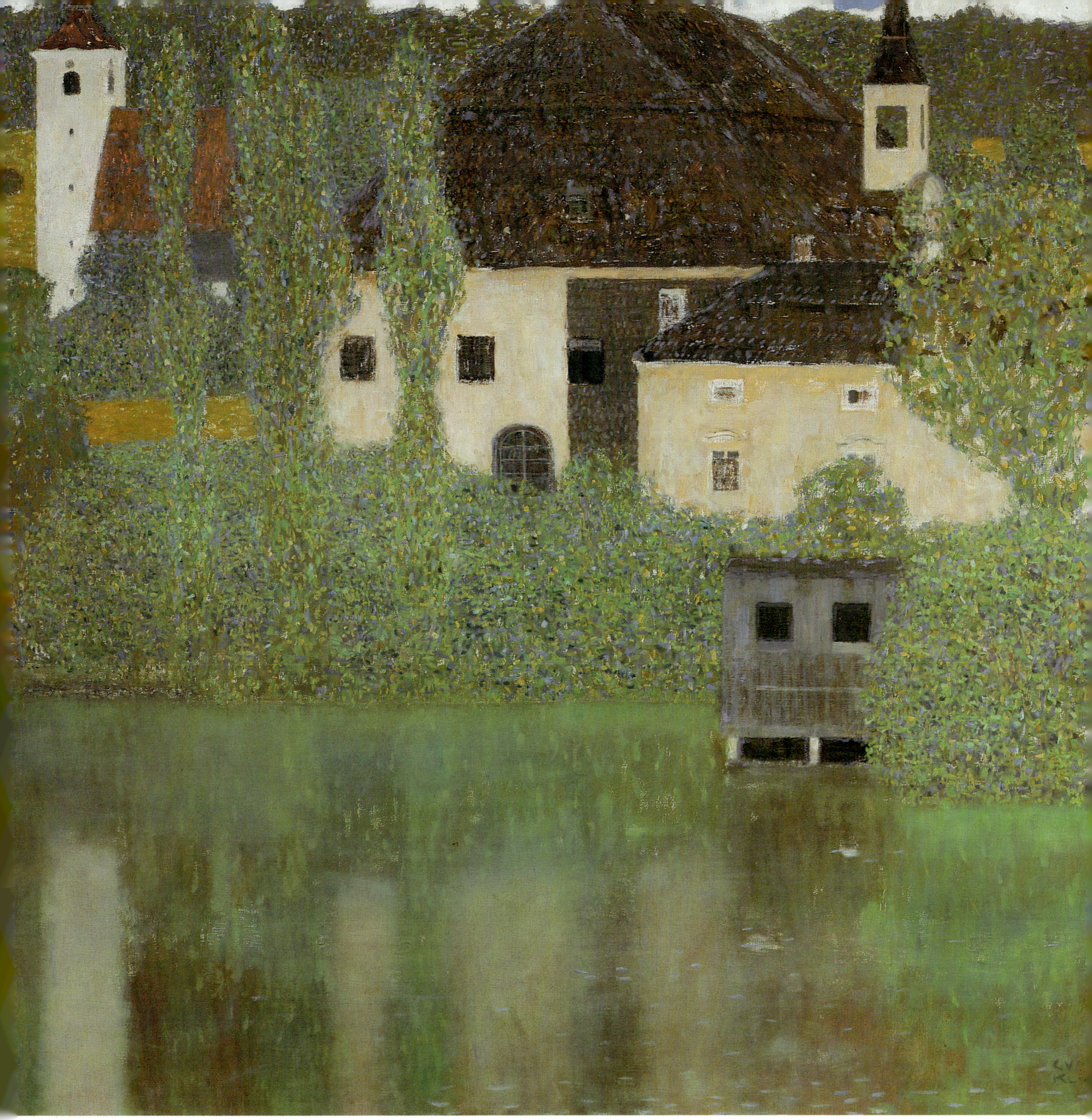

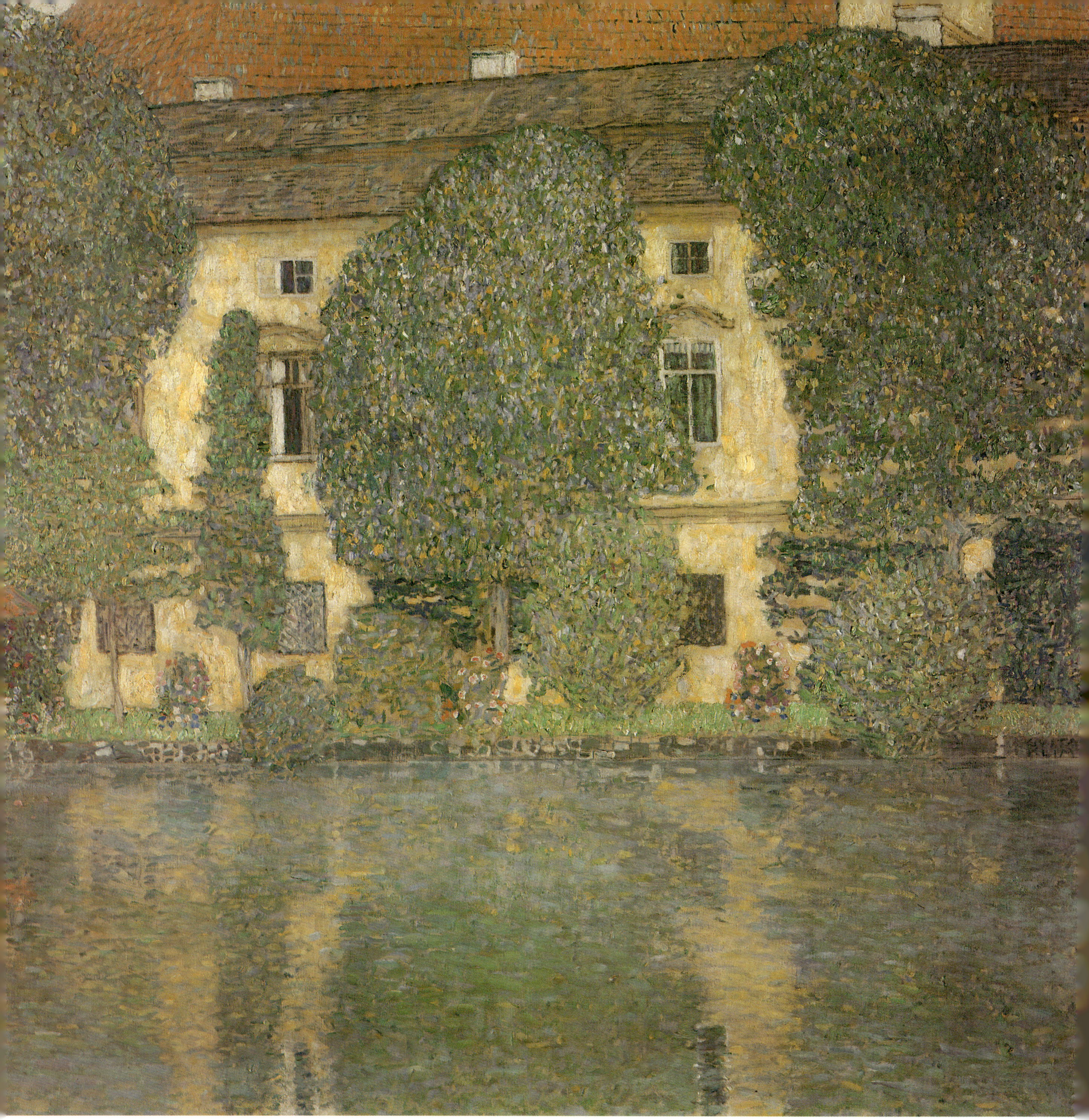

Even though the criticism of the faculty pictures seems unfounded in many respects, and the moral objections may nowadays seem somewhat ludicrous, nevertheless it must be conceded that the professors' objections had some justification. They wished to see their areas of study represented in the most important place in the university. Their feelings about their own branches of learning were positive, but Klimt's pictures left little scope for a positive view of science and learning. They offered no hope. They showed only the perils to which mankind is exposed. Therefore the professors' rejection of them is very understandable, even if their alternative suggestions, such as 'philosophers wandering in a grove', would not have been likely to result in great art.

The three pictures are of central importance in Klimt's work, partly because of the development of his style, partly because of the effect on his life, particularly on his manner of working. The circumstances and events surrounding the painting of the pictures led to his liberation as a painter. He freed himself from the importunities of others, and from commercial considerations, and from then on painted as he wished, turning down private as well as official contracts.

Today Klimt's attitude would be just what is expected, but it is important to remember his beginnings with the Company of Artists. Franz Matsch never took the crucial step to become a 'free' painter, and for Klimt things might easily have developed in a less radical fashion. One of the causes of radical change was the trouble with the faculty pictures.

41 Schloss Kammer on the Attersee I, c. 1908
Oil on canvas, 110 × 110 cm
Národní Gallery, Prague

42 Schloss Kammer on the Attersee III, 1910
Oil on canvas, 110 × 110 cm
Austrian Gallery, Vienna

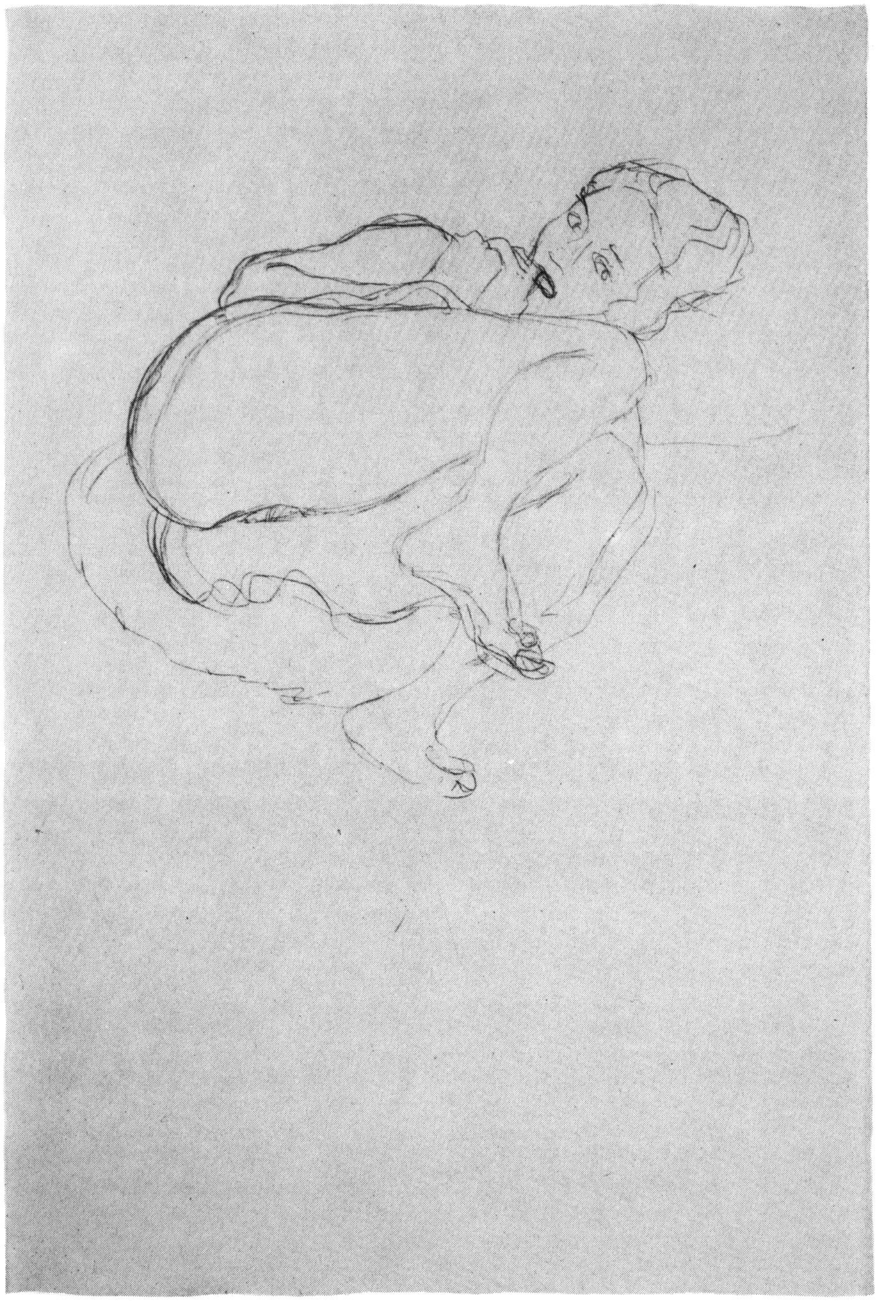

Huddled figure, 1914/15
Blue pencil, 55.2 × 36.5 cm

The Beethoven Frieze

"This has gone far enough, and anyone with the slightest sense of decency is filled with burning rage. What is there to be said about this painted pornography? It is an undeserved honour for it even to be described. For some subterranean locality in which pagan orgies are celebrated these paintings may be appropriate, but not for rooms to which the artists are bold enough to invite honourable ladies and innocent young girls.

The hideous gorilla, the shameless caricatures of noble mankind – those are no works of art, but an affront to our most sacred feelings! Are there no men left in Vienna to protest at such assassination?"[49]

This damning review appeared in a Vienna newspaper on 22 April 1902 in response to the opening of the fourteenth exhibition of the Secession. It was by no means an exception. There had been a steady flow of criticism since the violent polemics against the first two faculty pictures a few years before. The nudity which Klimt dared to portray went too far for the upright Viennese; but it was not only to the local press that Klimt's contribution was unacceptable. In Berlin the readers of the VOSSISCHE ZEITUNG could read the following description of Klimt's most recent work: "For this work he has drawn once more upon motifs and symbols from 'Medicine', which in this context appear repellent; he presents a disordered array of nastiness and horror in which only Klimt enthusiasts can see any rhyme or reason."[50].

The 'Klimt enthusiast' and art critic Ludwig Hevesi in turn spoke of Klimt's 'major achievement', of a delightful frieze . . . full of his bold, his majestic personality."[51]

As so often, contemporary opinion was divided; indeed, since the Secession public reaction to Klimt's work had always been divided. In this case he did not want his piece to be regarded in isolation; it was a subordinate part of a much greater idea.

The XIVth Exhibition of the Vienna Secession and Max Klinger's Beethoven

The Jugendstil artists' striving for unity of the arts at the turn of the century has already been described. They lived in the belief that the arts should permeate all of life, enhancing it with a transcendental quality and improving mankind. The idea of the total work of art was turned over and over in their minds, thought out in all its implications. Many plans were mooted but only a few were realised. The Vienna Secession, like other similarly minded Jugendstil groups, planned an exhibition which was itself conceived as a total work of art. Unlike many other groups and individuals, they succeeded in mounting such an exhibition.

The prerequisites for this exhibition were described in the catalogue to the XIVth exhibition: "First of all there must be unity of space, and this space must be enriched by paintings and sculpture which conform and contribute to the overall idea. The parts must be strictly subordinated to the whole. Logic enforces subordination to the character of the room and sustains the central idea."[52]

This central idea was provided by Max Klinger's statue of Beethoven, which was nearing completion in 1901. Some of the Secessionists were in touch with Klinger and were familiar with his project.

The painter, graphic artist and sculptor Max Klinger (1857–1920), who was born in Leipzig, had lived in Paris for several years (1883–1887) where he had been in close contact with the artists who later founded the Berlin Secession (1898). In 1893 he settled in his home city of Leipzig. His early work tended towards social criticism, but later he came to be one of the most noted Symbolists. His graphics were of particular consequence for the Jugendstil artists. As a sculptor he had worked most of all on portrayals of musicians; important works, other than 'Beethoven', were his memorials to Richard Wagner and Johan-

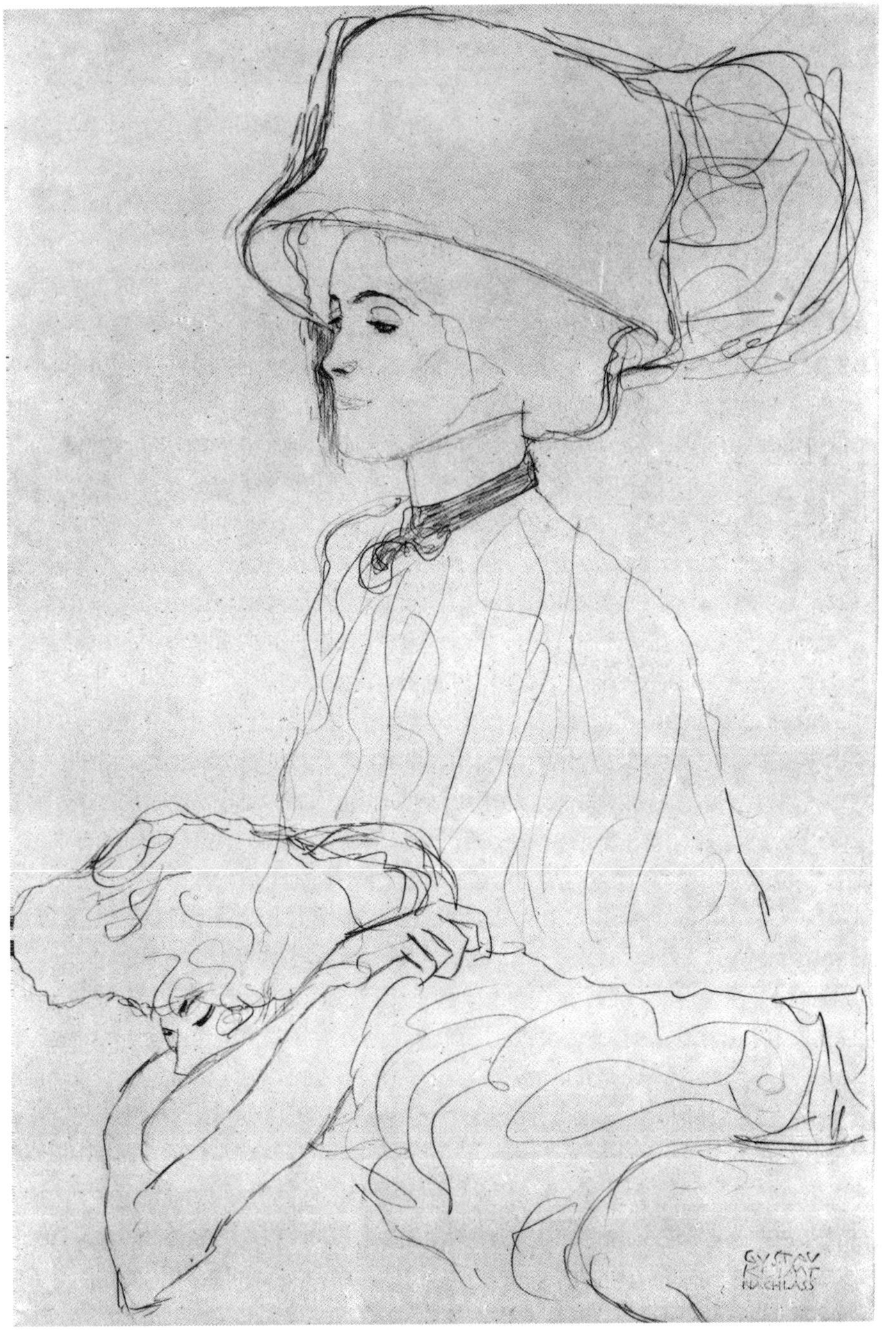

Sketch of tall hat and recumbent figure, 1907/08
Lead and red pencil, 55.9 × 37.1 cm

nes Brahms. In favouring these three composers he was in keeping with the tastes of his age. As a composer Wagner was influenced by Beethoven above all others, and he in turn strengthened public interest in Beethoven through his interpretations, particularly of the symphonies.

Klinger first began to think of a Beethoven statue in Paris, and he produced a first plaster model there, but the realisation of it took a long time. The size caused problems, but so did the diversity of the materials. On a rock pedestal of Pyrenean marble was a throne of bronze. In front of the throne crouched an eagle, also dark red, with eyes of amber. Beethoven, seated on the throne, was hewn in white marble from the Greek island of Syros. His robe, hanging loosely over the lower legs but leaving the body bare, was made of yellow and brown alabaster from Tyrol. The upper edge of the throne was adorned with the heads of four angels made of ivory; their wings were of fused antique glass, agate, jasper and mother-of-pearl, with an underlay of gold. The throne was richly decorated; there was relief on the outer surfaces of arm-rests and back, which made casting exceptionally difficult. Klinger had a Paris firm working on it, but there were repeated delays before the casting could be completed.

The public was informed about the project and awaited the results with keen interest, so it is not surprising that the Secessionists knew about it. From a correspondence with Klinger that began in 1900 it emerges that by the summer of 1901 at the latest the idea of an exhibition with Klinger's sculpture as centrepiece had begun to take definite shape. All the Secessionists' contributions had to be subordinated to 'Beethoven'.

The date was fixed for November 1901 and the preparation of the Secession's rooms began, but there were again delays with casting so that the Society was obliged to put on two more exhibitions in the meantime, as tactfully as possible. The walls of the exhibition rooms had already been covered with a 'second wall', painted and decorated with relief. It could not be dismantled without destroying these surface embellishments, as was indeed done when the exhibition was finally over. Walls and ceilings were covered with additional false fronts, which considerably reduced the space available but provided the opportunity of exhibiting without the visitor noticing what was concealed behind the exhibits.

From November 1901 to January 1902 the Secession presented to the Viennese public works by Scandinavian, Russian and Swiss artists, including Ferdinand Hodler (1853–1918) and Edvard Munch (1863–1944). The Dutch painter Jan Toorop (1858–1928) was given a whole room, with an exhibition of twenty-one works; he had exerted a marked influence on Gustav Klimt's development as a painter. In February and March of the same year there was an exhibition of works by artists from Austria and Munich, which in a sense was merely filling a gap. It was still uncertain when the Beethoven figure would arrive.

Only on 11 March 1902 was Klinger in a position to give a definite date; he promised the monumental piece for 12 April. On 13 April the Vienna ALLGEMEINE ZEITUNG carried the news that the individual pieces of the statue had arrived by rail and that two furniture vans had been needed in order to transport them to the Secession's rooms. There the pieces were put together under the personal supervision of the artist. On 15 April the exhibition finally opened and the statue was declared the most important artistic news of the year.

Klinger had broken with the memorial statue tradition that had prevailed since the Renaissance; the diversity of materials and colours alone made it necessary to look to classical antiquity for a comparable 'total work of art'. There one finds, for instance, Pausanias's description of the statue of Zeus by Phidias (not extant), which was made of ivory; the dark throne was covered with jewelled relief, as was the pedestal, and adorned with gold, ivory and brightly coloured stones. There were thematic links with this Zeus too, in asmuchas Klinger placed a sacred eagle at the musician's side; indeed, there is no trace of the human Beethoven except in the similarity of the head. The nudity of the figure caused an outcry, although contemporary heroes had often been displayed naked in nineteenth century compositions. Unlike other artists, Klinger did not shape his hero according to the classical ideals of beauty, a departure which was considered very daring even by his supporters. Only the relief ornamentation round the throne gave any suggestion of Beethoven's creative achievement. The contemporary critic Paul Kühn recognised in the Fall and in the pair in torment "the painful striving for knowledge and the pain of knowing". The crucifixion and the birth of Venus symbolise in his view "Love as the salvation of the world."[53]

At the turn of the century veneration of Beethoven was heightened almost to the point of idolatry, largely due to Richard Wagner and Friedrich Nietzsche, and it is only with this in mind that Klinger's statue and the entire exhibition can truly be understood. The statue, main exhibit and focus of the dominant idea to which all other arts had to conform in collaboration, stood in relative isolation in the main exhibition room. This emphasised the superhuman and timeless quality of the figure. The narrow ends of the room were decorated with two frescos, 'Night Falling' by Alfred Roller (1864–1935) and 'Day Breaking' by Adolf Böhm (1861–1927). The figure of Beethoven was turned towards 'Day Breaking', the implication being that the fresco was expressing the hope for a new future vested in the great composer. The decline of the old values in 'Night Falling' was emphasised by the manner in which Beethoven's back was turned on this picture. The timeless and sacral quality of both statue and frescos was intended to be complemented by the sensuous joy of human existence, which was expressed by fauns, nymphs, tritons and mermaids on embossed metal inlay work on the walls. On the pillars knelt female figures with wreaths, while two armchairs with carved gilt supports, decoratively painted, and two niches with fountains and figures of blue pressed concrete completed the room.

This main room was flanked by two smaller rooms. The one on the left was the entrance room and it permitted a first view of the central figure, but it also contained the frieze painted by Gustav Klimt. The frescos in the room on the right translated quotations from Schiller's 'Ode to Joy', the final chorus of Beethoven's Ninth Symphony, into painting; there were a number of separate scenes, painted by Ferdinand Andri (1871–1956) and Josef Maria Auchentaller (1865–1949). On the wall beneath the frescos, as also beneath Klimt's frieze, there was inlay work of jewelled ornaments, uniform in appearance because all were square-shaped, though there was a great diversity of materials. In keeping with the overall conception of unity, they did not in any way obtrude.

When the exhibition ended on 27 June the Beethoven statue was moved to Klinger's home city of Leipzig, having been purchased by the Leipzig museum. According to Klinger, a room was specially built

43/44 Three Ages of Woman, 1905
Oil on canvas, 180 × 180 cm
National Gallery of Modern Art, Rome

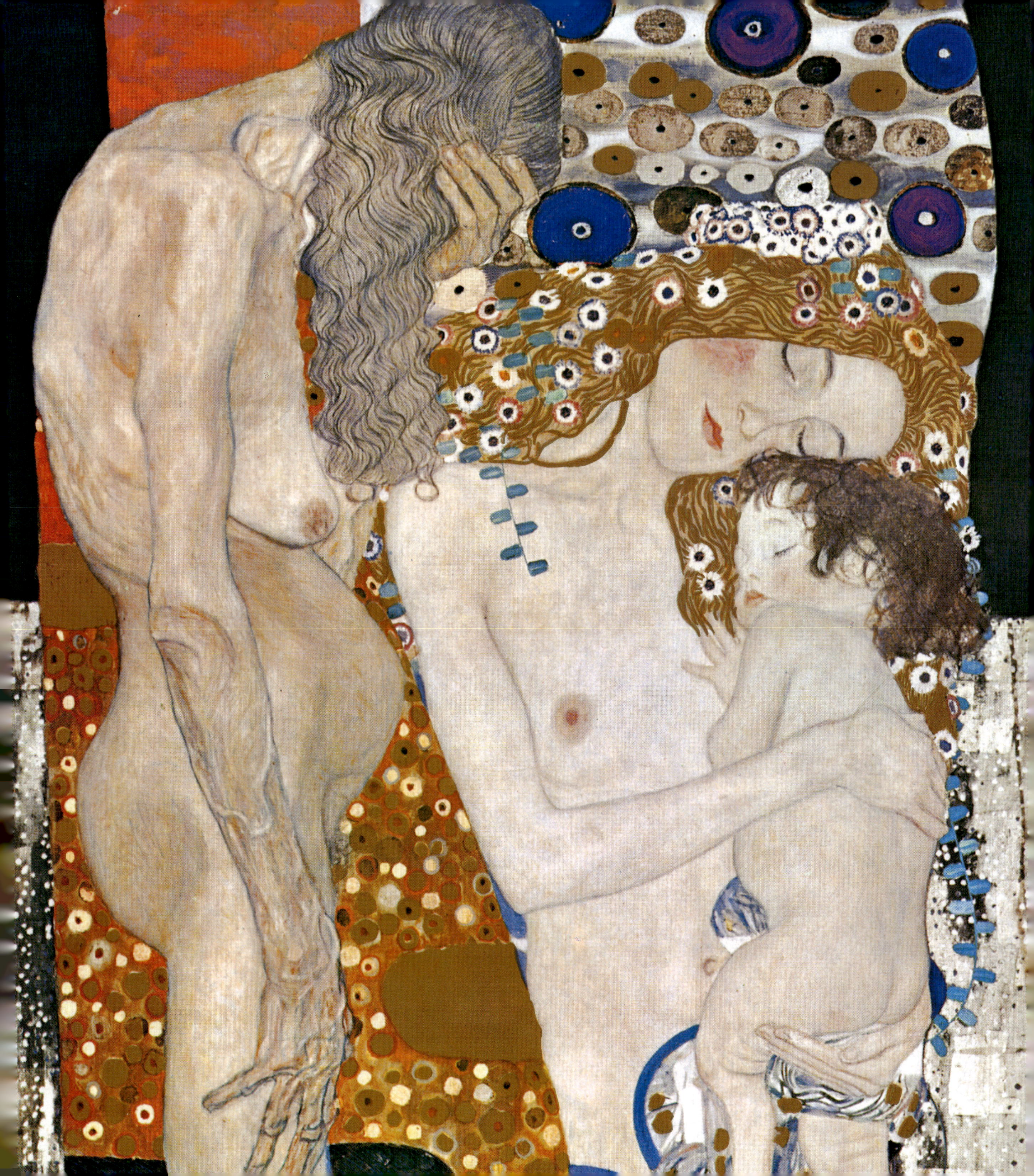

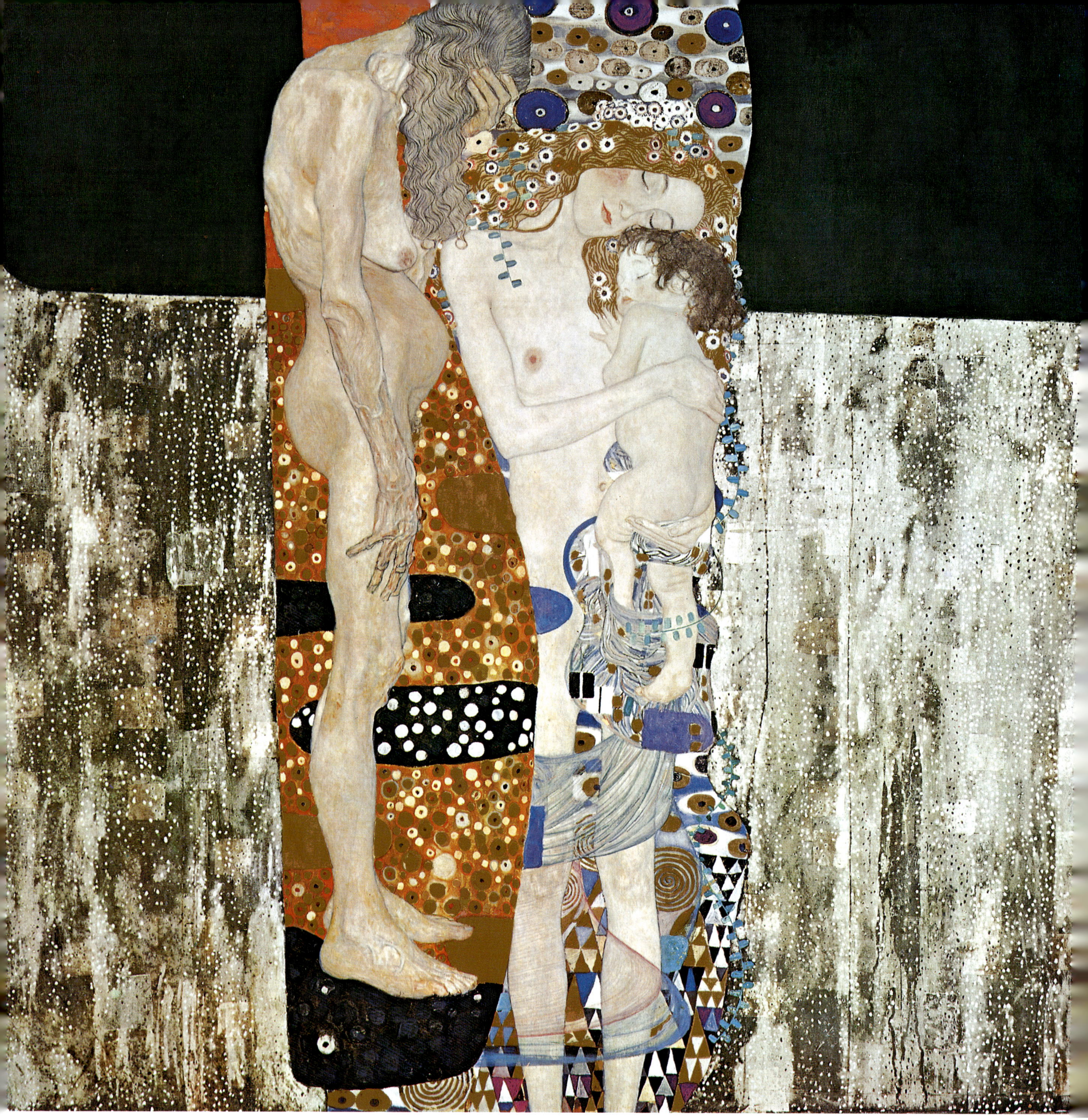

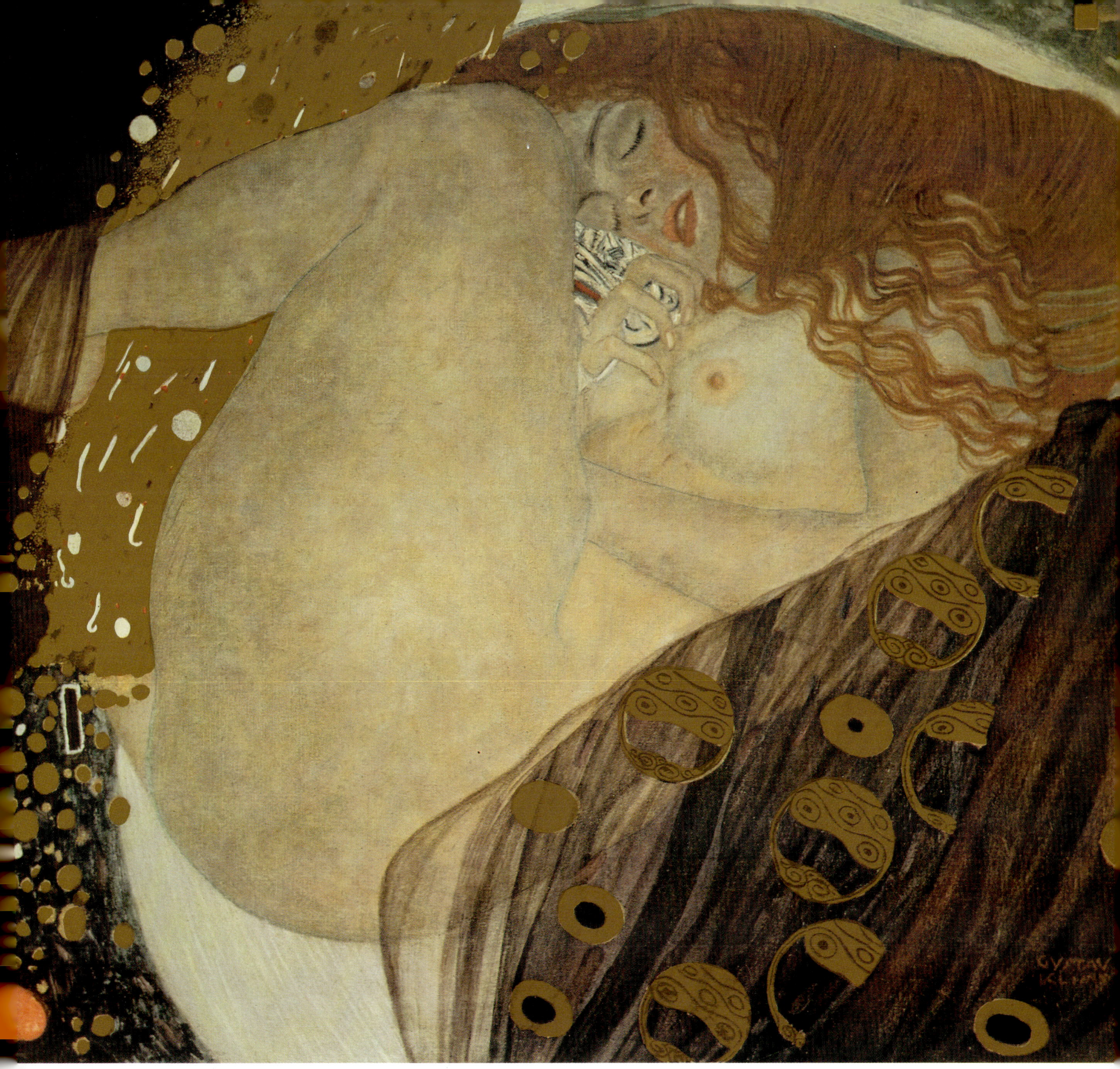

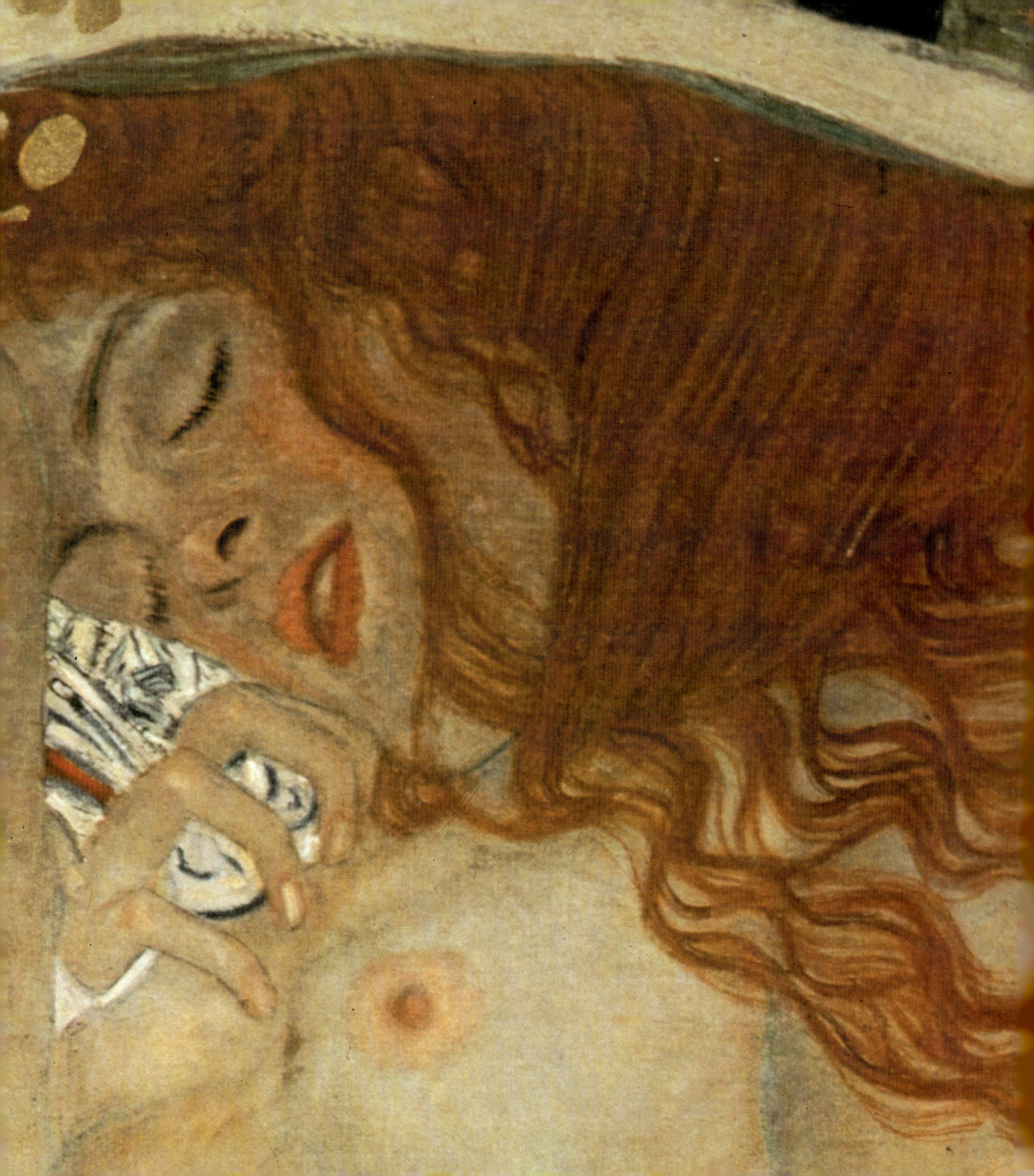

and 'Beethoven' was placed in the apse, preserving the sacral character of the figure so evident in the Secession's exhibition.

The frescos were destroyed, according to plan, so that they are documented only by a few black and white photographs. What happened to the jewelled ornaments is not known. Only Klimt's frieze was left in place for the XVIIIth exhibition of the Secession which was to be dedicated to the works of Gustav Klimt. After that exhibition the frieze, with the screens on which it had been painted, was sawn into eight pieces and sold privately; in 1915 it was acquired, together with the three hundred drawings which had preceded it, by Klimt's patron August Lederer; in 1973 it passed into public ownership. After long and complicated restoration work it was finally shown again for the first time as part of the Vienna exhibition 'Dream and Reality: Vienna 1870–1930' in 1985. For this purpose the room in which it had originally been shown was reconstructed. Afterwards it was moved to the restored Secession House, very nearly to its original surroundings, in which it is now on public display.

Gustav Klimt's Frieze

The sale of the frieze and the recent restoration work have preserved this monumental work which marks the beginning of Klimt's so-called golden period. This work and the faculty pictures form the real turning-point. At some points he takes up similar ideas in both series, but formally the frieze is far more advanced than the pictures.

Klimt, like Andri and Auchentaller, was inspired by Beethoven's Ninth Symphony, but he did not restrict himself to a few scenes; rather he made use of the interpretation provided by Richard Wagner, who was largely responsible for the symphony's great fame. The titles given to the separate sections of the frieze were provided by Klimt and listed in the XIVth exhibition catalogue.[54] The frescos covered the upper half of the two long walls and one narrow wall of the room, beginning on the long wall opposite the entrance so that the viewer's attention was immediately drawn in the right direction. Just below the

45/46 Danaë, 1907/08
Oil on canvas, 77 × 83 cm
Private collection, Austria

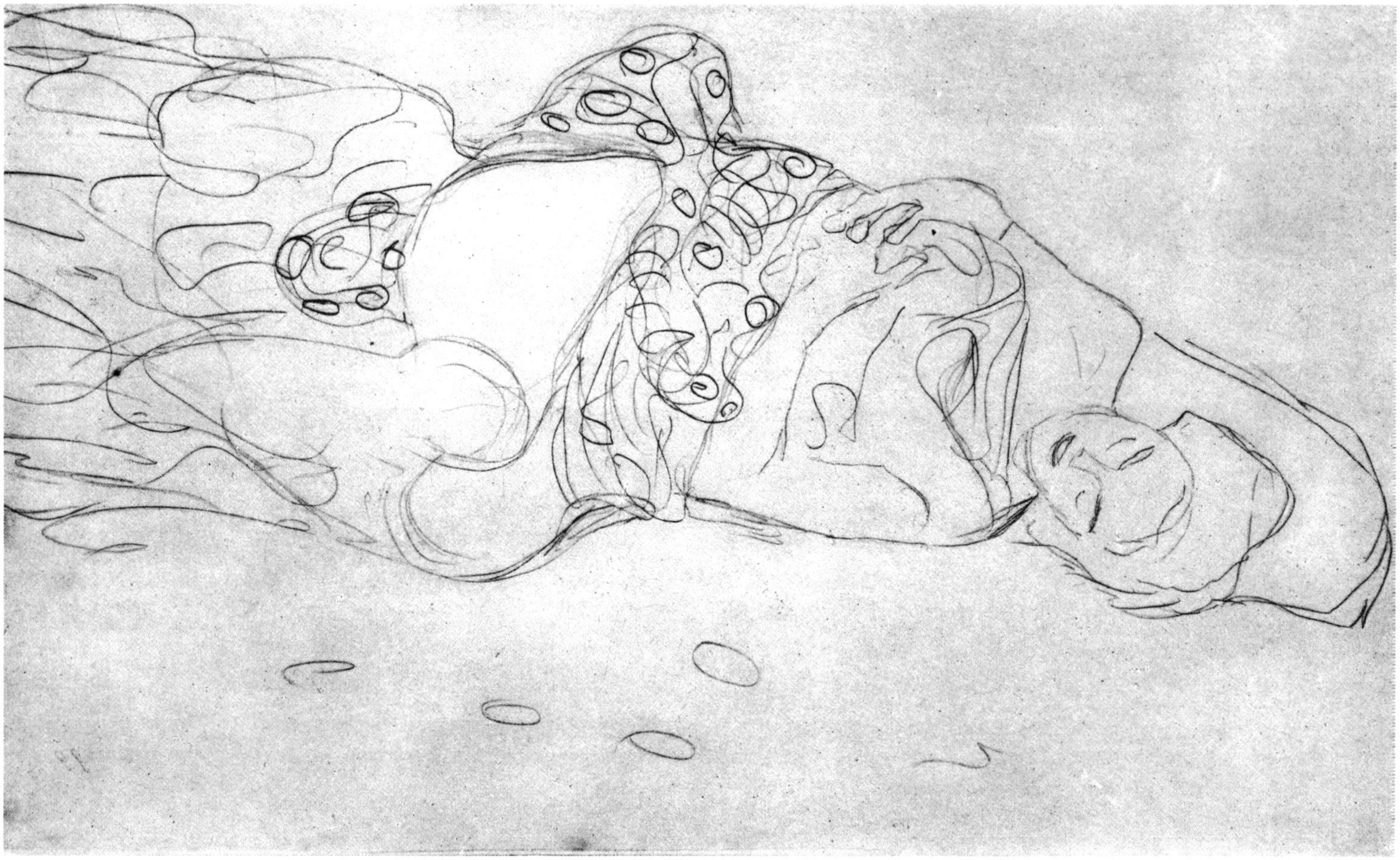

ceiling are floating figures personifying the 'yearning for happiness'. Their garments are light in colour so that only their brown or golden hair stands out clearly from the white wall. They are moving their hands in front of their heads as if they were swimming. The disproportionately long figures seem to consist entirely of head, arms and thin flowing garments which billow out behind them without appearing to conceal bodies. These figures continue for almost the whole length of the frieze. For the first seven metres there are no other figures, but then follows a scene which fills the whole space allotted to the frieze. Three haggard, nude figures, like those in the faculty pictures, symbolise the 'sufferings of weak mankind'. Two figures kneel with their arms

Recumbent figure turned half to the left, 1912/13
Pencil, 31.7 × 51.7 cm

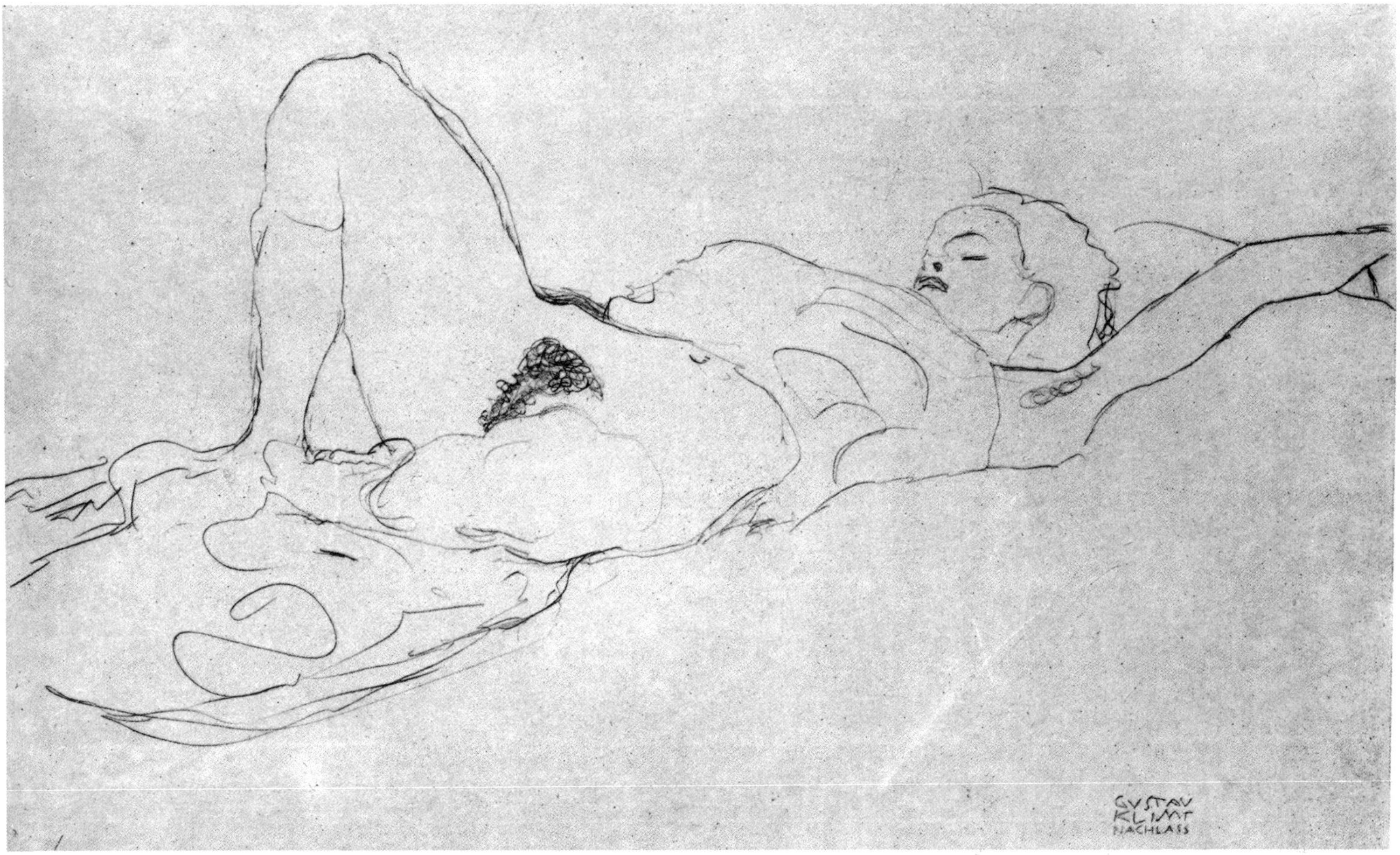

Recumbent figure, 1912/13
Pencil, 36.8 × 55.9 cm

stretched out petitioning, and behind them is a woman with folded hands. Just as with the creatures hovering over them, only their hair and the outline of their bodies stand out against the light background, so that they give the effect more of drawing than of painting. All the more striking is the hero in golden armour to whom they are turning; it is to him that they are making their impassioned appeal, but his back is turned and he gazes into the distance. His hand grasps a mighty sword. Behind him two women emerge from the mosaic-like background, against which the knight stands out and with which their robes are blended. Their hands and heads form a kind of halo round his head. Klimt described the group as 'the petition of weak mankind to the strong one in armour as external force, to pity and driving energy (the female figures) as inner force which can move him to champion the fight for happiness'. His posture does not suggest a refusal to answer weak humanity's petition; rather his gaze, directed towards the narrow wall, shows him already contemplating the struggle. 'Yearning for happiness' continues right to the end of the wall, resulting in a sharp focus on this single scene, scarcely three metres in width. Most of the remaining fourteen metres of wallspace are left empty except for the figures soaring just below the ceiling.

The narrow wall, by contrast, is entirely filled. It was above all the female figures on this wall which sparked off the criticism of the frieze quoted at the beginning of this section. Klimt put into the picture the 'hostile forces' against which the 'strong one in armour' must fight. The whole wall is filled with a gorilla-like monster, the ancient 'giant Typhoeus, against whom even the gods fought in vain'. On the left of his grimacing face, with staring eyes and enormous mouth, are the three gorgons, writhing like the snakes in their hair, whom Klimt erroneously presents as the daughters of Typhoeus. From them were derived the Erinyes in the faculty picture 'Jurisprudence' painted one year later. These naked women are again white, except for black pubis and golden breasts. The snakes writhing in their hair are gold. Above them can be seen the heads of 'Illness, Madness and Death', death-like grimacing female faces with flesh wasted to the bone. On the right of Typhoeus 'Lust, Voluptuousness and Intemperance' are trysting; the impurity of lust is expressed less by their nudity than by the facial expressions of the two female figures and by the luxuriant hair, which is coiled over the pubis of lust, again in the manner of a snake. Intemperance in her blatant nudity is quite simply ugly; apart from the fat belly on which the enormous breasts are resting, it is especially the gold jewellery that reveals her character. She alone wears a blue skirt with a gold ornament suspended from a gold belt, but it is fastened below the waist so that the belly seems even more gross. Behind these figures is the arm of the giant, supporting itself on a paw. The straight line of his supported lower arm is taken up again by the haggard figure of 'gnawing sorrow' which crouches alone before the body of the monster identifiable as a mass of snakes. Her long hair merges with

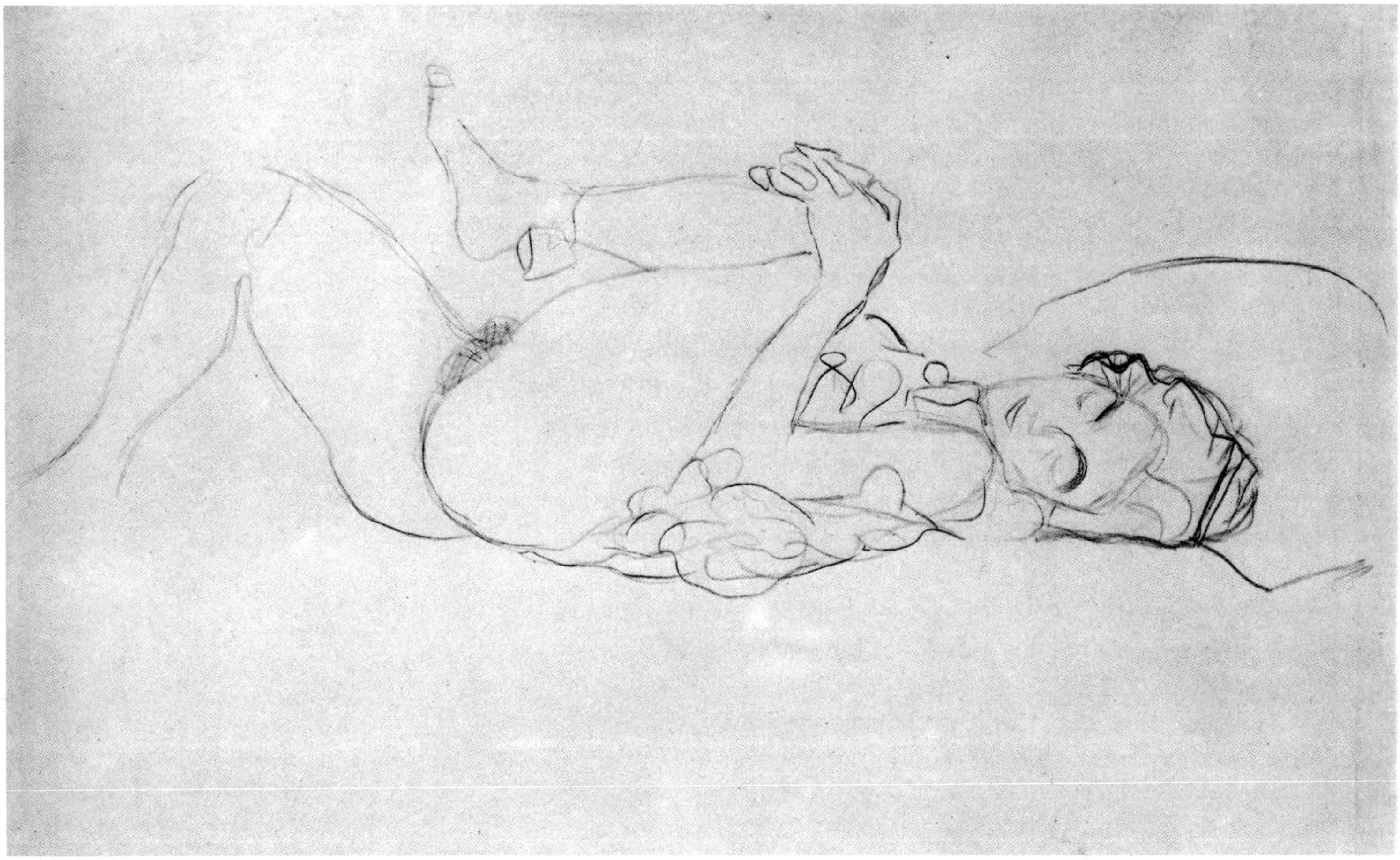

Recumbent figure turned to the right, 1913
Red and blue pencil, 36.8 × 57.2 cm

the black veils which hang loosely round her body, a further reminder of the first two faculty pictures. At the end of the wall 'yearning for happiness' reappears, for 'the yearnings and longings of men fly over the heads of the hostile forces'.

On the next long wall the soaring figures end with a small horizontal female figure in an ornamented gold robe with a musical instrument in her hand: 'yearning for happiness is stilled in poesy'. This figure of poesy with her dark hair and musical instrument goes back to the allegory of music which Klimt created for the supraportal picture in the

Palais Dumba in 1898 (see p. 83–85). Head and posture of the figure, painted without any background on the bare wall, are suggestive of Greek vase painting, which in turn suggests the spandrels and intercolumnar paintings in the Art History Museum.

Above poesy hover the figures which symbolise 'yearning for happiness', against a gold ground. The hair of the two figures, who have reached their goal, are of gold and adorned with gemstones, their hands reach upwards as if they now longed to halt their flight and come to a stop.

This is the end of the travels of 'yearning', and at this point the frieze breaks off. In the lower part of the wall an aperture allows a view of Klinger's statue. A few metres further along the wall comes the triumphant end of the frieze, with five delicate nude figures, one above the other, before a golden line. The three uppermost 'arts' reach upwards to the choir of angels in paradise. "The arts lead us to the happy realm in which alone we can find pure happiness, pure joy, pure love."

The choir of angels, made up of female figures in serried ranks, clothed in long gold ornamented robes and carrying musical instruments in their hands, stands in a meadow of brightly coloured flowers, singing Schiller's 'Ode to Joy' which brings to a close Beethoven's Ninth Symphony. In front of the choir, and partly concealing it from view, is the 'strong one in armour' who has now fulfilled his task, so that he has laid aside his armour and stands embracing a woman in a golden globe with a rose-bush behind it: "This kiss is given to all the world!" Sun and moon, personifying the female and the male principle, shine above them. As well as the opening lines, which contain the essence of the whole poem, Klimt takes up a sequence of lines close to the end of the ode: 'Yield to this embrace, ye millions,/This kiss is given to all the world!/Brothers, above the vault of heaven/There must dwell a loving father./Are you falling downwards, millions?/Do you sense your creator, world?/Seek him above the vault of heaven!/ Above the stars must be his dwelling-place.'[55]

As has already been mentioned, Klimt was following Richard Wagner's interpretation of the Ninth Symphony. Wagner not only revered Beethoven, he also began early on to write about his music; in 1870 he wrote extensively about him.

In 1846 Wagner conducted the Ninth Symphony in Dresden, and his interpretation won widespread acclaim, unlike earlier performances. For the concert programme he wrote a commentary, explaining his interpretation. It was on this commentary that Klimt's painting was based. Wagner's opening lines are taken into the frieze: "The first movement seems to be founded in a magnificently conceived struggle of the soul for joy, against those hostile forces that stand between ourselves and earthly happiness."[56]

These lines match the first wall of the frieze. The knight in armour is characterised by Wagner as follows: "We recognise a noble defiance, a manly energy and spirit of combat against the mighty enemy, which culminates in the middle of the movement in open battle with the antagonist."[57]

Just as the first wall matches the first movement of the symphony, so also is the second movement visualised in the painting of the narrow wall. In this movement Wagner hears the pursuit of another kind of happiness, in which the seeker loses his way, and he speaks of "scenes of earthly lust and voluptuous luxury."[58]

The third movement corresponds to the portrayal of poesy. At this point Wagner cites Goethe's 'Faust': 'Oh sound for ever, sweet songs of heaven! Tears fill my eyes, I belong to earth once more!'[59]

At the break in the frieze there is a pause for breath: then the choir joins the instrumental music. There can be no doubt that Klimt transposed the cesura and the fourth movement of the symphony into his final picture, but the frieze is more than just a theoretical comment on the theme.

When one listens to the music, many of Klimt's pictures spring to mind. Apart from the hovering 'yearning for happiness' and the delicate image of poesy, the final scene imprints itself most strikingly: the theme begins softly, with the lowliest figure of the arts, and becomes louder with the ascending figures raising their hands towards the choir, whose song then begins – the song of paradise. The voices become stronger and more insistent, culminating at the end of the movement in the repetition of the kiss for all the world.

Klimt has captured this gradual ascent to the highest point with his figures and with his choice of colours and the generous application of gold at the end. He has succeeded in visualising music in such a way that sounds become images and colours, and themes become scenes.

As with the faculty pictures, one may ask whether Klimt discovered the literary source material himself, or whether he was was encouraged to look in that direction. It is quite possible that Gustav Mahler, who revered both Beethoven and Wagner, and conducted the Ninth Symphony in the Secession's rooms the day before the opening of the exhibition, may have directed Klimt to Wagner's commentary, but there is no documentary evidence of this.

The description of the frieze will have shown that Klimt often re-used elements from his earlier works. The personifications which he had used during his years as a historicist painter recurred frequently in his work during the early years of the Secession, and it was through his work that Pallas Athene came to be the patron goddess of the Secession (see p. 96).

In the Beethoven Frieze and in 'Jurisprudence', the last of the faculty pictures, he used for the last time personifications from Greek mythology to portray archetypal situations in human life. From then on he used them no more; instead such themes as love and death were presented by means of large, often naked figures. The Beethoven Frieze combines both techniques: there are personifications such as poesy and mythological figures like the Gorgons and Typhoeus, but there is also the embracing couple in the last scene who either symbolise the 'kiss for the whole world', or, in Klimt's labelling for the exhibition of 1903, 'My kingdom is not of this world'.

Further comparison with the faculty pictures calls attention to the fact that in the frieze Klimt gives no suggestion of locality. He had placed 'Philosophy' and 'Medicine' in outer space, 'Jurisprudence' in hell, but in the frieze there is no placing of any kind. The figures are painted straight onto the plaster, which is often the only background.

Although the narrow wall often echoes 'Jurisprudence', yet each work is dominated by a quite distinct concept. The fatalistic view which runs through all three of the faculty pictures, and was one of the reasons for their rejection, has given way in the frieze to the striving for salvation. Therefore the frieze represents a turning-point in the artist's

47 Poppy Field, 1907
Oil on canvas, 110 × 110 cm
Austrian Gallery, Vienna

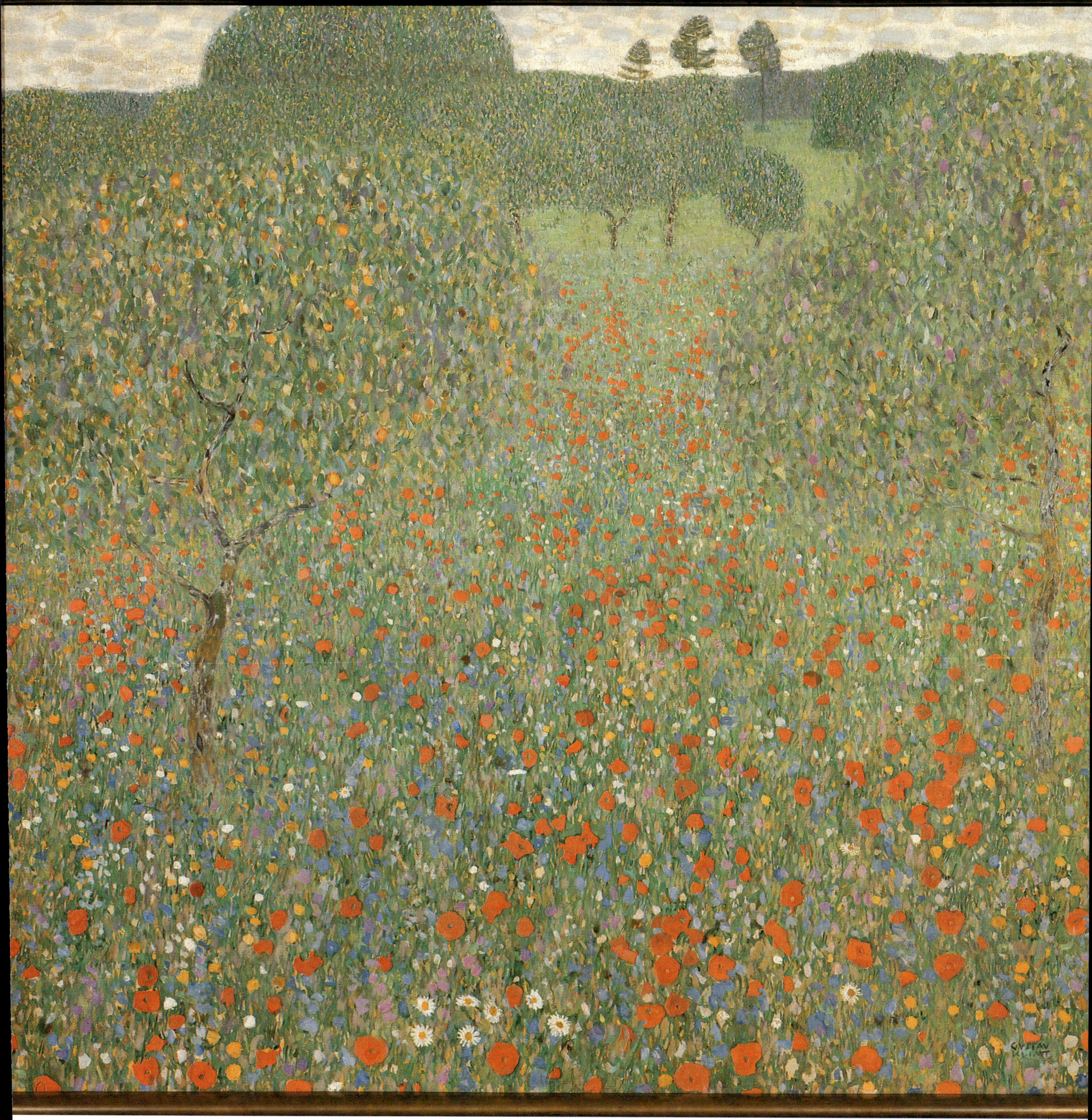

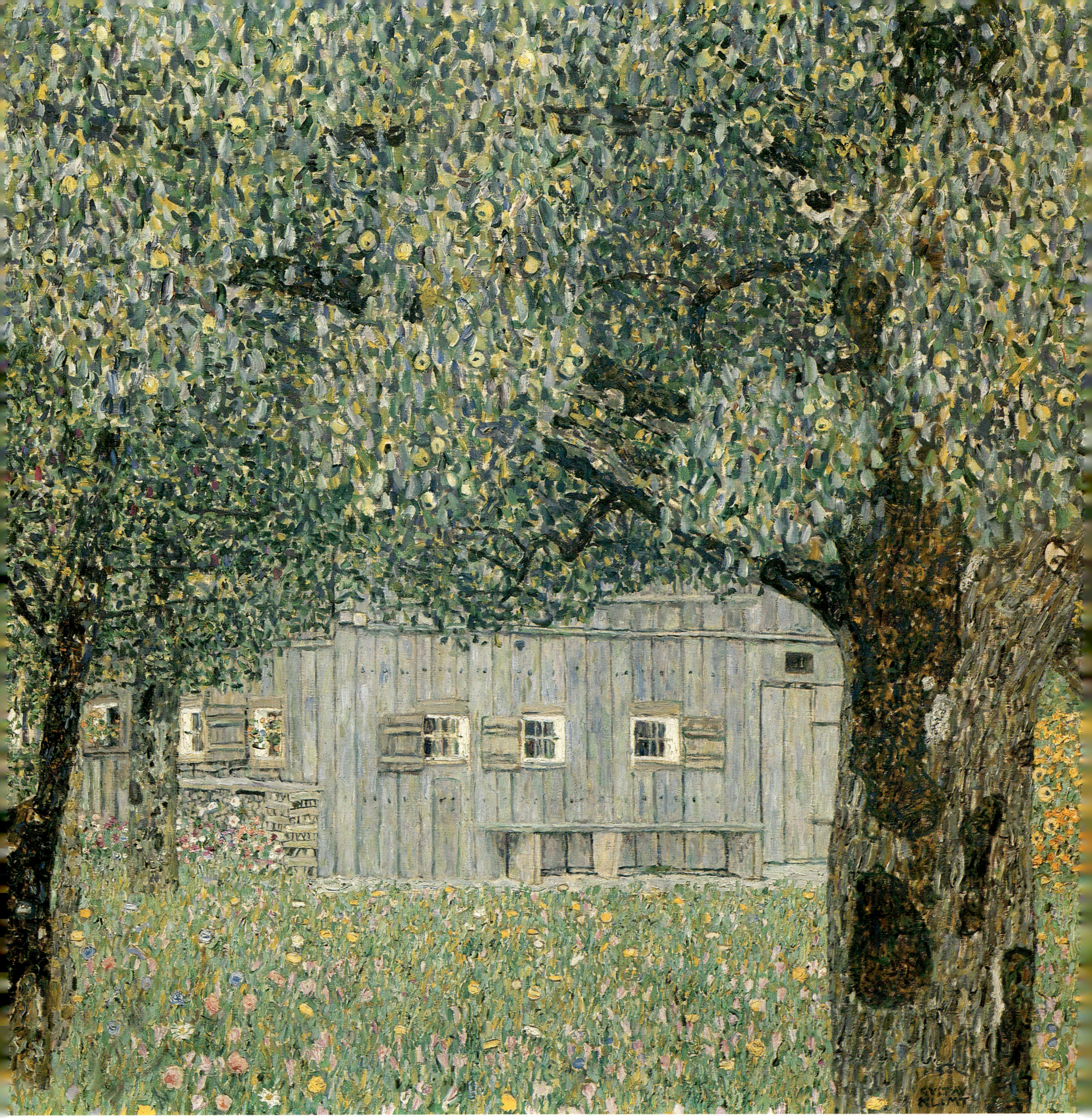

work, a point at which he may still make use of items from the earlier compositions, but not without substantially altering the line of thought.

Formally the frieze represents the final breakthrough to Klimt's linear style. Relinquishing perspective, he reduces his paintings to two dimensions. The art of the line is developed to the fullest extent, particularly in the figures personifying 'yearning for happiness'. These figures' robes are created by the line; it is through this technique that the sense of incorporeality is achieved.

The use of a variety of materials shows the tendency towards work in handicrafts, which is later manifested even more strongly in the Stoclet Frieze. Klimt painted with casein colours straight onto the plaster, but he also worked with gold and silver paint, and with stucco, mother-of-pearl, upholstering tacks, fragments of looking-glass, buttons and costume jewellery of brightly coloured polished glass. This gave rise to unusual reflections of light, which together with the abundance of gold gave a sense of enormous opulence. The alternating painting and drawing gave different kinds of emphasis to the figures, but also made the dominance of the line emerge even more strongly.

The Beethoven Frieze was not only an important milestone in Klimt's development as an artist, it was also an excellent demonstration of the notion of the total work of art, which was so vital an ingredient of Jugendstil thought. It was created as part of a whole, subservient to an overriding idea. This must not be forgotten when the work is viewed in its present-day isolation, remote from the original environment, although close to the original location.

48 Upper Austrian Farmhouse, 1911/12
Oil on canvas, 110 × 110 cm
Austrian Gallery, Vienna

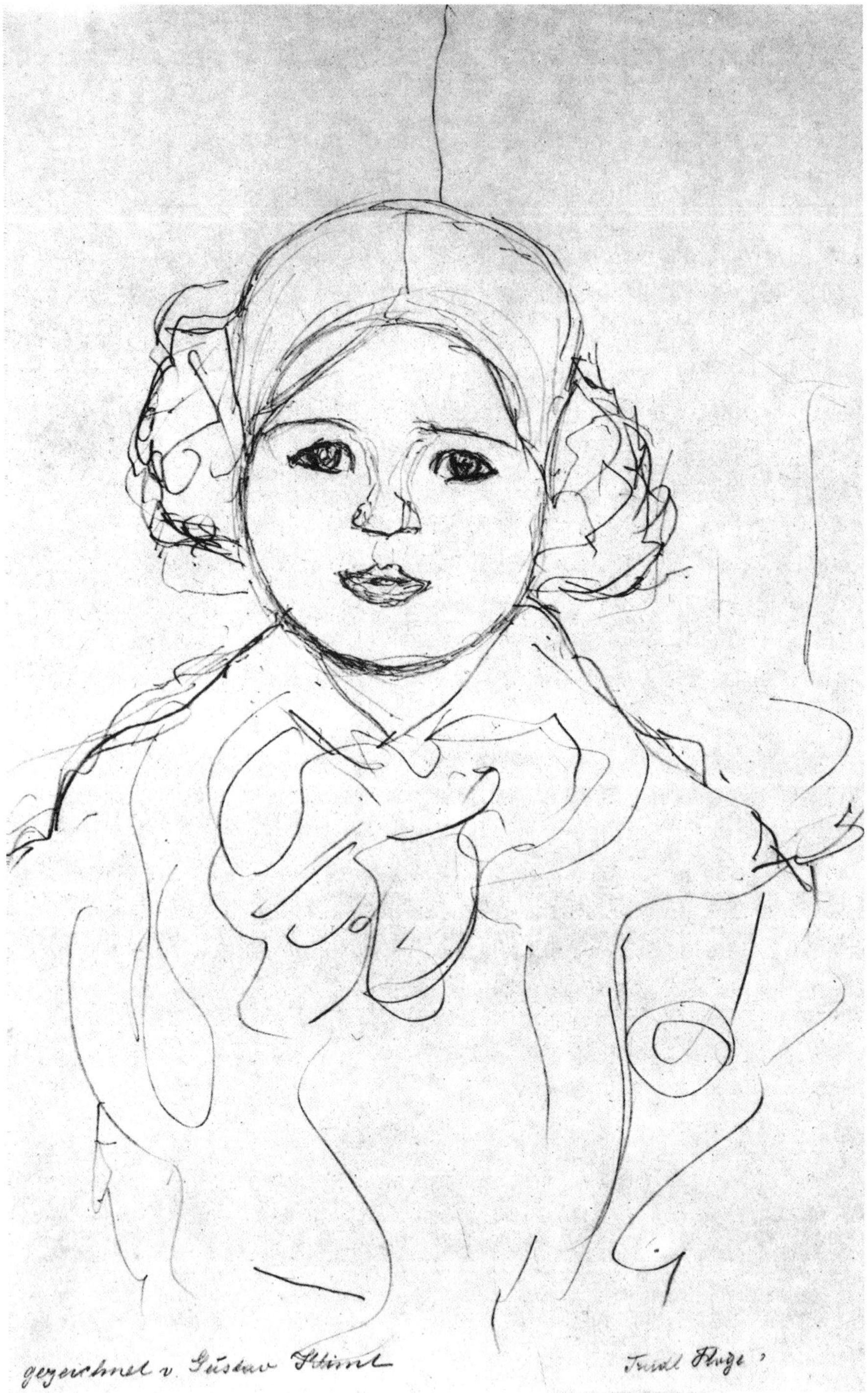

Trudl Flöge, 1916/17
Pencil, 55.9 × 36.8 cm

Emilie Flöge – Couturier and Companion

Gustav Klimt and Emilie Flöge probably met at the beginning of the 1890s. By 1897 at the latest they were united by close ties of friendship which lasted until Klimt's death. Neither Klimt nor Emilie Flöge left any written indication of the intensity of their friendship, so that biographers have been able to give free rein to their imagination and some have chosen to see in Emilie Flöge the self-sacrificing companion to whom marriage to the sensitive artist was denied. The possessions that Emilie Flöge left behind at her death were discovered in 1983, but failed to yield the hoped-for information about the relationship, although they do include the entire correspondence. In one respect her importance is beyond doubt: as a couturier she exerted a great influence on his fashion designing.

The Flöge Sisters' Fashion House

Emilie Flöge was born in Vienna in 1874 as the fourth child of Hermann Flöge (1837–1897), a master wood-turner who prospered in the meerschaum business. Apart from a brother Hermann about whom little is known, there were two sisters, Pauline (1866–1917) and Helene (1871–1936). Helene Flöge married Ernst Klimt in 1891, so that Gustav Klimt must have been in contact with the family by that time. After his brother's death he was appointed guardian of the infant Helene Flöge, child of the brief marriage. Emilie was at that time eighteen years old. Gustav Klimt must have become a frequent visitor to the house, and

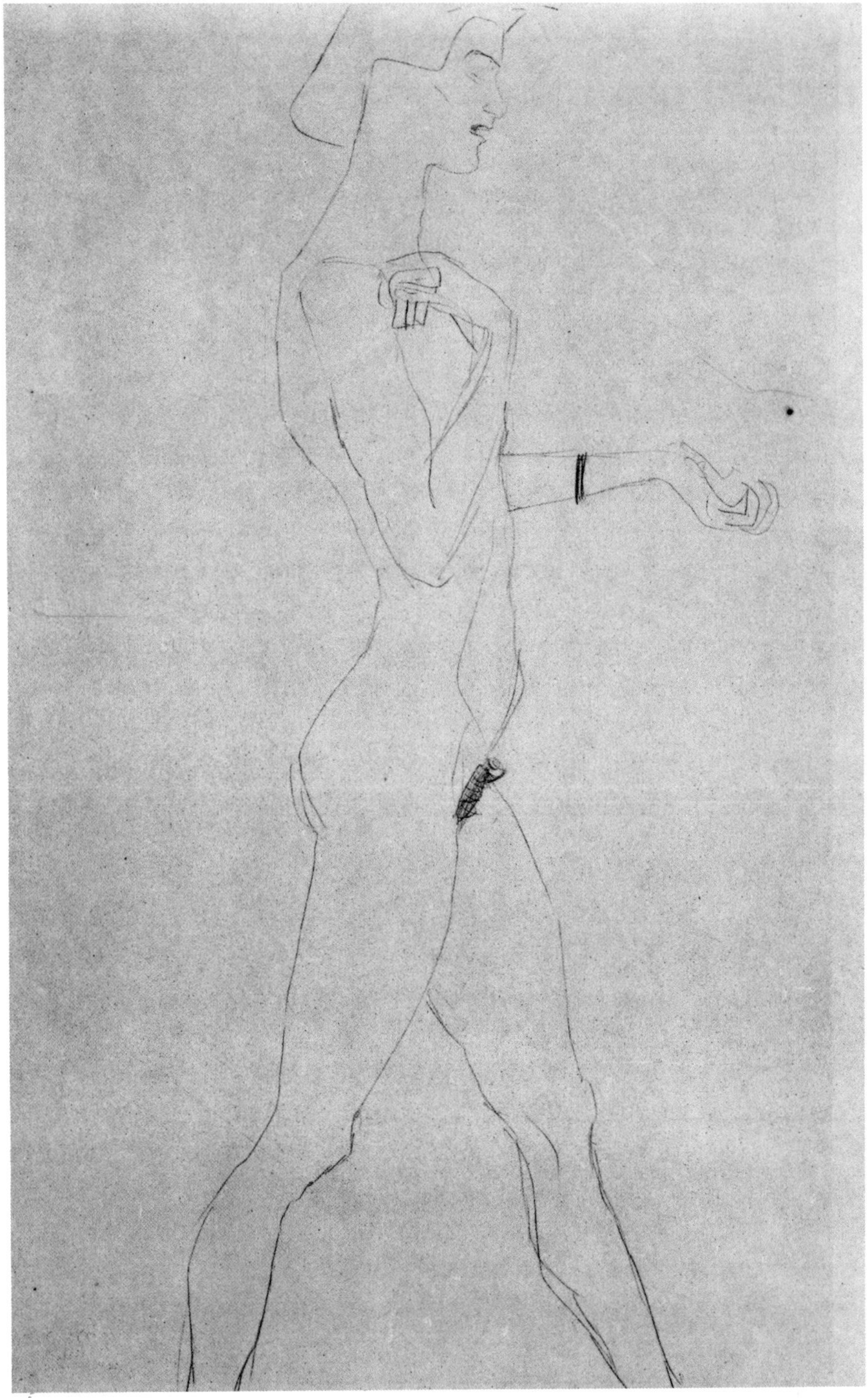

Striding woman, right profile, right hand on shoulder, left arm extended, 1906/07
Pencil, 55.9 × 37 cm

will have encountered not only his sister-in-law and his niece, but all the rest of the family as well.

In 1904 the three sisters founded a fashion house. It was rumoured that the father's business had declined and that he had insisted on his daughters receiving sufficient education and training for them to stand on their own feet. They apparently attended a dressmaking course together, which is surprising in view of the eight-year difference in age between Pauline and Emilie. At the end of the course they were asked, on the strength of an open competition, to design the clothes for the participants in a cookery exhibition and when this considerable task was completed they opened their own fashion house. Their brother Hermann is said to have helped them to obtain a licence in spite of their lack of the higher vocational qualifications which were strictly speaking required. The details of this story may be apocryphal. The difference in age between the sisters has already been mentioned; seven years passed between the death of their father in 1897 and the opening of the fashion house; considering how rapidly 'Flöge Sisters' became a well-known establishment in Vienna, it seems unlikely that all their skills were derived from a single dressmaking course. But there is no actual documentation of the events,[60] and one can only assume that at least one of the sisters received a thorough training. The account of the brother's assistance is not entirely convincing either: Pauline Flöge was already thirty-eight years old in 1904, and even Emilie was thirty; since they managed their business on their own in the years that ensued, there is no reason to suppose that they would have been incapable of setting it up themselves.

Be that as it may, the fashion house opened in 1904 in a large building on one of the main shopping streets in Mariahilf in the VIth district of Vienna. This district was dominated by the textile industry; there were weaving and knitting workshops, and here also were the earliest large stores offering ready-made clothes for sale. Then there were the small and medium-sized businesses, leathergoods shops and fashion houses.

The property in the Mariahilfstraße had been erected in 1895, with residential and business premises. The café on the ground floor gave the whole house its own earlier name of 'Casa Piccola', which was not at all fitting for this enormous corner building. Pauline, Helene and Emilie Flöge had not only their business premises there, but also a large apartment where they lived with Helene's daughter and their mother, Barbara Flöge, whose portrait Klimt painted as late as 1915.

The rooms were fitted up by the Vienna Workshops (see p. 193ff) which had been set up the year before. The design was Josef Hoffmann's. The interior suggested not only a certain exclusiveness, but also the relatively sound financial footing of the whole enterprise. The rent alone for the large apartment and business premises must have been very high, and then there was the costly interior decoration, a clear avowal of Jugendstil aimed at a quite specific class of customer.

Above the entrance hung a tesselated Jugendstil sign in blue and green, with black inlay lettering. The customer passed through a reception area to the main salon which was decorated entirely in black and white. The walls had a white egg-shell finish, with coloured paper inlay figures of fashionably dressed women designed by Koloman Moser.

The salon was furnished with two tables, high-backed chairs and glass show-cases, in which materials and national costumes from all over the empire and handiwork from the Vienna Workshops were displayed. Emilie is known to have collected the materials and national costumes; these same items were found with sample products from the Vienna Workshops when her possessions were discovered in 1983.

Another remarkable feature was the floor covering of grey felt, which was a sensational contrast to the parquet floor usual at the time. Next to the salon was the office where materials were stored and the bookkeeper worked. Here too the prevailing colours were black and white. From the salon another door led to the mannequin cubicle where the mannequin was dressed for the show. The changing rooms for the clients had adjustable mirrors enabling the ladies to see themselves from all angles, commonplace today but a novelty at that time.

Then there were three large workrooms in which at least twenty women were employed in 1932. The modern historian Christian Nebehay writes of eighty workers, but without quoting a source. Apart from this the sisters employed two cutters, a bookkeeper and a mannequin, and in their private quarters a cook and a chambermaid; a chauffeur drove the car for business and family purposes. It is on record that Emilie was herself an enthusiastic driver and liked "to drive the open Styr, which was painted yellow with black wings."[61]

The clients of 'Flöge Sisters' belonged to Vienna's moneyed class. In 1912 a gown made by a private dressmaker cost 40 crowns, and one bought ready-made from one of the large stores cost as much as 48 crowns. But a silk pleated skirt designed at Flöge's cost 190 crowns. However inexact such a comparison may be, it is clear that the fashion-house creations were for the moneyed classes only.

It is known that one of the Rothschilds was a customer in 1932. Other customers were the industrialists' wives Sonja Knips and Mäda Primavesi, whose portraits were painted by Gustav Klimt, and also various members of the Lederer family who were among Klimt's close acquaintances. Then there were numerous American customers.

Accounts of the running of the salon have survived only from the later period, when Pauline Flöge had already died and Helene Klimt, Donner by marriage, the daughter of Ernst Klimt, had been taken into the business. It seems that Emilie Flöge was the one with most energy and drive, and it was she who was responsible for the designs. Twice a year she travelled to the great fashion shows in Paris and bought from houses such as Chanel and Rodier materials and patterns, the latter usually requiring modification since most Viennese ladies were not quite the same shape as Parisiennes.

Emilie also gave directions to the cutters and pinned up the pieces when cut. For this purpose the salon had dummies stuffed to the exact shape of each client. Helene Klimt, the mother, received and advised the clients, and her daughter Helene Donner was responsible for the business side; she was in charge of ordering and for the remaining office work other than bookkeeping, for which they employed a specially qualified person. Helene Donner probably took over the responsibilities of her aunt Pauline. There was no man involved in the business.

Salon Flöge offered not only the latest fashions from Paris, but also the most recent designs from London together with many designs of

following page 182

The Beethoven Frieze, 1902

Long wall, left

Total length 1378 cm

"Yearning for happiness. The sufferings of weak mankind: mankind's appeal to the strong one in armour as the outer force and to compassion and ambition as the inner forces compelling men to take up the struggle for happiness."

Narrow wall

Total length 636 cm

"The hostile forces. The giant Typhoeus, against whom even the gods fought in vain; his daughters, the three gorgons. Disease madness, death. Sensuality and lechery, intemperance. Gnawing sorrow. The yearnings and longings of mankind fly over them."

Long wall, right

511 cm × 400 cm unpainted + 470 cm

"Yearning for happiness finds assuagement in poetry. The arts transpose us into the ideal realm, sole source of pure joy, pure happiness pure love. Choir of angels in paradise. Ode to Joy."

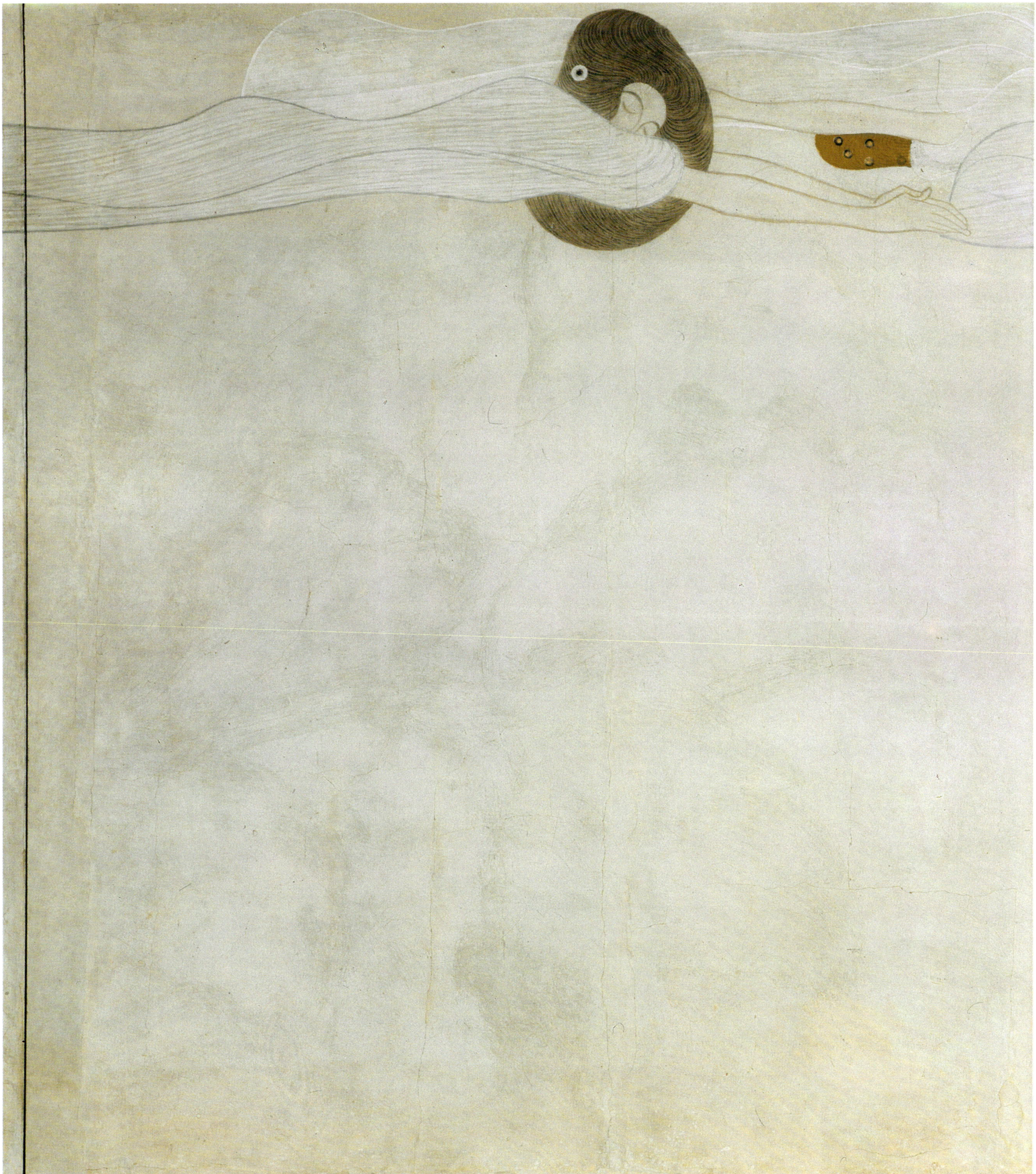

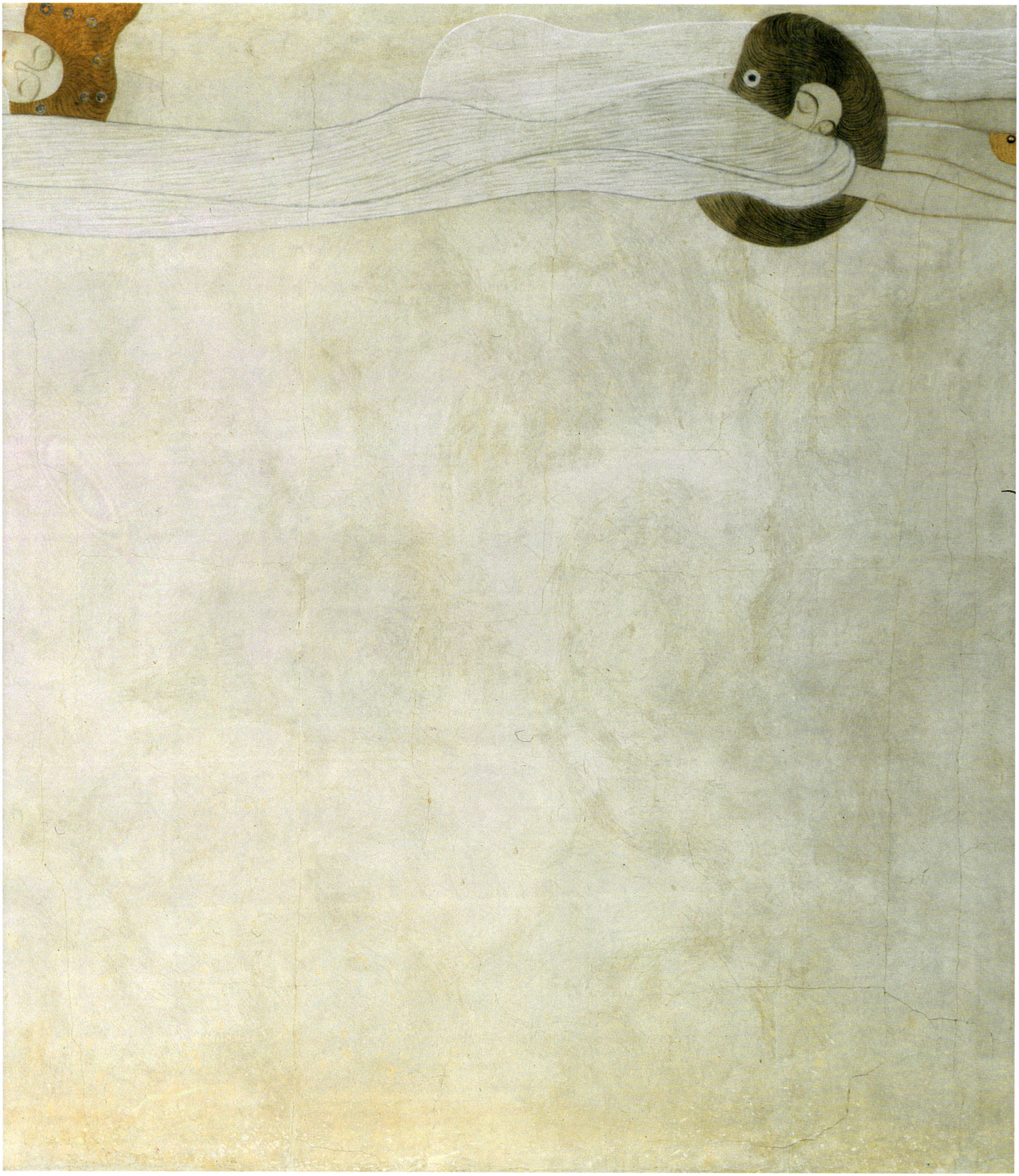

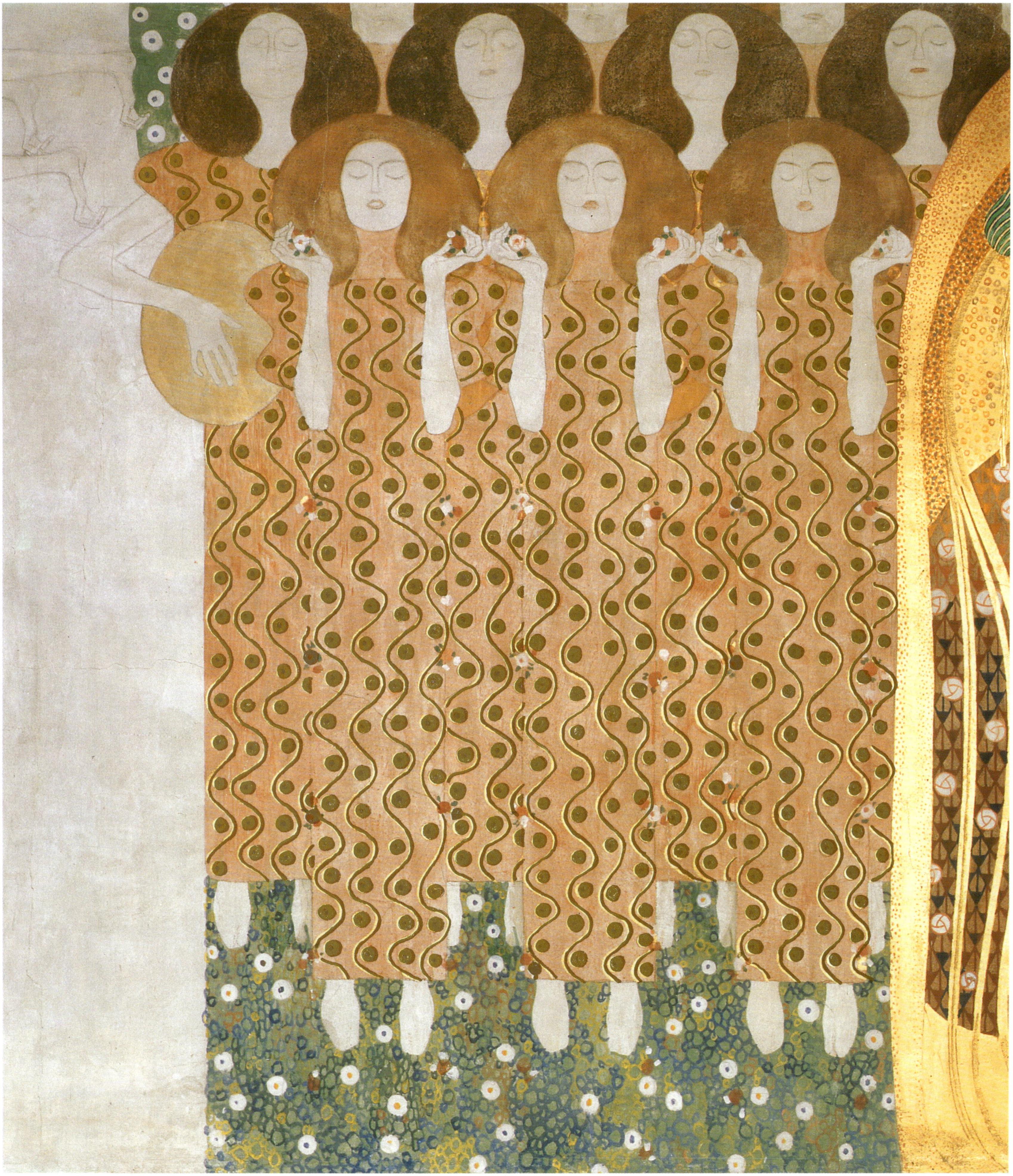

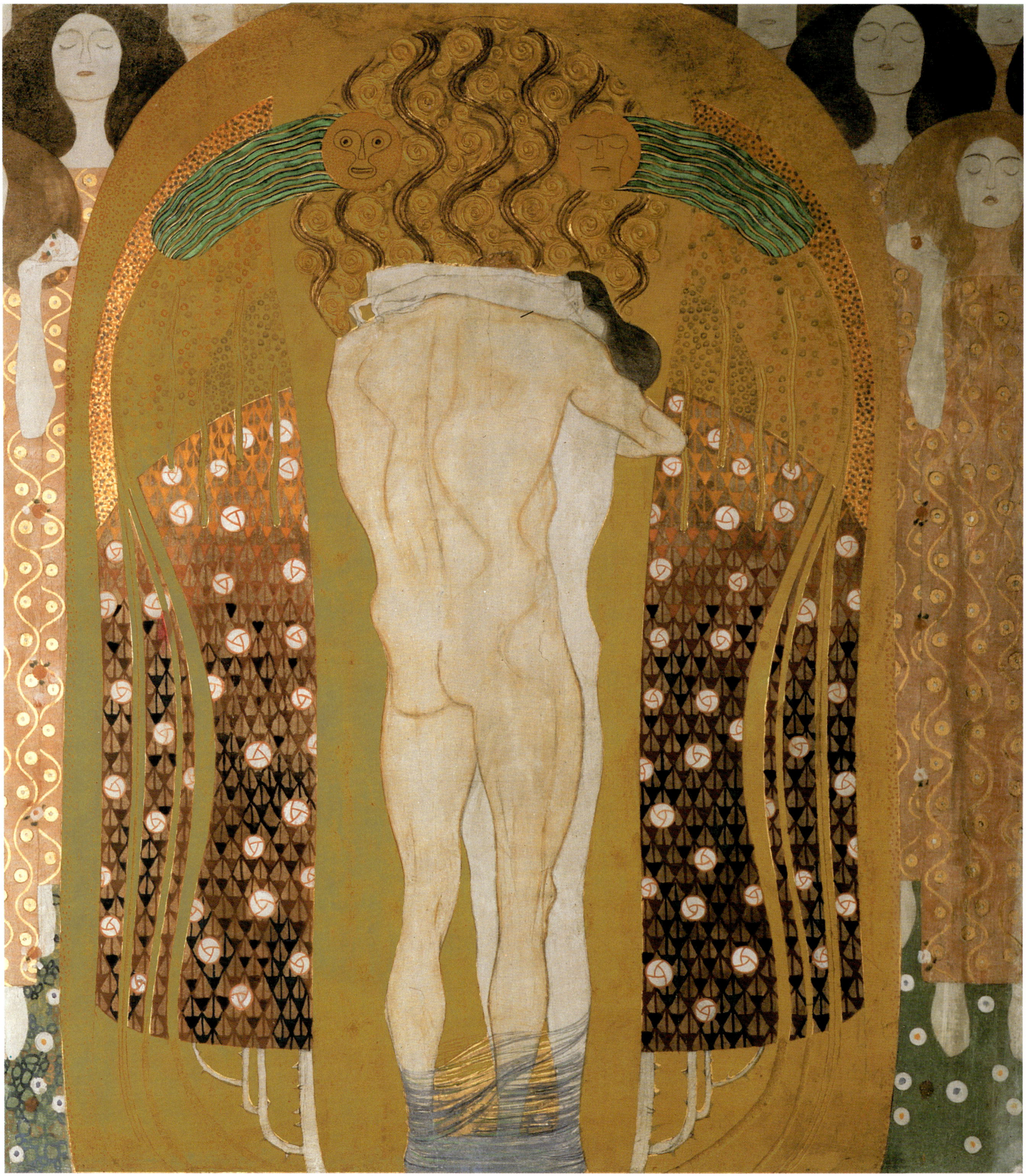

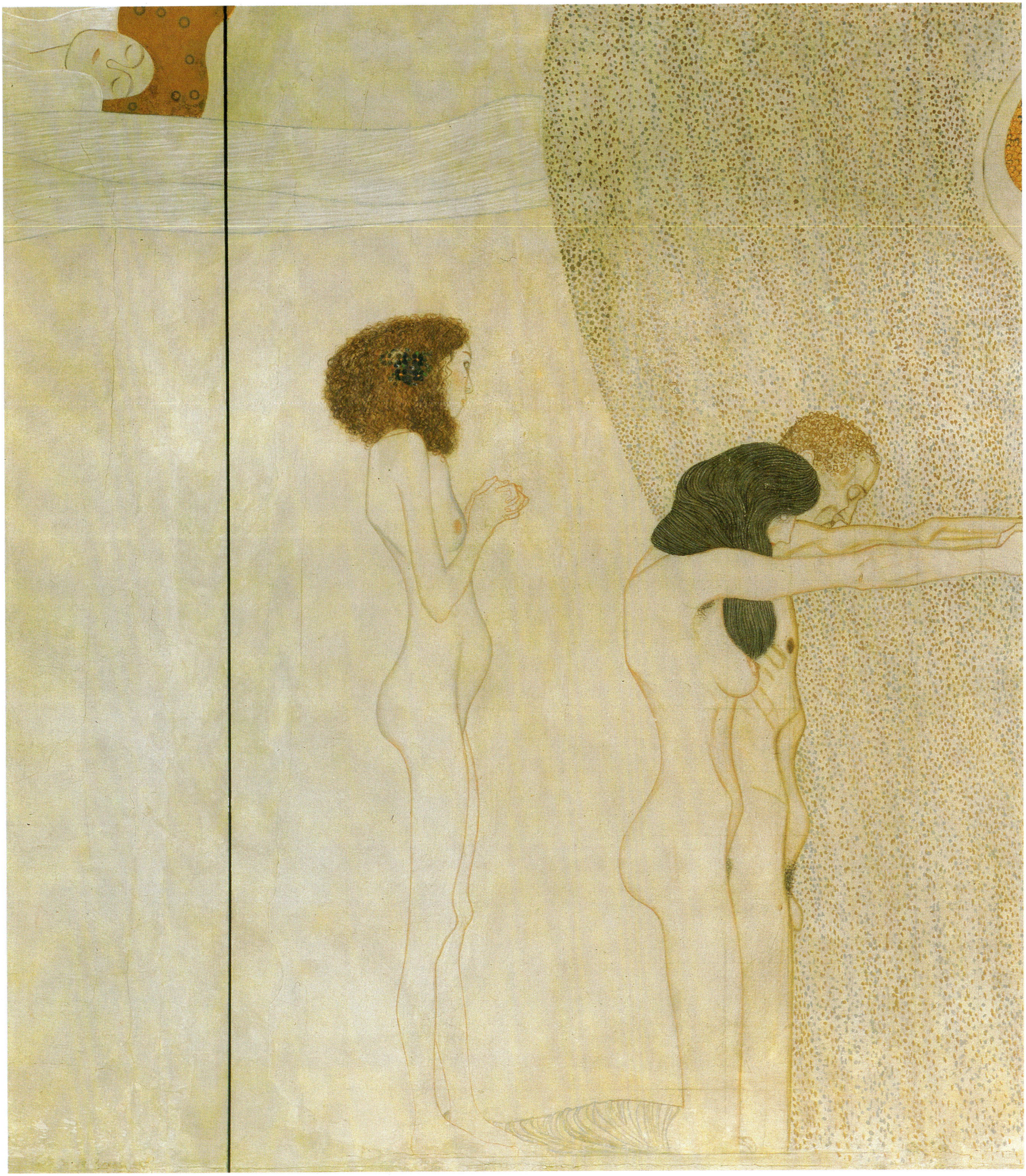

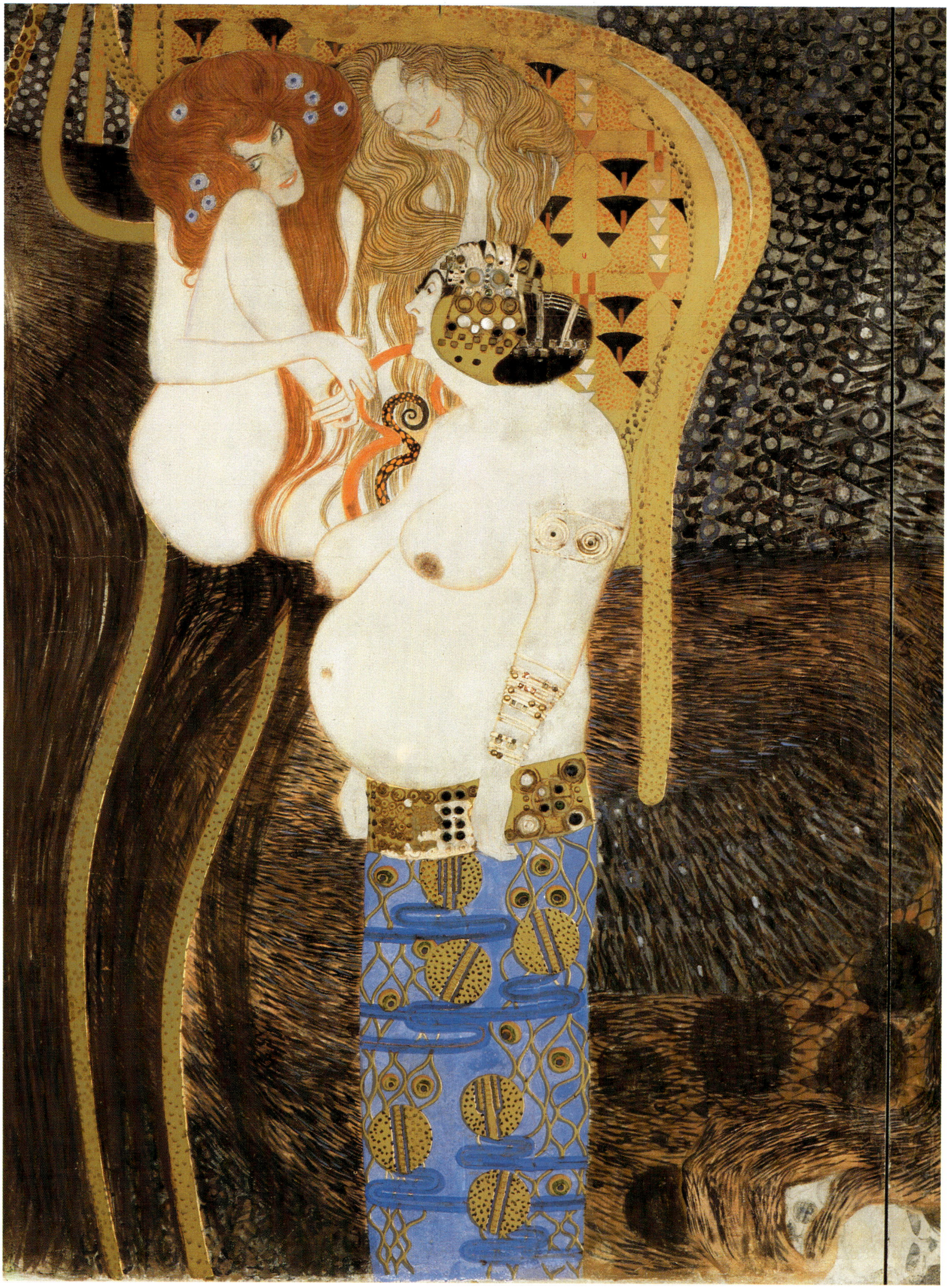

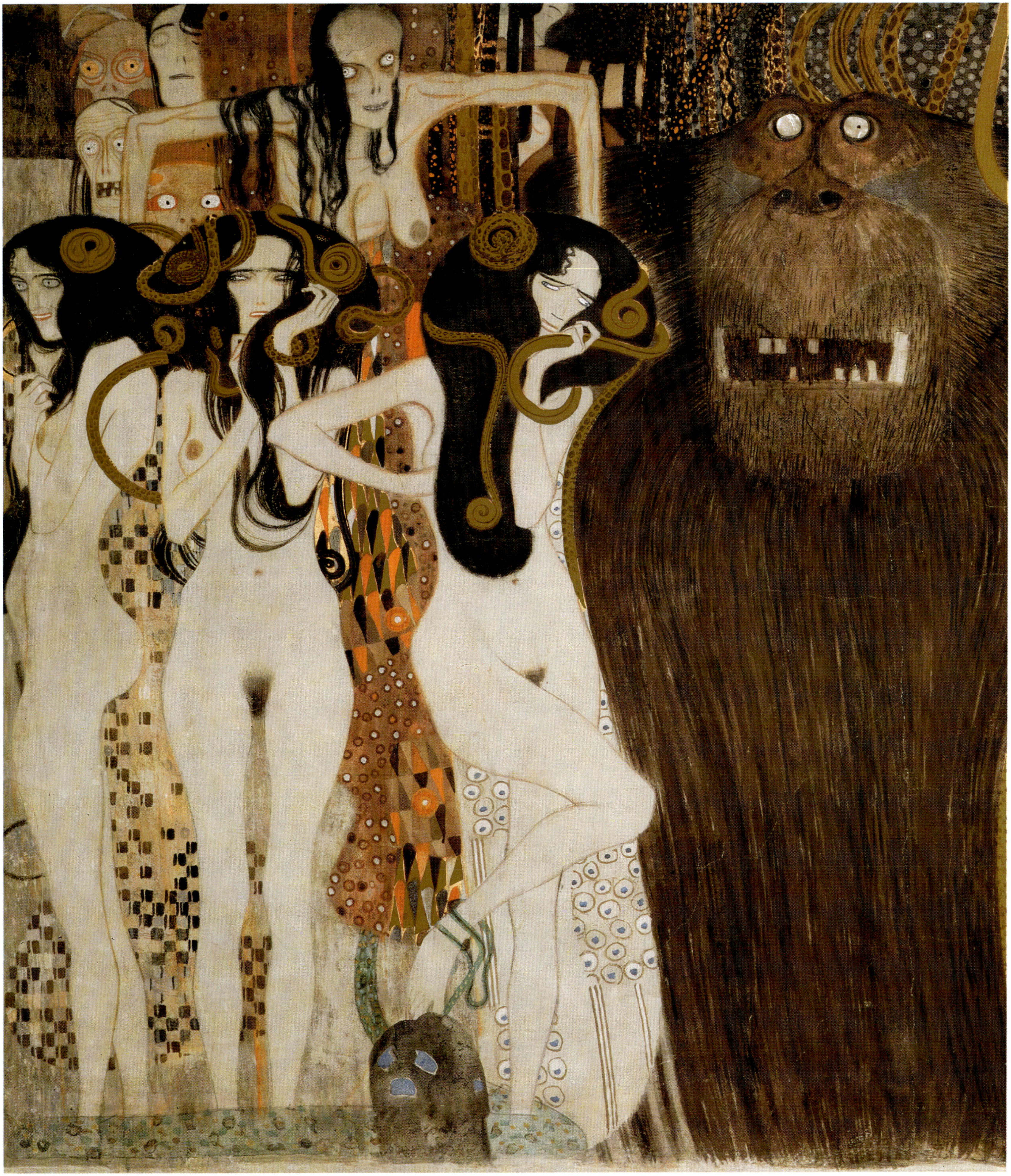

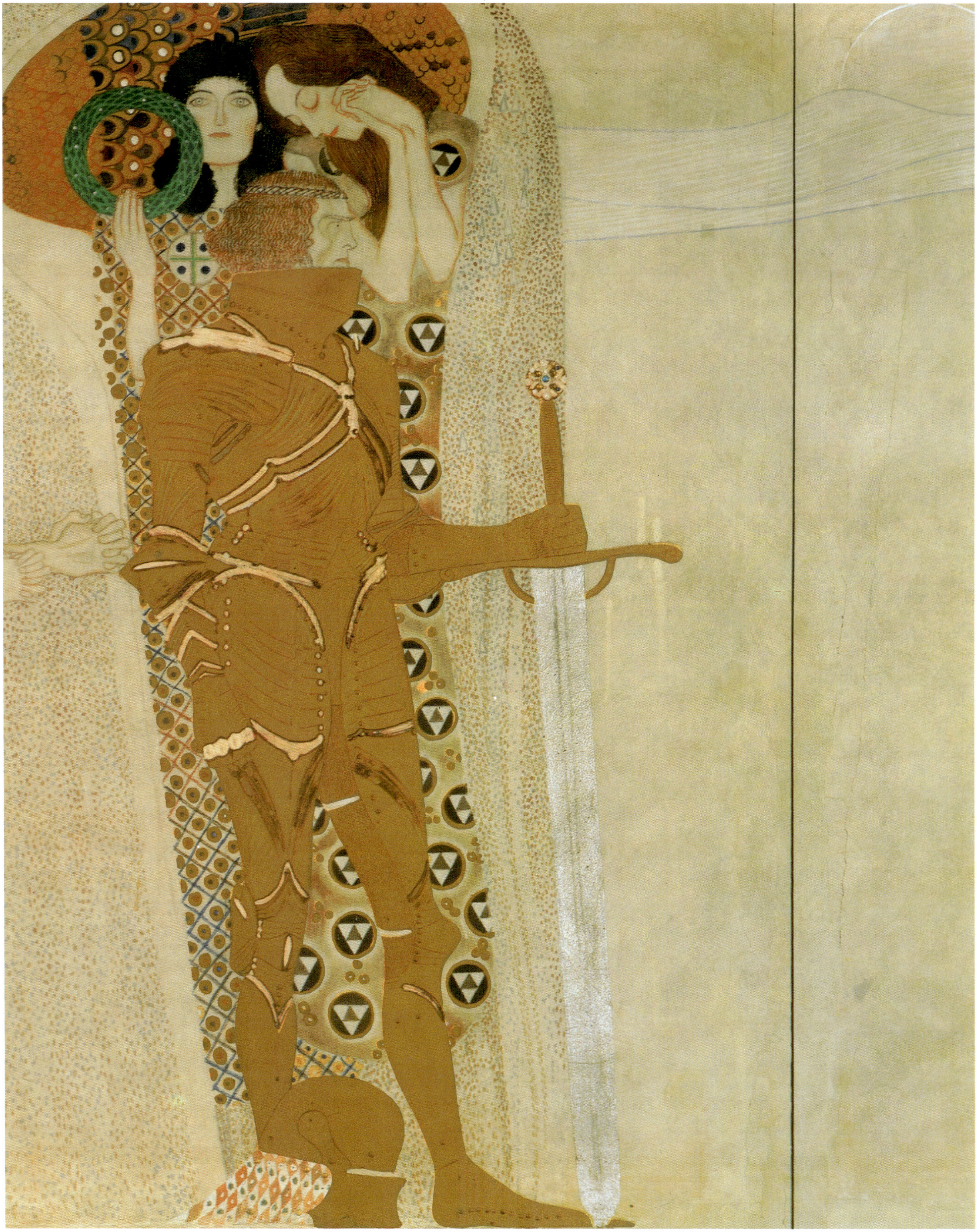

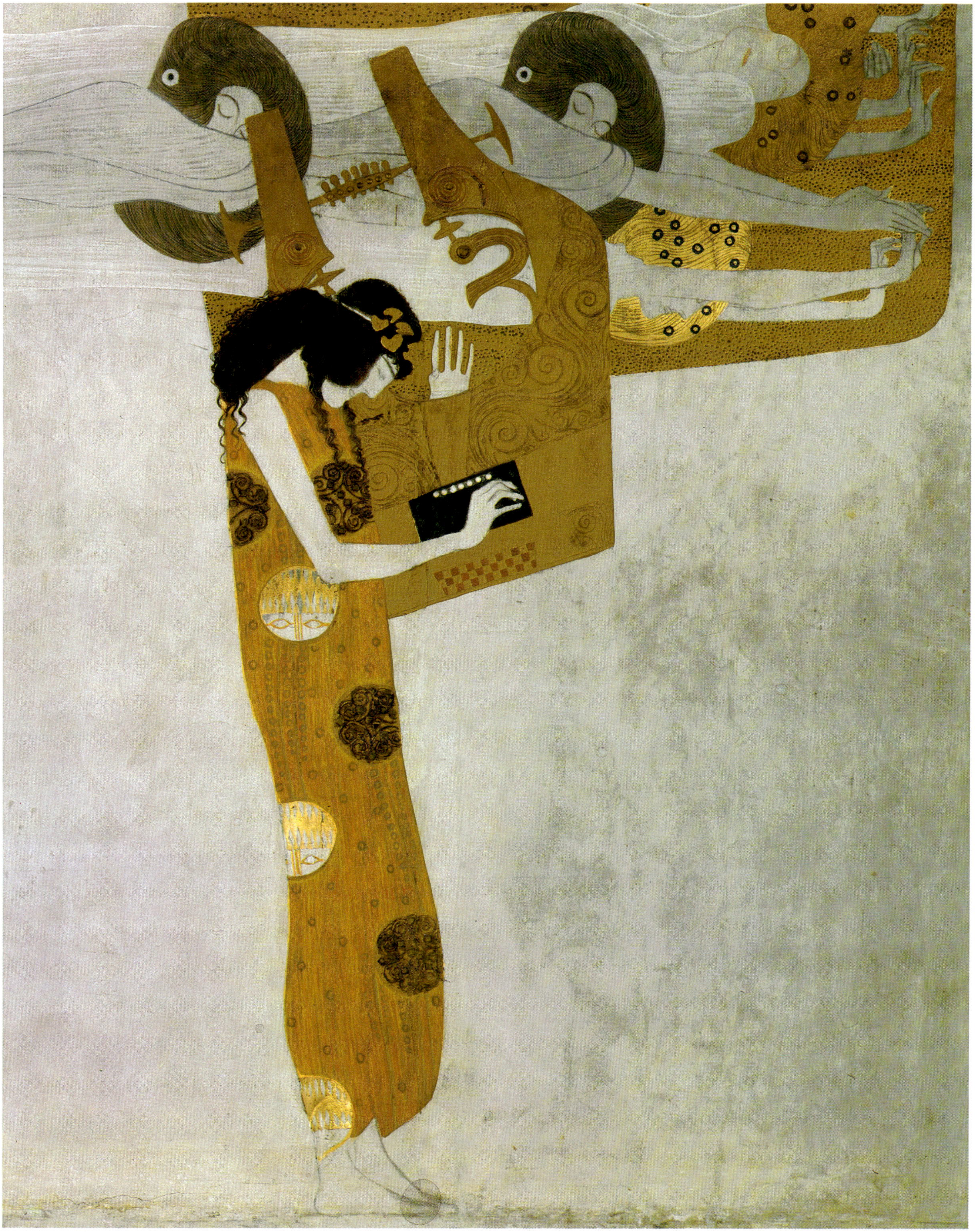

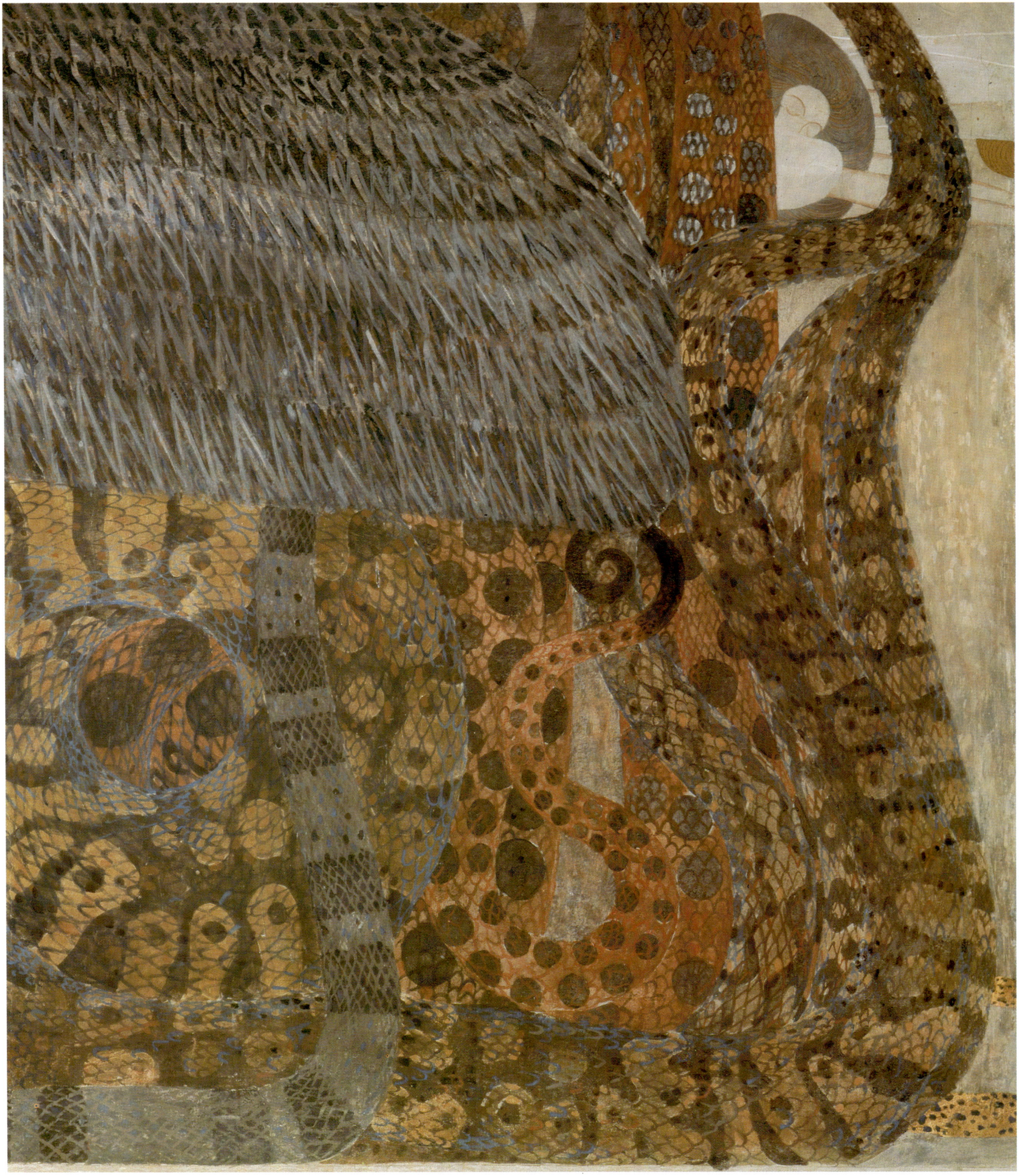

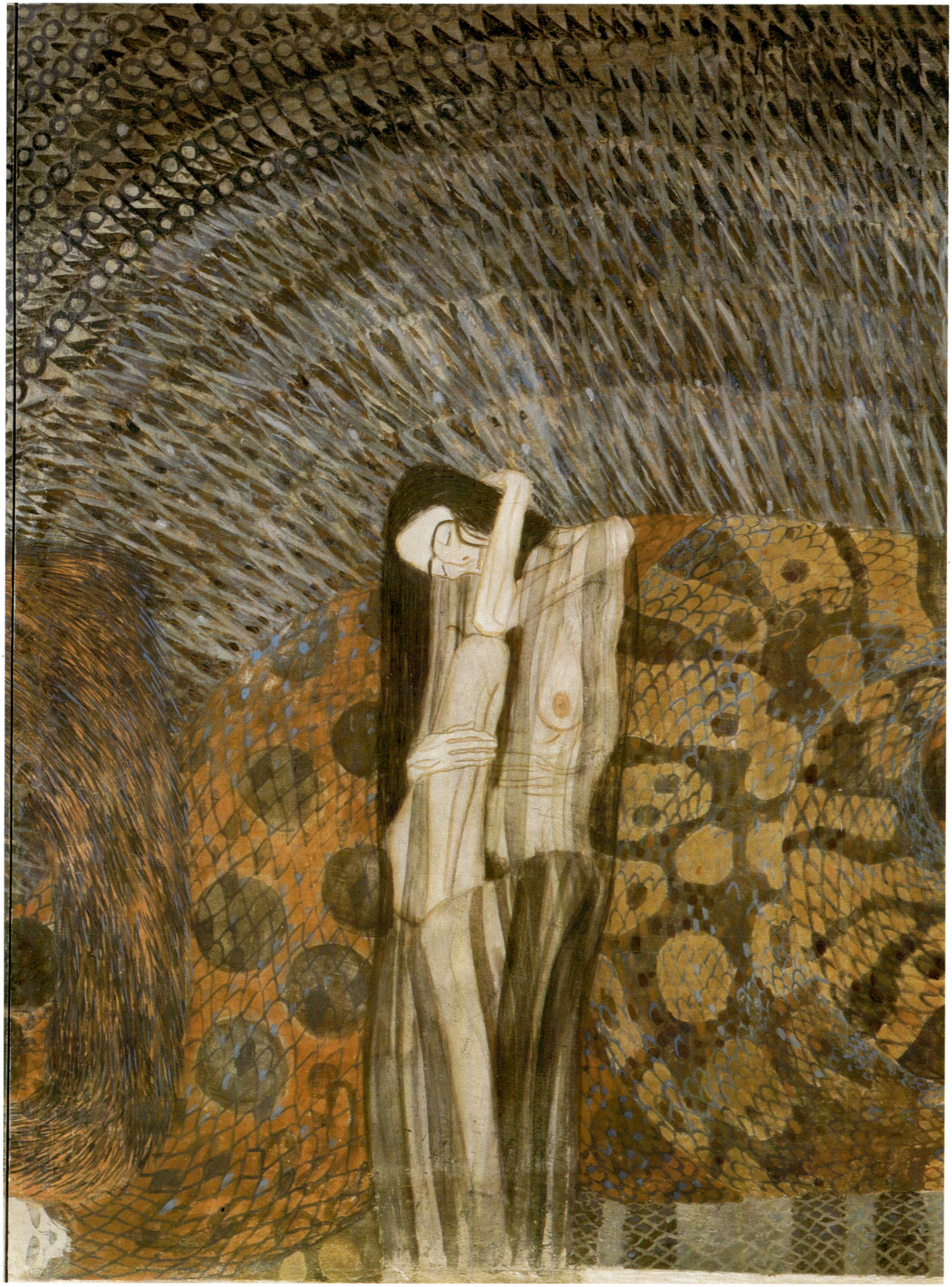

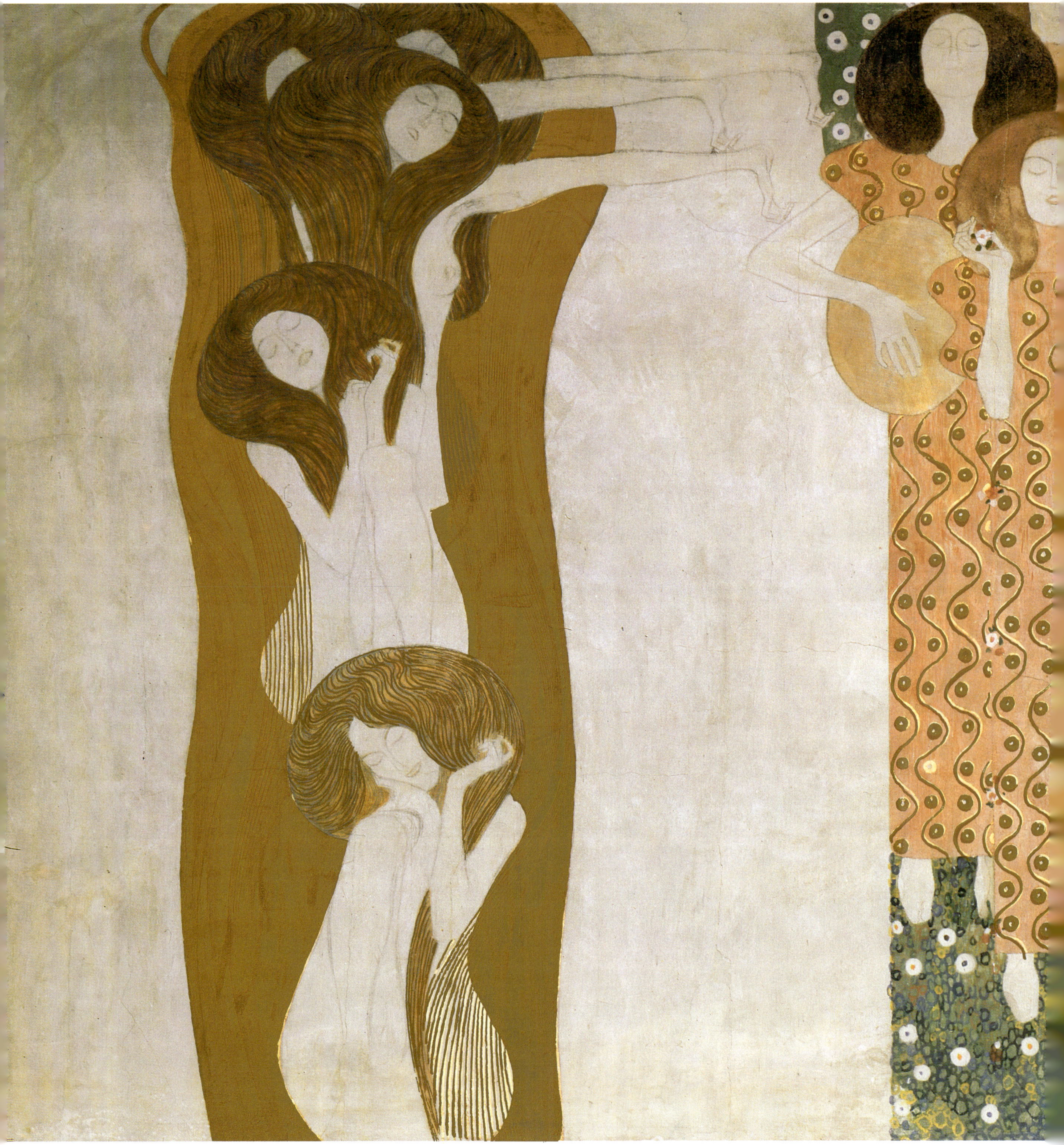

The Beethoven Frieze

Casein paint on refered ground, layered cane, stucco and gold overlay, ornamented (with semi-precious stones, pieces of glass and mother-of-pearl), charcoal, graphite, pastels. Seven sections, spread over three walls. Total area: 220 × 2400 cm.

The Beethoven Frieze, owned by the Austrian Gallery Vienna, is now again housed in the Vienna Secession premises.

their own. Emilie Flöge herself favoured 'reformed dress', with which, however, the salon would never have become one of the leading fashion houses in Vienna.

The reformed style arose from ideological and medical considerations. On the one hand, the image of the fashionable woman at the time was far removed from everyday reality. At the turn of the century the numbers of women working increased sharply, and not only because they needed the money. Many traditional household activities, such as the making of clothes and preserves, were greatly diminished by mechanisation. Women could fill their unoccupied time by going out to work.

One result of the increase in female workers was the women's movement, which rebelled against the dictates of fashion as well as against other strictures: "Calculating businessmen determine the appearance of women all over the civilised world, altering women's looks at will . . . One year we are shaped into a ball, the next year we are made thin as a rake, with every successful novelty accelerating the speed of change . . . This degradation was perpetrated most frequently in the enlightened nineteenth century, and the most respectable sort of women were to be seen playing their part."[62] The freedom fighters damned the corset as an instrument of torture and demanded a reform of fashion. Noted medical practitioners also spoke out against the harm caused to health by the corset, so that there was protest from different quarters.

In Europe it was the Arts and Crafts Movement that first designed long smock-type dresses with no waist, known at the time as 'reform clothes'. These clothes became a symbol of independence and casualness, asserting the individuality of the wearer and freedom from fashion.

Jugendstil centres in different countries took up this style of dress, and so it came about that it was propagated by the Secessionists in Vienna at the turn of the century. Gustav Klimt designed models which Emilie Flöge made, and also wore (see p. 192). It would be interesting to know whether she really favoured a fashion which conflicted so gravely with her chief source of income, but she left no record of her opinions, neither did her contemporaries.

The reform clothes were never in serious competition with the fashion of the day, and the public quite quickly lost interest in them. Parisian fashions remained.

'Flöge Sisters' survived World War I and continued to be one of Vienna's leading fashion houses for a further twenty years, but in 1935/36 business declined. The aristocracy was impoverished, and many of the industrialists were Jews who, if they had not already emigrated, were dispossessed in 1938 after the annexation of Austria by Nazi Germany. And so it was that in 1938 the salon had to close because of a total lack of customers. Emilie was the only sister still living, and towards the end she and her niece had run the business alone. They gave up the apartment in the Mariahilfstraße, but continued to live together until Emilie's death in 1952.

Gustav Klimt and Emilie Flöge

Although Gustav Klimt and Emilie Flöge had known one another since 1891 at the latest, Klimt's earliest extant letters to her are from 1897. From 1898 onwards he spent the summer months with the Flöge family beside the Attersee. In 1891 he painted his first portrait of Emilie. In 1893/94 he included her in his brother Ernst's easel painting of 'The Buffoon on the Impromptu Stage at Rothenburg' when he completed it (see p. 62/67). He introduced the Flöge sisters and his own sisters into the crowd, making Emilie specially conspicuous.

In 1902 he painted the only real portrait of her. It shows a tall, fine, slender woman in a long blue dress, richly ornamented, that veils the whole body. In 1908 this picture was sold to the History Museum of the City of Vienna. There is also a sequence of photographs taken partly by the Attersee, partly in Klimt's studio garden. The photographs show both Klimt and Emilie in reform clothes which Klimt is said to have designed.

Oral history has it that when Klimt suffered a stroke on 11 January 1918 he mumbled the words "Go and get Emilie". However, it was also known that Klimt had had relationships with various other women,

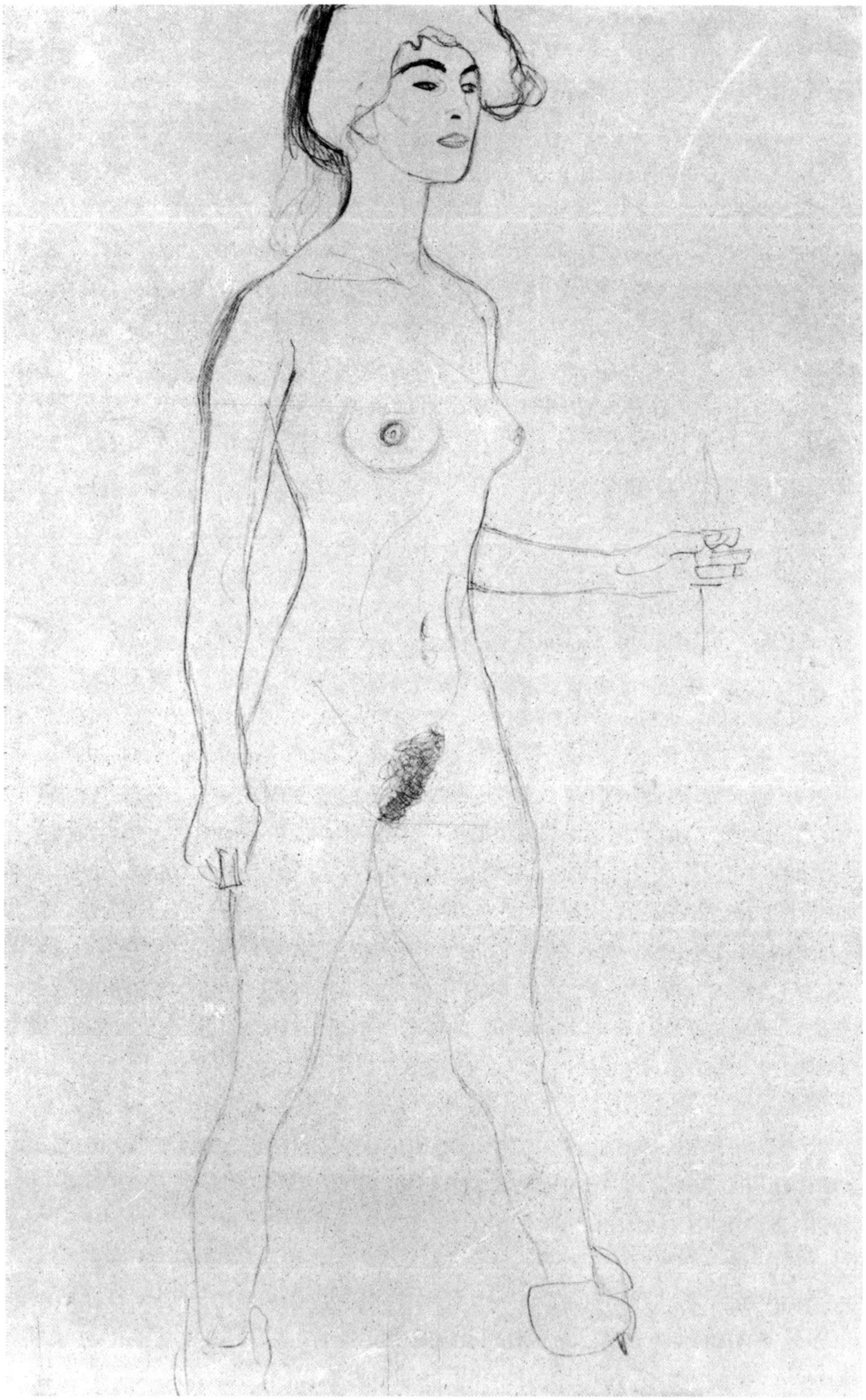

Striding woman, right arm dropping,
left arm extended, 1907
Pencil, 55.9 × 37.1 cm

usually models, and fathered three children whom he supported. After his death fourteen women put in claims on behalf of their children, said to be his.

People cobbled these bits of information together, and shortly after Klimt's death a description of Emilie Flöge was dreamt up, complete with a story of pure devotion. In 1919 it was possible to read the following account: "Klimt's power seems to be riddled with contradictions; he, whose chief characteristic was goodness, had to stand alone and face indifference and enmity though his greatest need was for love ... for many years he was tied to a woman by close bonds of friendship, but here again he was unable to say 'yes'. The erotic neurasthenia that quivers in some of his most deeply felt drawings is only too likely to have been charged with the most painful experience. Klimt did not dare to take on the responsibility of happiness, and the woman whom he loved for so many years was rewarded only with the right to care for him at the painful moment of death."[63]

On the basis of this 'right' – "Nothing marks the deep human bond between these two people better than the cry of the artist close to death"[64] – Emilie Flöge is made into "a wonderful woman, whose human warmth enabled her to give Klimt the unending and unshakeable friendship which was lacking with the many other women to whom his hot blood drove him time and time again." Klimt, on the other hand, "had to retain his personal freedom in order to create, and herein lies the simple answer to the question of why Gustav Klimt never married his Emilie Flöge ... all the more reason to admire this woman who devoted her entire life to the service of a great man, enabling him through her great sacrificce to pursue his vocation as an artist without hindrance."[65] It is said that after Klimt's death Emilie burnt whole laundry-basketfulls of letters. Since the discovery of her possessions in 1983 this seems unlikely; among them were found 399 communications from him to her, covering the time from 1897 to 1917.

Klimt was not a great letter-writer. Apart from three long letters, the communications consist almost entirely of postcards with short messages or greetings. Before he acquired a telephone the messages are just about theatre tickets; so on 9.1.1900: "Dear Emilie, 2 tickets for Fuhrmann Hentschel, greetings, Gust".[66]

Yet most of the cards were written when either he or Emilie were away from Vienna, the contents usually being restricted to the weather or his health (about which he was evidently very concerned most of the time) or the time of his return, or complaints that he has not heard, or not heard enough, from Emilie. Sometimes he wrote three or four times a day, especially when he was the one to be left behind in Vienna.

There is little information about his work, apart from some fairly detailed accounts of progress on the Stoclet Frieze in Brussels. Most of the time, if he mentioned his work at all, he just wrote that he was not making much progress. He scarcely ever referred to the subject matter of his pictures; he took her familiarity with them for granted: "I'll probably only finish one of the pictures, the larger one. Saturday as arranged! I need another 2 or 3 days for the other picture. Best greetings, Gustav".[67]

A comparison between these letters and those to Mizzi Zimmermann, with whom Klimt had an affair lasting from 1899 to 1903 and who bore him two sons, Gustav and Otto, suggests that Emilie Flöge was a very close friend with whom he stood on an equal footing. In his letters to 'dear Mizzi' he is lovingly condescending, he preaches to her and scolds her. The often very sparse messages to Emilie suggest that many things did not need to be spoken of between them, and at the same time that large parts of their lives were organised jointly: "Ministry of rail transport today – have to go on Monday 12.45 – still a lot to do. Spoke about Bruno H. – won't be very easy – support for the application granted. Weather good All the very best Gustav".[68]

A few of the cards refer jokingly to other women. On 23.10.1909 he wrote from Paris: "Fled to the Parisiana – at least some pretty women to look at – saw the first young women in Montmartre (cocottes of course) but at least not wrecks".[69]

From Paris his journey continued to Spain. Several cards mention that he has not yet discovered a beautiful Spanish woman. On the same journey he wrote one of his few long letters, which contains the only passage in the whole correspondence suggesting that they were lovers: "Now I look forward with royal pleasure to my silly little Midelinchen, Midessa etc. – perhaps she'll come to the station – I'll be with her

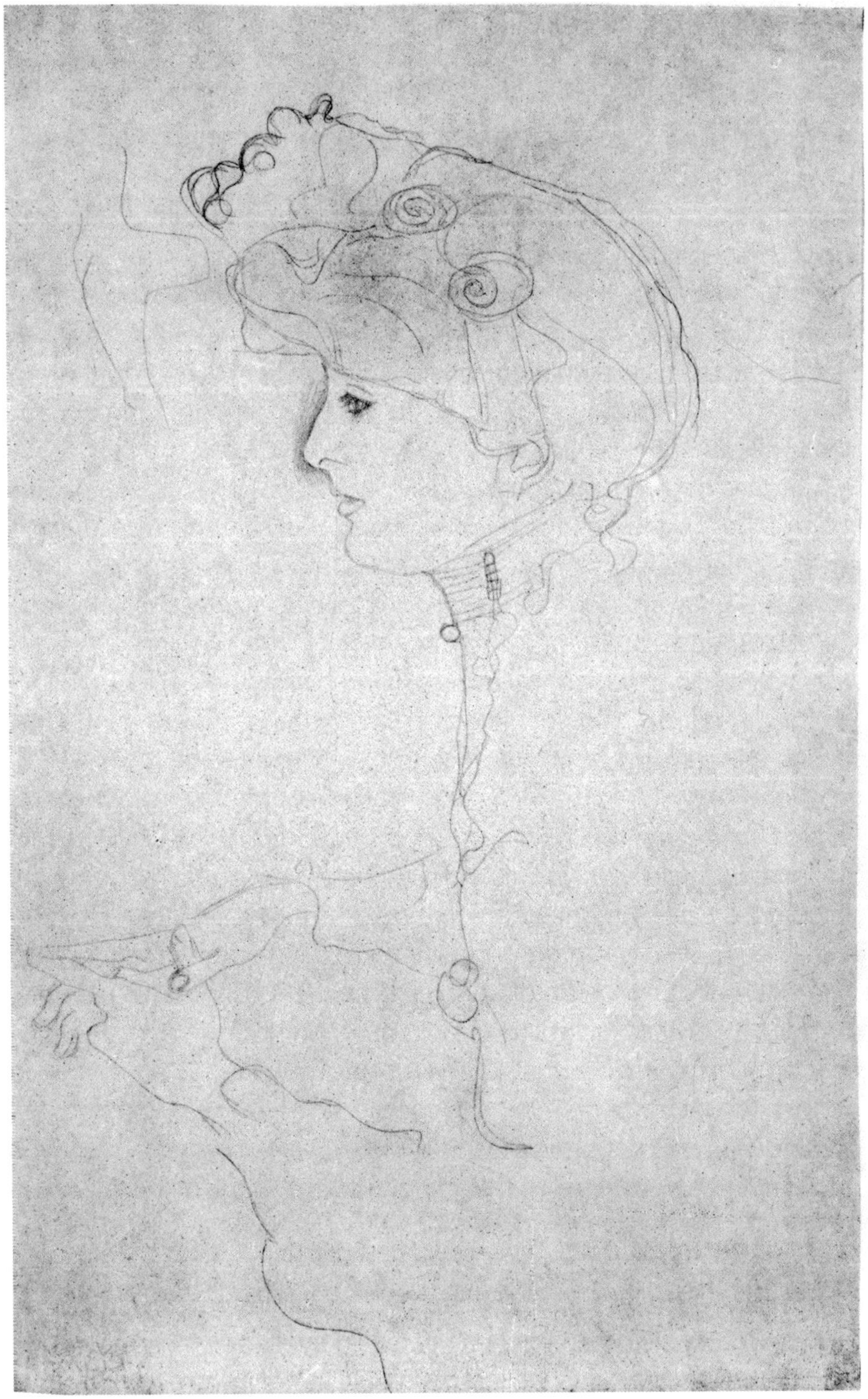

Half-sketch of woman, left profile,
1906/07
Pencil, 55.2 × 34 cm

anyway on Thursday. The first and the last night in Spain I dreamt of her. Do you remember the agreement about the letter? Everything's that way! All the very best Gustav".[70]

The letters do indeed show a very close friendship between the two, and it was probably more than friendship. It does not seem necessary to take very seriously later comments of neighbours at the Attersee, which have recently been published, such as: "Emilie and Gustav – they were never a proper loving couple, they never had an affair! Never! That's why Emilie was such a bundle of nerves all her life, there's no other explanation for it"[71]. It is quite possible that such remarks were made out of consideration for members of the Flöge family still living at the time.

It seems right to question the stereotyped image of the freedom-loving Gustav and self-sacrificing Emilie. The story can be read in several different ways. Emilie Flöge was not always there; she was an independent woman who had work to do which involved regular trips to London and Paris.

It is possible to speculate further. At the beginning of the twentieth century freedom in love was being propagated in various circles; Wassily Kandinsky (1866–1944) and Gabriele Münter (1877–1962) lived together in Munich, and later in Murnau, without a wedding certificate. The ideas of the psycho-analyst Otto Groß (1877–1920) fell on fruitful soil, particularly in Schwabing, the artists' quarter of Munich, and were passed on from there to Ascona. There a fluctuating group of people had settled on Mount Verita and were experimenting with different lifestyles. One of Otto Groß's aims was to convince people of the value of loving each other more freeely, without the constraints of marital fidelity and jealousy. In his eyes a woman had the right to choose the father of her children freely, even if she was married. He and his wife lived according to this principle, as did numerous friends and devotees, who mostly lived in Schwabing. Many of them moved for shorter or longer periods to Ascona.

Ideas from Schwabing and Ascona reached Vienna. It is possible that Emilie Flöge was just as unenthusiastic about relinquishing her freedom as Klimt is said to have been about relinquishing his. She is likely to have known about his other relationships; perhaps she was

61–66 Working Drawings for Stoclet Frieze, 1905/1910
Tempera, water colours, gold paint, silver bronze, crayons, pencil, white paint, some gold leaf and silver leaf, on paper; with handwritten instructions
Austrian Museum of Applied Art, Vienna

61 Expectation, 193 × 115 cm

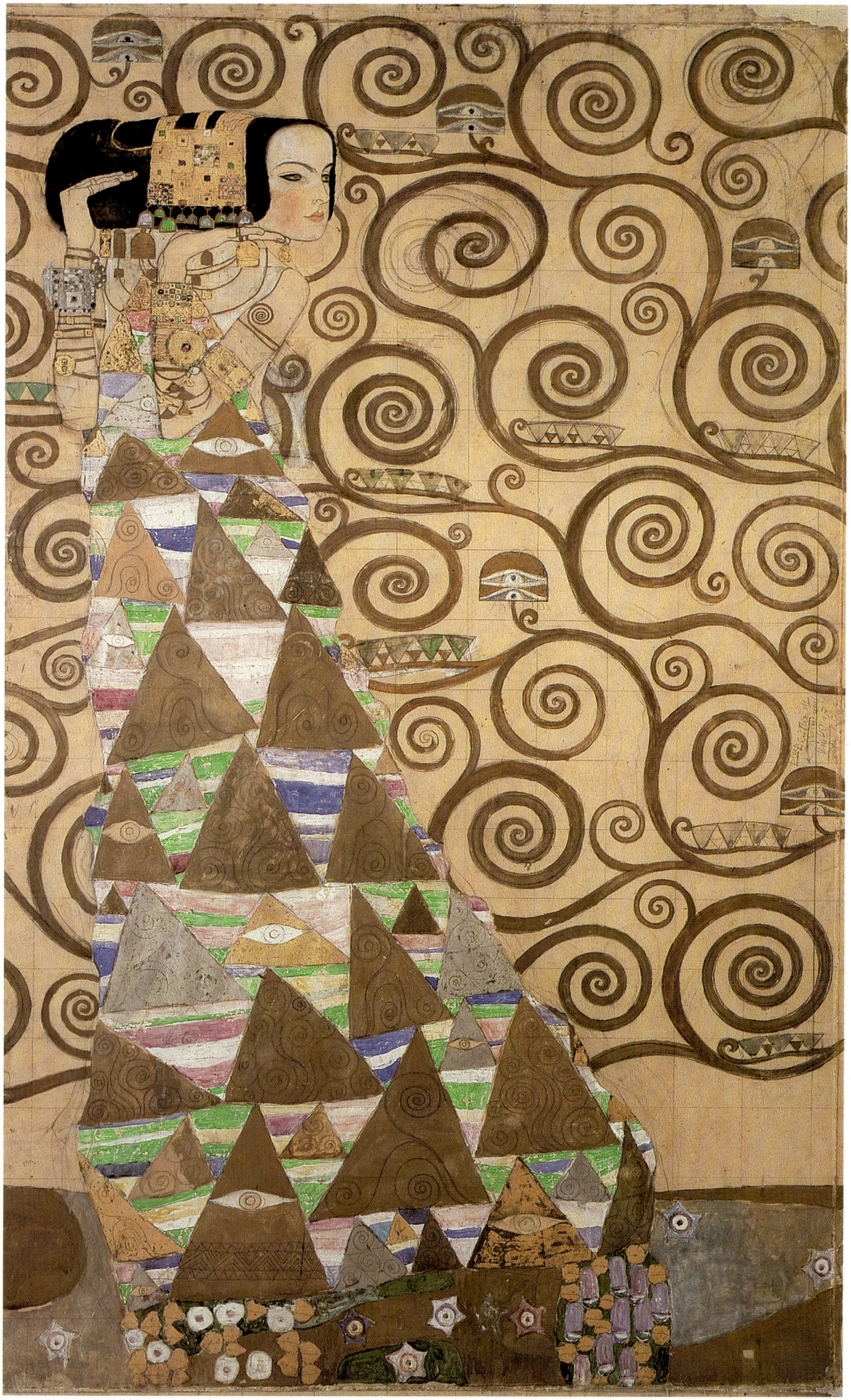

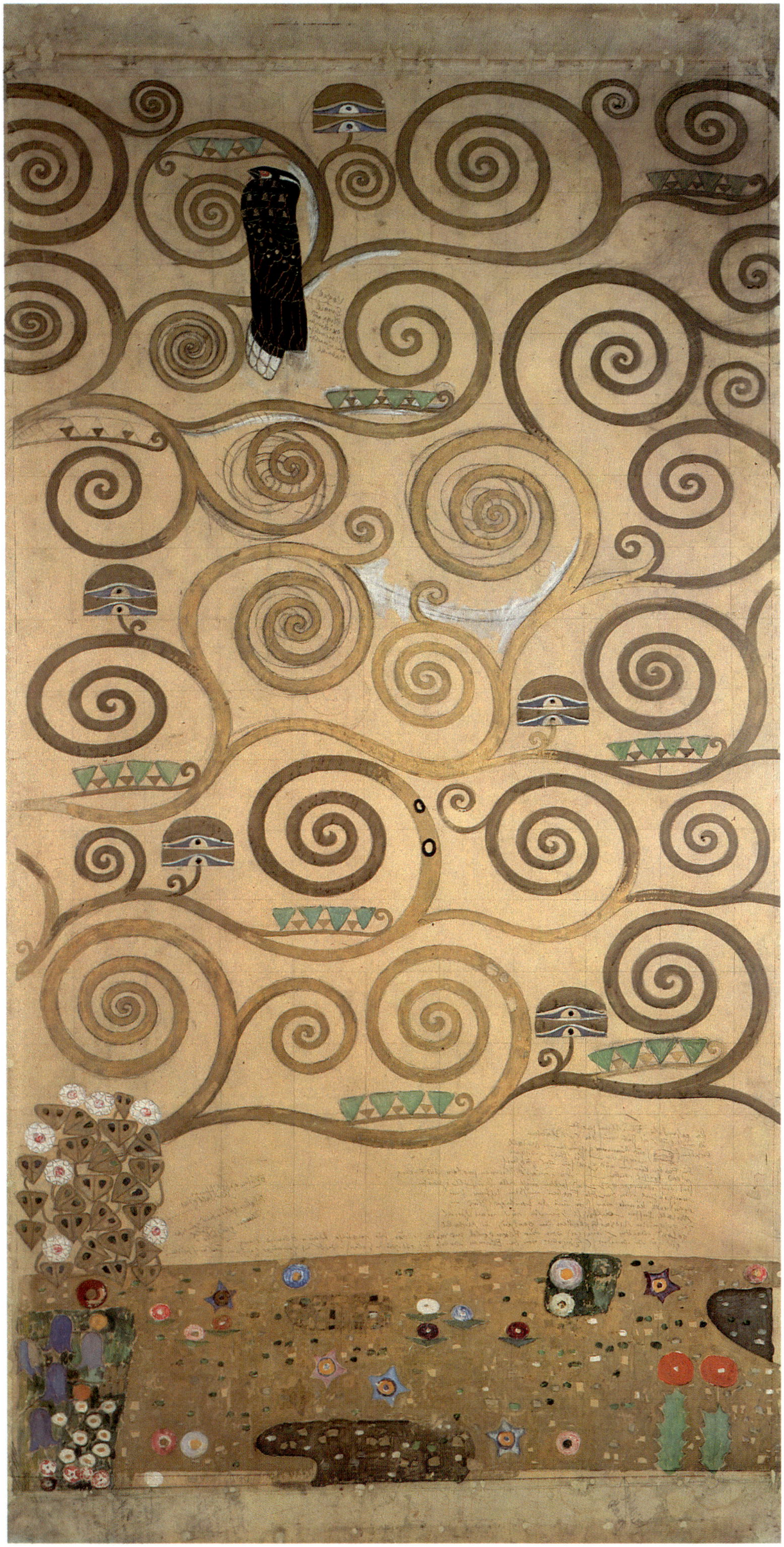

able to accept them totally. Comments such as "Emilie will never have looked at another man either before or after his death, although he could never descend to anything so bourgeois and despicable as a proposal of marriage"[72] seem entirely unjustified. Speculations of all sorts proliferated for many years, but no satisfactory documentary evidence for any of them has so far come to light.

The fact is – and this is all that matters – that Gustav Klimt and Emilie Flöge were involved in a relationship which enabled both to draw into their own creative lives ideas from the other's sphere. This is what makes the relationship interesting.

It is likely that Klimt encouraged the Flöge sisters to have their salon decorated and furnished by the Vienna Workshops. Some of the items from the Workshops which have been found among Emilie Flöge's possessions were collected by her, some were presents from Gustav Klimt, as is shown by old bills. In turn Klimt's interest in materials and in fashion-designing will have been encouraged by Emilie. Some of his designs were published in the journal 'Deutsche Kunst und Dekoration' in 1907, and he will have learnt a great deal from Emilie while working on them. Klimt's reform clothes, for instance, are lighter and more elegant than those of his artist colleague Henry van de Velde. They present "a more successful synthesis of theory and practice than earlier experiments... partly because in this case the collaboration is between artist and couturier, not between artist and dilettante. Klimt's clothes... take up touches of fashion and deliberately include them: the high collar, wide flounces and delicately falling pleats. Light patterned materials, flounces and frills decorated with geometrical ornament, are also to be found... they particularly suit Emilie Flöge, who wears them."[73]

It is not clear how Gustav and Emilie apportioned their work on the designs. It is quite possible that they did them together. The clothes were tailored in the Flöge salon; Emilie wore them and Gustav took photographs of her in them. One novelty was that these photographs were taken out of doors, in Klimt's studio garden.

Klimt himself usually wore a long smock, of which he possessed a fair number. These smocks – reform clothes for the man – will also have been made in the Flöge salon. One such smock, made of a

62 Tree of Life, left, 197 × 105 cm

Mexican material, was found among Emilie Flöge's belongings. Klimt's clothes designs will have contributed to the opening of a fashion department in the Vienna Workshops in 1911, and in this project also Emilie Flöge will have been involved.

Emilie Flöge and Gustav Klimt worked independently of one another for the same social class in Vienna. She provided clothes for the wives of rich industrialists, he painted their pictures. At times their paths will have crossed, and each will have benefited from the contacts of the other. All this is more important than fruitless enquiries into the exact nature of the friendship between them.

The Vienna Workshops

From foundation to liquidation

In 1903 the architect Josef Hoffmann and the painter Koloman Moser founded the 'Vienna Workshops – Manufacturing Association of Vienna Craftsmen', with the affluent businessman Fritz Waerndorfer (1868–1939). The two artists had also been prominent founder members of the Vienna Secession. It was largely thanks to them that the status of handicrafts rose. The amazingly consistent adjusting of decoration and furnishing in the exhibition rooms of the Secession, always finely attuned to the pictures exhibited, was the particular achievement of Josef Hoffmann. The design of VER SACRUM owed much to the initiative of Koloman Moser.

Early success with the arts and crafts business had spread far beyond Vienna, and resulted in official support being given to them. They were appointed to professorships at the School of Arts and Crafts in 1899 and 1900 respectively. As early as 1901 some of their students founded the association 'Vienna art in the home', which set itself the task of '"countering the fragmentation of talents through an organisation which will strive to make tangible use of developments, ideas and experiments by means of shared work in a shared cause"[74]. They undertook interior designing and decorating jointly, and were successful in so doing. Having official support, they were given premises in 1903 in which they could work together and display their products. This institution, probably initiated directly or indirectly by Hoffmann and Moser, may be seen as a forerunner of the Vienna Workshops.

More important, however, was the contact with London and Glasgow which was brought about by the VIIIth Secession exhibition of

November and December 1900. Hoffmann initiated a contrastive presentation of arts and crafts from Austria and from abroad, as had been done several times previously with exhibitions of paintings. The director of the School of Arts and Crafts, Felician von Myrbach (1853–1940) put them in touch with Charles Robert Ashbee, who had founded the London 'Guild of Handicraft' in 1888, with the intention of putting into practice the ideas of Ruskin and William Morris (see p. 26/27).

It was thanks to Ashbee that Mackintosh and his wife Margaret Macdonald from Glasgow were persuaded to contribute to the Vienna exhibition. In spite of frequently cited remarks on the enthusiastic reception that the foreign guests enjoyed, the Viennese actually received these visitors rather coolly; even Ludwig Hevesi, who favoured the Secession, could not refrain from criticism. He wrote of Ashbee's extraordinary furniture, which appeared to have arrived from a square-shaped planet, with "everything upright, right-angled, at ninety degrees"[75]. His criticism of the Scottish exhibits was even sharper: "One of the interiors in the exhibition is beyond our ken . . . it never actually takes shape, but rather it remains in its embryonic state, and its pieces spin themselves out into black and gold threads which do nothing more than delineate the space that could have been filled, or is said to have been filled . . . The room is white, the furniture is black, everything made of wood is smooth, thin, narrow . . ."[76]

Nevertheless, between the artists and craftsmen themselves a friendly association was formed, and Hoffmann and Moser were influenced by the geometrical forms of the Scottish artists.

For Waerndorfer it was not the first meeting with Mackintosh, for he had paid the Scotsman a brief visit in Glasgow two years before. Waerndorfer was the son of a rich Jewish family who had made a considerable fortune in cotton. In 1900 he was sent on a tour of Europe; in England he was supposed to be learning about the textile industry, but instead he used the time to find out about modern art, and arts and crafts. He had been put in touch with the Secession through Hermann Bahr, and he particularly cultivated the acquaintance of Klimt, Hoffmann and Moser. He owned a number of Klimt's paintings, especially early ones. He bought 'Hope I', which is discussed below.

In 1902 Myrbach and Hoffmann were sent abroad by the Ministry,

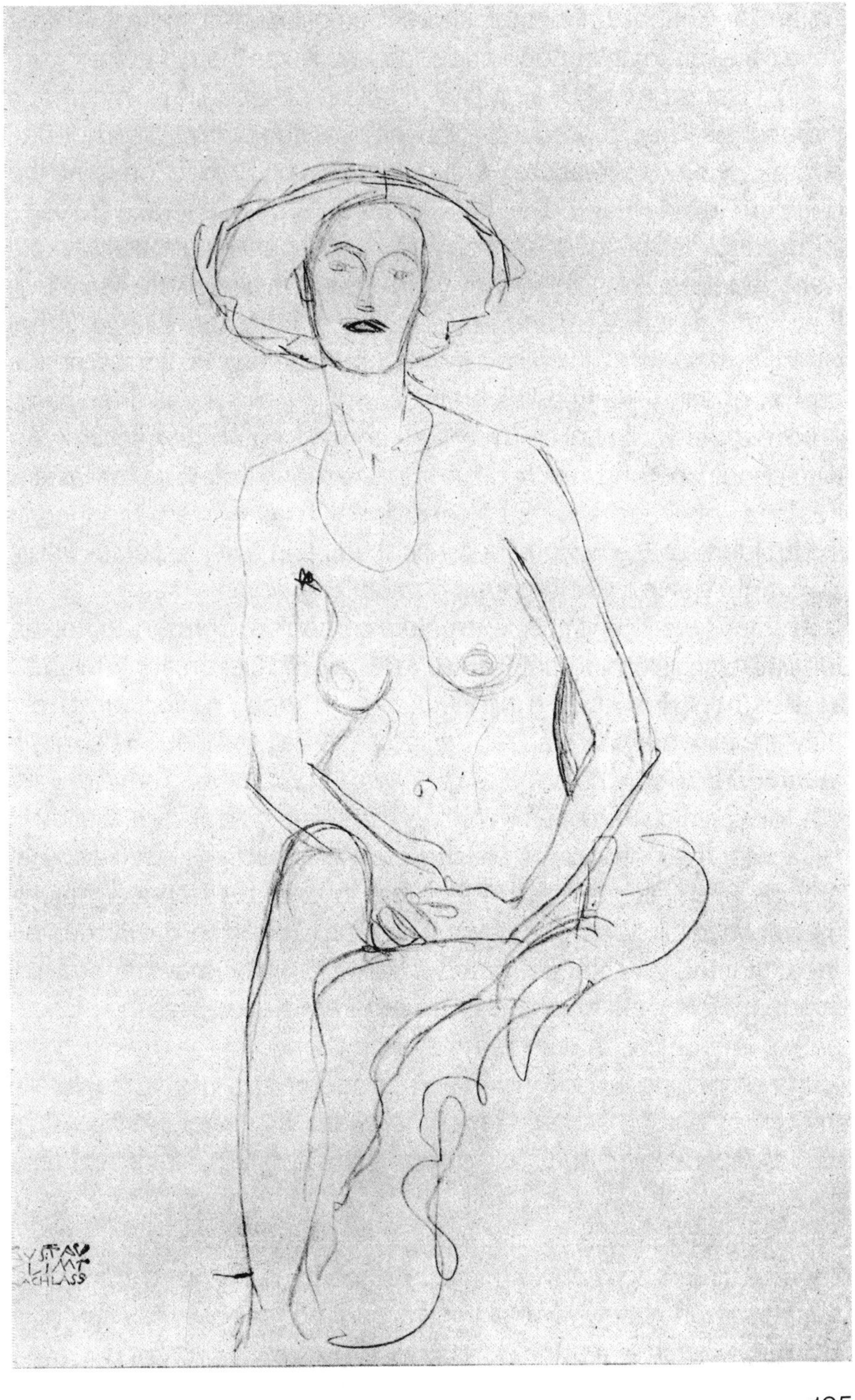

Seated female figure, front view, 1908
Pencil, 56.5 × 37.2 cm

so that they might further their knowledge of arts and crafts, and their travels took them to London and Glasgow. It was there that they were finally inspired by what they saw to set up co-operative workshops themselves. The necessary capital was provided by Fritz Waerndorfer, and he was made treasurer, while Hoffmann and Moser became the directors. In May they moved into three rooms, of which two were used for production, the third as office. A silversmith and two metalworkers were engaged. By October they were already in a position to expand; they moved into spacious premises, with workrooms for different types of metalwork, for bookbinding and leatherwork, for carpentry and lacquering. Hoffmann's architect's office and a buildings office adjoined the workshops. They were concerned about healthy working conditions, and their sanitary fittings, among them English lavatories and washrooms, were so sensational that they were reported in the art journals. Each workshop was fitted up in a distinct colour of its own, right down to order forms and delivery notes.

The first reactions to this new venture came from Germany, where in 1904 the Darmstadt journal 'Deutsche Kunst und Dekoration' included a lavish article introducing the Vienna Workshops. The first public display of their work took place in Berlin that same year. In 1905 people in Vienna were given the opportunity to visit the Workshops as part of the 'Art Tours' which had been started by a philanthropical organisation in 1902 with the purpose of making private collections accessible to anyone who was interested. Soon these tours were extended to include public institutions. The interest aroused seems to have been so great that the Workshops issued a leaflet in which they announced their principles and objectives. This programme exposes the inescapable contradictions of the whole undertaking.

In the opening section the authors condemned mass production in their time: "A flood of boundless proportions is threatening the whole world, caused by shoddy mass production and the unthinking imitation of old styles in arts and crafts. We have lost touch with the culture of our forefathers, and are buffeted backwards and forwards by a thousand desires and considerations. As machines replace hands, so businessmen replace craftsmen. It would be madness to attempt to swim against this current."[77]

Then they justified their attempt: "Nonetheless, we have founded our workshops, which are to be for us the still point, the home territory, amidst the cheerful sounds of the craftsmen at work – extending a welcome to all who declare themselves followers of Ruskin and Morris. We appeal to all those to whom culture in this sense seems valuable, and hope that unavoidable errors will not deter our friends from supporting our aims." They spoke of the "intimate contact between public, designer and craftsman", and in the spirit of this co-operation they proposed to have the signatures of designer and craftsmen on all the objects they made, an intention which had effect only for a short time.

Their products were above all to be purpose-designed and useful, which was more important than decorative appearance. In the early days especially, Moser and Hoffmann designed clear forms with no unnecessary embellishment. Pure geometrical shapes, above all the square, and the frequent use of black and white rather than other colours, were characteristic of their work, and it was in this style, influenced by Mackintosh, that they decorated and furnished the Flöge salon.

They were more interested in good design than in costly materials. They favoured semi-precious stones because of their vivid colours. Of metals they wrote: "We love silver and gold because each has a shine and lustre peculiar to it; in our opinion copper is just as valuable to the artist as precious metals... The idea, and the value of creative work must once again be recognised and appreciated. The craftsman's products must be measured according to the same criteria as the painter's picture and the sculptor's statue." The increased importance attached to arts and crafts, then as now, was explicitly stated, and the intention was that they should be accorded the same importance as fine art, but this was never actually to be achieved. There was a further far-reaching illusion: "We cannot compete with cheapness, and we do not wish to; cheapness is attained at the expense of the worker, and we consider it our most pressing obligation to grant the worker joy in creation, and to ensure that he leads a life worthy of mankind. All this can only be achieved one step at a time."

Such intentions were laudable, but naïve. They could only apply to the few workers in the workshops, and they increased the price of the products. No worker would ever have made his purchases in the Vienna Workshops, even supposing that one or other of the pieces might have appealed to him.

After lengthy discussions of the processes of bookbinding and carpentry, in which they claimed that superior quality justified the high price of the products, they turned to the idea of life within a total work of art, just as William Morris had done: "It cannot be enough for us to purchase pictures, no matter how splendid they may be. The spirit of our time must be reflected simply but beautifully in the appearance of our towns, our houses, our rooms, our cupboards, our utensils, our clothes and our ornaments, in the words we use and in our feelings: otherwise we fall far short of our forefathers, and our weakness cannot be disguised by lies."

These ideas, typical of Jugendstil artists and practitioners all over Europe, could only be put into practice by a small section of society because of financial constraints. Moreover, such claims presupposed the superiority of the artist over life, as was demonstrated by the anecdotal account of the need for a fashion department in 1911: women in their accustomed clothes simply did not fit in the interiors created by the Workshops, with the result that clothes had to be designed which were in keeping with these surroundings. Such reports, in which there was some truth – the Stoclets wore clothes from the Vienna Workshops in their palais – might be good-natured, but this was not always the case. There were some scathing critics, and Adolf Loos wrote in 1900: "The architect was so full of the best intentions that he had thought of absolutely everything in advance ... The rooms were comfortable, but very hard work, especially for the brain. So the architect watched over their life in the first few weeks, to make sure that no mistake was made ..."[78]

More than forty years later, in 1946, the art critic Karl Scheffler wrote: "... a casually dressed individual could disturb the effect of an interior of this sort. Anyone living in one of these houses needed instructions for use."[79]

These criticisms reveal the inherent problems in the concept of life as a total work of art. Man becomes the slave of his environment, and

63 Tree of Life, centre,
193 × 102 cm

64 Tree of Life, right, with bush,
194 × 118 cm

(Working drawings for Stoclet Frieze; see p. 188)

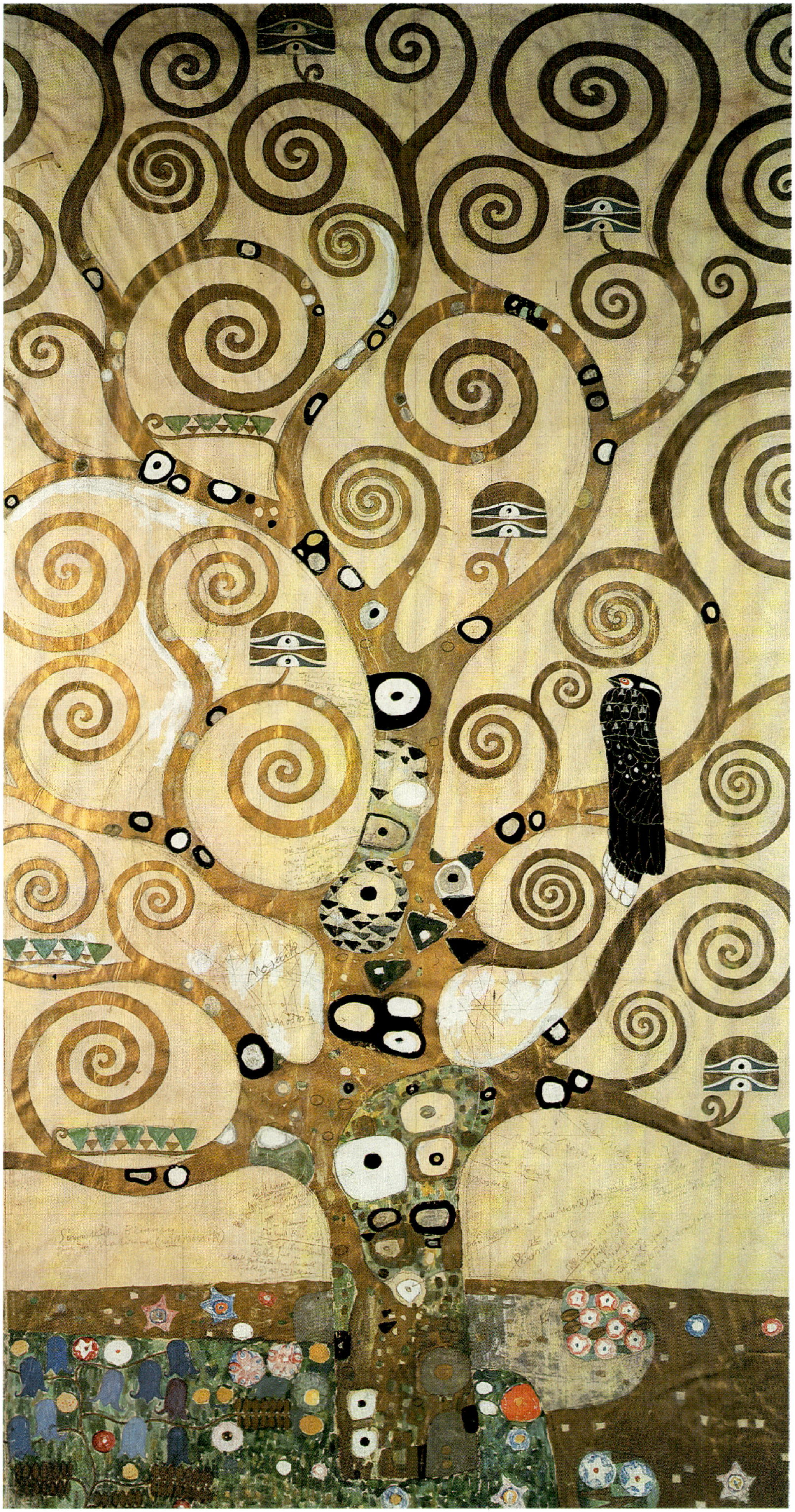

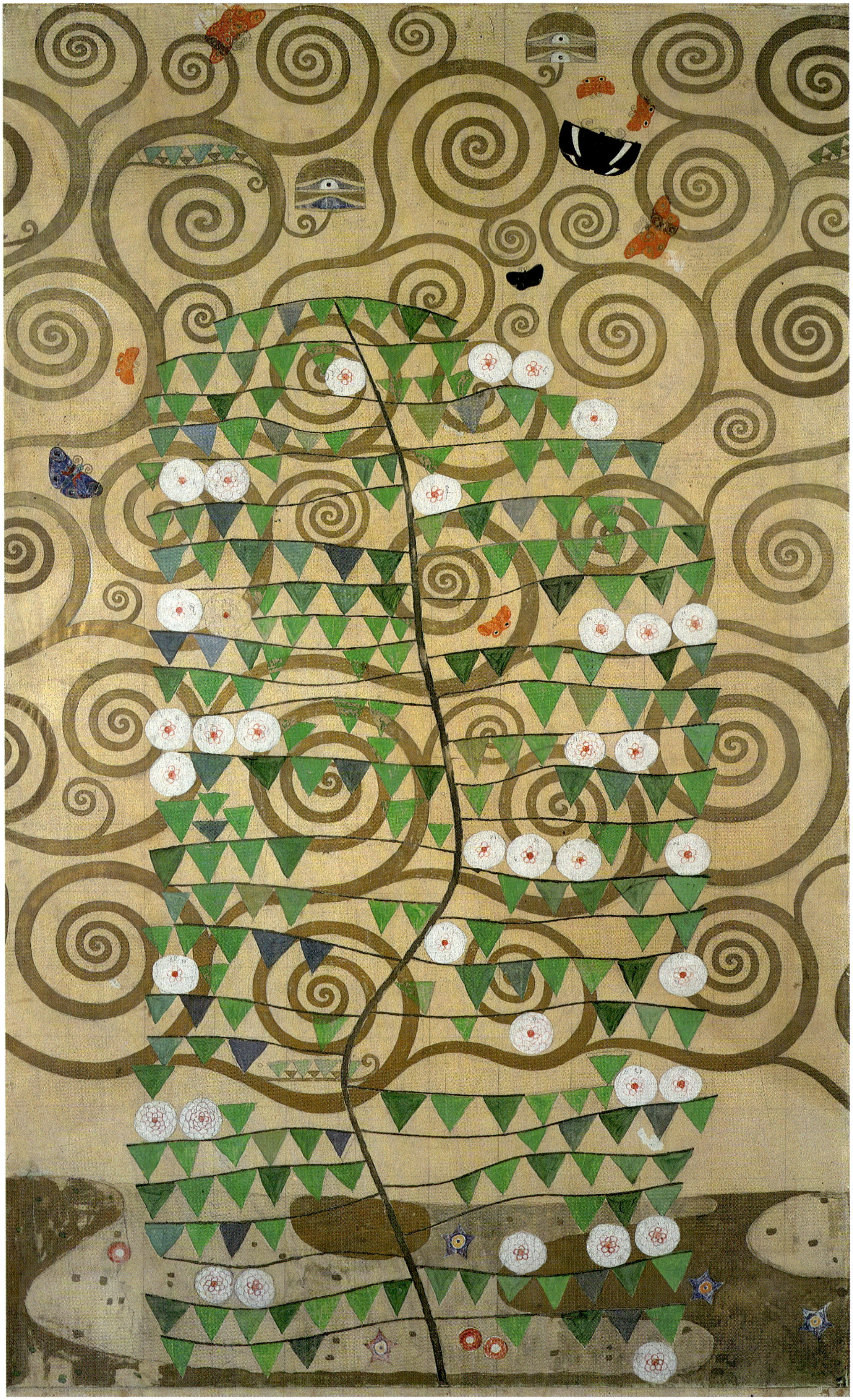

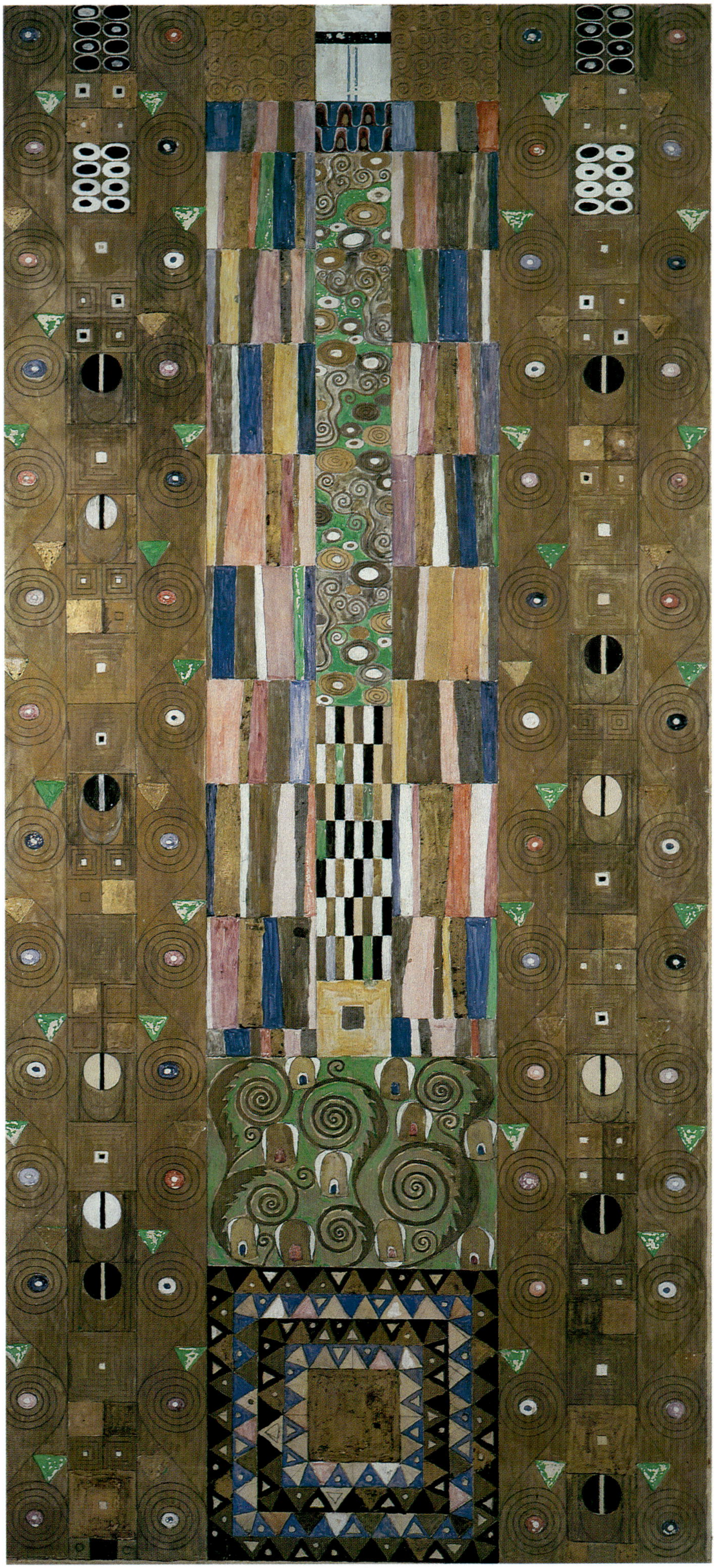

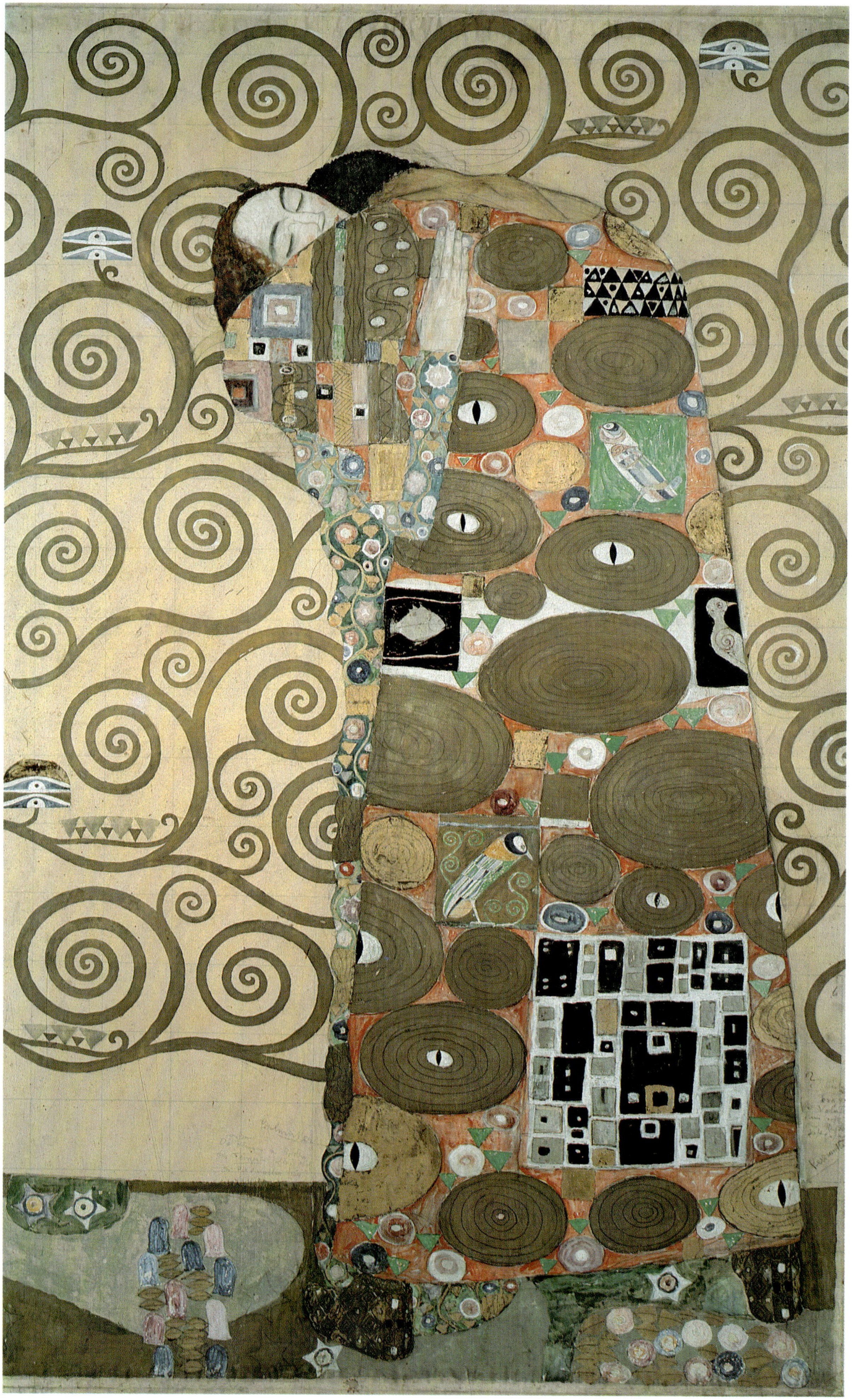

must adapt himself to suit it. Individuality, often possible only to a very limited degree, and only in one's own home, must be forgone.

The conclusion of the Workshop programme showed defective self-knowledge: "We do not pursue a will-o'-the-wisp. We stand with both feet on the ground, and ask only for work."

In reality the artists were not capable of making proper calculations; they did not have the necessary business ability. The estimates provided for their customers often fell far short of the actual costs. To begin with they received their big contracts largely from friends. In spite of their later successes, with branches operating in Zurich, Berlin and New York as well as in Vienna, they needed regular injections of capital in order to keep the business going.

In 1907 one of the directors, Koloman Moser, left the Workshops. Apart from administrative difficulties, the main reason for his departure was that his wealthy wife had once more been asked to put money into the firm. After he had gone the style of the Workshops changed; severe geometrical shape and functional ornament gradually gave way to sweeping curves with decorative adjuncts. Since Hoffmann on his own was not strong enough to insist on his wishes being followed, the style was less uniform, or, to put it in a positive fashion, more varied than in the early years.

By 1914 Fritz Waerndorfer's fortune had been entirely used up, and he gave in to family pressure, left the Workshops and emigrated to America where he became a farmer. His correspondence shows that in spite of his enormous losses he was still attached to the Workshops and deeply regretted his departure.

In an attempt to escape from the pecuniary difficulties, the Workshops became a limited company, in which the most important customers became shareholders, but this led to financial complications which ended in 1932 in liquidation. The largest shareholder, the industrialist Otto Primavesi, lost his entire fortune in this process.

Although the Vienna Workshops were not a viable company from a financial point of view, they exerted a significant influence on the development and status of arts and crafts. Their effect on twentieth century design can still be felt, and our perception of style owes a great deal to ideas which were formulated at the beginning of this century.

65 Narrow wall, 197 × 91 cm

66 Fulfilment, 194 × 120 cm

(Working drawings for Stoclet Frieze; see p. 188)

Commissions and challenges

As has already been mentioned, the large commissions came in the early days almost entirely from friends and acquaintances. In 1903 Josef Hoffmann and Koloman Moser designed and furnished the Salon Flöge. Gustav Klimt will have made the introductions. In 1904 they were commissioned by Margarethe Stonborough-Wittgenstein to decorate her apartment in Berlin. Her father, Karl Wittgenstein (1847–1913), was one of Vienna's major industrialists, and he was one of those most involved in building the Secession House. In 1905 he commissioned Klimt to paint a portrait of his daughter (see p. 239ff). In the same year the Vienna Workshops altered and refurbished his hunting-lodge in Lower Austria.

There were more such contacts and connections. The cousin of the journalist Berta Zuckerkandl, who outspokenly championed Gustav Klimt, the Secession and the Vienna Workshops in the Vienna 'Allgemeine Zeitung', turned to Hoffmann when he wanted to have a sanatorium built. The Purkersdorf Sanatorium was built in 1904–1905 with the collaboration of the various artists and craftsmen. Hoffmann designed a flat cuboid building. The only ornament on the façade was a narrow strip of blue and white tiles. The clinic rooms were equipped with the newest inventions in medical technology and hygiene, while the day-rooms – reading-room, games room, writing-room, lounges and dining-room – were decorated and furnished with the elegance appropriate to the moneyed classes who were likely to use them.

In 1905 the Workshops won their largest contract of all: the building, decorating and furnishing of a palais in Brussels for the industrialist Adolphe Stoclet. This building is still intact, and is of particular interest because of the mosaic frieze which Klimt designed for it (see p. 218ff). For the Workshops this contract meant that they felt they could really expand. They realised their dream of a total work of art with the 'Cabaret Fledermaus' in 1907, a project with which they hoped to extend their sphere to include music and drama.

The cabaret bar was adorned with brightly coloured tiles put together in a gaudy pattern. The actual theatre, with only 300 seats and therefore too small to be viable financially, was decorated in restrained

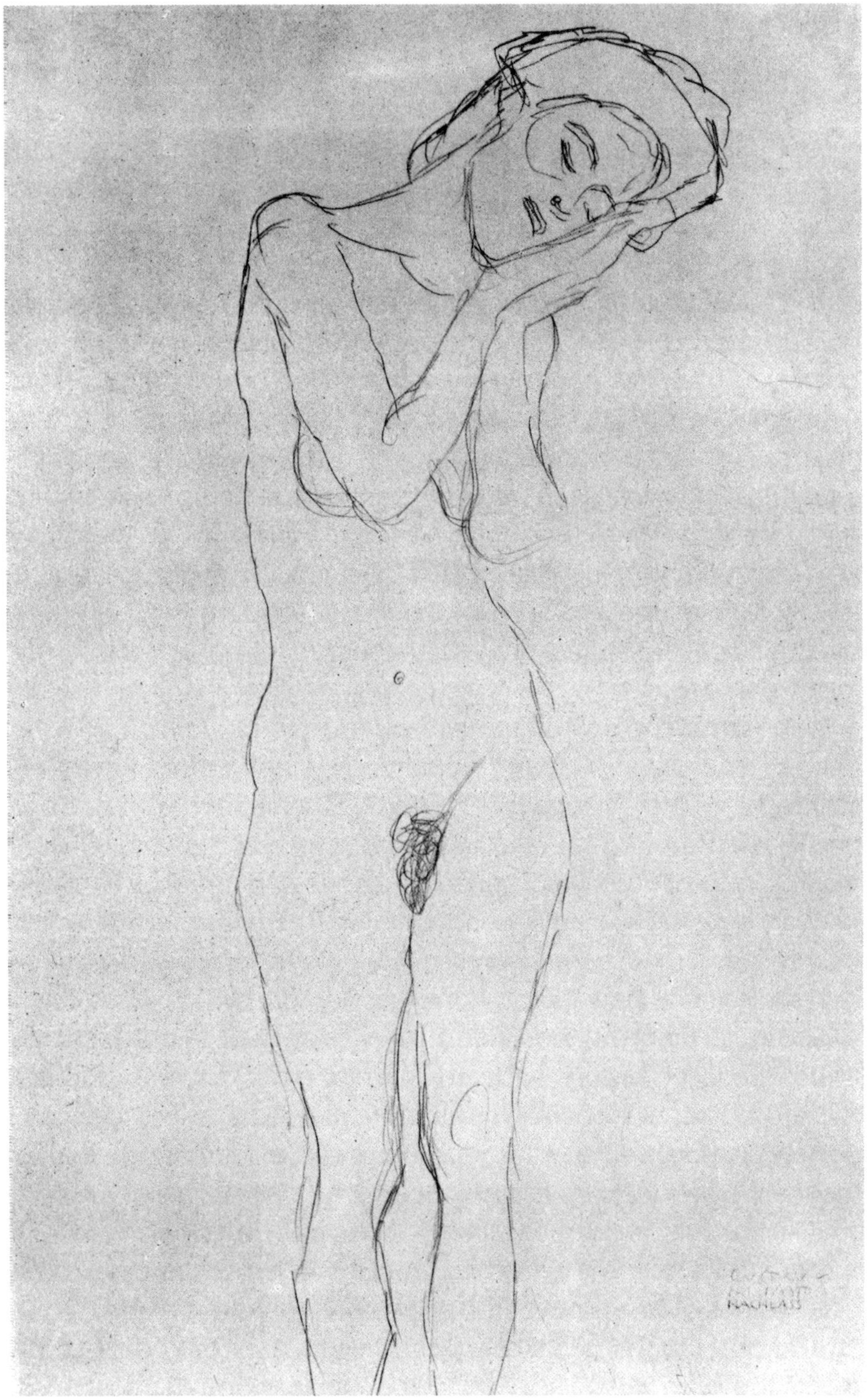

Girl, front view, hands against her cheek, 1910
Pencil, 55.9 × 36.2 cm

grey and white tones. Ludwig Hevesi described the rooms enthusiastically: "A new cabaret in Vienna... But an artistic cabaret. Not a low haunt, ... rather an artistically responsible establishment favoured by muses properly dressed in the most recent fashions from nowhere, where a cultivated man need not feel bored, or may at least feel bored in his own preferred fashion... The two main rooms are downstairs: bar and theatre...

The bar is a room unlike any other that I have ever seen, an original masterpiece of the decorative imagination. He who is a wallpaperer at heart would be driven to contemplate suicide. The walls are covered right up to the top with unique mosaics, colourful as colour itself, fantastic as fantasy, an irregular pattern which looks as if large and small squares of majolica, each one a different colour, had come together haphazardly... There are more than seven thousand of these tiny tiles, and in every imaginable shade of colour, applied with uninhibited artistry, to take full effect. And one thousand of these little squares are decorated: with pictures, drawings, vignettes, symbols, caricatures, jokes, portraits..."[80]

Viennese authors who had already spoken out in favour of the Secession wrote for Cabaret Fledermaus; among them were Hermann Bahr, Peter Altenberg (1859–1919), Egon Friedell (1878–1938) and Roda Roda (1872–1945). Oskar Kokoschka (1886–1980) was working at the time for the Vienna Workshops, and was allowed to display his series of 'Indian Legend' pictures. The programmes for the cabaret performances were printed in the Workshops, and postcards with motifs from the various shows were produced.

Soon after the first introduction of the postcard as a cheaper alternative to the letter, picture postcards and art cards became popular, leading to a regular boom in cards in the nineties. The first collectors' society was followed shortly by the first specialist journal in 1895. The Vienna Workshops began to produce cards relatively late, in 1907. By 1932 there had been more than a thousand cards designed with motifs drawn from the art exhibition of 1908, the Emperor's jubilee celebrations of the same year, the Cabaret Fledermaus or the Vienna Workshops' branches in other cities. After the addition of the fashion workshop there were also many cards with fashions and costumes.

Gustav Klimt sent many of these cards to Emilie Flöge when she was on her travels.

Graphic work of a utilitarian sort was also undertaken. The Workshops printed invitations, announcements, advertisements, monograms, personal note-paper and 'Ex Libris' labels. Firms could order their own stationery. The Flöge trademark was designed by Klimt, and reproduced by the Workshops.

From 1906 the programme was extended to include menus, place-cards and wine-labels. This new line was prompted by an exhibition of table-ware. In the catalogue it was said that "the dining-table offers one of the many daily opportunities for artistic involvement. It is too important a matter to be left to serving-maid or butler."[81]

There were tables laid for every purpose, from wedding feast to nursery. Koloman Moser designed special baking tins for the exhibition, and had cakes baked in them for display. In the press there appeared the customary praises, written for instance by Hevesi and Zuckerkandl, but there were satirical comments as well: "Our little women will soon have to decide whether they are going to order their biscuits from the Galerie Miethke, from the Secession or from the Artists' House . . . In order to carve meat in the new style it is necessary to have ruler and compasses; the dumplings are turned on the wheel and the only pure doughnuts are the poppy-seed ones in the new improved style of Kolo Moser . . . Here madness is espoused to geometry."[82]

It is the same criticism as was expressed in connection with the interiors. The demand that daily life should be viewed as a total work of art made the artist into a dictator, necessitated 'instructions' for the artist's customer, and excluded the majority of the population. It is doubtful whether the Vienna Workshops collaborators ever became fully aware of this, but their catalogue for the art exhibition of 1908 was less specific and no longer referred to serving-maids and butlers.

The Art Exhibition of 1908

There was a pageant in the summer of 1908 in honour of the emperor, as there had been in 1879. The earlier pageant had celebrated the emperor's silver wedding, whereas this one was in honour of the sixtieth anniversary of Franz Joseph's accession. There was no histrionic artist such as Hans Makart to take charge of the pageant this time, although artists, among them Oskar Kokoschka, were drawn into the preparations. The 1908 pageant was to be a display of the peoples and folklore of the empire, which provided little scope for the city guilds or the artists, so that they decided to pay homage in a different, more lasting way.

On a site reserved for the construction of a new concert house designed by the firm of architects Fellner and Helmer, they organised with some assistance from the state the largest exhibition that had ever taken place in Vienna. The organisers were those artists who had left the Secession in 1905. Gustav Klimt was appointed president of the committee. The exhibition was devoted to Austrian art in all its different manifestations. In 1909 the spectacle was again staged, but this time with foreign works of art. This was the last time that Gustav Klimt presented an exhibition to the public.

Josef Hoffmann was again responsible for the design. He built several pavilions, with a total of fifty-four rooms, set between terraces, courtyards and gardens. A coffee house and a summer theatre completed the facilities. Above the entrance could be read the familiar slogan "To each age its art, to art its freedom", which had been removed from the Secession House after the departure of Klimt and his group. Ludwig Hevesi, with whom the slogan had originated, made chaffing remarks: "Hm! That looks so familiar. Have I read it somewhere before? Oh yes, it used to stand large and clear at the Secession House, over the door. All the musing muses of the vegetable market knew it off by heart... then they modernised the Secession by becoming rather less modern, and pulled down any disturbing inscriptions... and here is this honest old war-cry, resurrected in this far more suitable place..."[83]

Gustav Klimt, never one to waste words, introduced the ideas and aims of the artists at the opening of the exhibition in a brief speech which was printed in the catalogue. He emphasised that he and his group had had no place to exhibit their work for four years, and then spoke of the function of this exhibition: "As is well known, we do not see the exhibition as the ideal way of establishing contact between artist and public; we would far rather achieve this by fulfilling major public commissions. But as long as officialdom is preoccupied with economics and politics, the exhibition is the only path open to us, and we must be most grateful for all the public and private assistance which has made it possible on this occasion for us to show that during all the years when we could not exhibit we were not idle, but . . . worked all the harder, with greater intensity, to develop our ideas."[84]

He pointed out that they were not a society or a brotherhood, but had simply come together informally "united by the conviction that no area of human endeavour is too small and insignifacant to offer scope to art, that, as William Morris said, the humblest object perfectly made contributes to the beauty of this earth, and that the progress of civilisation is grounded in the permeation of the whole of life with artistic purpose."

The art exhibition, he said, did not want to present "final goals attained in an artist's life", but to document "the present state of civilisation in our empire." Klimt also wanted a new definition of 'the artist': "We understand this to mean not only the one who creates, but also the one who is capable of experiencing what has been created and who can appreciate it. For us 'the artists' are the community of those who create and those who enjoy. And that this community really exists, and is thriving and strong in youth and vigour, because of its purity of heart and mind, is shown by the fact that this house could be built and this exhibition opened in it."

At this point Klimt was repeating the general statement that the Vienna Workshops had incorporated in their programme of 1905 – a demonstration of his closeness to its initiators. The last paragraph is particularly interesting because in it Klimt uses three key phrases – 'those who create', 'those who enjoy' and 'youth' – which had been employed in the programme of a young group of architects in Dresden two years earlier. These five young men had formed themselves in 1905 into the 'Brücke', and in 1906 they published the manifesto which was destined to become famous: "Believing in progress, in a new generation of those who create and of those who enjoy, we summon youth. And, as youth, holding the future in our arms, we intend to liberate ourselves from the old established forces. Anyone who transmits directly and truly the creative force that is in him, is one of us."[85]

Klimt belonged to an earlier generation and to a different school, one which the young Expressionists had determined to overcome, and there is no evidence that he was familiar with the manifesto as these artists were still relatively unknown. This makes the parallel all the more striking.

The exhibition offered a comprehensive display of all the different branches of the art of style. There was painting, where Gustav Klimt was predominant with a whole room devoted to his pictures, and then architecture, sculpture and graphics – arts practised and recognised for centuries. But there were also special sections for posters, graveyard art, ecclesiastical art, theatre art, arts and crafts and fashion. There were even two rooms showing children's toys and children's play. It was the first opportunity for the Viennese art teacher Franz Cizek (1865–1946) to introduce his far-reaching principles of art education to the public; they are still relevant today.

Cizek was a pioneer. His basic tenet was that every child possessed artistic abilities which could find expression if it was not forced into a mould. In his school, which became an extension of the School of Arts and Crafts in 1903, the teacher had to keep a low profile, to avoid being perceived by the children as a teacher. With the materials at their disposal the children exercised their innate creativity. Sometimes subjects from daily life were suggested, but the children decided how to treat them. This form of art education was new. Cizek's method rapidly spread all over the western world, and it also prompted many artists to think about children's art and to profit from these reflections. Paul Klee (1879–1940) is a famous example of this.

The Vienna Workshops had a room of their own at the exhibition, and a show house with loggia, hall and five rooms was built by Hoffmann and decorated and furnished by the Workshops. Even the gar-

67/68 Adele Bloch-Bauer I, 1907
Oil on canvas, 138 × 138 cm
Austrian Gallery, Vienna

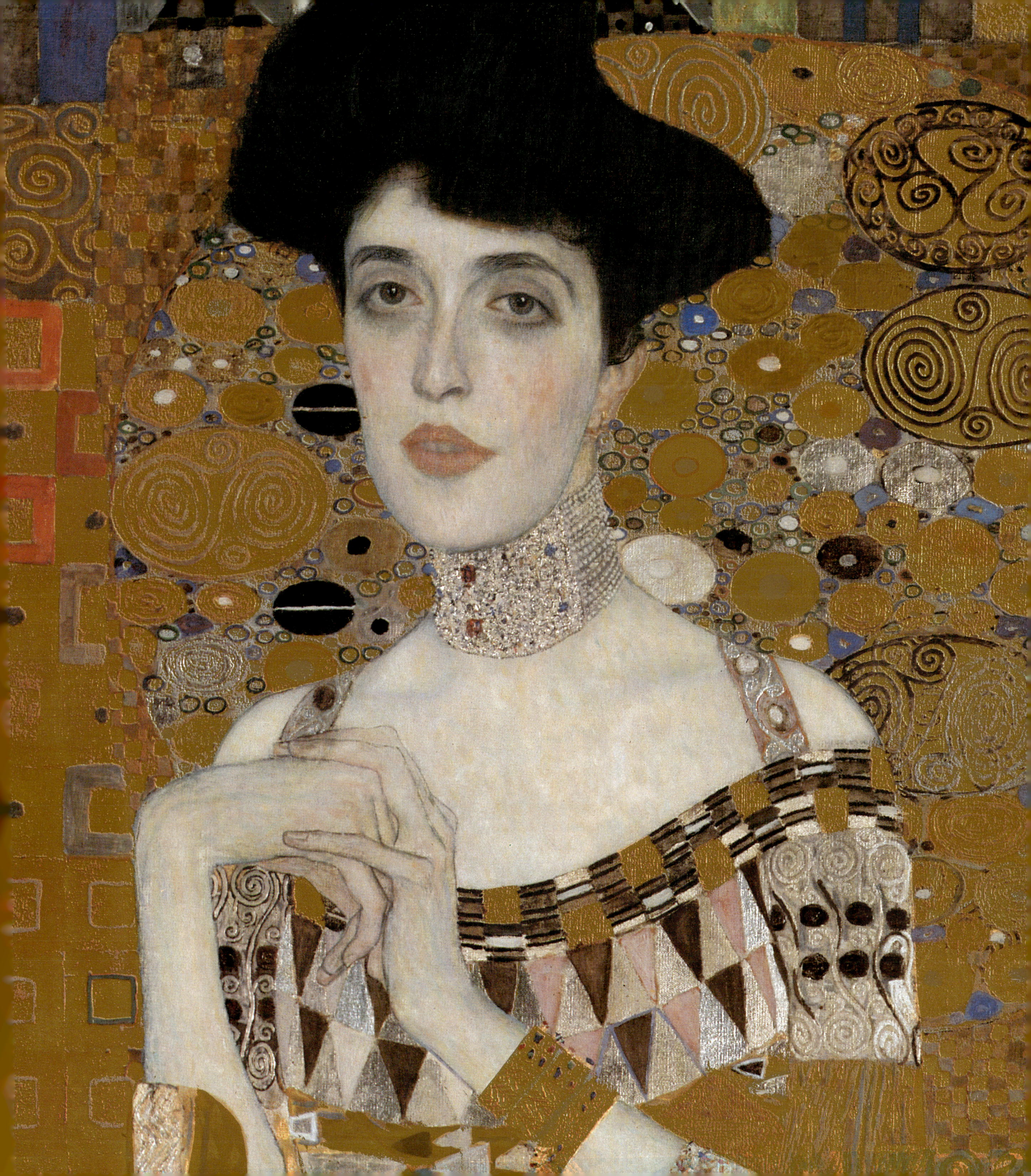

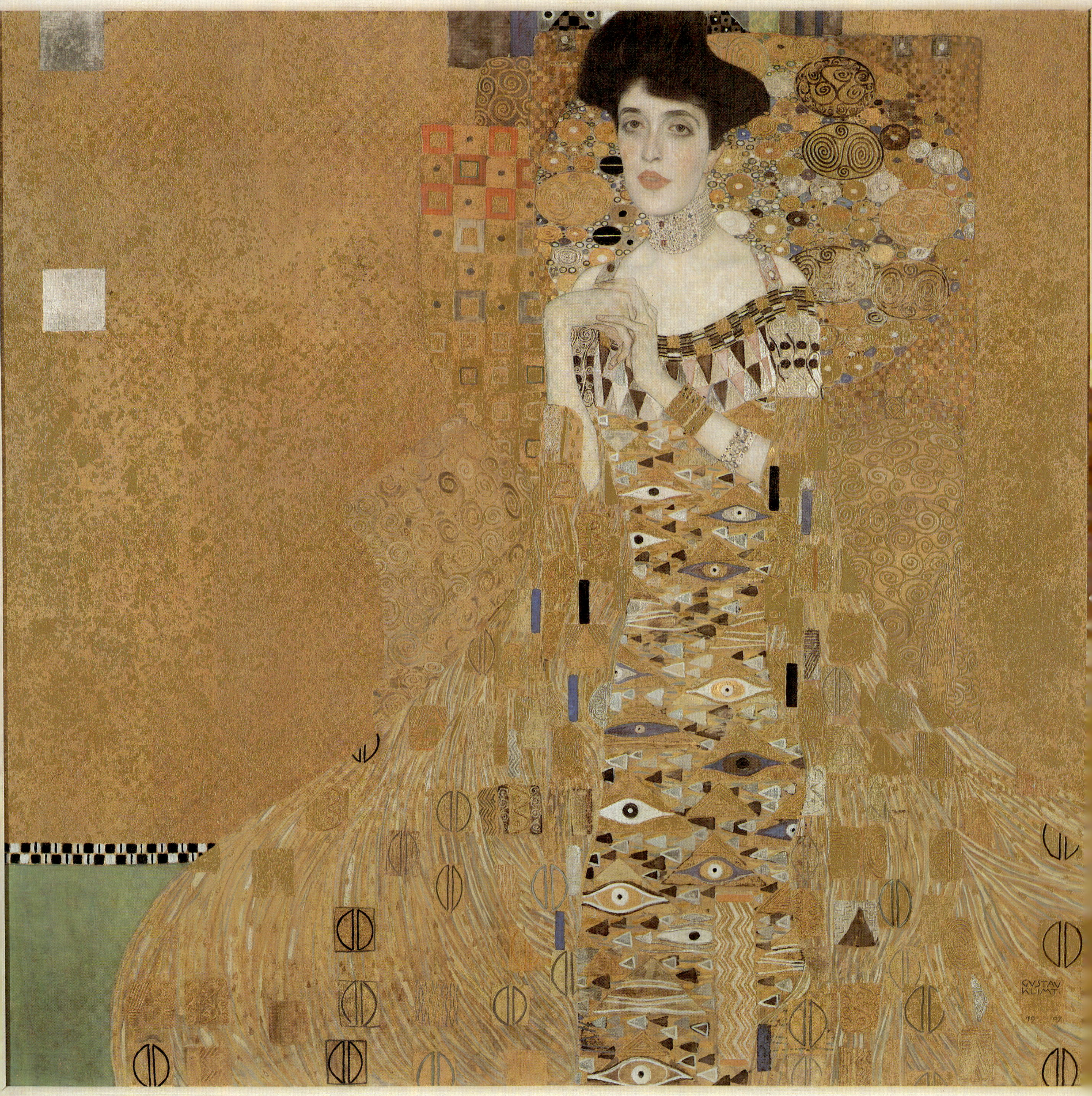
GVSTAV
KLIMT

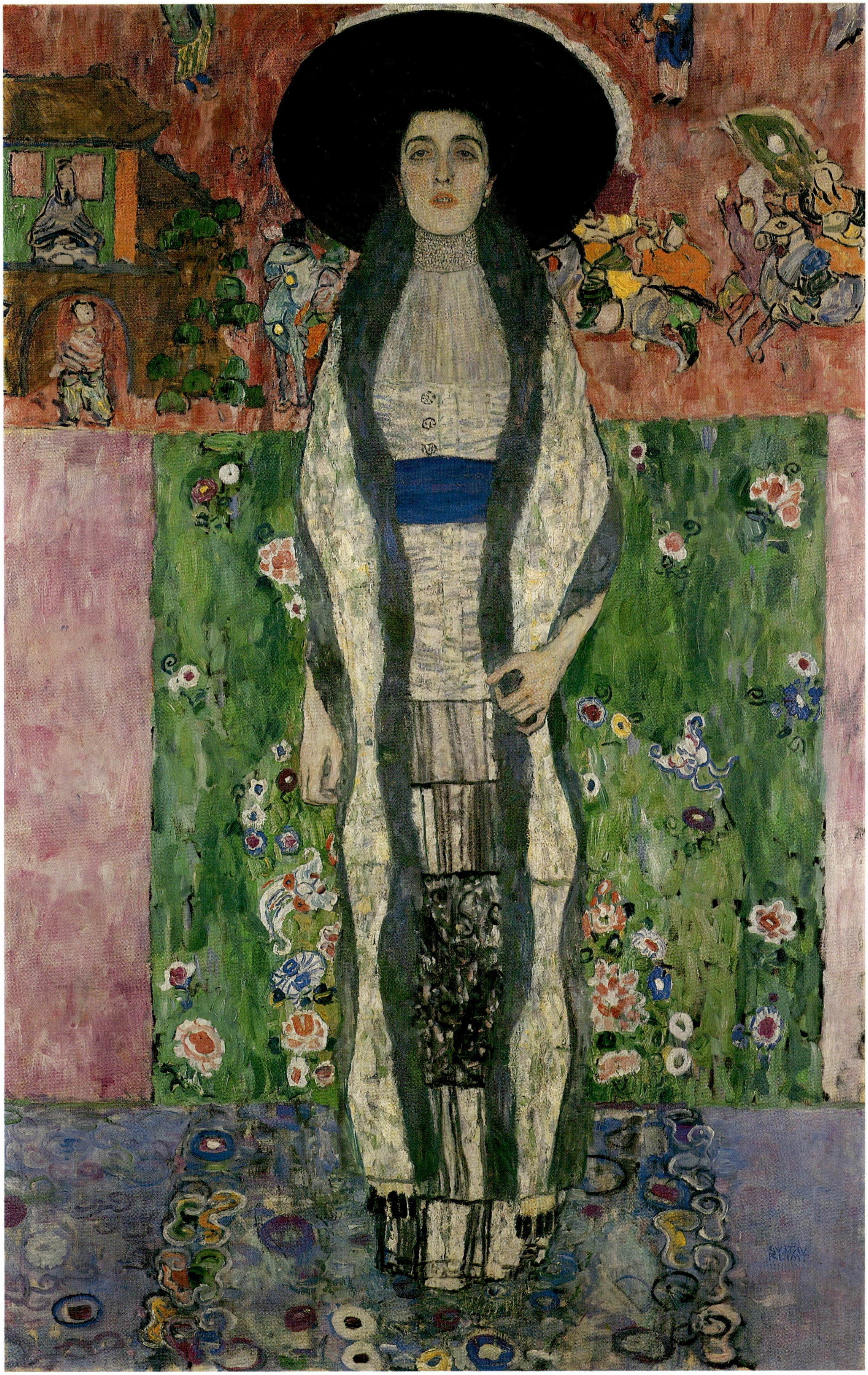
GVSTAV
KLIMT

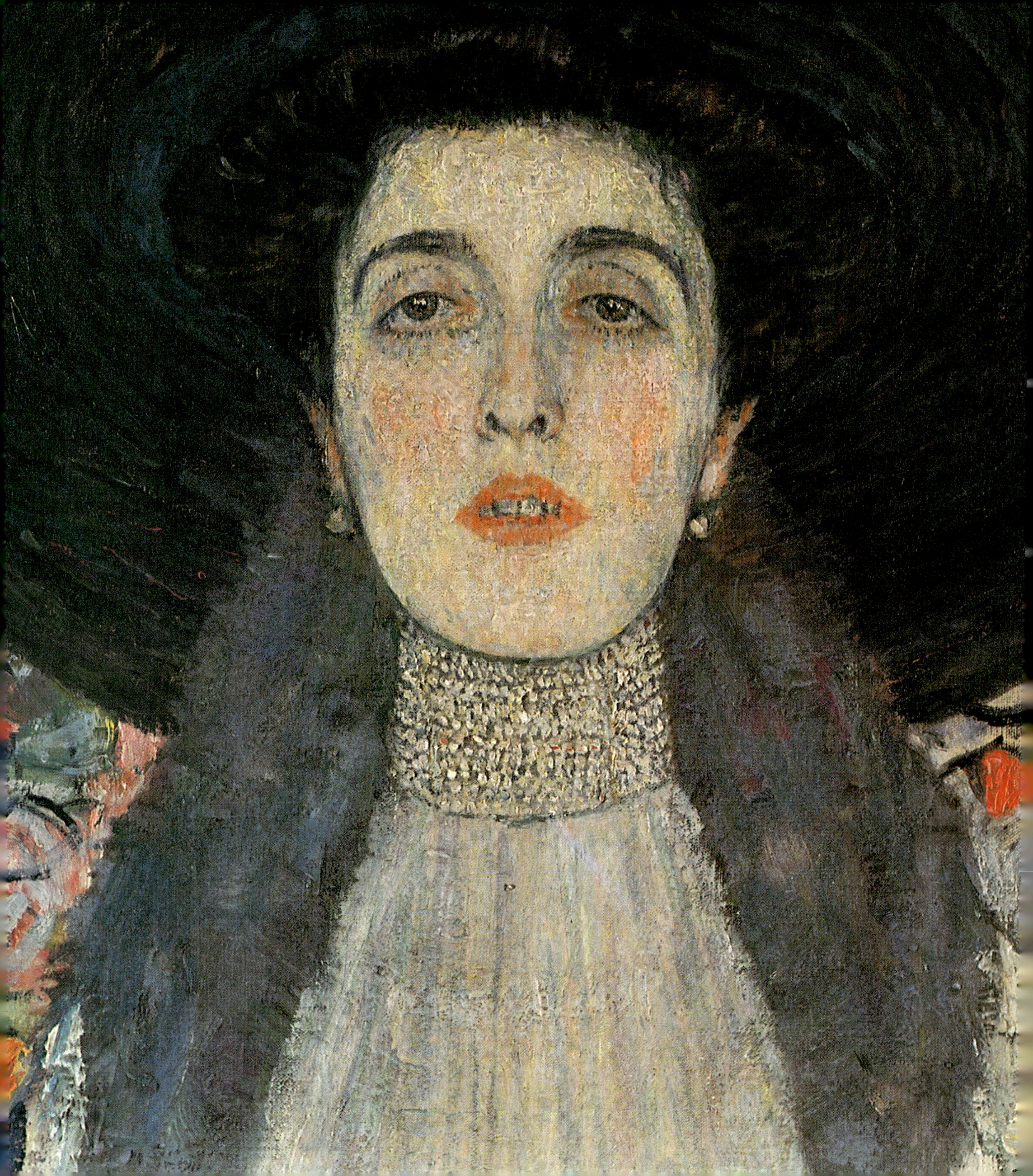

den was part of the display; in the garden theatre there were regular performances during the two months of the exhibition. Here, too, the idea of the total work of art prevailed.

The central focus of the exhibition was room 22, designed by Koloman Moser, in which sixteen paintings by Gustav Klimt were on display. In the adjoining room were some of his pencil drawings. Apart from Klimt's famous 'The Kiss', exhibited here for the first time, he showed his best-known portraits, a few landscape paintings, the 'Three Ages', 'Danaë' and the two versions of 'Water Serpents'.

Peter Altenberg described this room as the 'Gustav Klimt cathedral of modern art' and bestowed upon the individual pictures the ultimate accolade: "These portraits of women embody the most tender romanticism of nature. They are as poets rapturously dream of them – gentle, delicate beings, who never fade, yet never find salvation! Their hands are the expression of a charming spirit, childishly light, yet gracious and kind! All of them are beyond the pull of lumpish earth, however they may be in the reality of day and hour. All of them are princesses for better, gentler worlds... Are you an upright, tender friend of nature? Then allow your eyes to feast on these pictures: country gardens, beech woods, roses, sunflowers, poppies flowering! The landscape is treated as the women are, elevated, exalted, romantic! This is right, this is sacred, visible even to the sceptics with their faded joyless eyes! Gustav Klimt, a mysterious blend of primeval peasant and historical Romantic, praise to you!"[86]

'The Kiss' was bought directly from the exhibition by the Modern Gallery. By chance the Vienna Workshops also came to be represented in the museum: responsibility for the Museum of Art and Industry, and for the various schools and colleges of arts and crafts attached to it, was transferred from the Ministry of Education to the Ministry of Public Works. In spite of the reservations of the museum director, the minister insisted on the purchase of various items from the exhibition, in particular of products of the Workshops. Although the art exhibition was a success for Klimt, Moser and Hoffmann, those who were now 'the young' caused a great stir. Thanks largely to Klimt's support, Kokoschka and, in 1909, also Egon Schiele were able to show their work, which met with violent criticism, even from Ludwig Hevesi.

69/70 Adele Bloch-Bauer II, 1912
Oil on canvas, 190 × 120 cm
Austrian Gallery, Vienna

The art exhibition of 1909 included contemporary art from abroad and Klimt's most recent work, as well as the works by Kokoschka and Schiele. At the end of the summer the pavilions were dismantled and work on the concert house began. The exhibition offered the public the last opportunity to see the so-called 'Klimt group' in action. Their works were never again displayed together, and in 1909 there came another milestone: Klimt's 'golden period' came to an end; he turned aside from Vienna Jugendstil and his style became more decorative-expressionistic. Yet the members of the Klimt group continued to work closely together. Adolphe Stoclet gave them a further opportunity to realise their notion of the total work of art.

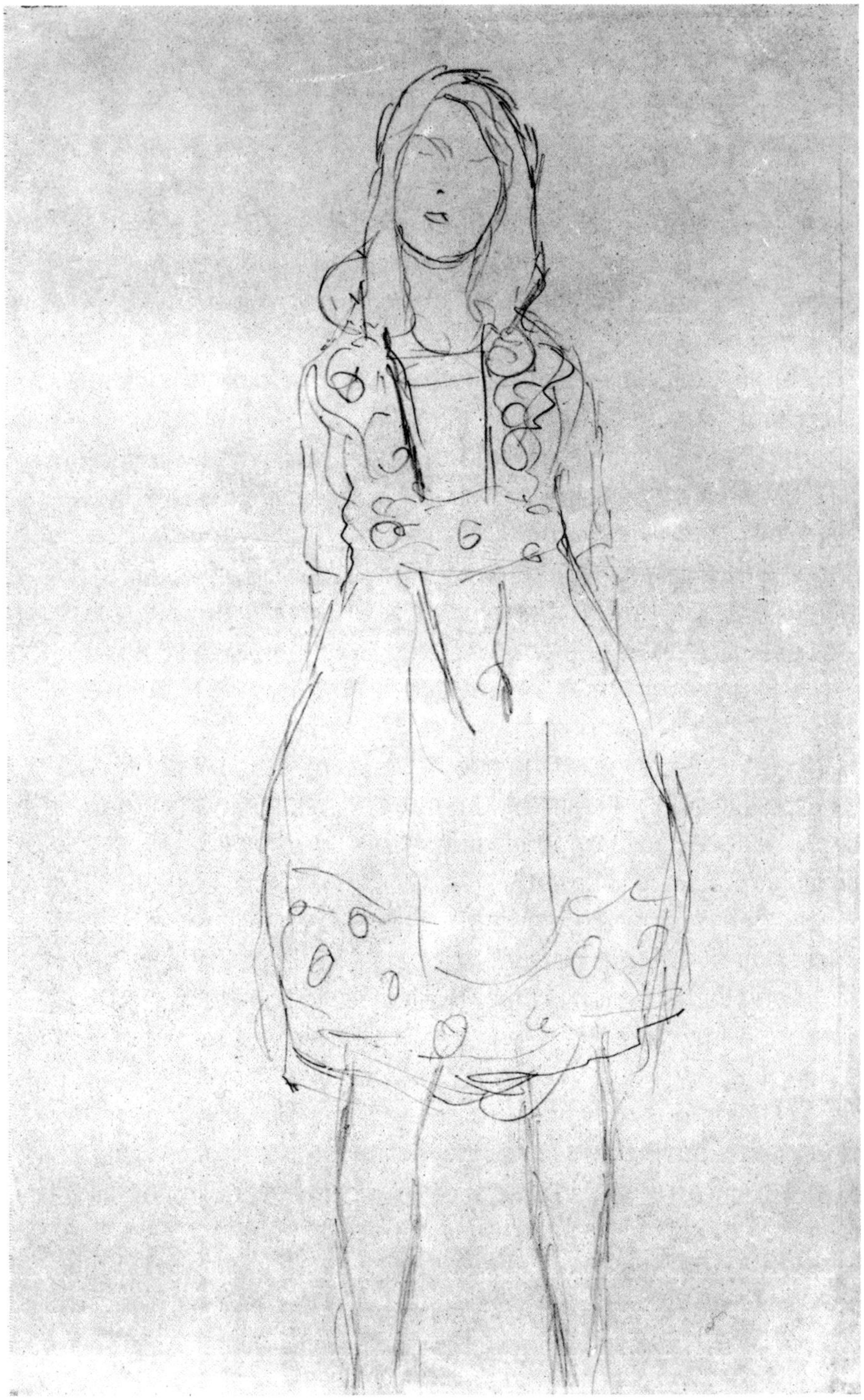

Mäda Primavesi, 1912/13
Pencil, 56.1 × 36.8 cm

The Palais Stoclet and Gustav Klimt's Frieze

The magnificent Palais Stoclet is the only house still standing that was designed, decorated and furnished by Josef Hoffmann and the Vienna Workshops. It can be designated the 'permanent exhibition of the Vienna Workshops'. Paradoxically it is in Brussels and not in Vienna that the visible effects of the notion of life as a total work of art, propagated by Gustav Klimt and the artists with whom he worked, can still be seen today.

In 1904 Adolphe Stoclet, the son of a Brussels manufacturer, was living with his wife Suzanne in Vienna. He was enthralled by the villas built by Josef Hoffmann, and he became acquainted with the occupant of one of them, Carl Moll, with a view to getting to know the architect. Moll put Stoclet in touch with Hoffmann, and Stoclet had the idea of building a villa in Vienna himself. At this point, however, Stoclet's father died, and the son had to return to Brussels in order to take over the family business; he commissioned Hoffmann to build a palais for him in Brussels. It was to be provided with every luxury; the price was not a subject for discussion.

Stoclet never revealed the cost of the palais, and he evidently took care to destroy all relevant documents. The materials alone must have cost a fortune, quite apart from the work, which was carried out by artists as well as workmen.

The contract required more collaborators than usual, as Berta Zuckerkandl could report in October 1905. First she listed Gustav Klimt, and then went on to say: "The immediate reason for the expansion of the firm is a contract which attests the high reputation abroad of modern Viennese art. A Brussels magnate has commissioned Professor Hoffmann to build him a private palais in that city, and has entrusted the decorating and furnishing entirely to the Vienna Workshops. Klimt is to give free rein to his decorative imagination. The other artists will take care of the remaining interior down to the very last detail."[87]

It took eight years for the building to be completed. The severity of the smooth marble façade was relieved by gold cornices, the roof was finished with copper. To the east of the living area is a tower crowned with four monumental figures in copper. To the right of the tower, in a one-storey extension, are the kitchens and garages. The actual living quarters are on two floors, with attic extension above, and cellaring beneath the entire building complex. At ground level is the entrance to an enormous hall, which extends upwards to include the upper storey. From the hall there is access to a music room complete with stage, and to a long dining-room in which Klimt's frieze is to be found. Salon, breakfast-room and smoking-room are relatively modest in size. On the first floor are the main bedroom suite complete with a splendid marble bathroom, four children's rooms and a room for the nanny. The attic is divided up into many small rooms, offering an additional children's room, four servants' bedrooms, three guest rooms and a small study which does not seem likely to have been much used, being so small and away from the main living quarters.

The walls of the reception rooms are finished in malachite, marble or onyx; parts of the floors are fitted with inlay work, with matching carpets specially woven. Chairs and sofas are covered in goat's leather. Light is provided by innumerable lamps specially created to fit the different rooms.

The names of those who worked on these interiors under Josef Hoffmann are not known. He must have delegated some of the responsibility, for everything was provided by the Workshops, right down to kitchen equipment, crockery and cutlery. Several artists were involved in interior design and decorating. When the designs did not please Stoclet, he chose others.

Stoclet already possessed a large collection of Egyptian and other antiquities, Chinese paintings and bronze figures, African carvings and Italian pictures painted on wood, mainly of the fourteenth century. These works were to be housed chiefly in the large entrance hall, and had to be incorporated by Hoffmann in his overall design.

The dining-room was some fourteen metres long, and a bay at the narrow end led out to the terrace. Four high French windows gave a view of the garden, and also gave the only natural light. The floor is of black, white and brown-shaded tiles. The dining-table, which can seat twenty-two people, stands on a carpet woven in browns and olives, with lengthwise rhomboid patterning emphasising the length of room and table. The walls are faced with yellow Paonazzo marble streaked with green, except for the lower parts of the long walls which are entirely taken up with sideboards of black Portovenere marble. The narrow wall opposite the bay is given a matching wedge shape by means of fitted cupboards, so that both ends of the room are triangular. The absence of right angles again emphasises the length of the room. A small distance above the sideboards is Gustav Klimt's frieze, in seven-metre sections. The frieze breaks off at the transition to the bay, but is taken up again in the middle of the bay with mosaics 183 × 89 cm in size.

Klimt provided the working sketches for the frieze, the Vienna Workshops were responsible for producing it. He worked on it for five years, and towards the end his correspondence with Emilie Flöge suggests that it had become tiresome. Instead of spending the whole summer with her by the Attersee in 1910 he had to stay on in Vienna to complete the working plans. Since the spring the mosaics workshop had been engaged on the project. On 26 June he gave vent to his exasperation: "I should spend the whole summer here working, after all the stupid work for Brussels – I'm afraid I'll have to come back to Vienna several times."[88]

The working plans were actual size, with precise directions to the craftsmen. They were done in tempera, water colours, gilt and silver bronze, chalks, pencil and opaque white. In its final form the frieze consisted of fifteen sheets of white marble, seven along each long wall and one in the bay. The marble is inlaid with copper and silver plate, corals, semi-precious stones, gold mosaics, enamel and coloured fayence. The cost of the materials must have been approximately 100,000 crowns at the time, and Klimt's fee will have been a comparable sum. When one considers that a top civil servant at the time earned approximately 7000 crowns a year, it is possible to have some idea of the vast cost of the whole palais.

Klimt's working plans were executed by metalworkers and goldsmiths at the Vienna Workshops, by enamellers at the School of Arts and Crafts, by Vienna Ceramics and by craftsmen at the Leopold Forstner mosaics workshop. "...all of the above are exceptional craftsmen, of which no other city can boast in such numbers. Gustav Klimt insisted on employing them. He makes the utmost demands on their technical skills, on their ability to understand and translate his designs, on every aspect of their work. And the end result is made all the more impressive by the fact that there are no models, no precedents; never before has an artist attempted to cover a wall with such splendour, such wealth of colour, such exquisite gems and enamel and gold and incrustations of pearl."[89]

Berta Zuckerkandl was not exaggerating. And Klimt watched very carefully over the execution of his working plans. When the design had been transferred to the marble, with drilling of the lines, Klimt studied the contours of the material once more with great care and made such adjustments as he found necessary.

For the craftsmen, too, the frieze meant an enormous amount of work. Each of the two rose-bushes, for instance, contained 200 enamel leaves in different shades of green precisely determined by the artist. Klimt himself was worried about the expense, as is shown by one of his letters to Fritz Waerndorfer: "I knew right at the start that the whole thing would be damned expensive and said so – not much to be done about it. As I said before, it might be a bit cheaper to have some of the flowers in glass or mosaics rather than enamel . . . am working harder than ever – just Stoclet, only Stoclet – haven't started a single landscape. Costing me vast sums."[90]

The frieze makes Klimt's penchant for arts and crafts more clear than do all his pictures. In the Brussels frieze there is none of the 'action' which had prevented the Beethoven Frieze from becoming pure decoration. On both sides of the room, the golden branches of the tree of life reach out over the whole length of the wall, ending in volutes with stylised two-eyed 'blossoms' in between. In each tree, three birds of prey perch close to the trunk. Without this trunk in the centre, the whole would appear to be an abstract volute pattern. Klimt had seen ornamentation of this sort in 1903 in Ravenna, where he made a very close study of the early mediaeval mosaics.

The gold ground out of which the tree grows is covered in flowers of every colour; towards the bay on either side a stylised rose-bush with triangular leaves and round flowers grows in front of the tree. Butterflies fly round the roses. Towards the entrance hall on either side is a dancing girl whose arms are adorned over and over with gold finery. Her brightly striped dress, which leaves the shoulders free, is strewn with embossed metal triangles, between which the two-eyed flower pattern recurs. One dancing girl has her face turned towards the tree, while her body moves in the opposite direction. She represents 'Expectation', the girl on the opposite wall 'Fulfilment'. Only the face and one arm of 'Fulfilment' are visible, her body being veiled in a long flower-patterned dress, and covered for the most part by a man in a long loose robe who is embracing her. Most of the ornamentation of the man's robe is round in shape and black, interrupted by a square pattern just above the hem, with black squares and other rectangular shapes on a white ground.

All the round floral ornamentation makes this square pattern striking, even disturbing. Klimt is certainly alluding here to Moser and Hoffmann's favourite motifs and colours, but it is not known why he should have done this at this particular point. The 'picture' in the bay was seen until very recently as purely ornamental mosaics, in which geometrical shapes in a wide range of colours stand out against a gold ground. It is now thought to represent a human figure without eyes, modelled on a comparable figure by Koloman Moser. This conjecture cannot be dismissed out of hand. Not once did Klimt work in a wholly abstract manner, which is one reason why scholars have found it difficult to fathom this part of the frieze. As yet no interpretation of the man without eyes has been put forward. The theme of expectation and fulfilment is in part reminiscent of the Beethoven Frieze, particularly if the three birds of prey in the tree of life are seen as threatening.

A comparison with the two other monumental commissions reveals, however, a striking difference; in the Stoclet Frieze, the chief focus is not on content but on ornamentation. Klimt himself saw this as "the final stage of my ornamental development".[91] This marks a return to the decorative and ornamental activities of the practitioner of Arts and Crafts, emphasising once more the equal validity of Fine Arts and Arts and Crafts.

Although the designs for the palais were displayed several times in Vienna – for instance at the art exhibition of 1908 – Klimt refused to have the frieze exhibited in public after its completion: "No! I can do without the petit-bourgeois back-biting and debasement of this work,

71/72 The Black Feather Hat, 1910
Oil on canvas, 79 × 63 cm
By permission of Galerie St Etienne, New York

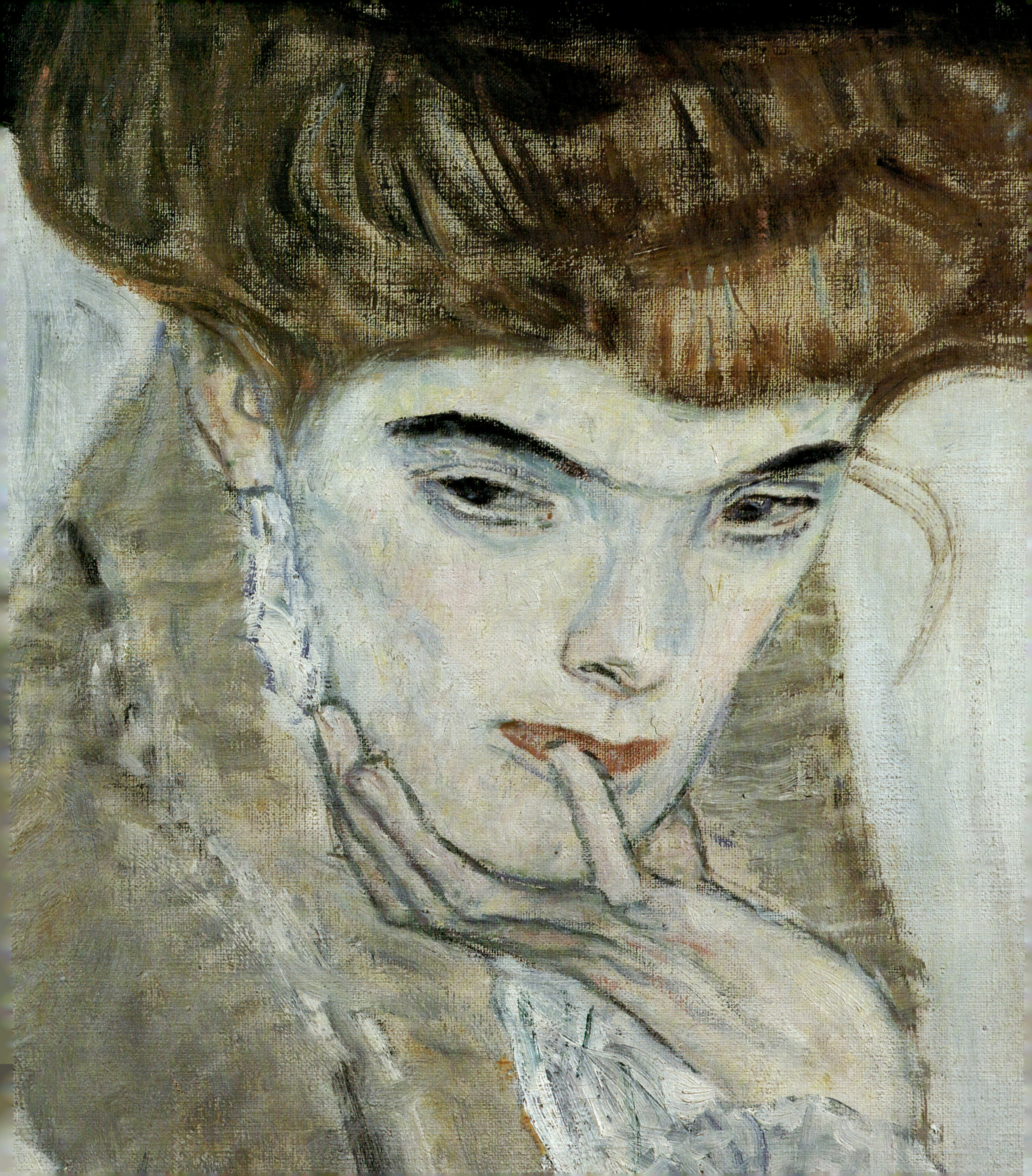

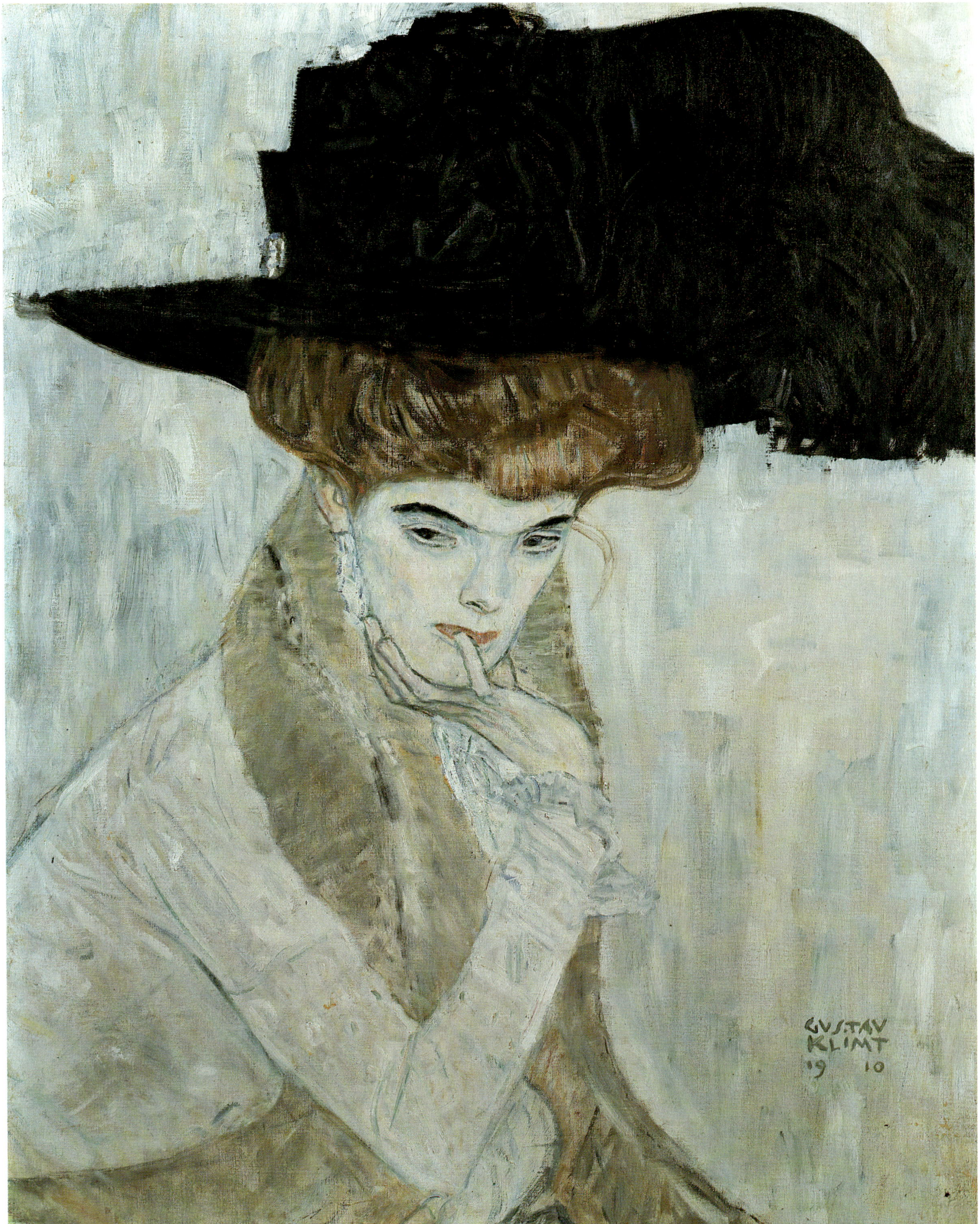
GUSTAV
KLIMT
19 10

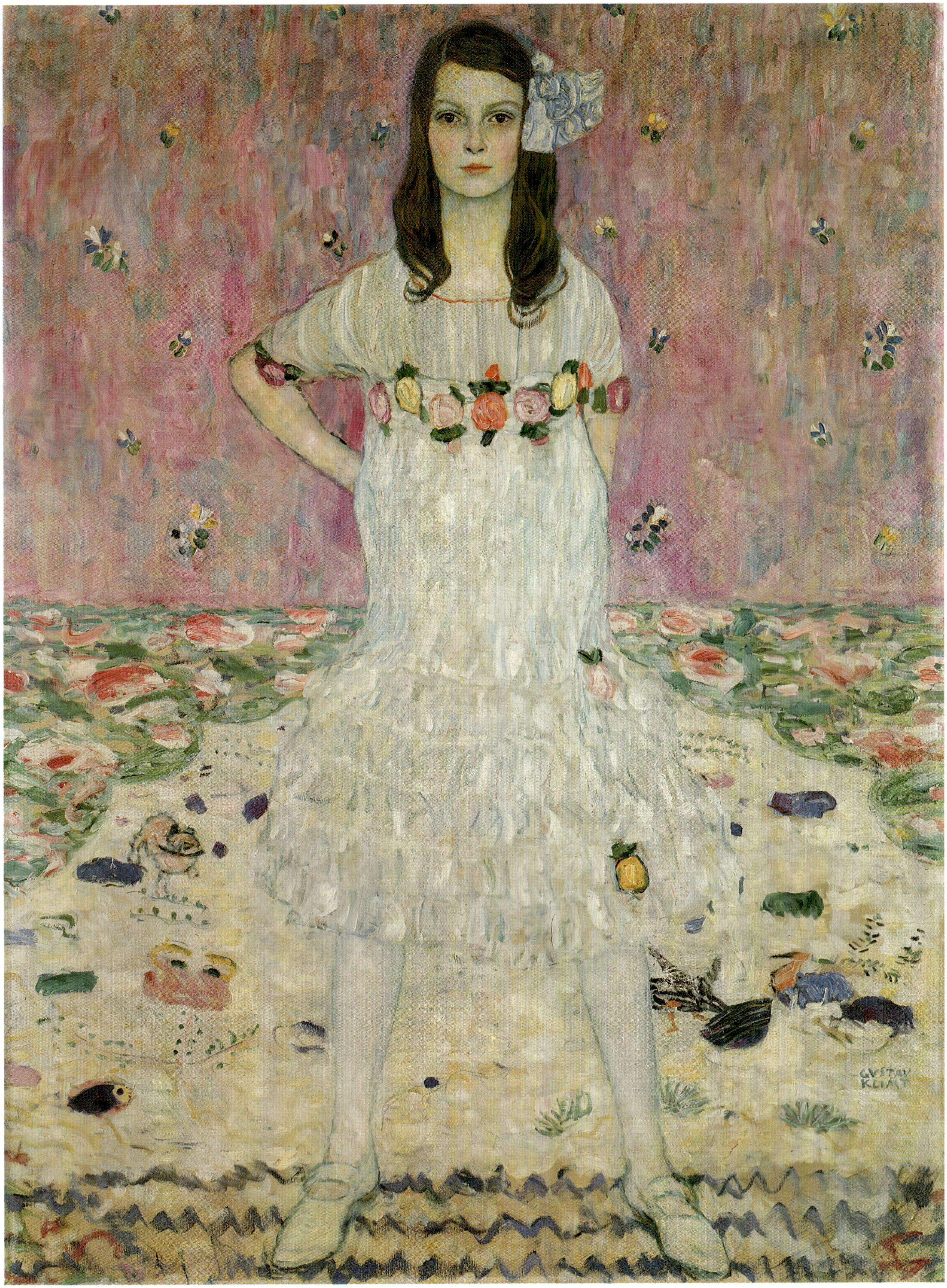
GVSTAV
KLIMT

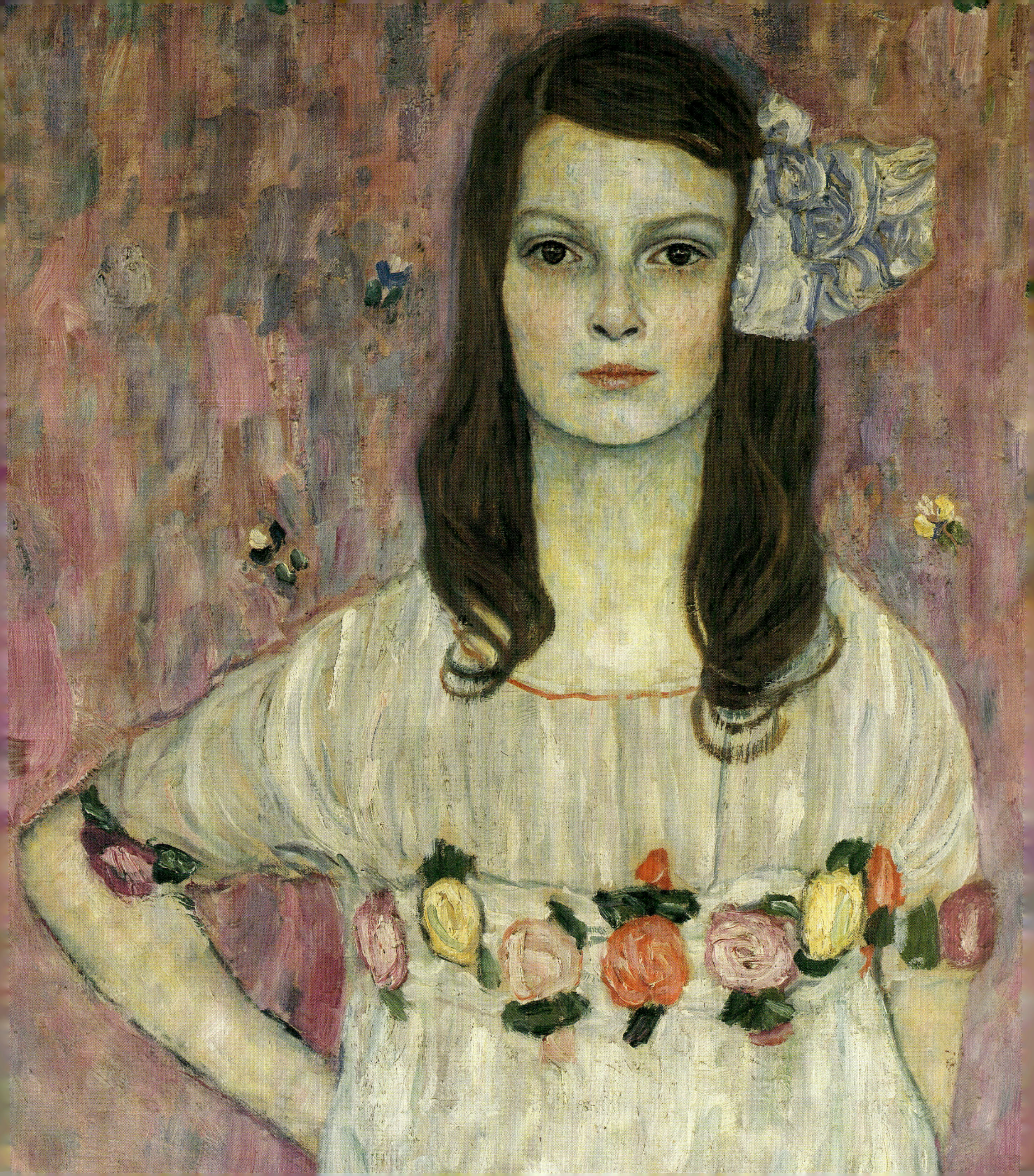

which is probably the final stage of my ornamental development, a work involving so many years of trial and struggle, to which so many craftsmen have contributed to the best of their ability in a spirit of quiet and patient self-sacrifice. My friends will be able to see the work in my studio."[92]

Nevertheless, the frieze was viewed in Leopold Forstner's workshop not only by close friends but also by various connoisseurs who expressed an interest. Arthur Schnitzler (1862–1931) noted in his diary entry for 20 October 1911 that he had seen the frieze there.

In 1914 Klimt made the journey to Brussels. From his correspondence with Emilie Flöge it is apparent that he was to paint portraits of Adolphe and Suzanne Stoclet, but for some reason this never happened. On this occasion he was able to see the palais for the first time, with his frieze.

On a postcard showing the interior he wrote to Emilie Flöge: "The Stoclet house is really very very beautiful. The photographs don't give any idea of it. The garden too is much lovelier than expected, and all the new planting. At the moment there aren't many flowers, tulips etc. are over, the roses, of which there will be a great many, and all the other things aren't flowering yet. And when I walk round the room and look at things I get a violent reminder of 'Kammerl' (Kammer, by the Attersee), of the wall, of the joys and sorrows of that time, of lots of things, and I long for it all. This photograph is a bad picture... Some things I could have done differently – lots of things the workshops could have done differently. The wall could have done with a lot more gold."[93]

It is not surprising that Klimt was not entirely satisfied. He always found it difficult to say that a picture was finished, and relinquish it, which was the reason why so many of the commissions he was given dragged on for so many years. The Stoclet Frieze had provided him with a unique opportunity to apply his art in the service of a single grand idea. He had created a piece for a specific room, where it would be displayed permanently, not for a temporary display like the Beethoven exhibition of 1902.

All the designers and artists had worked together, creating in Brussels the Vienna Jugendstil's single surviving total work of art,

73/74 Mäda Primavesi, c. 1912
Oil on canvas, 150 × 110 cm
Metropolitan Museum of Modern Art

fully represented by its chief proponents, Josef Hoffmann and Gustav Klimt.

It is a testimony to the collaboration of architect, painter and craftsmen, advocated and practised by the Vienna Workshops.

'Woman'

'Woman' occupies a central place in Klimt's work, isolated at times, at other times part of larger compositions. The pictures give some idea of his personal attitude to women.

The picture of the auditorium of the old Burg Theatre (1888) had established his reputation as a painter of beautiful women, which soon resulted in private commissions for portraits. He continued to paint portraits of women, usually of the wives of wealthy Viennese industrialists, for the rest of his life, though the total number of portraits is less than might have been expected.

The allegories of the early years often involved the portrayal of the 'femme fatale'. The symbolical nature of many of these pictures is emphasised by the metamorphosis of the female figure into water spirit – mermaid, fish, water-snake – or by the introduction of women from classical antiquity or from the old testament, such as Danaë, Leda or Judith. Three times Klimt turned to the difficult subject of pregnancy. In pictures such as those concerned with love and death, which often contain numerous figures, the female figure is usually predominant, at least at first glance.

The drawings are also important; more than 2000 have survived, providing a more prolific sequence than the paintings. Klimt did preliminary sketches for his oil paintings, but there are also a great many drawings in their own right, particularly of the female nude.

'Man' does not have the same importance in Klimt's work. After 1896 there are no individual portraits of men, although their rôle in the cycles of pictures, and in the pictures on the themes of love and death, is often important, an example of which is the knight in the Beethoven Frieze. As 'observers' men are often present in the pictures of women.

The Portraits

Portraits of women recur throughout Klimt's oeuvre as nothing else does, and they therefore provide suitable material for an analysis of his style. The fact that there are not actually very many of them can be accounted for by Klimt's slow rhythm of working; the complete inventory of his works only reaches no. 222. Between 1883 and his death in 1918 he painted twenty-six portraits which are listed as such. Then there are some paintings of women for which he probably used his models; these pictures show the artist pursuing other interests, and tend to present types rather than individuals.

Klimt's first portrait was not a commissioned work but a picture of his sister Klara, a conventional half-length portrait with dark background. The face is shown in three-quarter profile, the gaze from the corners of the eyes catching the eyes of the viewer.

Ten years later Klimt had completed the large projects in the Burg Theatre and the Art History Museum, and had made a name as one of the Ring painters, which resulted in the first commissions from Viennese society. The portraits he painted in the years that followed still kept to a conventional plan, although in retrospect it is possible to see the beginnings of his own individual style.

In 1898 he painted the 'Portrait of Sonja Knips'. For the first time he used the square shape canvas he increasingly favoured, and which was so important for the Vienna Workshop artists, particularly for Koloman Moser. Sonja Knips is sitting in a park or garden, on the edge of a light-coloured chair, in the right half of the picture. Beside her, orchids with their leaves reach up into the picture and form a background for her head. The orchid motif recurs in two flowers in the upper left corner. The light earth contrasts with the dark background, which has some red in it on the left. There is something mysterious about the dark, irregularly applied colour, which casts shadows on the light earth. There is the merest suggestion of a pond in the background. Against this background Sonja Knips sits in a sumptuous pink dress with high neck and ruffles, narrow waist and full skirt. The lower edge of the picture cuts off the bottom of the skirt, which is therefore not visible, any more than are the feet. With her left hand Sonja Knips grips the

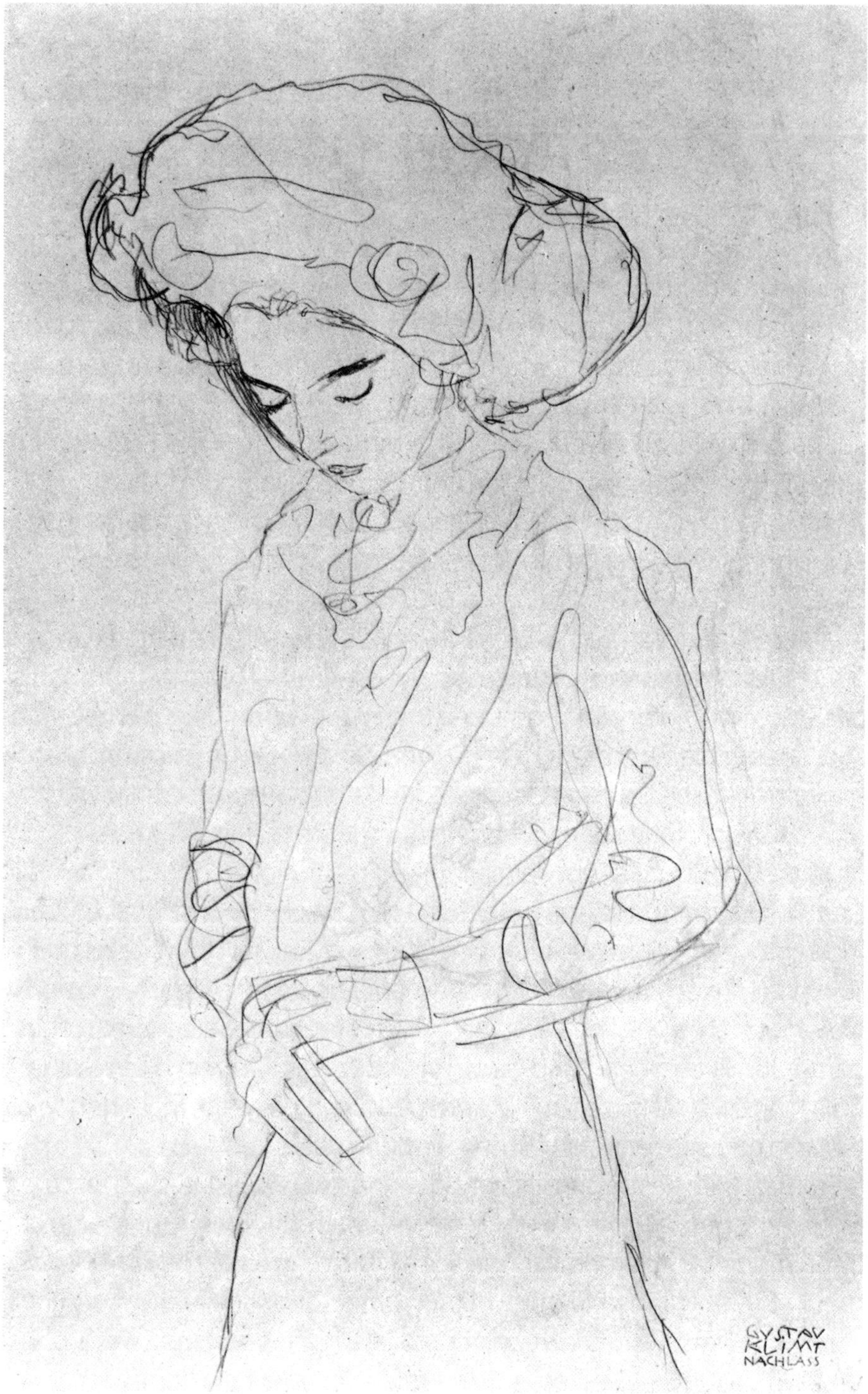

Girl with downcast eyes, 1910/12
Pencil, 55.9 × 37.1 cm

armrest, as if she were just about to get up, and this impression is strengthened by the way she sits on the edge of the chair, but contradicted by her right hand which rests quietly on her leg clasping a red booklet. Nor does the expression on her face suggest that she is about to move; she gazes straight ahead out of the picture, disquieting in her immobility.

This portrait is the only one with a hint of landscape in the background. Klimt painted many landscapes, and many people, but kept the two distinct, which makes this portrait truly exceptional. It was painted at a time of upheaval, when Klimt had abandoned historicism but not yet found his own style. In the same year he painted his first landscape pictures. The orchids and the pond in the portrait represent a subdued symbolism, hinting at sumptuousness and mystery.

There are Impressionist traits in the treatment of the figure, as in the supraportal 'Schubert at the Piano' in Palais Dumba, painted one year later, where they are even more pronounced (see p. 83–85). This is clearly the transitional phase between historicism and Klimt's brand of Jugendstil. The square picture becomes increasingly important in his later development, although the experiment combining portrait with landscape does not recur. The contradiction between immobility and movement in the figure was succeeded in the portraits that followed by an increasing tendency towards static incorporeality.

In the same year he painted his niece Helene, daughter of his brother Ernst and Helene Flöge. The face in profile is almost entirely hidden by the page-boy haircut, the upper body is only sketched in. The puffed material of the dress makes it seem as if the child's body were not there at all. The careful drawing of face and hair makes a stark contrast; it is as if head and body had nothing to do with one another. This tendency becomes more and more marked as the importance of the garments increases in the later portraits.

In 1899 Klimt was commissioned by the industrialist August Lederer to paint a portrait of his wife, Serena Lederer. Mention has already been made of Lederer's importance as Klimt's greatest patron; the two men were also close friends. In the course of time Lederer acquired many of Klimt's important paintings, of which a number were confiscated in 1938 – the Lederers were Jews – and burnt in 1945. The portrait of Serena Lederer, however, is still in the possession of the family.

As well as the square picture, Klimt had come to favour the high rectangular shape, a tendency which was first noted in 'Love' and in the portrait of the actor Lewinsky (see p. 81). The dark area in which Lewinsky stands is set off diffusely against the light background, with no suggestion of spatiality. The figure almost seems to hover or swim in a vacuum rather than stand in reality. In the portrait of Serena Lederer this impression is strengthened by the long falling robe, curving forward at the lower edge. The feet are covered, so that there is no suggestion at all of the figure standing firmly on anything. Face, upper body and arms are the only visible parts of the body; the rest is lost beneath the flowing robe. It is interesting that Klimt painted Serena Lederer in 'reform dress' at this date; she seems to have picked up the new 'fashion' very early. It is impossible to know whether this resulted from her own preference, or whether it was Klimt's idea to portray her in this dress which was so conducive to the creation of incorporeality.

There is no record of another portrait until three years later, when it is astonishing to find, in the portrait of Gertha Felsoevanyi, a similar approach. In the meantime Klimt had created the Beethoven Frieze, and the disagreements about the faculty pictures were very far advanced, but the artist was probably still prepared to make concessions to those who commissioned portraits privately. This was later less and less the case.

In the portrait, again in high rectangular shape, the background colours echo the colours of the figure, which fills almost the entire space in such a way that the upper edge of the picture coincides with the edge of the coiffure though the feet are cut off at the bottom. The necessary distance is restored by the remoteness of the figure. Again the body is veiled in a long falling dress; the head, and the hands folded in her lap, are all that is flesh and blood in a billowing surge of white and light blue colour. Against the light colours, reduced to a few tones, the face with the red mouth and reddish-brown hair stands out very strongly. Looking closely, it is possible to see that the face is made up of tiny dots. Klimt is again using Impressionist techniques, which he seemed to have given up in the Beethoven Frieze. It was characteristic of him in his times of transition that he took up traits of his own earlier styles.

In the same year he painted his companion Emilie Flöge. This is another of the few portraits that he painted without commission. The background is resolved into abstract areas of colour, organic rounded shapes in contrast to the severe geometrical ornaments Klimt favoured later on. Against the blocks of colour the human figure seems to be caught between great crags. The clear colours of her dress stand out against the subdued browns, greenish pinks and dark blues of the background. Again the figure takes up most of the picture, and her coiffure is even cut off by the upper edge, but she has moved up more into the centre so that the lower edge of the dress can be made out. The long reform dress is resolved entirely into ornamentation. The turquoise-coloured material is covered for the most part in blue volutes, gold circles and squares and innumerable little white dots. The head is framed by ornamentation of rhomboids and circles in turquoise, red, blue, black and yellow, giving the effect of a halo. One hand rests where the hip might have been. The body is turned towards the right but the eyes look straight forward out of the picture, catching the eye of the viewer. The closed lips give an impression of firmness. In spite of the stylised incorporeality there is an air of self-confidence emanating from this woman, and that is what Klimt was aiming to convey.

It is safe to assume that Klimt captured those characteristics of his companion which were, to him, the most important. Yet the picture did not appeal to the Flöge family, in particular it did not please Emilie Flöge, so that it was sold to the City of Vienna History Museum in 1908. Klimt commented briefly on this sale on two postcards which he sent to Emilie Flöge at the Attersee, where she was already spending the summer vacation: "Today you're being 'cashed', or perhaps 'converted into money' – got a ticking-off from Mother yesterday . . . Mother is outraged and is ordering a new portrait to be delivered at the first possible opportunity"[94].

So at least Klimt's mother disapproved of the sale. It is not known why Emilie Flöge objected to the portrait. Whatever her reasons, it is clear that the first era in which even Klimt's detractors were prepared to

75 Avenue in Schloss Kammer Park, 1912
Oil on canvas, 110 × 110 cm
Austrian Gallery, Vienna

76 Apple Tree I, 1912
Oil on canvas, 110 × 110 cm
Austrian Gallery, Vienna

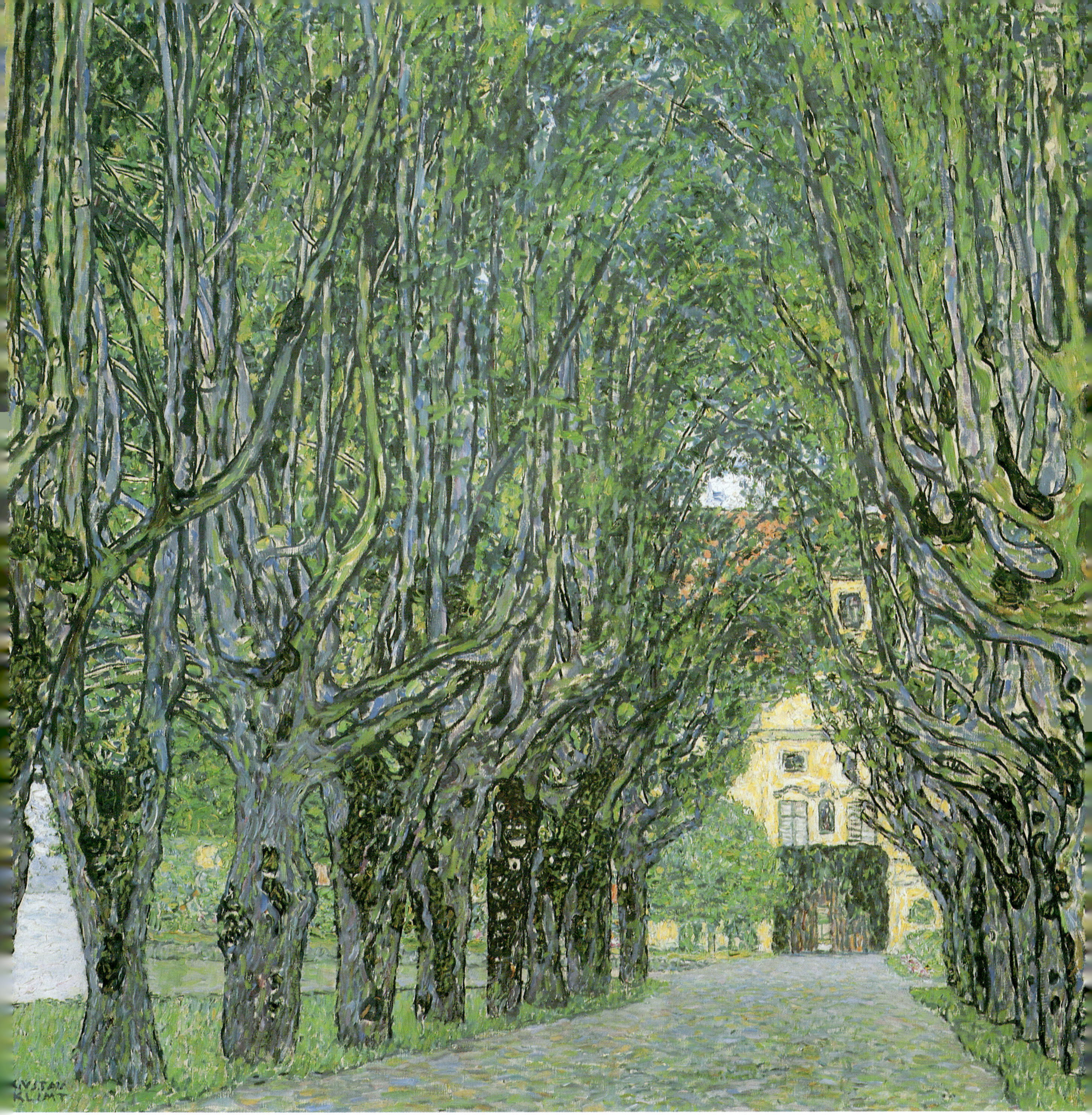

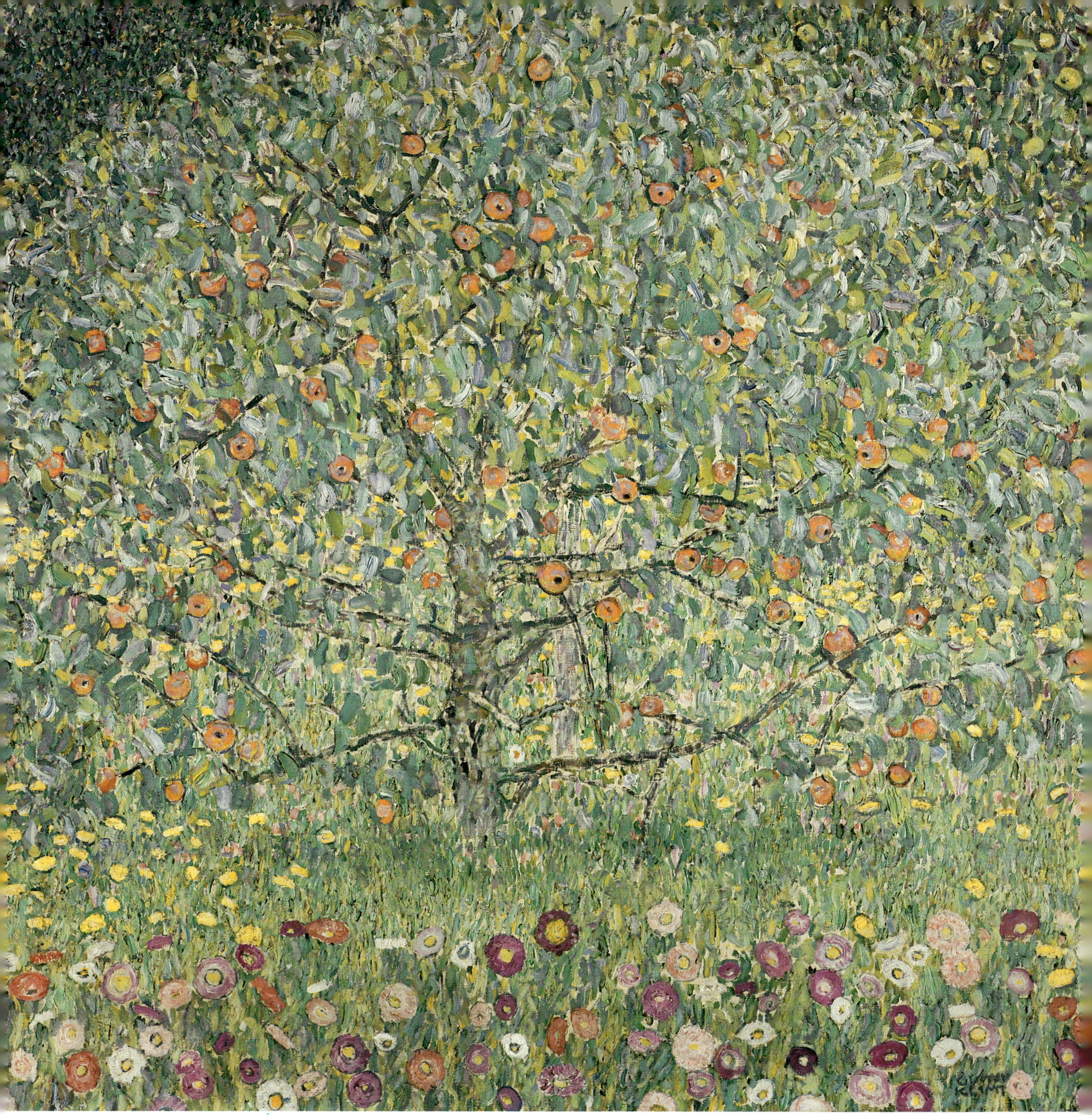

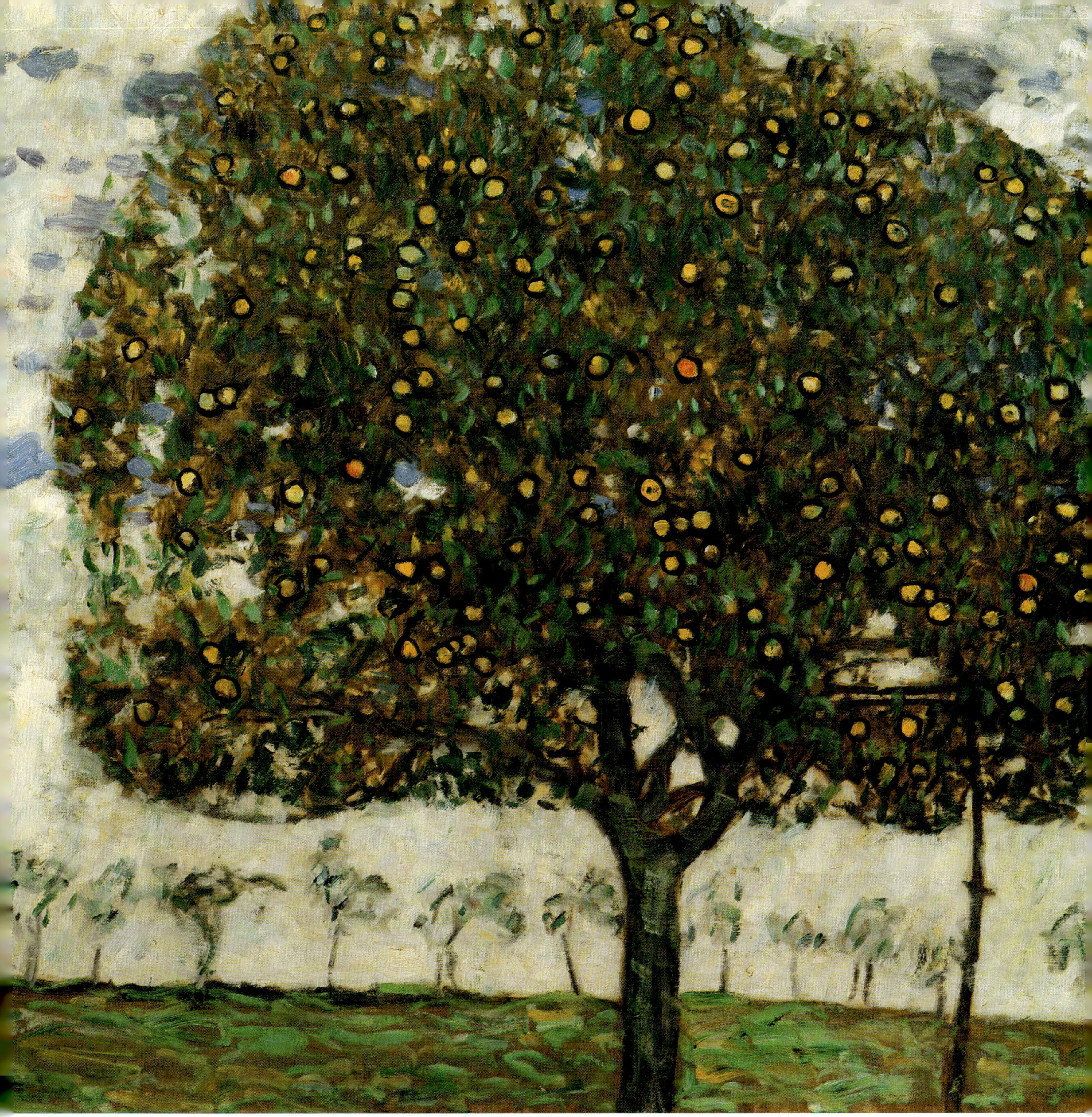

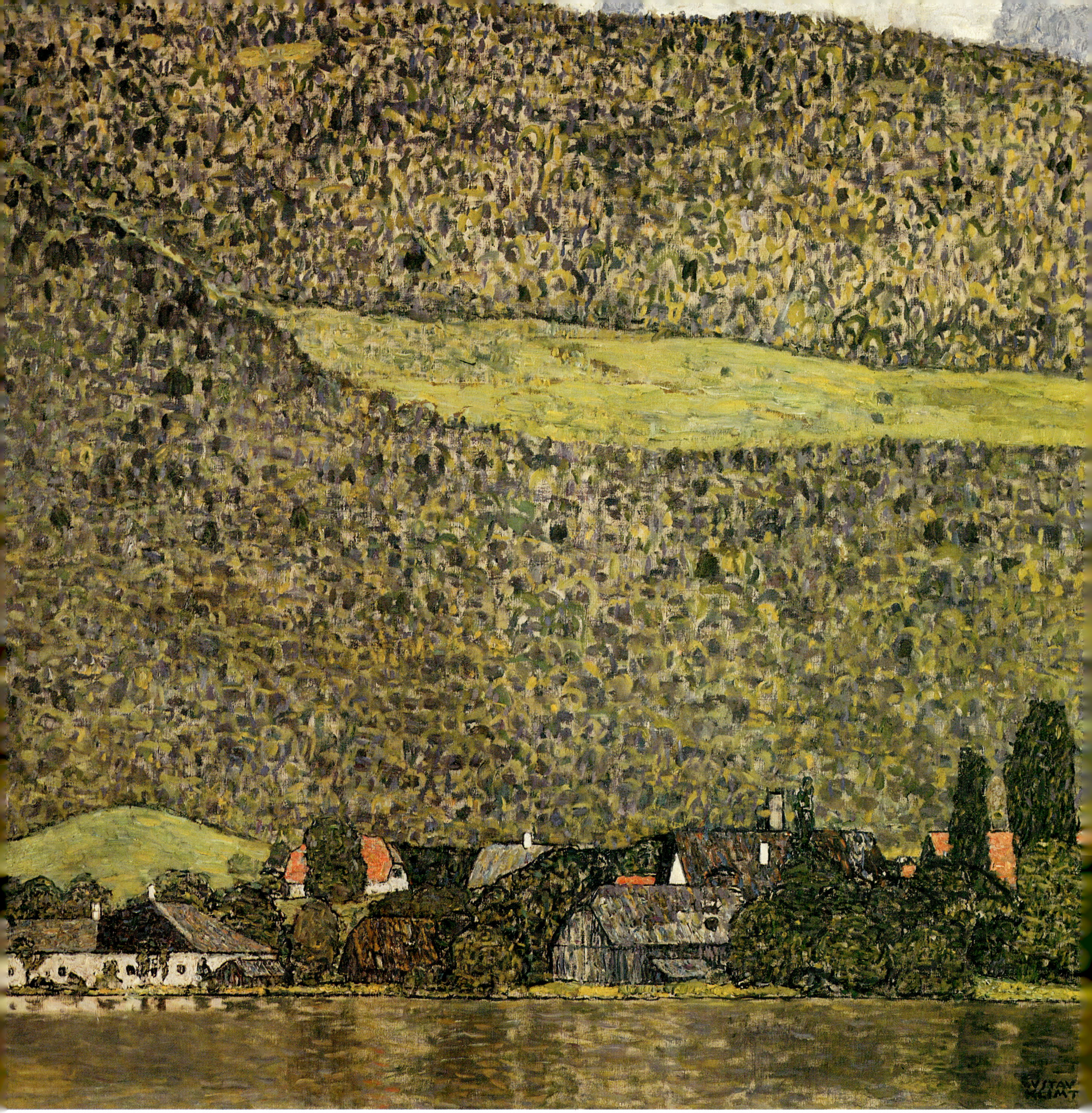
GVSTAV
KLIMT

77 Apple Tree II, c. 1916
Oil on canvas, 110 × 110 cm
Austrian Gallery, Vienna

78 Unterach on the Attersee, 1915
Oil on canvas, 110 × 110 cm
Rupertinum, Salzburg

admire his portrait painting was over. Margarethe Wittgenstein, whose family commissioned Klimt to paint her portrait, was the next to refuse to accept her own picture.

Karl Wittgenstein was mentioned above in connection with the Vienna Workshops (see p. 204). He had emigrated to America in 1865 to seek his fortune, but had returned to Vienna two years later and become one of the great steel barons. He extended hospitality to a great many artists and musicians, in particular Brahms and Mahler. He was so generous in his support of the Secession that he was commemorated in the entrance hall to their building, alongside the artists Rudolf von Alt (1812–1905) and Theodor von Hoermann (1840–1895). After the 1903 Secession exhibition of Klimt's works the Wittgensteins purchased the picture painted the same year, 'Life a Battle', which was exhibited there for the first time, and was later re-named 'The Knight in Golden Armour'. The commission for the portrait of the Wittgensteins' youngest daughter must have been given a short time later.

In 1904 the Klimt began with the preliminary sketches, and had the portrait more or less ready. He let the family have it to look at, on the understanding that it was not yet finished; the enormous fee of 5000 guilders he would not accept before completion. In 1905 he asked to have the preliminary sketches and picture so that they could be included in an exhibition, and he undertook to make improvements to the picture.

In the meantime Margarethe had married the American Stonborough, had moved with him to Berlin and was expecting her first child, so that she was not available to sit for him, and he altered only the background. The picture hung only for a short time on the walls of the Wittgensteins' house before being taken down and handed over to the Austrian Gallery on permanent loan. From there it passed to the New Gallery in Linz, but the city authorities in Linz were unable to raise the sum demanded for it by the Wittgensteins. In 1960 it was acquired by the Neue Pinakothek in Munich, the only gallery in the Federal Republic to own two pictures by Gustav Klimt.

The portrait of Margarethe Stonborough-Wittgenstein is a further milestone in the development of Klimt's painting. The organic ornamentation in the portrait of Emilie Flöge has been superseded by more strict geometrical patterns. The background is made up of right-angled shapes, with one exception. The green 'grass', not seen in perspective, is edged by a black band decorated with small silver squares, which could be interpreted as a skirting-board. Above this is a light blue 'wall', interrupted two-thirds of the way up by a white beam flanked by two rectangular copper shapes. Above this are bands of black-and-white and bright blue, rather like a piano keyboard. Above the white beam and in front of the blue strip of wall is a flat arch painted white with brightly coloured circles on the inside. The arch is framed by blue and black volutes on a gold ground. This background looks forward to the constructivist painting of the 1950s or 1960s, and derives from the association with Koloman Moser and Josef Hoffmann, as do the techniques Klimt used in the Stoclet Frieze. Klimt transposes the experiments of the Vienna Workshops to the medium of painting. The geometrical shapes which dominated the interiors designed by the Workshops at this time are given here in paint, and all sense of spatiality is lost. Without the female figure in the centre, it would never occur to anyone to describe the green area as grass, or the narrow black band as a skirting-board.

Again the human figure takes up almost the entire picture. The principles which Klimt had developed since the painting of Sonja Knips have been sustained. Again the figure is veiled in a long dress, revealing only head, shoulders and hands. This time it is a dress of white moire velvet that negates the corporeality of the human figure, and again the dress reaches right down to the ground and is cut off by the frame in the vicinity of the feet. The head is framed by the arch-like ornamentation, the suggestion of a halo less pronounced than in the portrait of Emilie Flöge, but still discernible. The hands are folded in front of the body. The figure is turned to the right, but this time the face stays in three-quarter profile so that the eyes seem to gaze into the distance. The lips are lightly parted.

Margarethe Wittgenstein's bearing and facial expression make her seem coolly aloof with an air of expectancy, but also far removed from reality. The portrait may well have been in keeping with Klimt's general view of women, but it was not in keeping with Margarethe Wittgenstein's character. She is known to have been a very strong-minded woman, ready to break with convention when possible. She took a strong interest in science and mathematics, as well as in philosphical tracts, literature and art. "In her youth her interests were far-flung and unselective, she had to try everything out; as a young woman she worked for a time in Professor Emil Fischer's chemistry laboratory in Zurich, later studied mathematics and ... various other things ... "[95].

No wonder, then, that she did not care for the portrait. "Klimt tried in vain to soften Margarethe into a yielding figure in a stylized setting. There are dissonances within the very work itself which reveal that that is not what she was, not even in her youth."[96]

The next portrait, painted a year later, coincides with the beginning of Klimt's so-called 'golden period'. The 'golden style', with which he is chiefly associated today, lasted only for four years. 'Fritza Riedler' for the first time displays a self-contained area of gold worked into the background, which again consists of geometrical shapes in different colours, but this time geometrical patterns are placed within the shapes, a technique reminiscent of arts and crafts. Fritza Riedler sits in a fauteuil which is ornamented over and over with eye pattern. This and the warm, dark colours give a quite different character to the human figure and to the whole picture. Nevertheless, the distinctive features of presentation remain the same as in the preceding portrait.

The art historian Werner Hofmann wrote of this portrait: "The figure has the aloofness of an icon. If there is a body beneath this dress, it can only be in the narrow space between flattened fauteuil and wall decoration ... The levels of reality seem interchangeable, the gracious lady hovers uncertainly between the second and third dimension. She is merged into the decor and yet stands out against it, the ornamental aura offers her to us as an exquisite work of art and makes her remote from us as a person. Klimt paints a woman who conforms to her decorative environment, thereby becoming herself a work of art." Hofmann sees three artistic realities merging with one another: "The work of art 'portrait' reproduces a work of art within a work of art inasmuch as it presents a person as work of art within an environment imagined by the artist, which is a further artistic reality, consisting of mosaic wall and fauteuil. The painter and his model become part of the 'brotherhood of artists' which encompasses 'those who create and those who enjoy'."[97]

Hofmann shows how Klimt puts into practice the principles he advanced on the occasion of the opening of the art exhibition of 1908 (see p. 209/210).

He went one step further in portraying Adele Bloch-Bauer, wife of the captain of industry Ferdinand Bloch. Her portrait represents the 'golden period' more fully than any other, and is also, interestingly, the last portrait of this period. There are preliminary drawings from 1903/4, but the portrait was not painted until 1907, so that he must have taken a very long time over it.

The characteristics of Klimt's style in this period are carried to extremes in this portrait. At first glance it seems that, except for a small green patch at the bottom on the left, the picture consists entirely of gold and ornamentation, out of which rise a woman's face and hands. Looking more closely it is possible to make out a fauteuil, the back of which resolves into mosaics. Adele Bloch-Bauer sits in a golden dress which is hardly distinguishable from chair and background. In the middle of the very ample folds of the dress is again a band of the eye-pattern which goes back to Egyptian sources and was much used by Mackintosh and Macdonald, from whom Klimt presumably derived it.

Even more than in the preceding portraits, face and arms seem detached from the body; they float without anchor in a sea of gold and ornamentation, almost, it could be said, disturbing it. The identity of art and life, fulfilled at the highest level in the total work of art, is disturbed by the appearance of an individual's face. A woman could more easily be absorbed into the picture than a man. The permeation of life by art was 'a man's dream', it was men who tried to achieve it. The part that 'woman' had to play in this led to various elaborations on the differences between the sexes: "In a civilised culture woman is the most costly luxury . . . and at the same time the most precious work of art; man shaped her into the incarnate reflection of his deepest desires, his boldest dreams, his most passionate striving – the living likeness of his creative imagination."[98]

The portrait of Adele Bloch-Bauer shows an affinity with these ideas.

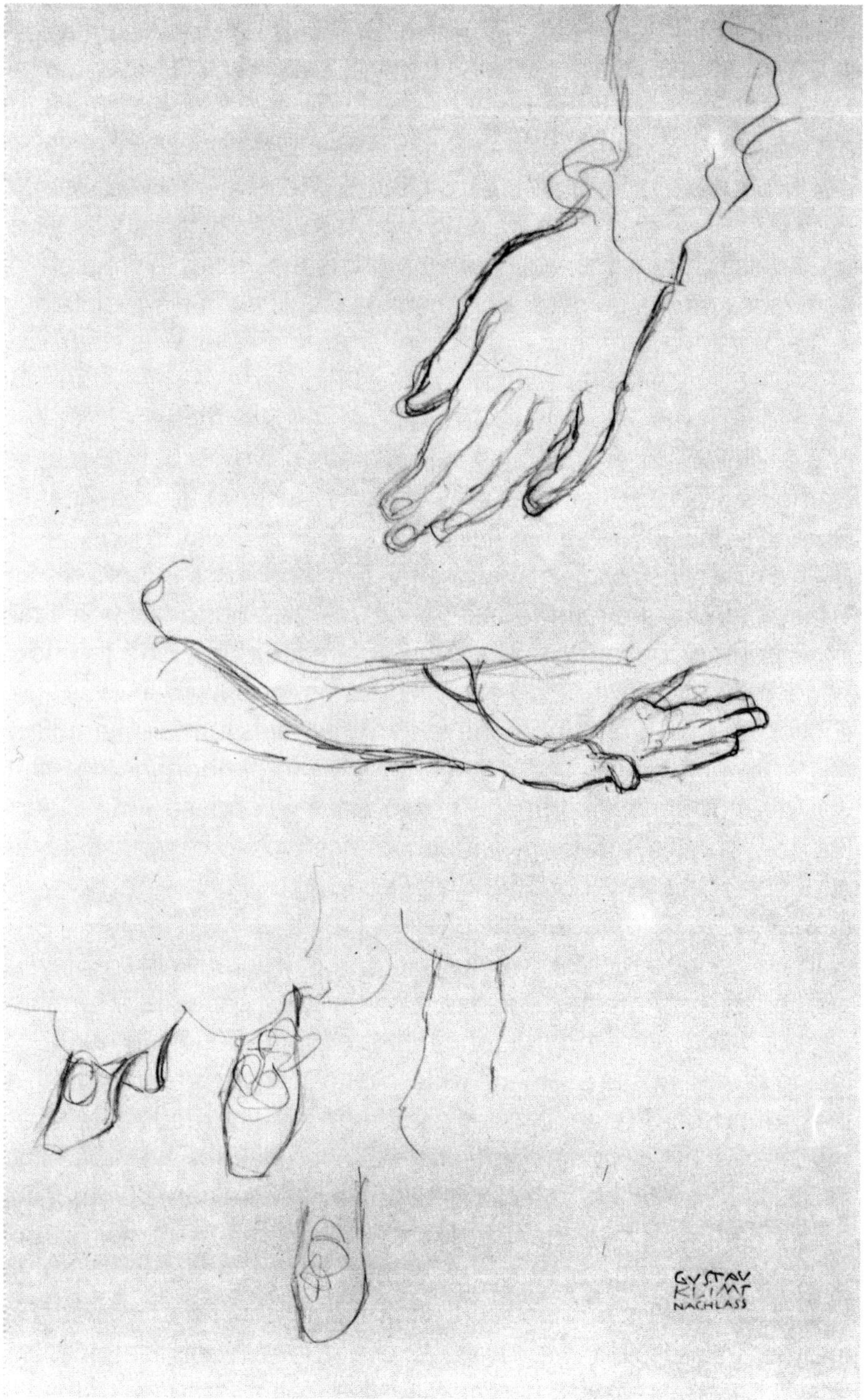

Left hand, right hand with breast, shoe studies, 1914
Pencil, 57 × 37.5 cm

The figure is part of the decoration, is subsumed in it. It is probable that Klimt had read the book 'Sex and Character' by Otto Weininger (1880–1903), which appeared in Vienna in 1902. The author had extreme notions of the differences between the sexes; the book had run through twenty-eight issues by 1932. In Weininger's eyes, woman had no soul, no ego, no morals, no logic, but was distinguished by her boundless primeval sexuality. She had "no sense of depth or height, of acuteness or straightness, in fact no 'sense' at all"[99]. He maintained that woman's awareness was derived from man. Nor was she really capable of anything that could be termed 'thought'. "Woman's thought is a gliding in and out of things, a tasting of the outer surface . . . savouring and nibbling, trying things out, no grasp of what is right. Because woman's thought has this quality of tasting, taste, in all its senses, is woman's chief characteristic . . ."[100].

This widely held view of woman can be discerned in Klimt's works, in his pictures of the 'femme fatale' and in his drawings even more than in his portraits, but of the portraits the picture of Emilie Flöge, the independent woman, is the only one which is free of it. Women were fighting for their independence. The reform dress was a small example of this; another example, on a different level, of great importance to Klimt, was his companion's management of a fashion house. Man's reaction to woman's increasing independence was to demonstrate his superiority in every possible way, reducing woman to a body, to sexuality. It will be necessary to return to this later.

In his portraits Klimt combines this view of woman with the view of woman as 'holy mother'. The latest portraits are particularly reminiscent of paintings of the madonna. 'Adele Bloch-Bauer', in her front-facing seated posture with the wide folds of her dress falling towards the ground, has frequently been compared with late mediaeval Italian madonnas, although she does not have the halo of the preceding three portraits, which gives those women likewise something of the aloof, unapproachable quality of mother and object of worship so frequently found in the portrayal of woman.

In 1909 a radical change in Klimt's style can be observed. He stopped using gold in his pictures, except in the still unfinished Stoclet Frieze, the brush stroke became wider, less calm. Klimt came close to

Expressionism, though without really becoming an Expressionist painter. The cause of this change is not known. Perhaps it had something to do with Klimt's openness towards the young painters Oskar Kokoschka and Egon Schiele, to whom he gave the opportunity of showing their work at the art exhibitions of 1908/9. There is no portrait painted in 1909, the year of radical change; it is worth looking instead at the picture of an unnamed model which Klimt painted without commission that year.

The 'Woman with Hat and Feather Boa' is quite unlike the portraits that preceded it. The prevailing dark shades of green show in the background, unclearly, the silhouette of a town. There are a few dots of yellow and red against the dark. The background is almost entirely covered by the head and shoulders of the lady. The face is not only framed, but also half covered by the feather boa. The dark blue trimming of the hat is cut off by the upper edge of the frame. Red hair escapes from beneath the hat, spreading out sideways like flames. From beneath the half-closed eyelids the gaze is directed down towards the right, so there is no contact with our eyes as we look at her. The lower third of the face is covered by the feather boa, leaving only a part of the bright red upper lip visible. There is the faintest suggestion of a coat, merging with the background.

Yet this seductive woman is more tangible than the women in the commissioned portraits. She is less static, less unapproachable, less incorporeal, nor is she integrated into a decorative frame. In this picture Klimt has relinquished the ornamentation so characteristic of his style. It returns in his later pictures, in quite a different form.

In 1912 he painted a second portrait of Adele Bloch-Bauer. This time light colours prevail. The arrangement of the areas of colour harks back to the geometrical ornamentation of the 'golden period', but they are filled with motifs drawn from Chinese painting, which must have exerted a great influence on Klimt. In a later picture, the portrait of Baroness Bachofen-Echt painted in 1916, he used as background a section of a Chinese robe. Adele Bloch-Bauer stands on blue ground which, with its stylized flowers, gives the effect of a water-lily pond. She stands facing the front, dressed in a tight-fitting dress over which she has a fur wrap moulded to the contours of her body, reaching right down to the ground. She has the air of a wooden doll. The background gives the impression of separate parts, put together but lacking in unity; it is almost as if the whole picture could be taken apart.

Shortly before his death Klimt began to paint more traditional portraits. In the unfinished picture 'Johanna Staude' of 1917/18 the half-figure is placed against a neutral background, as in his early pictures. The colours, however, are gaudy rather than subdued: Johanna Staude is presented in an extravagantly patterned coat with a fur collar against a yellowish-red background. She faces the front, looking straight out of the picture. It would be a mistake to attach much importance to the emptiness of her gaze, as the picture was still unfinished at Klimt's death; the face still needed the painter's final touches. Nor is it likely that the background had been given its final colours; a comparison with the half-figure painting of a young girl completed not long before this time supports this view. The girl's figure is turned towards the right, but she is looking straight out of the picture. The colours of the green-blue background are applied with much more differentiation, and the figure stands out very clearly against them.

These late paintings are not only very different from the earlier works – and it will be seen that the same applies to the landscapes – they are also less successful. The last ten years of Klimt's life are marked by his search for a new style. This development was not complete when he died at the age of 56.

The 'Femme fatale'

Earlier chapters discussed Klimt's treatment of allegorical figures. Pictures such as the 'Allegory of Sculpture' and 'Greek Antiquity II' contributed to the development of his style. They also led to a view of 'woman' different from the picture conveyed by the portraits. In them Klimt was working not towards the presentation of 'the plaything' or 'the mother', but towards the 'femme fatale'. The transition from allegory to 'femme fatale' is noticeable in 'Pallas Athene', whose threatening quality was put into words by Ludwig Hevesi (see p. 96). It is most

79/80 Judith II, 1909
Oil on canvas, 178 × 46 cm
Gallery of Modern Art, Venice

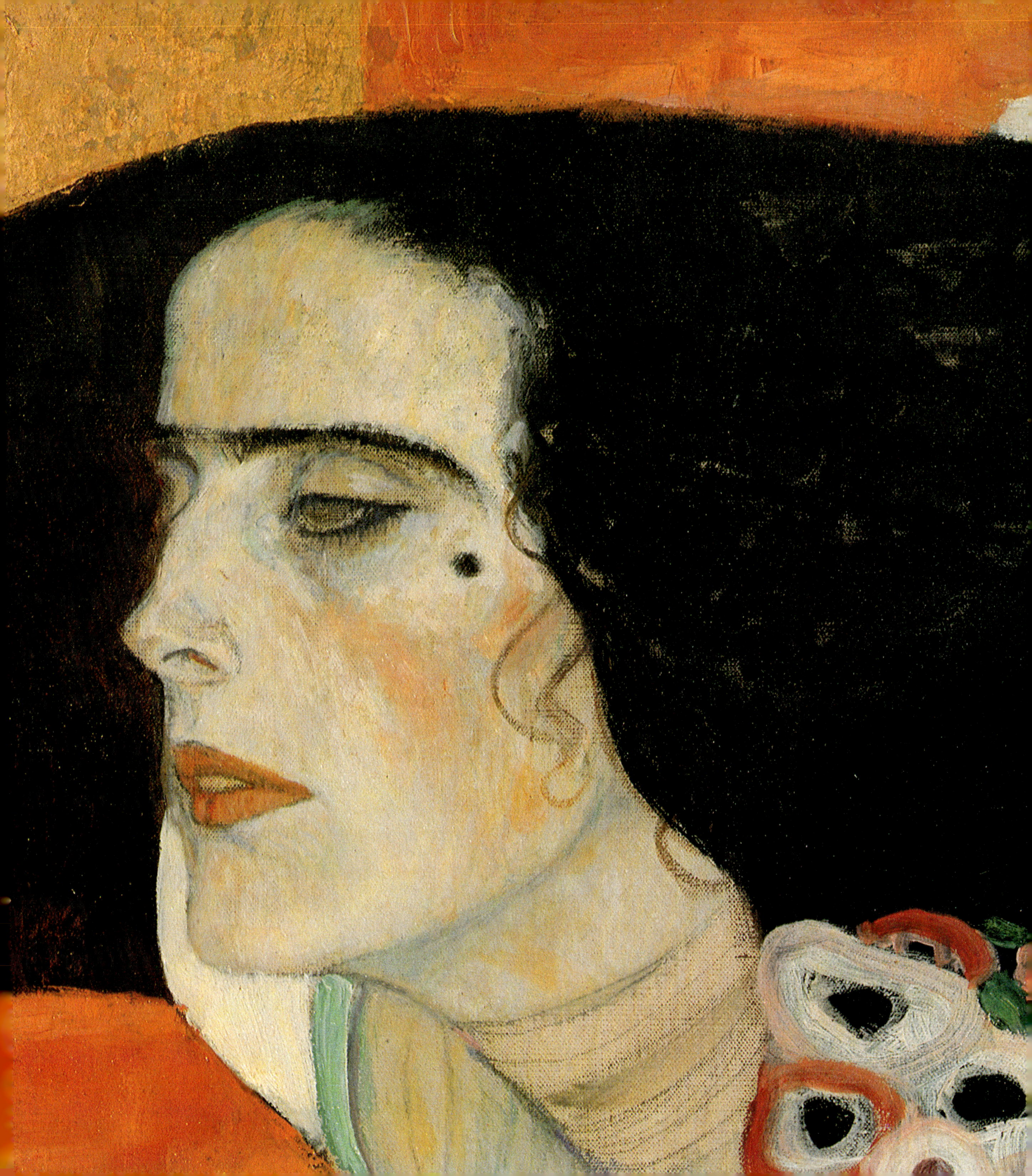

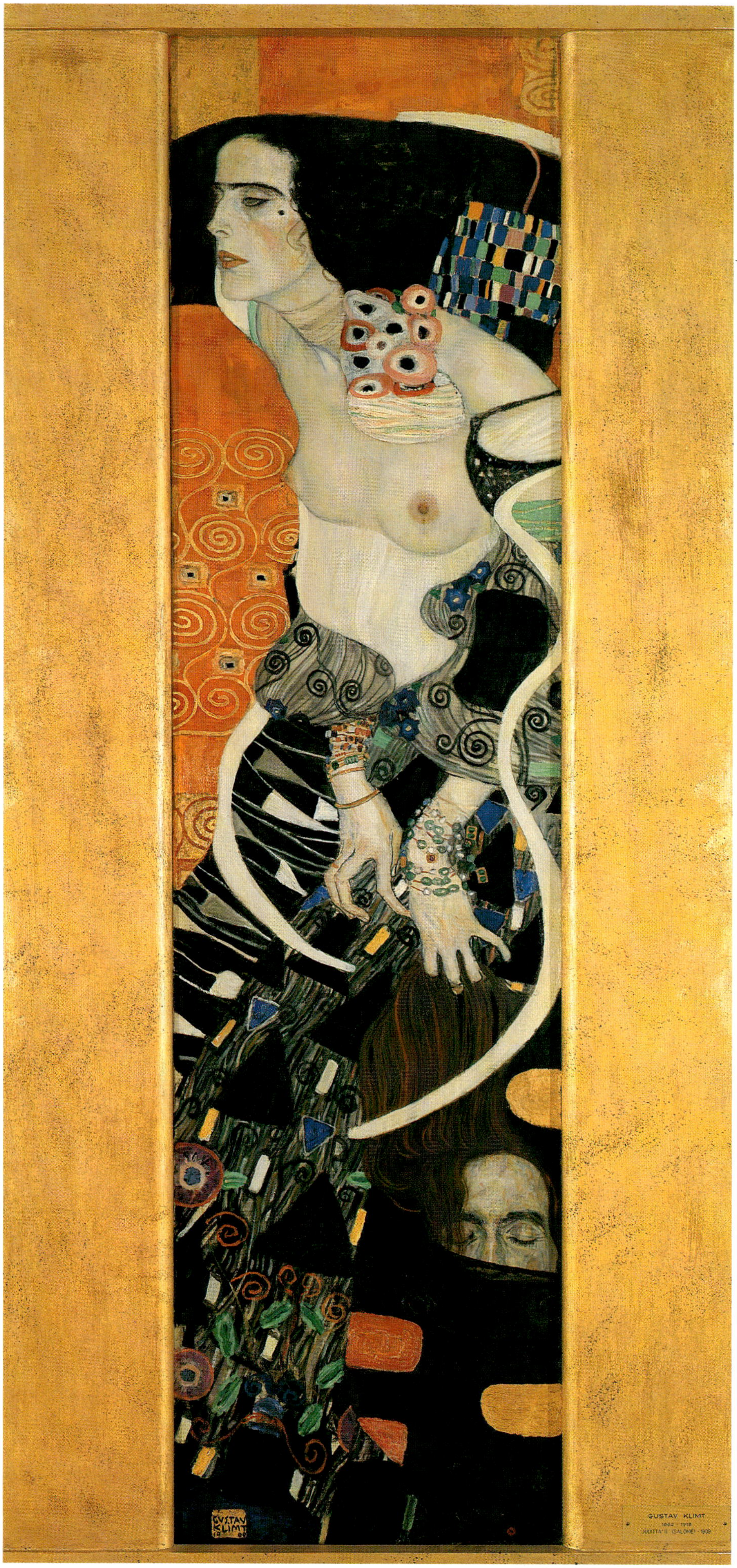
GUSTAV KLIMT

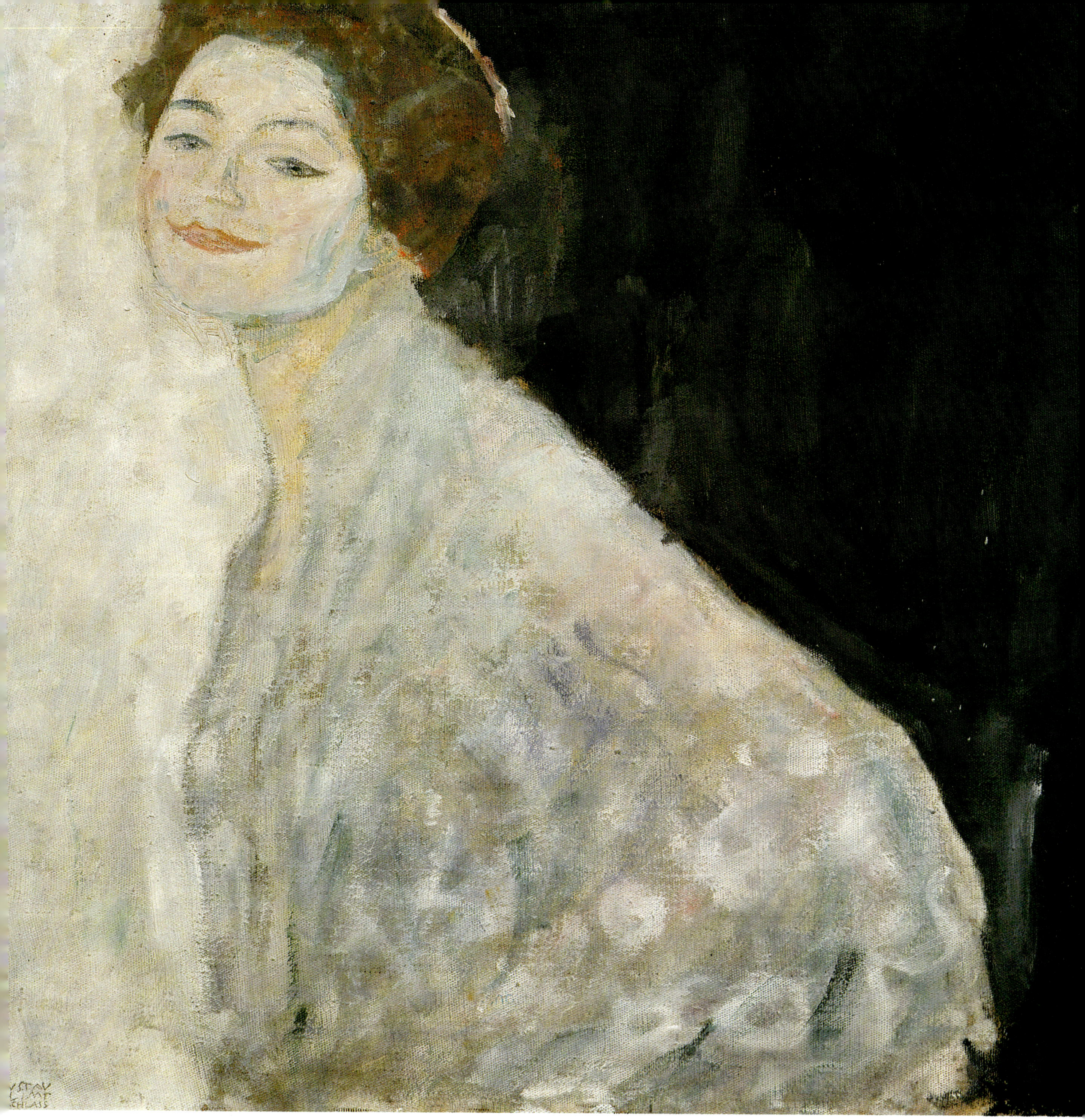
VSTAV
LIMT
CHLASS

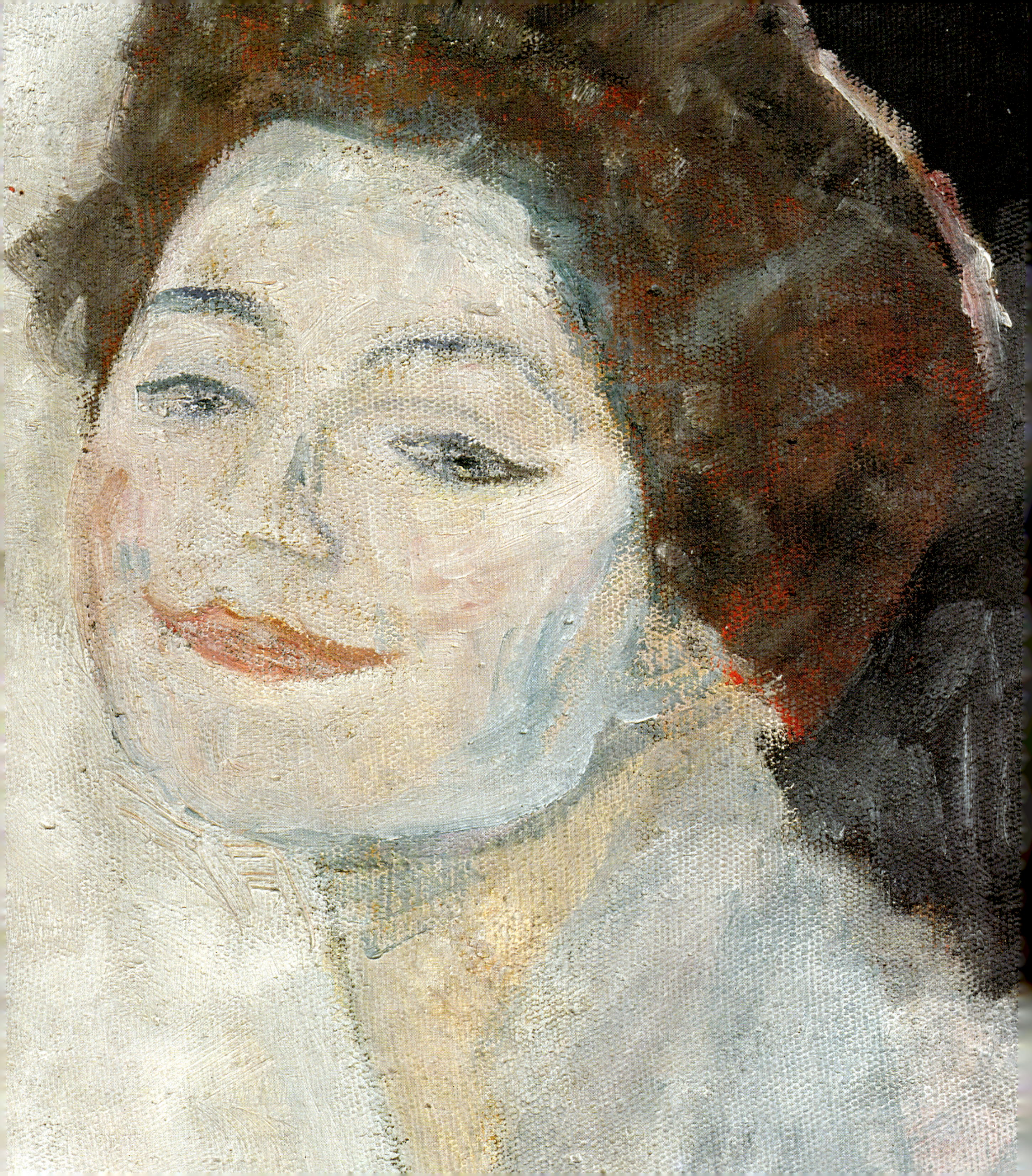

81/82 Portrait of a Lady in White,
1917/18 (unfinished)
Oil on canvas, 70 × 70 cm
Austrian Gallery, Vienna

relevant at this point that Hevesi saw in the Greek goddess gazing so threateningly out of the picture a living woman, a "Secessionist of today". This figure developed in Klimt's subsequent pictures into the woman who threatens man, as well as into the woman whose chief characteristic is her sexuality.

In 'Judith I', painted in 1901, Klimt kept the frontal presentation of 'Pallas Athene'. Against the background of gold trees, with vegetable ornamentation in the upper half of the picture and a green area in the lower half, stands a figure whose body is cut across at the level of the pubis by the lower frame. Except for a wide collar of gold and a gold girdle covering her hips she is naked, though a cloth falling over her right shoulder covers one breast. From beneath half-closed lids her eyes look at us, her lips are parted. In her hand she holds not the staff or the spear of an Athene but the head of Holofernes. The 'man-murdering woman' is not shown, as so often, at the moment of his death or shortly after it, with the bloody sword in her hand. Only the half-recognisable severed head at the bottom right edge of the picture indicates that Judith has killed Holofernes. She is not the war-like heroine who liberated the Jews, but a sensuous and lascivious woman.

There is no suggestion in the painting that the liberation of her native city from the Assyrians besieging it had caused her to kill. This is the woman whom lust turns into a seductress, and who then becomes passive once more. "The man-threatening sexuality of the woman turned back on her; being perceived as the one overcome by her own feelings facilitated the metamorphosis of mythical threat to sex object."[101]

Klimt's contemporaries suggest such an interpretation. Felix Salten wrote in 1903: "This Judith ... is a lovely Jewish lady of the day ... who turned all men's heads towards her at every première. A slender sinuous creature with smouldering fire in her dark eyes and a cruel mouth ... puzzles and powers seem to slumber in this alluring woman, energy and violence impossible to curb if the glowing coals dampened by bourgeois society were ever to ignite. An artist has stroked the fashionable clothes from their bodies, taken one of them and presented her to us adorned with her timeless nudity ..."[102]

Although this picture, 'Judith I', has 'Judith and Holofernes' embossed on its metal frame, it was often referred to, even during Klimt's lifetime, as 'Salome'. Salome only caused caused a man's death, did not kill him with her own hand.

In 1909 Klimt painted another Judith, also frequently referred to as Salome. Like most of the female figures he painted at this time, she turns towards the right and seems to be dancing, giving further justification to the alternative title. Holofernes' head is sticking half out of the sack in which Judith has smuggled it out of the Assyrians' camp.

The figure is neither so threatening, nor so seductive nor so passive, as the one in 'Judith I'. It lacks the most powerful characteristics of the earlier picture, the challenging gaze and the nudity; only the breasts are exposed to view. Nor is Judith touching the head directly. She holds the sack with the tips of her fingers, as if she wants to get rid of it. The 'femme fatale' is more assured, more at one with herself in spite of the dance, more subject than object.

One of the themes that recur, particularly in Klimt's drawings, is lesbian love. It occurs only in a few of the paintings; 'Mermaids', of 1899, can be numbered among them, but 'Water Serpents I', painted between 1904 and 1907, deserves closer attention.

Two embracing female figures are framed between water snakes, against a background of brightly coloured ornamentation. From the hips down the two girls, closely entwined, are clothed in such a way that the material seems a continuation of the body. In this way only the breasts are revealed. The tender embrace, the absorption of the two bodies in one another, is prevented from yielding a wholly positive picture by the presence of the snakes, one of which is thrusting its head into the foreground on the right. The snake as a symbol not only of female sensuality but also of evil draws attention to woman as a sexual object, to her availability, and in the context of lesbian love to her function as 'femme fatale'.

Availability is also one of the themes of 'Danaë'. Klimt will deliberately have selected this story of the begetting of Perseus by Zeus in the shape of a shower of gold. The shower of gold falls between the legs of the sleeping, naked Danaë. There can be no more cogent display of the availability of woman and the dominance of man.

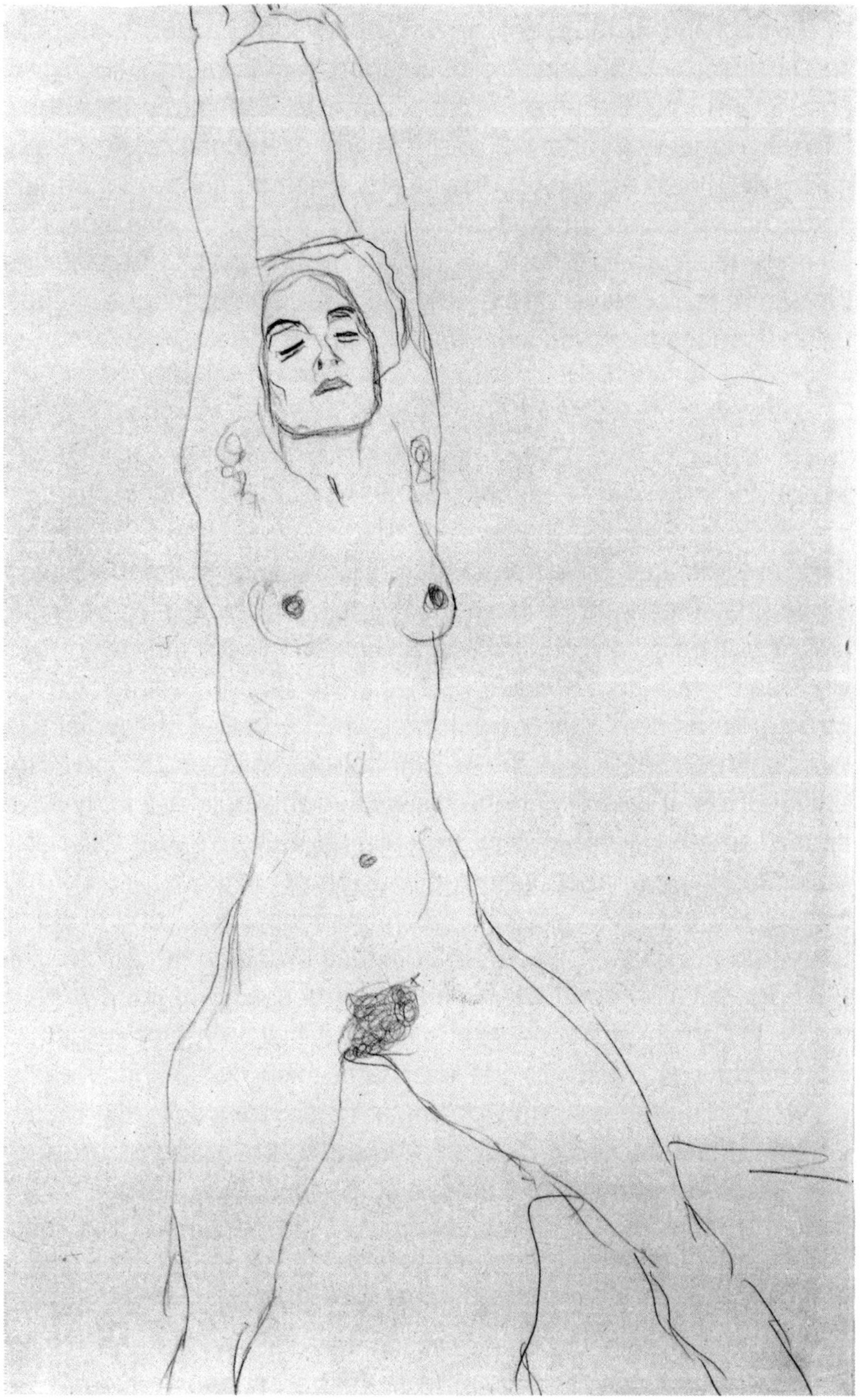

Female figure, front view, arms raised, 1914
Pencil, 55.6 × 36.8 cm

The subtlety of the presentation in pictures Klimt painted from about 1900 to 1910, which makes them so appealing, is later relinquished. The 1912–13 picture 'Virgin', also known as 'The Girls', shows five female figures in a variety of postures and even contortions, mostly nude, on a bed adorned with flowers. Only the central figure lies spread out in the middle, clothed in a long dress. She is sleeping. There is no symbolism here, no subtlety of suggestion, but rather, as Kirk Varnedoe observed in the New York exhibition catalogue 'Vienna 1900', voyeurism and sensuality.[103]

'Hope I'

Klimt's pictures of females suggest a view of woman located some where between 'mother of God', 'costly plaything', 'femme fatale' and sexual object. All of these are combined with the themes of love and death in a picture Klimt completed in 1903 for the Secession exhibition of his works. Minister von Hartel, who had acted as mediator in the disagreements about the faculty pictures, intervened, and Klimt did not insist on displaying the picture, which would probably have caused an even greater outcry. The painting shows a nude woman far advanced in pregnancy. It was unthinkable at the time to let a proud mother-to-be display herself in the manner that has become customary in our own time. There would certainly have been a scandal.

Shortly after its completion Fritz Waerndorfer bought the picture and hid it behind folding doors in such a way that only select guests, of whom Ludwig Hevesi was one, ever came to see it: "On that evening we were sitting together and looking at the severe works of art in the Waerndorfer collection. One large picture is shut away behind hermetically sealed folding doors, so that no profane eye may see it. The picture is Klimt's famous, or infamous, 'Hope', namely, that most extremely expectant, interesting young woman whom the artist dared to portray unclothed. One of his masterpieces."[104]

Rumour gave the following account of its genesis: the model Herma had not been seen in Klimt's studio for a long time; since he favoured her for his studies of figures in motion – "there is more beauty and intelligence in that girl's bottom than in many girls' faces"[105] – he made inquiries about her; it turned out that she was pregnant and did not dare to appear in the studio although the whole family depended on her earnings. Klimt sent a message saying that he urgently needed her for his work, which caused a great stir among the other models and in the Academy of Art. "Other people were soon equally disturbed, especially Klimt's fellow artists, art historians and critics. Nonsense! Infamy! Filth! Perversion! Baseness! Shamelessness! Swinishness! – all these abusive criticisms and many more poured down on the master like hailstones."[106]

The annalist who recorded all this more than fifty years later went on, after he had described the picture itself, to say: "Klimt had no words to say in defence, in the face of all this hypocritical abuse, uncomprehending indignation, slobbering vilification . . . But his models, who had heard all about the help that he had given to the 'unfortunate' Herma . . . and to numerous others, would all have gone through thick and thin for him from that time on."[107]

People's anecdotes about famous contemporaries must always be regarded with suspicion, especially when there has been no written record of them for such a long time. It may be that Klimt behaved generously towards his models – there are plenty of stories along those lines – but in this there may have been an element of voyeurism.

Klimt had painted a pregnant nude in 1901 in 'Medicine', and the theme recurs frequently, from that time on, in his drawings. In 'Medicine' as in 'Hope' the figure is turned towards the right, so that the abdomen is displayed in full profile, with hands folded on the belly "as if she were trying to protect the unborn life."[108]

This bearing is typical of the pregnant woman, and Klimt will have observed it with his customary sharpness of perception, not only in this model but also in the women who bore his children.

Klimt did not focus only on the figure of the pregnant woman from 'Medicine', but also on some of the other figures, which in the earlier picture pose a threat to the whole of mankind – here, to the unborn child. Behind the central figure a narrow blue band with gold dots suggests the hope that is associated with the birth of a child. But behind it lurk various aspects of danger, for instance in the form of a monster reminiscent of Typhoeus in the Beethoven Frieze. Other deadly threats appear in the two figures of sickness and death, which symbolise the gravest peril for mankind in 'Medicine', and in two leering faces for which no satisfactory interpretation has been offered, but which certainly have to do with the temptations or dangers to which the child not yet born will one day be exposed.

The pregnant woman has turned her face away from the dangers around her and looks out of the picture, at us. The flaming red hair adorned with flowers, the questioning and challenging look in the wide open eyes, may well suggest the 'femme fatale' rather than a woman in need of protection. The face harmonises with the curves of the buttocks and the lovely slender legs, starkly contradicted by the upper body and belly. Over the years, the picture has, for many people, become "the private icon of madonna-like pregnancy"[109]. Hevesi saw it as a "deeply moving creation. How proudly the young woman walks in the sacredness of her condition, surrounded by sordid scowling faces, by the lascivious blaspheming demons of life... but she fears no attack, she treads undeterred the path of horrors, preserved unblemished and unblemishable by the hope in her womb... A symbolic picture,... a coming together in a single focus of every possible kind of emancipation."[110]

Arthur Roessler sees only motherhood, displayed not in the customary manner "but entirely naked, as living vessel in which the hope of mankind, safe in the warmth of mother's blood, grows towards the time when it will be raised from mysterious darkness to the light of day."[111] This line of thought continues into modern art history: "The fear which adheres to all life from the beginning is made visible in Gustav Klimt's picture of hope: a naked girl far advanced in pregnancy, trusting in destiny as she carries her child... the thought of hopelessness forces itself on our attention, to be disarmed by the expression on the face of the woman, who offers herself in complete unquestioning surrender, transcending all possible doubt."[112]

All these interpretations focus on the idea of pregnancy rather than on what is actually to be seen in the picture. The woman in her startling form symbolises both lasciviousness and motherhood. The figures in the background, bearing less on the sexual object than on the unborn child, and the blue band take up themes from the Beethoven Frieze. The blue band can be equated with 'yearning for happiness', the background figures with 'hostile forces'. But the positive prospect given by the Beethoven Frieze is lacking in this as in Klimt's other pictures. Theme and date suggest that the symbolic aspects of the painting may refer back to the short life of Otto Zimmermann (22.6.1902–11.9.1902), the second son of Mizzi Zimmermann and Gustav Klimt. When Klimt first worked on the composition in 1902 he planned to place the figure against a landscape background, then against a carpet-like pattern. It is quite probable that the theme was suggested by Mizzi Zimmermann's pregnancies. The death of their little son led to a change of plan. But the elements he introduces are not new, they can be traced in much of his work.

In the faculty pictures life and death were thematically treated, as were the three ages, and in reduced form they recur in 'Hope'. They can be found also in 'Procession of the Dead' (1903), 'Three Ages of Woman' (1905) and 'Death and Life' (1911/16). They are hinted at in various other paintings.

As in the case of 'Judith', Klimt was evidently unable to let the subject go, and he painted a second version in 1907/08. Again there are radical differences between the two versions. In the second one the pregnant woman is clothed in an exquisitely patterned dress, reminiscent of the ornamentation in the Stoclet Frieze. The allegorical figures are less sharp, and seem more incidental than threatening, just as Holofernes' head in the sack was less threatening than in the first picture. 'Hope II' and 'Judith II' both have figures turned to the right, the dress revealing only the breasts, the gaze averted. Both these women seem at peace with themselves, even if they are stylized to the extent of becoming elements in the ornamentation, like the figures in the portraits painted at the same time. As in the Stoclet Frieze, on which Klimt had begun to work, life becomes indistinguishable from decorative adjunct.

'Judith I' and 'Hope I' have more content, veiled as this may be in symbols, which means that no comparison between the earlier and later pictures can be more than rudimentary. There seems to be a direct link between 'Pallas Athene' and these pictures, although Klimt expresses his ideas with increasing directness. The threatening goddess becomes the man-killing object of lust, which in turn undergoes a metamorphosis. 'Hope' shows pregnancy, the fruit of active lust. Klimt's view of woman emerges in these three paintings, and even more clearly in the drawings. 'Hope' is one of the key pictures, containing within itself more levels of meaning than most of his other work. This multiplicity has been disregarded in the past.

The drawings

There are more than 2000 drawings known to be by Klimt, many of them female nudes. This phenomenon is treated briefly at this point; a later chapter studies 'the draughtsman'. Apart from the female nude, shown from different viewpoints, Klimt drew lovers in various postures, women united in lesbian love, masturbating women, demonstrations of sexual organs, pregnant women with and without a man.

Klimt's view of woman is shown in these drawings more clearly than in the paintings. One aspect above all others is frequently in the foreground: the total availability of the woman for the man. The man – in this case Klimt – presents the woman as passive sexual object. Usually her body is made available to the man who enjoys her while she sleeps, or lies quietly. It is man's fantasies, not woman's, that are excited by these displays, including those of lesbian love.

Not enough is known about Klimt or his environment for any detailed discussion of these matters to be possible.

But public response to the pictures is interesting. They were recently subjected to a precise analysis, from which extracts are reproduced here; the extracts are informative both about Klimt and about those who have written about him, particularly art historians. Apart from the inherent eroticism of these drawings, one of the most distinctive qualities was found to be the freedom of the women portrayed, indicating "a liberation of woman from the inequitable ties of bourgeois morality".[113]

83/84 Portrait of a Lady, 1916/17
Oil on canvas, 60 × 55 cm
Gallery Ricci-Oddi, Piacenza

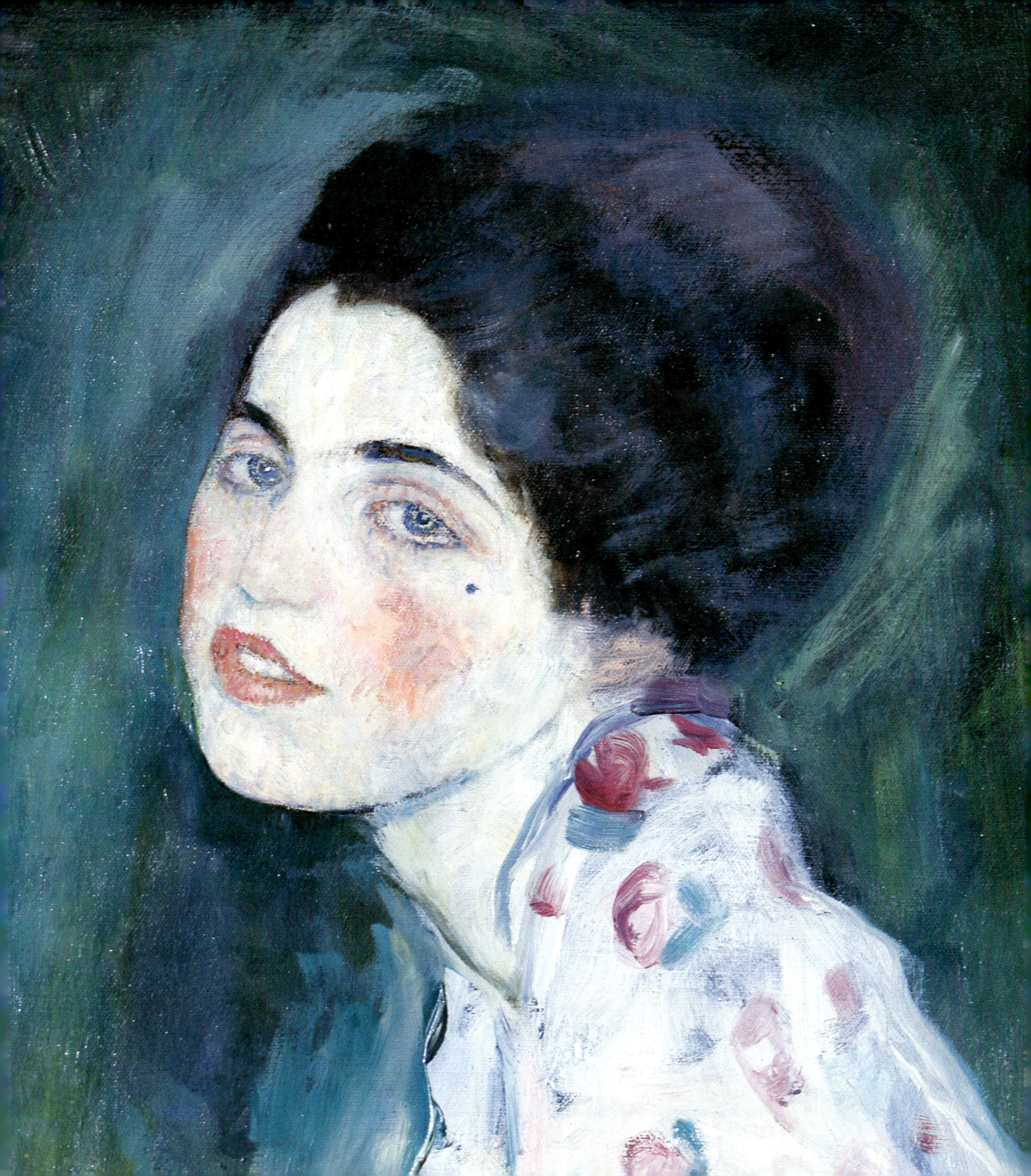

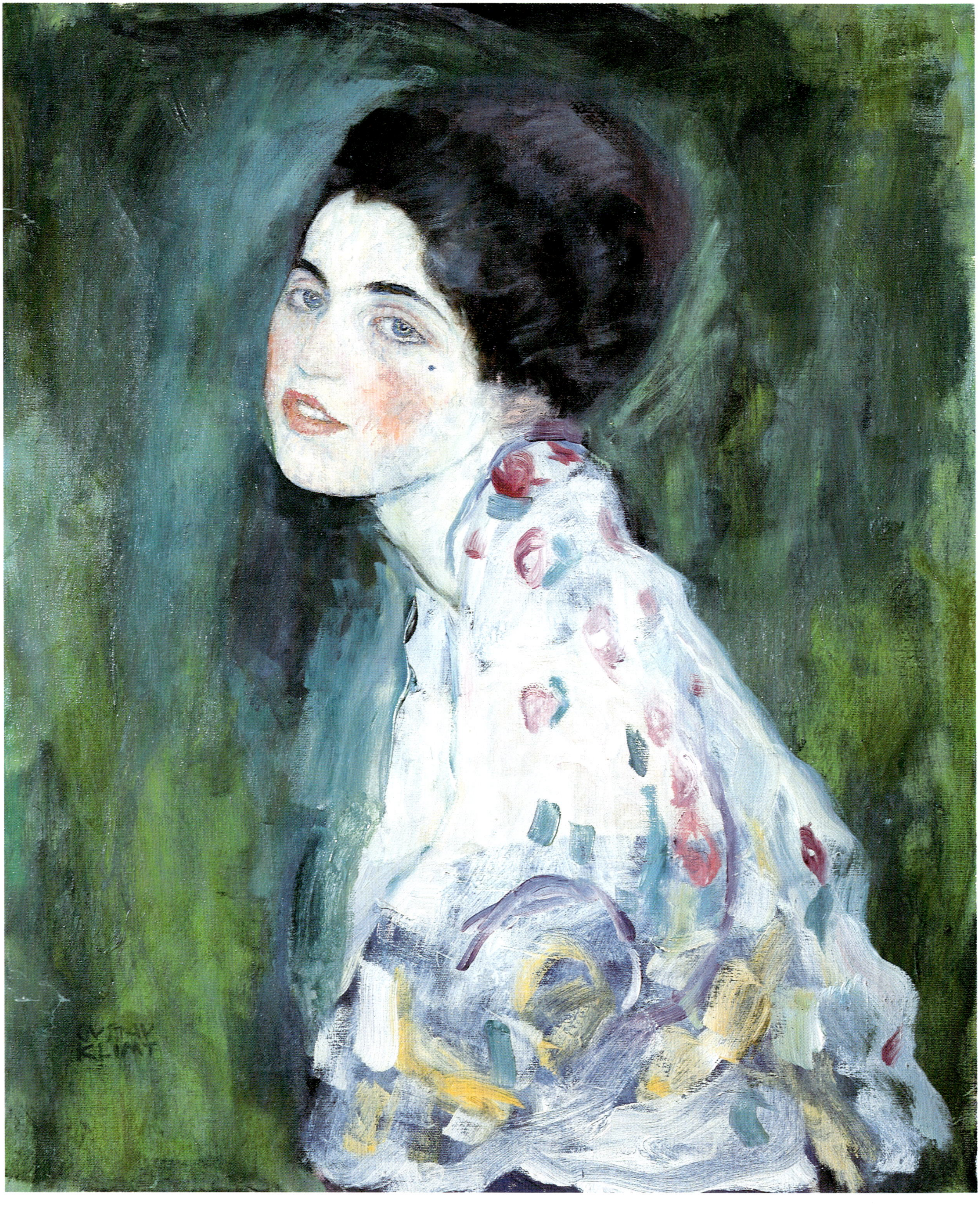

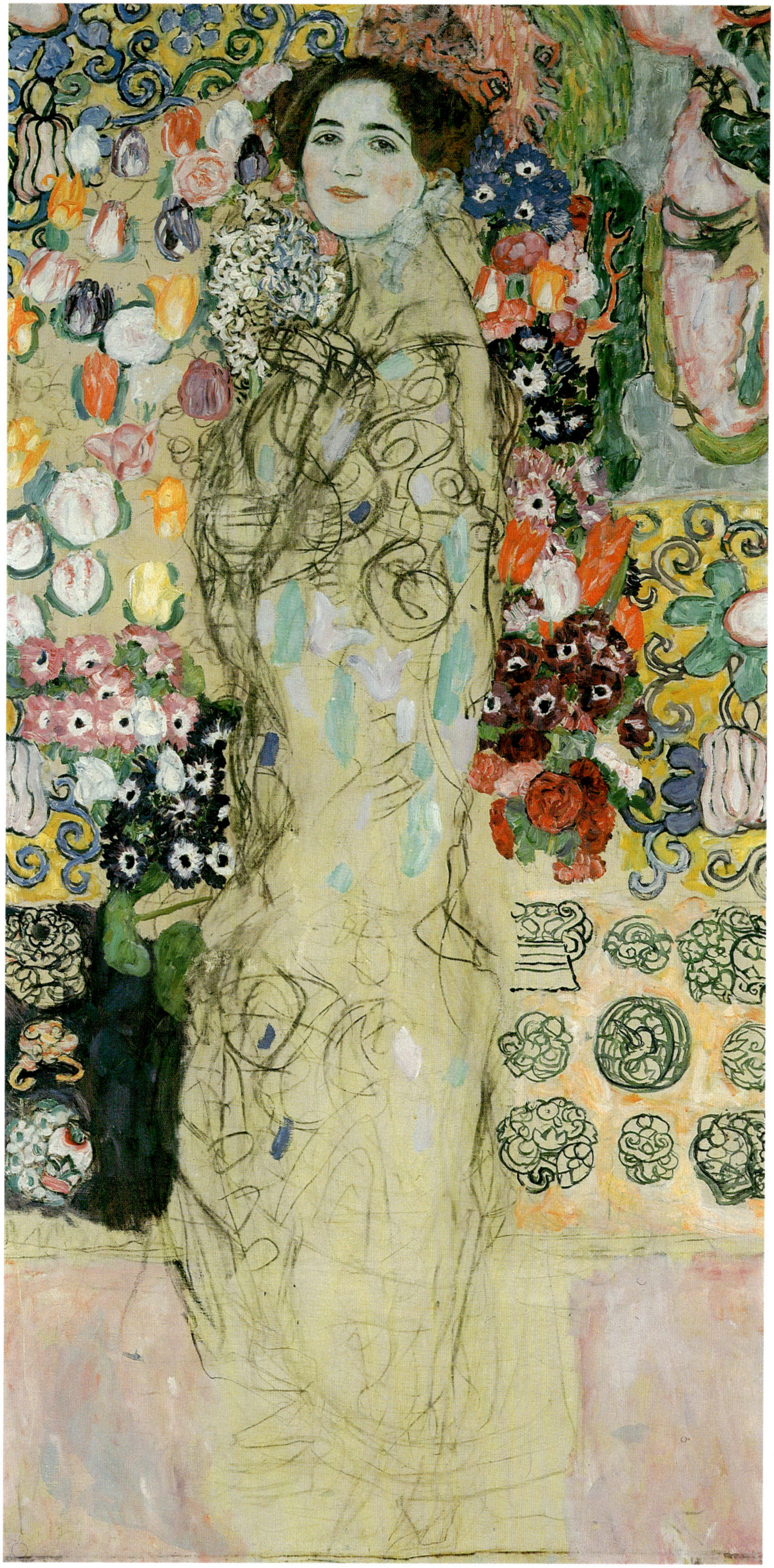

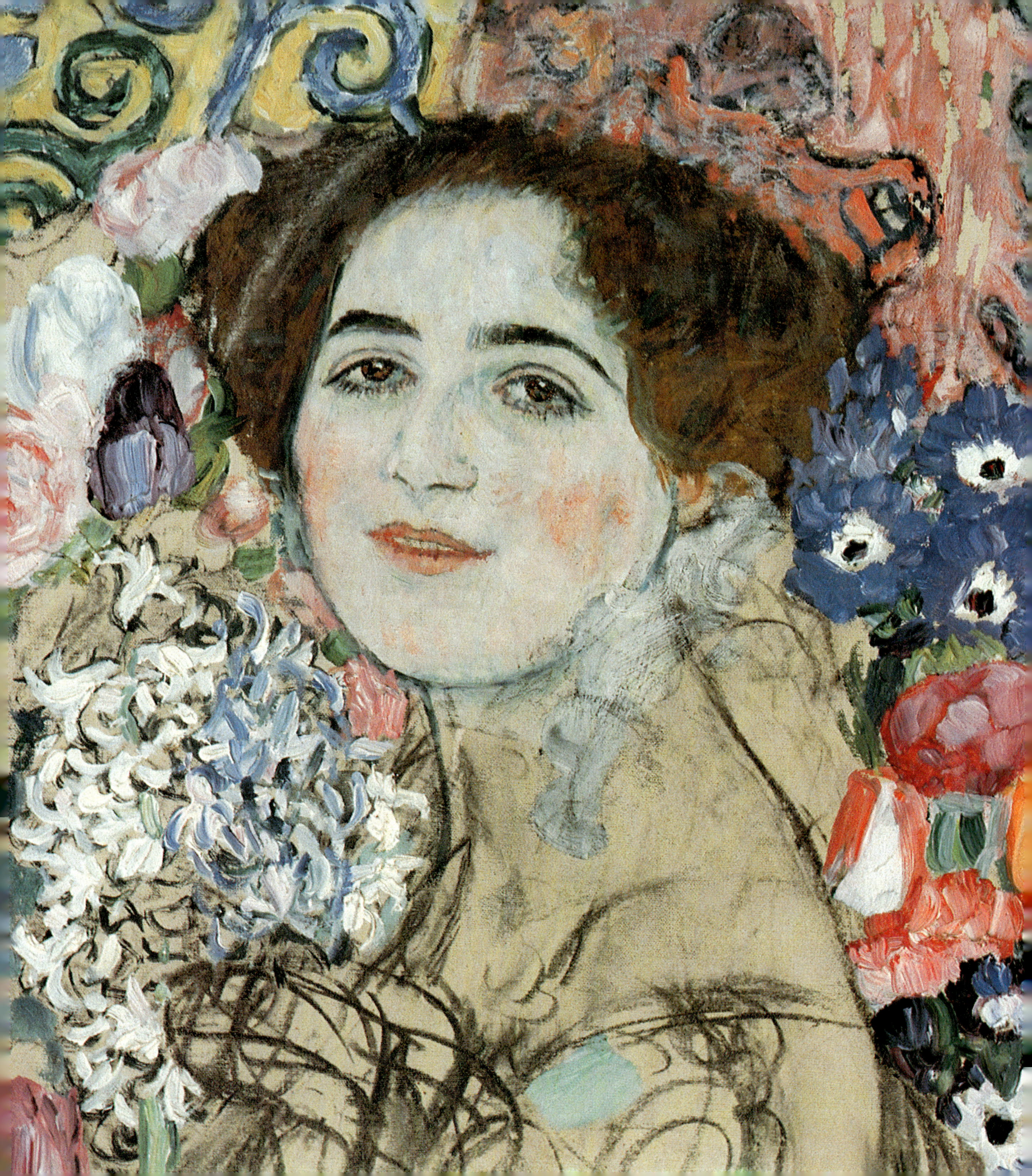

The fact that these drawings were done by a man seems to have been forgotten. The Viennese art historian Gottfried Fliedl has studied the various different interpretations offered and comments: "What is celebrated so enthusiastically as 'erotic' turns out to be the artistic scenario of man's view of woman. Neither the portrayal of the varying states of the human psyche nor the full scale of the differentiated expression of erotic and sexual sense impressions can be seen as the 'actual' themes of the drawings. They are the product of a limited interest in woman reduced to a few instances of sexual sensitivity... A great many drawings have recently come to light, and if it is the ones showing couples and groups of women, showing sexual relations between women and masturbating women, which are polished up for public display, then that is an indication of continuing and at times blatant voyeuristic interest in seeing woman displayed exclusively as a 'creature of instinct' driven by the sexuality taken to be her 'actual nature'."[114]

Woman is defined in the drawings only by her sexuality, often controlled by man. "'Liberation'... is to be seen more in the freedom given to 'man's eyes', in a discarding of taboos in artistic representation, in an extension of man's invasion of the most private moments of female sexuality, legitimised in the name of art."[115]

These observations give reason to doubt the thesis "that Klimt's art alters traditional moral notions, breaks through them in an emancipatory way. Even if we leave out of consideration the comprehensive control of an artist over his model which forbids any thought about her emancipation through art, the existence of such concerns at the end of the century presupposes a corresponding receptivity in society at that time."[116]

The investigation of Klimt's view of woman has not yielded satisfactory results as yet, because the environment of the time has not been taken into consideration: "... many of Klimt's nudes... display both the wish for unrepressed sexual expression and at the same time the regressive male image of woman as merely sexual creature of nature... the gently aesthetic subtlety with which this problem is treated in Klimt's art, and the virtuoso nature of this treatment... evidently cut short even today the inquiry into the social and cultural conditions in which Klimt developed 'his' view of woman."[117]

85/86 Portrait of a Lady, 1917/18 (unfinished)
Oil on canvas, 180 × 90 cm
New Gallery, Linz

These quotations show how difficult it is to grasp fully Klimt's view of woman. Various aspects have emerged during the discussions of the portraits, the 'femme fatale' and 'Hope'. They have shown that Klimt's attitude is not always the same, which is hardly surprising since he seems to have related to different women in very different ways. On the one hand he seems, like many others, to have been convinced by the tenets of Otto Weininger, on the other hand he portrayed his companion Emilie Flöge as a woman of great self-assurance, giving her a unique position above the level of all the others.

Margarethe Stonborough-Wittgenstein is known to have possessed a good measure of self-confidence, but Klimt saw her differently. He applied 'his' view of woman to her, and had to accept that the result did not please her.

Klimt's view of women was undoubtedly determined in part by his close relationships with them – he lived all his life with his mother and two of his sisters – and in part by the besetting fear of seduction. His view of women includes elements of motherhood, of the mystery of motherhood and of the exploitability of the woman as a plaything and sexual object. The independent woman is represented only by Emilie Flöge.

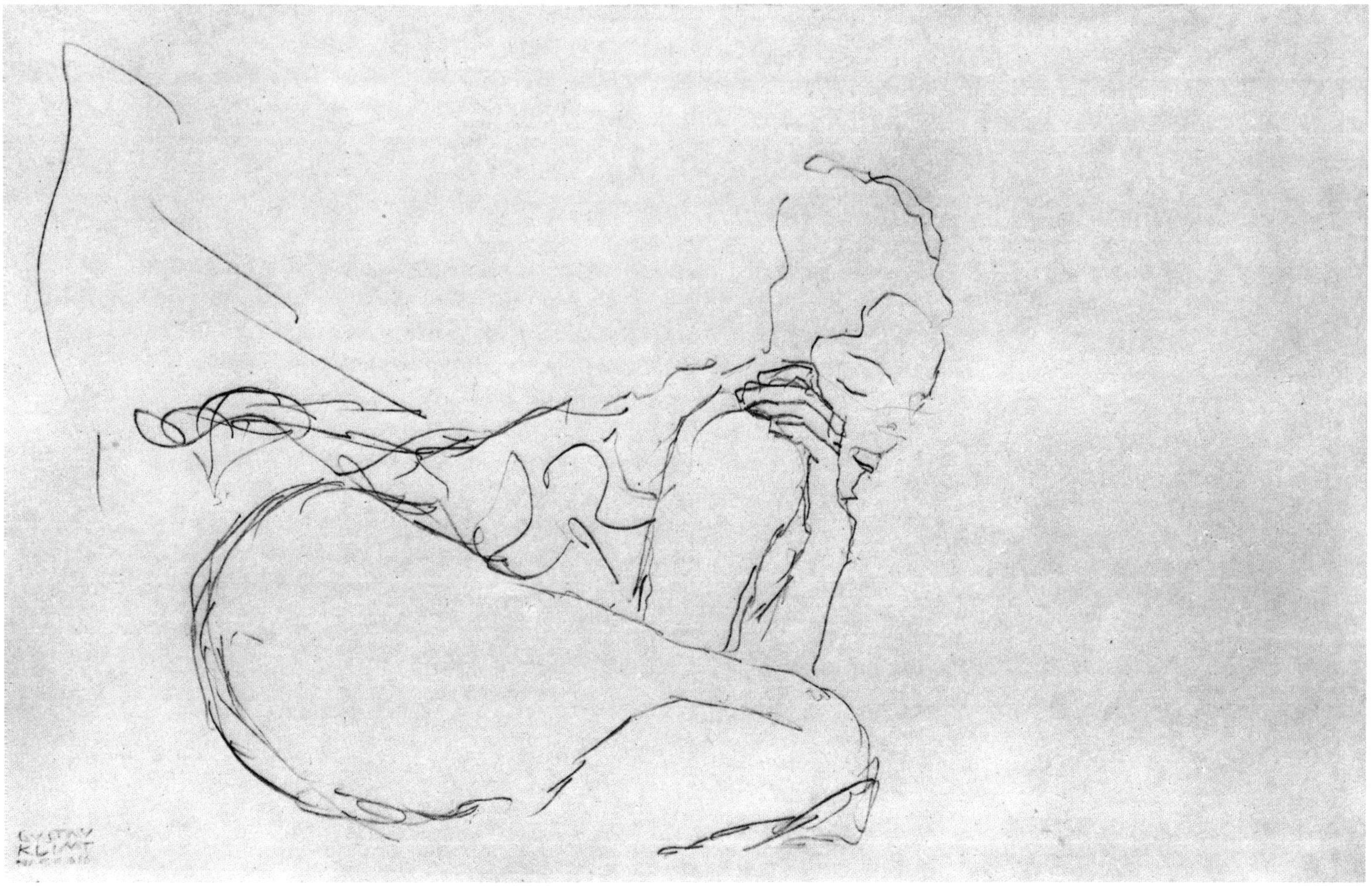

Half-figure, sleeping. c. 1915
Pencil, 36.7 × 55.9 cm

'The Kiss' – theme and variations

In the art exhibition of 1908, there was a painting on display in the room (No. 22) reserved for Klimt's pictures, which the artist himself had entitled 'Lovers', and which is generally known today as 'The Kiss'. It passed straight from the exhibition to the Austrian Gallery, and Ludwig Hevesi wrote at the time: "The recent good Klimt news caused me to return to the exhibition. The Ministry of Education has purchased Klimt's 'Lovers' for the Modern Gallery... Education minister Dr Marchet... has rendered our modern art a notable service by this purchase."[118] Of the Klimt room and the picture itself he wrote: "This Klimt hall at the exhibition is the most remarkable painted assortment seen in Vienna since Makart's Dumba room. A purely painterly painting, not possible before Makart, a specific phenomenon of colour... The Modern Gallery's new lovers stand in a sea of flowers, like Homer's old Zeus on Mount Ida when Hera embraced him once more and a carpet of flowers broke forth from the earth. And the lovers wear festive robes, just right for a festival of love. The whole world is festive again... The special Viennese modulation of feeling, newly arrived, is at long last to be recognised as the people begin to discover there's a place in their hearts for Klimt. Not long now and he'll be 'our Klimt'."[119]

Hevesi compared Klimt to Makart, Vienna had a new prince of painters. 'The Kiss' did not present society with a scandal, as so many of Klimt's pictures did. On the contrary, the painting was received with enthusiasm from the beginning, as is shown by the immediate sale. It has remained Klimt's most famous work, and has also become in a sense a symbol of Vienna Jugendstil, which has resulted, however, in extravagant marketing that has recently provided an opportunity for satire:

"Klimt's painting 'The Kiss', reproduced with high polish, adorns aesthetic niches in bourgeois apartments as well as spartan cabinets in experimental communes. It is televised and broadcast all over the world as 'a living picture', promoted by the organisers of the Opera Ball on the occasion of the Vienna Philharmonic Orchestra's New Year concert, and serves time and time again as a commercial for the series 'How we Austrians love'. Vastly enlarged, a reproduction, with additional fantasy landscape, decorates the walls of a villa outside Vienna. Imbued with additional magic powers, it becomes an instrument for the soul-mending efforts of a Viennese lady psychoanalyst: her couch clients find themselves lying beneath a poster of 'The Kiss' as they are questioned about their inner life."[120]

The picture, painted on gold ground reminiscent of Byzantine icons, before which the golden lovers in a meadow of flowers embrace, arouses hope and longing for harmony and happiness. Looked at more closely, and particularly with its precursors in mind, it reveals other components too, which expose the dubiousness of this illusion.

In 1895, twelve years prior to the transitional phase in which he now was, Klimt had painted the picture 'Love' (see p. 81). In the earlier picture the lovers are shown in profile, the man holding the woman in his arms and bending his head towards her. His face is in shadow so that the expression is unclear. The light falls on the face of the woman, her head is tilted back, her eyes are closed, she offers her mouth to be kissed. The man is the strong, active, dominating partner, while the woman is presented as the devoted, expectant object. The heads hovering above the pair point not only to the ages of man (childhood, youth, old age), but also to the ever-present threat of death.

In the first of the three faculty pictures, 'Philosophy', the figures soaring in space include a pair of embracing lovers (see p. 314). As in 'Love' the two figures are shown from the side, but here the man is not larger than the woman. His face is hidden against her shoulder, only her face is visible. His muscular back affirms his male strength, the woman's body is almost entirely covered by her long hair and the figures beneath her. There is no actual kiss, but a tender embrace which is part of a whole, symbolising growth, ripeness and decay.

In the Beethoven Frieze (see p. 60) the kiss signifies fulfilment after the victory over the hostile powers. As in 'The Kiss' the lovers stand againt a gold ground, which breaks into the meadow of flowers on which the choir of angels is singing. Behind the lovers is a rose-bush. Klimt had used roses in 'Love' as well. As in 'Philosophy' the lovers are naked, but here the man's strong muscular back entirely conceals the woman's body. She has her arms round his neck and pulls herself up towards him, while he bends down towards her. Nothing of their faces, or their kiss, can be seen, but it can be felt. The man is again the strong and active partner. It was he who, as the knight in golden armour, vanquished the hostile forces. His reward for the victory in battle is the love that awaits him, personified as a woman. Her womanhood is more important than her individuality; neither her body nor her face can be discerned.

The last precursor of 'The Kiss' seems to be 'Fulfilment' in the Stoclet Frieze (see p. 66), though it is in fact likely that Klimt worked on both pictures at the same time. The Stoclet Frieze was finished later, but preparations had begun in 1905. The ideas for both pictures were probably developed at much the same time.

In the Stoclet Frieze the lovers stand on a meadow of flowers, the rose-bush flowers far away at the other end of the wall, but is there. As in the Beethoven Frieze the man's body covers the woman's, though her face and one hand are visible. Life is symbolised by the great tree, the three birds of prey pose a minimal threat. The dominance of the man is expressed above all by the magnificent ornamentation of his robe. The wide-cut neck reveals the top of the same muscular back as in the Beethoven Frieze. The woman again has her eyes closed, but her head is on the same level as his. As in 'Philosophy' we see not a kiss but a tender embrace.

At first glance 'The Kiss' seems to have little in common with these other pictures. Before a gold ground which takes up the whole of the background, so that the scene seems set in heaven as in late mediaeval paintings on wood, a pair of lovers stand, or kneel, in a meadow of flowers. The meadow extends into the picture from the left, but takes up no more than two thirds of the lower part of the picture. It ends abruptly, suggesting that the lovers are poised on the edge of a precipice. The threat symbolised in the other pictures by death, hostile forces and birds of prey, here takes the form of a precipice over which the lovers might fall at any moment.

In spite of the gold background the lovers are framed, as in the Beethoven Frieze, by a golden aureola, which the broad-shouldered man covers on his side with his long golden robe, so that it is visible only above their heads and at the side of the woman; beside her slender body it forms a continuous vertical line with the edge of the precipice, symmetrically balanced against the breadth of the man on her other side. The man's golden robe is adorned chiefly with black, white and grey rectangular shapes, the woman's with round ornamentation within which round stylised flowers are painted. It is noteworthy that the woman's robe is tight-fitting, revealing the curves of her body. She kneels turning towards the man, towards the left, her bare toes braced against the edge of the precipice. Her shoulders are drawn high, her head is tilted back, turned sideways so that she faces straight out of the picture, her eyes closed. The flowers adorning her hair are drawn right round her head, enclosing it in a circle, giving the sense – as in some of the portraits – of a halo. The man, whose posture is masked by the wide folds of his gown so it is not possible to see whether he is standing or kneeling, is scarcely taller than she. He clasps the woman's head in both hands. His body turns lightly towards the right, his head is inclined towards her mouth for the kiss. As in 'Love' his face is in shadow, and is further obscured by the turn of the head towards the kiss. The womans holds his right hand in one of her hands, her other arm is round his shoulders. Her closed eyes and the anatomically impossible position of the head make her seem 'lifeless'. Her passivity reduces her once more to an object. The sexual element is suggested by the contours of the body, not otherwise found in Klimt's work at this time.

Most revealing is the curve of the buttocks seen through the robe. It is remarkable too that the feet, which Klimt almost always covered at this period with long dresses, are not only shown but are also seeking to grip the ground with symbolic force.

Although the man is seen from the front, he strongly resembles the figures in the Beethoven and Stoclet friezes. His manly strength is felt in the broad neck revealed by the robe, his male dominance is evident,

87/88 The Virgin, 1913
Oil on canvas, 190 × 200 cm
Národní Gallery, Prague

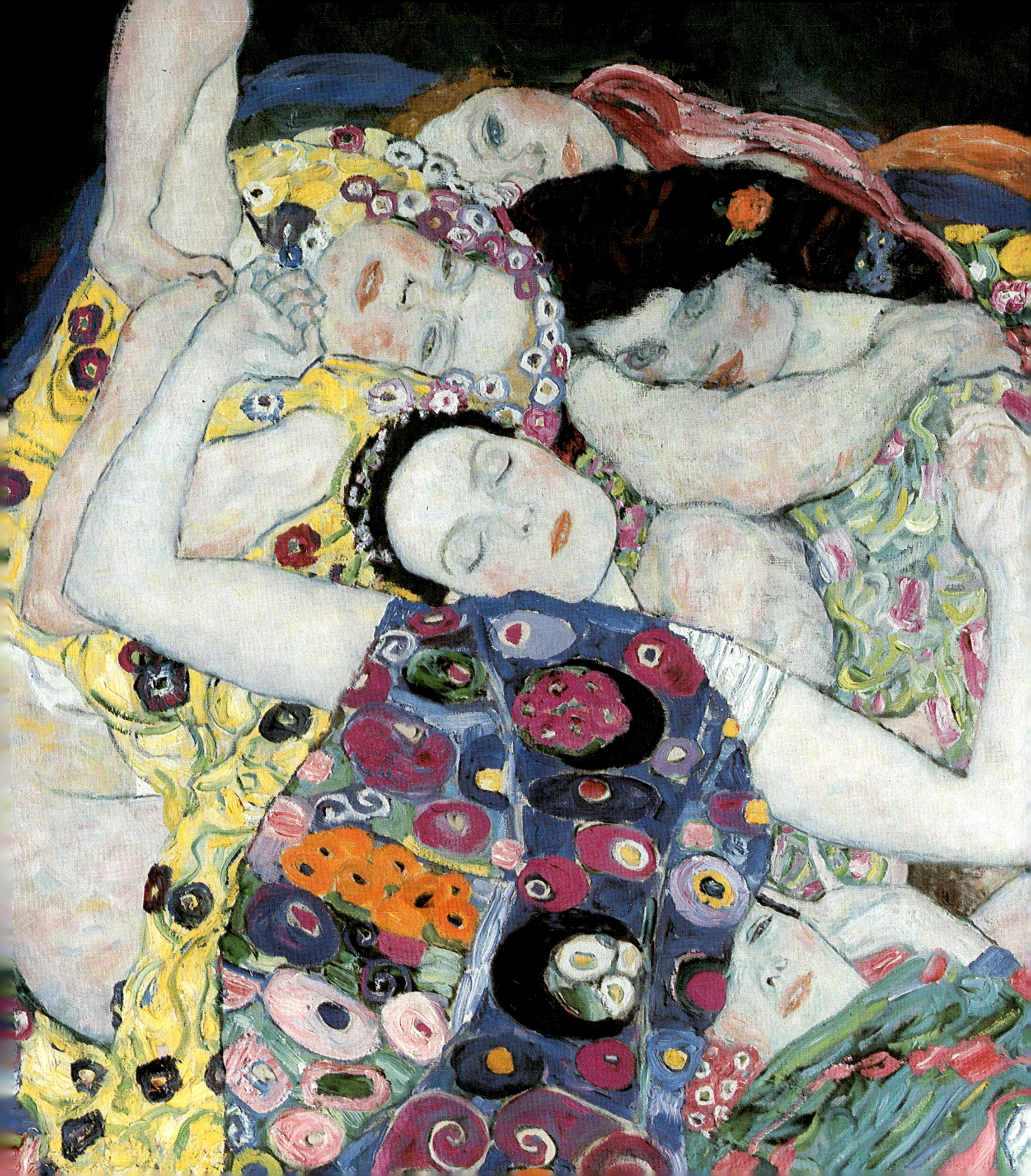

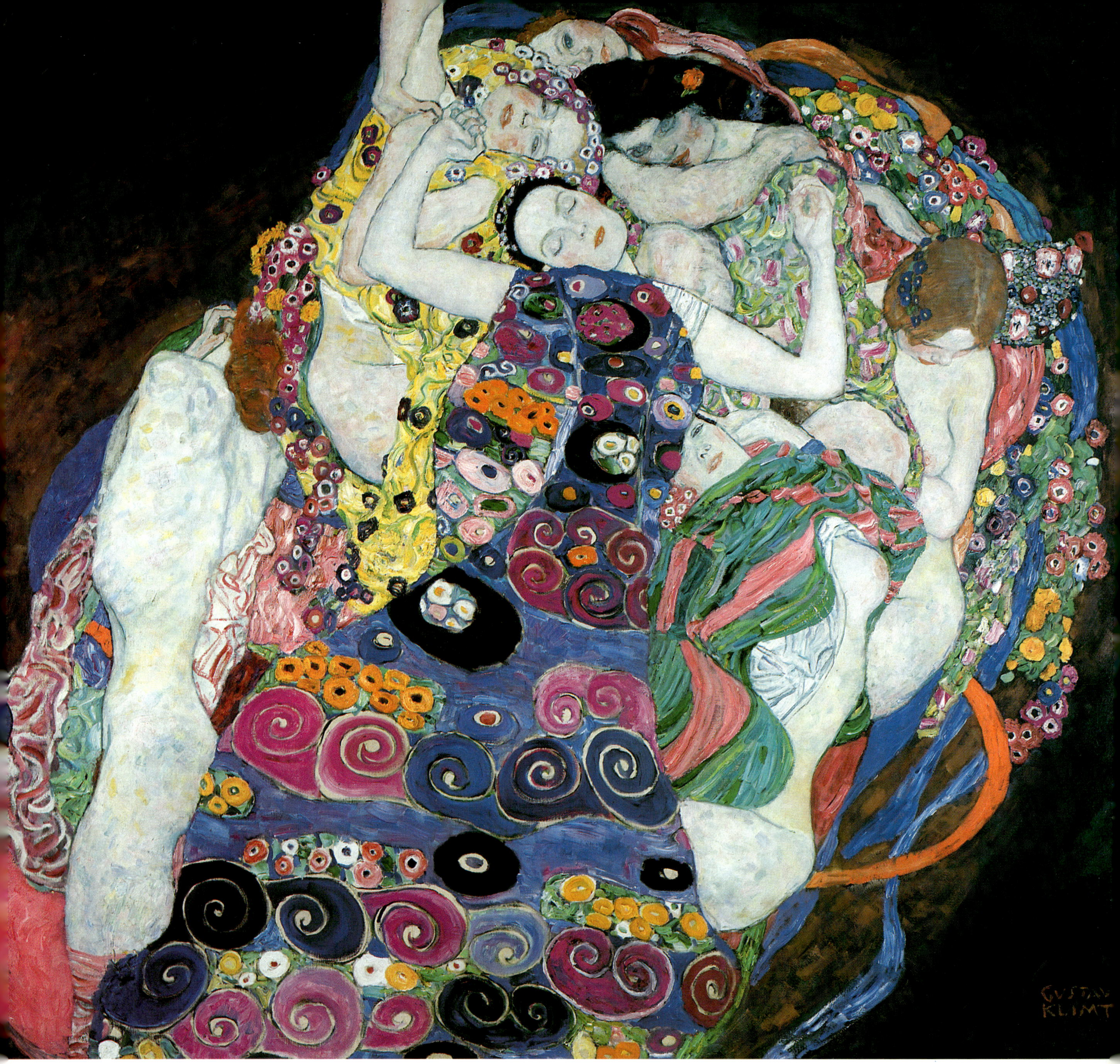
GUSTAV
KLIMT

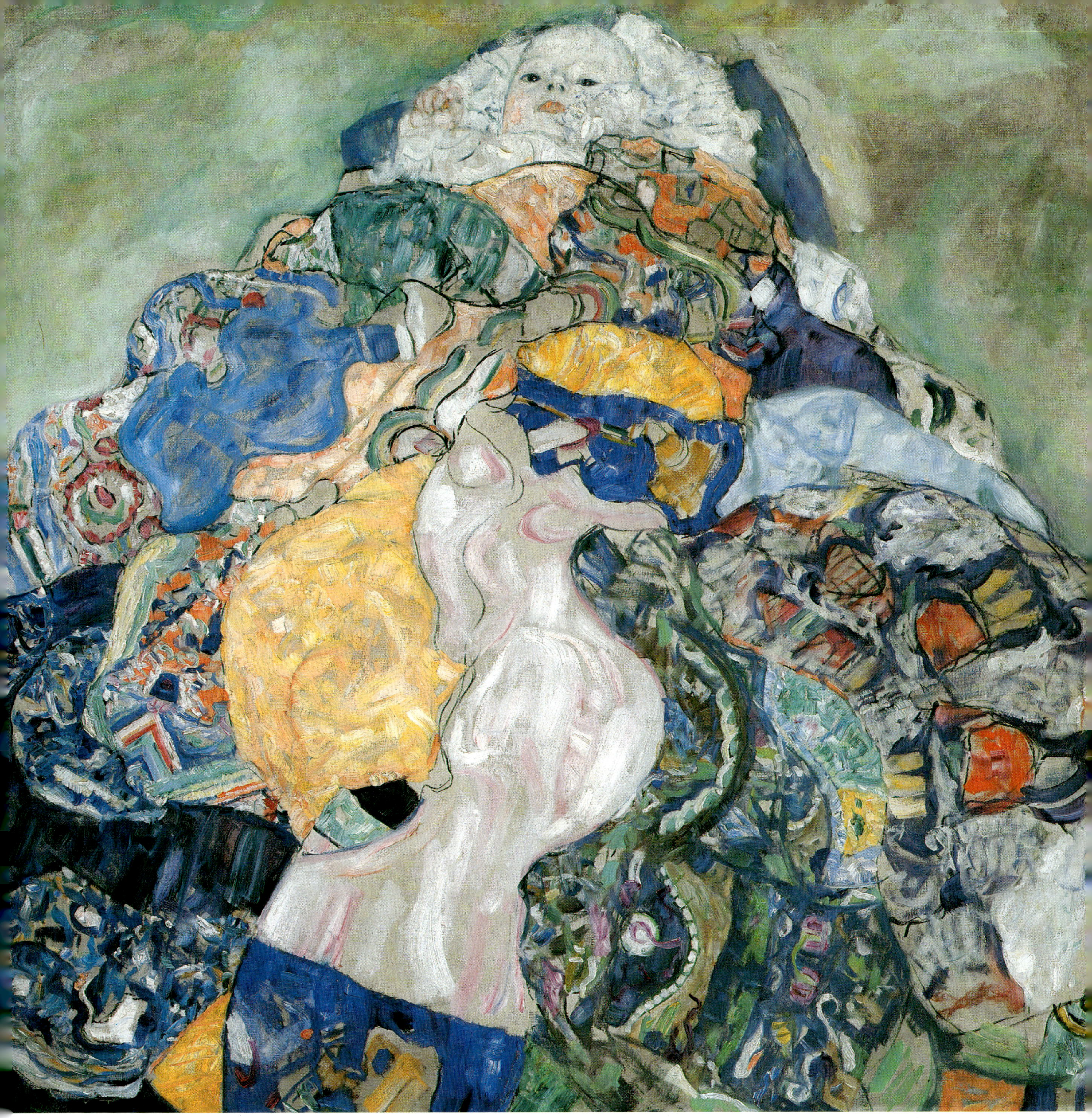

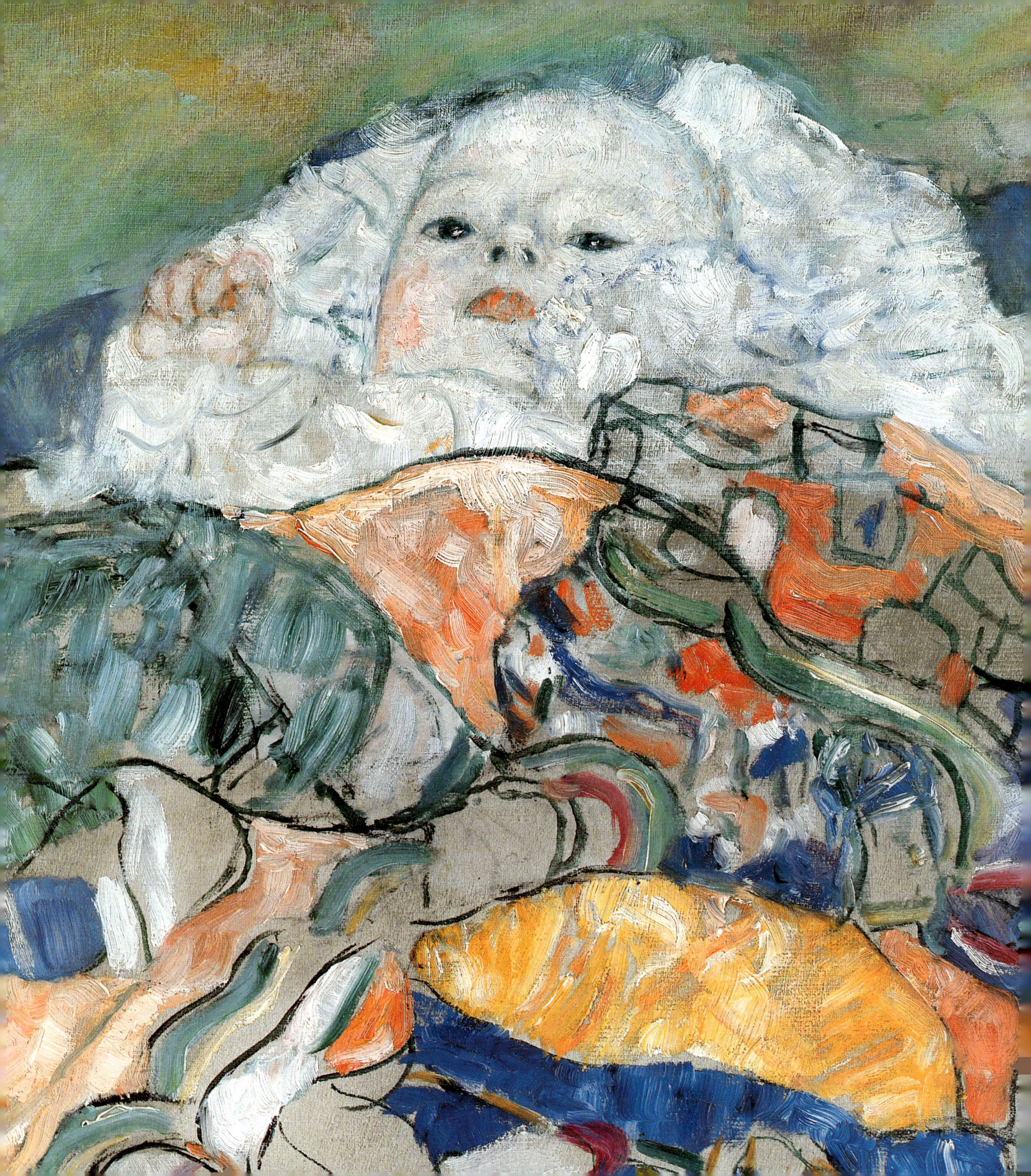

89/90 Baby (Cradle), 1917/18 (unfinished)
Oil on canvas, 110 × 110 cm
National Gallery of Art, Washington

compelling the woman back into the rôle assigned to her by Otto Weininger.

According to the recently published notes of a former model from Salon Flöge, Emilie Flöge saw in this couple Klimt and herself. A 1917 sketch-book has come to light with a little sketch of lovers embracing, and "Emilie" written in large letters beside it. Klimt was averse to painting his own features, which could explain why the man's face is shown not only in profile but also in shadow.

The desire to see in this most famous of Klimt's pictures something of his own life is in this way fulfilled. The picture can be taken to show not only the idealisation of love, but the exaltation of the artist's own love.

In a Klimt monograph of 1942 the picture was interpreted as follows: "Two lovers arise in this picture from an Arcadian meadow full of flowers, their clothing incorporeal, resolved in arabesques, decoration in the highest sense of the word; only faces and hands are of the earth, framed in a sacramental aureole of pure gold. The mystery of union with nothing withheld,the soul all-pervading in the image."[121]

Reading descriptions like this shows how intense the longing for personalisation of the figures must have been, and the notes and sketchbook will have brought satisfaction. Yet it would be a mistake to see in 'The Kiss' only a self-portrait of Klimt with Emily Flöge. It must be kept in mind that there is no portrait likeness in these two figures, and although there is sometimes a private ingredient in Klimt's pictures, they never display his feelings openly but always contain a far greater measure of more general meaning. So it is interesting to know that the lovers can be seen as the artist and his companion, but this detail of knowledge is of little importance in understanding what the picture is, more generally, about.

In the light of the subject matter of 'Love', 'Philosophy' and the Beethoven Frieze it seems remarkable that in 'The Kiss' only the precipice symbolises peril. It would be an over-simplification to say that at this period Klimt was relinquishing symbolism in favour of ornamentation, and that therefore there was less of a message to be conveyed. The painting seems to occupy too significant a position for this to be the case.

In the art exhibition of 1908, where 'The Kiss' was shown for the first time, it hung next to 'Three Ages of Woman'. This picture not only has the same dimensions as 'The Kiss' (180 × 180 cm), it is also comparable in composition. Right and left sides of the picture are unfilled, the background is composed of areas of colour. In the centre are the three ages of woman before a yellow-gold field strewn with gold discs. There is a suggestion of flowers. A shrunken old nude represents old age. She is shown from the side, her face turned away so that only her hair can be seen. Her posture expresses despair at the end of life, her body shows all the signs of decay. To the right beside her a young woman faces the front. Her head is inclined to one side, her eyes are closed. With her temple resting on the sleeping child's head, she hugs and holds it closely to her. The baby's sex cannot be made out as its body is pressed close to the mother. As in 'Philosophy', growth, ripeness and decay are represented, though in this case only through women. The male is missing. 'The Kiss' and 'Three Ages of Woman' supplement one another, and together they yield the key message of so many of Klimt's pictures. Looked at together, they show the love that leads to procreation, human life in its different stages, and the threat of death that can strike at any moment, through perils (the precipice) or through age. It is necessary to consider the possibility that Klimt conceived of the pictures as a diptych, a unity. The different times of composition (1905 and 1907/08) are not so surprising, for Klimt was a slow worker, and these two or three years are not long compared with the time he spent on the three faculty pictures or on the Stoclet Frieze.

'The Kiss' will remain Klimt's most popular picture, its appeal undimmed by interpretations, comparisons and the search for sources, its fascination unchallenged, though scholars are still at odds over its meaning. In the New York exhibition catalogue of 1986 it was suggested that the picture affirms the power of love and unifying sensuality, in which extravagant ornamentation becomes part of the subtle interplay of certainty and uncertainty, individuality and universality.[122]

Quite a different view is put forward by the Viennese art historian Gottfried Fliedl in his essay on public response to Klimt: "This very popular picture 'The Kiss' should not just be enjoyed as the icon of

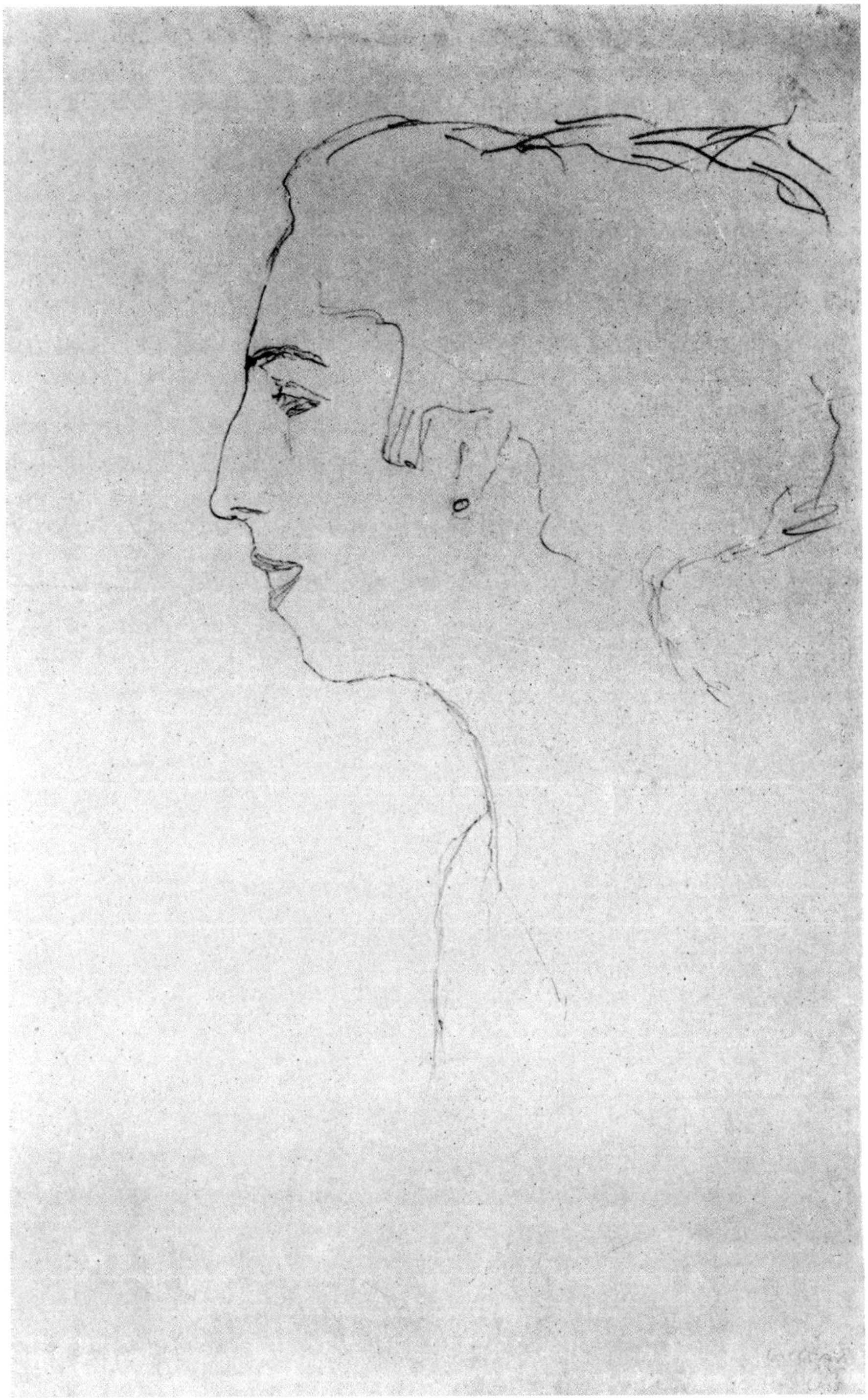

Woman's head, left profile, 1914
Pencil, 55.2 × 36.8 cm

Jugendstil bliss restored. One should not yield entirely to the seductive promise of the monumentally isolated and apparently harmonious relationship between the two lovers . . . The longing for a non-violent relationship between the sexes and for a non-violent relationship to nature appears in a dream, metamorphosized: the yearning of which the picture speaks is presented by the picture itself as something which can never be fulfilled. The aggressive defining of the male – which is revealed on close scrutiny – and his dominance over 'the female' destroy the conditions necessary for the successful relationship on which the hope of the picture believes itself founded."[123]

Some of the complexities of the picture have been worked out, others are still obscure. Much research remains to be done.

Landscape painter

Klimt's pictures of landscapes, in the widest sense of the word, form a distinct group, and it is surprising that so little has been written about them. Klimt is known chiefly for his portraits of women, the portrayals of the human condition, the Beethoven Frieze, and above all 'The Kiss'. Yet his 54 landscapes, often mentioned only in passing, make up almost a quarter of his work. When one considers that the first landscape painting dates from 1898, and that after that time he completed only 124 paintings – most of the more important ones – it becomes apparent that the 'nature' pictures make up almost half the works of this productive period. It is all the more surprising that they have received scant attention.

That Klimt did not begin any sooner to paint landscape pictures can be explained by the nature of his training, by the commissioned work undertaken by the 'Company of Artists' and by the fact that he began relatively late to spend the summer months in the country. In 1897, the year in which the Secession was founded, Klimt was thirty-five years old and had made a name for himself as one of the Ring painters. From that time on, with only a few exceptions in his latter years, he spent the summer with the Flöge family by the Attersee, the first landscape painting being completed in 1898.

The Vienna bourgeoisie liked to spend the summer months in the Salzkammergut, the Salzburg region. Many had their own places there, others rented the same accommodation year after year. When the Flöge sisters acquired their own house by the Attersee, or when they began to rent rooms there, cannot be ascertained from the contradictory evidence that has survived. Certain it is that they usually left for the country sooner than Klimt did. He was often delayed by delivery deadlines and his postcards to Emilie suggest that he did not like staying behind.

Sooner or later he packed his things, above all canvas and paint, and set off. There are several cards written in July 1907 in which he laments the need to finish a picture, yet cannot leave it as it is. At the same time he was drawn to the Attersee. "... I've already packed up a lot – just need to put it in the basket – but the pictures!" (9.7 1907) "Rotten day all round – getting nowhere with work – perhaps I'll put off delivery until September, no good otherwise. Lots of packing done already." (10.7) "... last go at the picture – not so much lack of time, just isn't any good, that's the trouble ..." (11.7) "Can't do anything with the picture – I've ordered them to collect it on Monday – Saturday as arranged." (11.7, evening) "... Packing, shopping, finishing the picture, a haircut – lots of wonderful things – in spite of winding everything up!" (12.7, morning) "Studio bag packed – picture case not yet obtained. Sleeper promised. Looking forward to seeing you." (12.7)[124]

In the country Klimt, who must have been very athletic, enjoyed rowing and sailing. Later he was one of the first people in Austria to acquire a motor-boat. There are photographs both of expeditions on the lake, sometimes with Emilie Flöge, and of country walks with her and with other friends.

The environment in which he spent the summer months is the 'nature' of his landscape paintings. The pictures were always at least begun in the country, though some were completed in Vienna. This explains the absence of winter landscape paintings. All the pictures taken from nature reflect summer or autumn moods.

Letters written to Mizzi Zimmermann in Vienna between 1900 and 1903 give an account of Klimt's daily routine in the country: "Early in the morning, about 6, sometimes a bit earlier, or a bit later – up I get – if the weather's good I go to the forest – paint a little beech wood (if the sun's shining) with a few conifers, till round about 8, then breakfast, and after that a bathe, very careful – then a bit more painting, of the lake if it's sunny, of the view from my window if it's not ... by that time it's noon, after lunch a nap ... before or after tea another bathe in the lake ... after tea more painting. – a big poplar at dusk with a storm brewing ... dusk ... evening meal – then early to bed and up again early next day. Sometimes a little rowing gets into the daily programme to shake up the muscles a bit."[125]

So the day was carefully apportioned between work and relaxation. The account suggests that he worked on several pictures at once. Other letters to Mizzi Zimmermann tell how he spent the first few days by the Attersee relaxing, not painting, but could not put up with that for long. "Today I'm going to begin work again in earnest – I'm looking forward to it, doing nothing gets boring after a bit."[126]

Although Klimt painted many landscapes, only three landscape drawings have survived; they are in the few sketchbooks that have come to light, in which Klimt tended to capture first ideas in hasty drawings. There were presumably more landscape sketches in the books that were destroyed by fire in 1945. Yet there was no need here for preliminary studies of the various aspects of a picture such as he made above all for paintings of the body. As the correspondence shows, he painted out of doors directly onto the canvas. Often he hid his easel in the bushes in order to take up painting at the same place next day. In later years he went out on the lake in his motor-boat and painted from there. This was closer to the practice of the Impressionists than to the later French painters of Emile Bernard's circle, who rejected painting in the open air (see p. 36).

It is significant that in his landscape painting Klimt is closest to Neo-Impressionism and Pointillism. A tree, a lake, a meadow was composed of tiny delicate brush-strokes though, unlike the French, Klimt used not pure colours but various shades of one tone. It was relatively late that he started applying colour more vigorously. Hevesi termed Klimt's Pointillist manner 'trout-stippling' and explained it as follows: "One of Klimt's new landscape paintings is called 'Storm Brewing'. A deep dark picture: apparently. On the right a fine poplar, ascending all black: apparently. Looked at more closely it turns out to be stippled all over like trout, if one may use such an expression. It is sprinkled with yellow, blue, green and mauve, but it looks black."[127]

Just as in the portraits and in all the other pictures in which human figures are portrayed, with one exception, nature does not exist – apart from some very stylised flowers and trees in a few works – so also in the landscape paintings there is no trace of mankind, nor indeed – with one early exception – of animate life in any form.

The four first pictures of 1898 and 1899 are the only upright ones.

After that the canvas was always square. The square was the preferred shape, alongside the high rectangular format, for many of his other pictures also, particularly during the so-called 'golden period'. The early landscape paintings are all "typical of the traditional landscape picture in 'atmosphere', with muted colour and melancholy, entirely redolent of the contemplation of the inner peace of nature remote from the tumult of time..."[128]

'After the Rain' of 1899 is the last high rectangular landscape picture. Although an early one of the landscape paintings, it already shows many of the elements that characterised the later ones. On a meadow in full bloom grow several trees a little way in front of a stream in the background. The far bank of the stream can be seen through the tree-trunks. The tree-tops are cut off by the upper edge of the picture, so that only the trunks of most of them are visible. There is no sky or horizon. In a sense it is wrong to speak here of a 'landscape'. Klimt has painted items from nature – trees, meadows, little ponds – but not landscape as such. He used a viewfinder to look for motifs, "... a little piece of cardboard with a hole cut in it..."[129]. Later on the piece of cardboard was replaced by ivory; he always had his viewfinder with him.

The unusual feature of 'After the Rain' is that there are hens pecking for food on the meadow, introducing into the picture the animate life that is entirely lacking in Klimt's other landscape paintings. The artist was still feeling his way. Just as he included landscape in one portrait only ('Sonja Knips'), so 'After the Rain' must be seen as his only attempt to bring animate life into a landscape painting. From this point on he kept the two areas strictly separate. His landscapes became peaceful and meditative, reflecting the refreshing peace of his own summer months. In Vienna he dedicated himself anew to themes revolving round life and death.

The square format of all the landscape paintings from 1900 on helps to make them objects of meditation, conveying a sense of balanced calm which is strengthened by the paintings themselves. One senses the meditative quality of all these paintings in one of them particularly: 'Farmhouse with Birch Trees' of 1900. The farmhouse is scarcely discernible, lying hidden amongst fruit trees in the background. The square picture is dominated by the green meadow, with

91/92 Johanna Staude, 1917/18
Oil on canvas, 70 × 50 cm
Austrian Gallery, Vienna

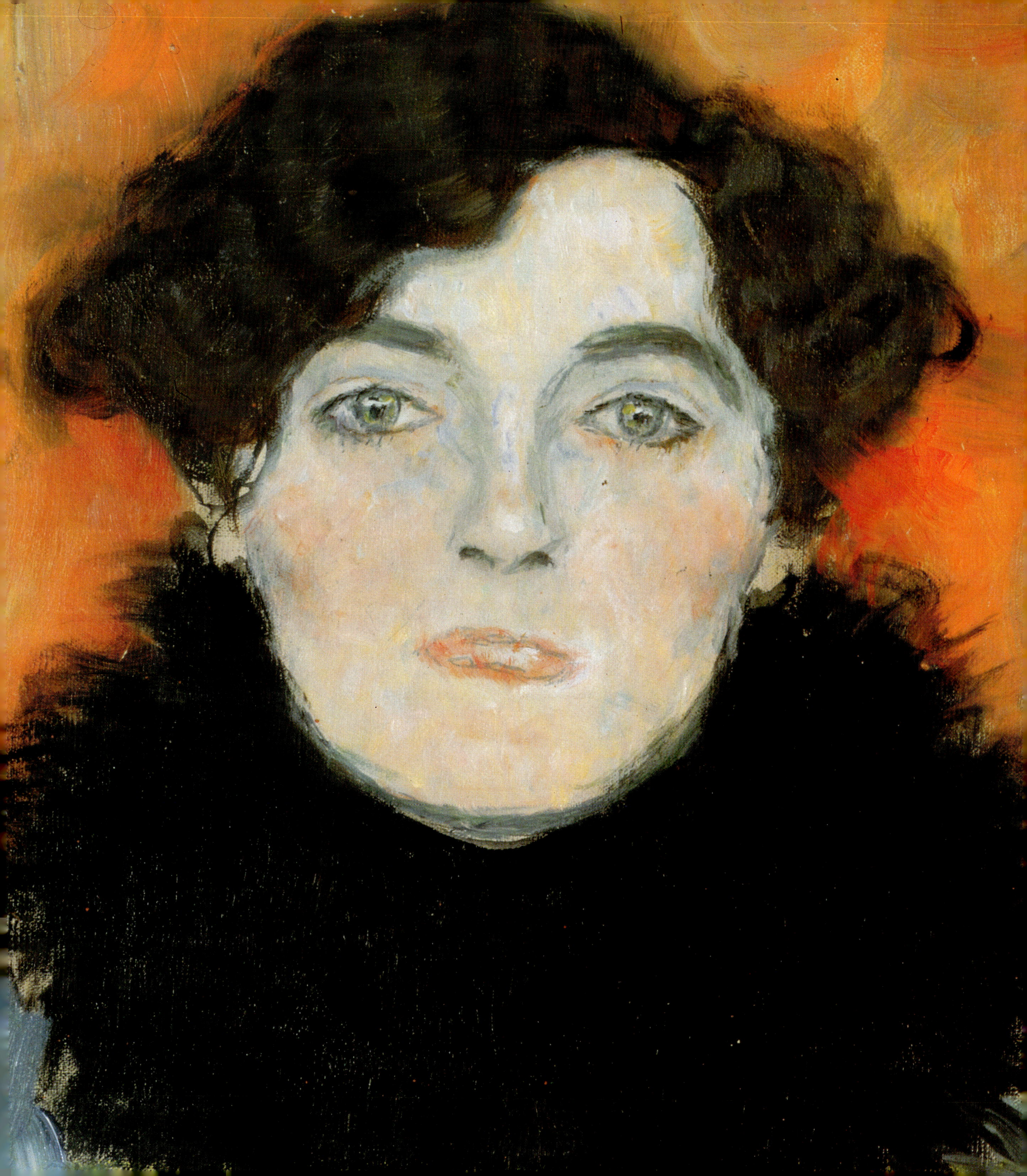

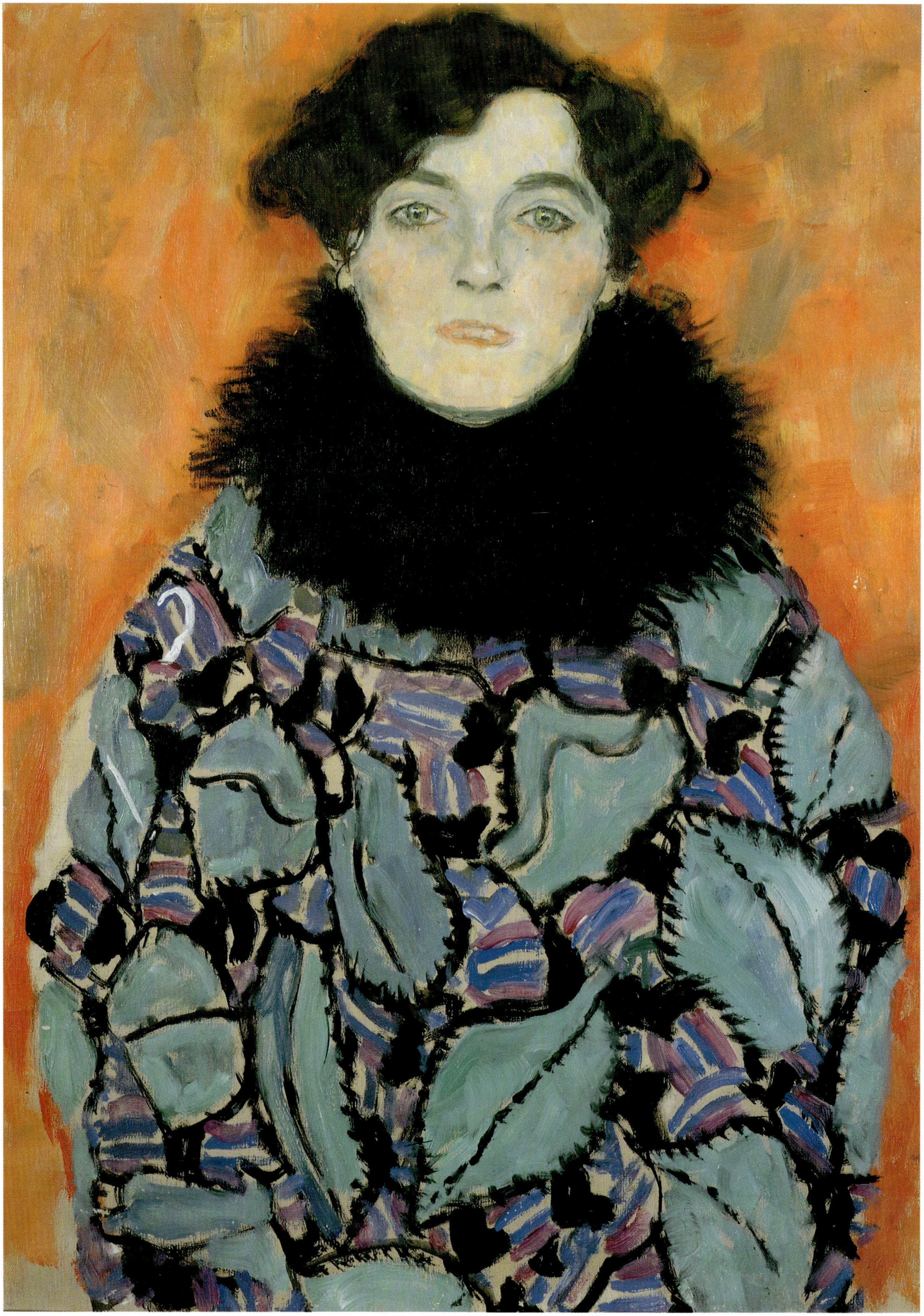

the slender trunks of four birches. The tree-trunk most in the foreground is cut off by the edge of the picture not only at the top but also by the root at the bottom. No branch or leaf gives an illusion of these birches swaying or dancing.

Klimt applied a similar technique in 'Beech Forest I' of 1902. Again the trees reach up to an unseen sky; only the beeches far to the back have leaves. Through the forest the horizon is visible, very close to the top of the picture. The forest floor is covered with leaves and twigs. The picture demonstrates what is meant by the terms 'Neo-Impressionist' and 'Pointillist' in connection with his landscape painting. Looked at from very near, the forest floor resolves into tiny different-coloured brush-strokes; only from a distance can the eye recognise twigs and leaves. A year later Klimt began to differentiate trees according to their girth, and they began to develop a life of their own as individual living organisms.

In 'Birch Forest' powerful roots as well as slender tree-trunks rise out of the leaf-covered forest floor. Variations in girth of the trunks give the trees a certain individuality previously lacking. The leaves lie on the ground, the trees are bare. Detached from the branches and decomposing on the ground, organic matter is in the process of dying. Death and life are thematicised here more cryptographically than in the pictures of people.

It is significant that these forest pictures were painted at the time when the dispute over the faculty pictures was reaching its climax (see p. 120). There is a heavy melancholy about them. The same can be said of the pictures of water painted during this period. In all of them the horizon is high up in the picture, the trees on the bank can be seen more clearly in their reflection in the water, but the reflection itself is fragmentary. In his landscapes Klimt wanted to grasp the essence behind the optical reality. Water was vital as "the female bringing forth all organic life"[130].

In 1905 the dispute over the faculty pictures reached a conclusion: Klimt had decided not to work for the state any more. The commission for the Stoclet Frieze provided the possiblity of creating part of a total work of art which, unlike the Beethoven Frieze, would last. Cheerfully coloured flower pictures, such as the two farmhouse gardens, reflect this change for the better. It is probable that work on the Stoclet Frieze also increased Klimt's tendency to resolve objects into particles of colour in his landscape paintings. The 'Poppy Field' of 1907 seems at first glance to be a sea of colours composed of the tiniest elements (mosaics), stabilised only by the sky, which is for once visible. The foreground extends upwards to the top quarter of the picture. In a meadow full of red poppies, blue cornflowers and white daisies, a few flowers stand out clearly. In the background the meadow seems to have been mown, and the trees with their green and yellow foliage stand out against the sky, so close to one another that they seem to form a kind of wall, on the left of which there is a hill crowned with trees that reaches right up into the sky. By different stylistic means Klimt achieves the same effect of detachment as in the portraits painted during this period, in which everything except face and hands dissolves into ornament ('Adele Bloch-Bauer I', 'Fritza Riedler'). Klimt used gold only once in a landscape painting, namely in the 'Golden Apple-Tree' of 1903 which was destroyed by fire in Schloss Immendorf in 1945, with the faculty pictures.

The change in Klimt's style which took place around 1910 affected his landscape painting. He painted several pictures of Schloss Kammer, from different viewpoints on land and lake. Although he did not abandon detailed studies of natural phenomena, at this stage he introduced larger cohesive shapes, such as the Schloss. The changes in style can be illustrated particularly well from the last of these pictures. The 'Avenue in Schloss Kammer Park' was painted in 1912. Klimt has rejected a bright palette in favour of a few tones. Yellow mixed with green prevails. A tree-lined avenue leads in the direction of the Schloss, sections of which can be made out in the background. The main focus is on the trees lining the avenue, which incline towards each other at the top, forming an arch. Nature becomes architecture in this "masterly and solemn work"[131]. Klimt has given up all the delicacy and lightness which characterised so many of the earlier landscapes. No slender tree-trunks ascend towards the heavens; instead thick gnarled trees with branches spreading sideways grow up out of the earth.

During these years Klimt did also paint 'proper' landscapes, both by

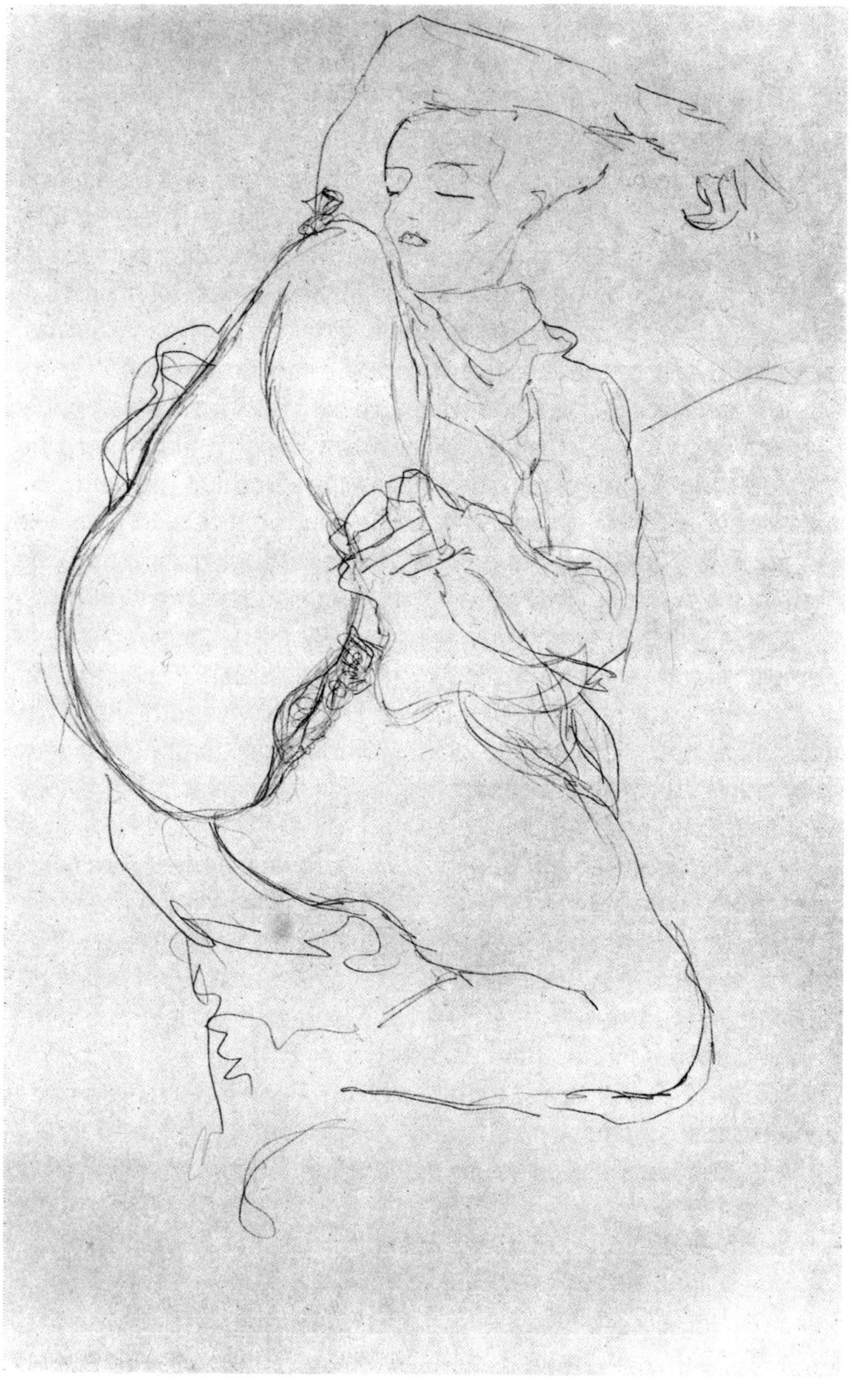

Recumbent half-figure, 1914/15
Pencil, 57.1 × 37.5 cm

Lake Garda where he exceptionally spent the summer months of 1913, and in the subsequent summers by the Attersee. The return to more traditional forms, noted here in the study of the landscape paintings, was evident in the portraits as well.

The comparison with the portraits can be carried into particulars. Thomas Zaunschirm (*1943) has recently observed that in many instances the composition of a landscape painting relates to the composition of a particular portrait. Detailed investigations still have to be carried out, but the comparisons made so far seem to carry conviction, as for instance between 'Emilie Flöge' and 'Beech Forest I', or between 'Fritza Riedler' and 'Farmhouse Garden'. It seems quite possible that in these pictures of nature Klimt was re-working material from the preceding winter's work in Vienna. In the summer paintings he enjoyed himself, experimenting, working things out, relaxing. He was free from the dreaded deadline pressure, except during the one summer when the Stoclet Frieze had to be finished and he worked on it by the Attersee. He may have made a deliberate decision to work during the summer months only on the landscape paintings, on themes that did not weigh him down. These paintings have all the makings of an independent oeuvre. Although in composition they may be linked with the other pictures he was painting at the time, their style is all their own.

Klimt has recently been described as "one of the most significant landscape painters of his time... He saw in landscape the means of entering a mood, a sort of creative stimulus like a 'jewel', a 'firework', he saw the landscape's structure and the unfolding of elemental biological life forces, but the secret of his art as a landscape painter lies in the manner in which these different ways of seeing are layered and interlaced... the landscape was for him a place of contemplation, source of joy but also of sorrow."[132]

Klimt's landscapes convey a facet of the artist's personality not shown by the other pictures, one which contributes to the overall view. The meditative quality suggests a different, more tranquil 'yearning for happiness' than that, for instance, of the Beethoven Frieze. These paintings do not have the weight of meaning associated with many of his other pictures. Yet there is still an element of Symbolism. It is likely

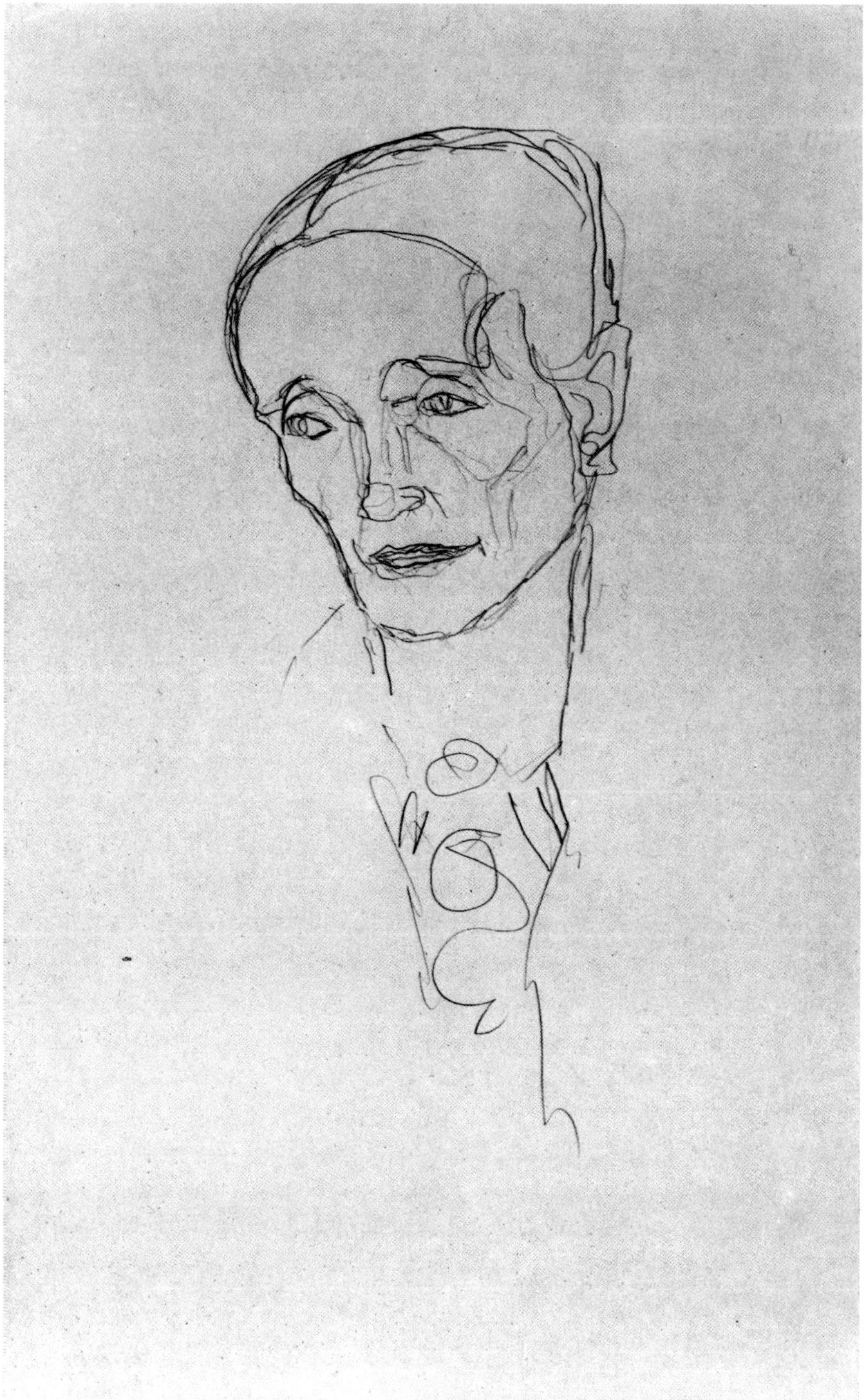

Head of old woman, 1915
Pencil, 56.5 × 36.8 cm

that they owe their distinctive character to the fact that Klimt turned his attention to landscape painting only when he was far away from Vienna, seeking solace in nature, and finding there more response to the 'yearning for happiness' than in the great city.

Draughtsman

Reference has frequently been made in the preceding chapters to Klimt's drawings. They were of great importance in his early development, and they helped to illuminate the many different aspects of his attitude to 'woman'. The remarks that follow refer not to individual drawings, but to the medium in general.

The evidence of Gustav Klimt's draughtsmanship is fragmentary. Most of the 3000 known examples, particularly those completed after the turn of the century, are rapid sketches rather than autonomous drawings. This is particularly interesting since his original training was as a drawing teacher. Drawing occupied most of his time during the early years at the School of Arts and Crafts, either as part of the course or in the first commissioned works negotiated for him by his teacher Michael Rieser. His development towards Symbolism and Jugendstil could be followed most clearly in the drawings. In the finished drawings for 'Allegory and Emblem' his affirmation of Jugendstil is complete; 'Tragedy' of 1897 was the direct model for the picture 'Pallas Athene', painted one year later, which became the 'trademark' of the Secession.

After the founding of the Secession Klimt drew illustrations for VER SACRUM, but very sparingly. During its first year of publication there were fourteen illustrations by him, but during the five years following only five more. Most of the later drawings are sketches.

The sketch-books deserve careful attention. It has long been known that fifty of these books were destroyed in 1945 by fire and until recently it was assumed that there were no sketch-books left. Now three have come to light, of which two have so far been published. One is a very early one which was in the possession of Sonja Knips, and which she is holding in Klimt's portrait of her; the other is the last Klimt used, from

22.6.1917 to 2.1.1918. He always had his sketch-book with him, so that he could note anything that caught his attention, using the book as a kind of diary.

The 1917 sketch-book includes studies and sketches for paintings of the sort found also on the loose leaves that have survived, but also quickly noted ornaments, flowers and landscapes. It is probable that he used his sketch-book whenever he went anywhere, for instance in the country, by the Attersee, or in the town, on his daily outing to the Café Tivoli, where he breakfasted. If he had an idea over breakfast, he made a note of it. His route from the Tivoli to his studio took him through the park of Schloss Schönbrunn, and it is quite likely that he lingered, sketching a flower or a plant in his little book. In the studio he drew on loose leaves, of which the 3000 that have survived are surely only a part.

The post-1900 studio drawings are exclusively of the human body, mostly rapid sketches in which he recorded a certain posture or detail of movement. From the turn of the century he repudiated the broken line which he had favoured since 1890, and restricted himself usually to the outline. In his studio there were always a good number of models "who, while he stood silent before his easel, wandered up and down, stretched and blossomed, ever ready to respond to the master's sign and be still when he spied a posture, a movement, that his sense of beauty demanded must rapidly be drawn."[133]

"There was always a model waiting in the next room, sometimes several, so that he could pick and choose what he wanted for the endless variations on the theme of 'woman'... He might just draw a face, a hand, a torso, or one slight movement perceived from nature's in exhaustible source."[134]

Although there are some contradictory details in these two eyewitness accounts, and the comments on the availability of the models seem more like myth than reality, it is clear that Klimt drew very rapidly. Yet he needed an enormous length of time to paint a picture. He always drew a great many sketches for any subject. For the first portrait of Adele Bloch-Bauer, for instance, there are more than a hundred surviving sketches.

The drawings were done very rapidly, and Klimt does not appear to

93/94 The Dancer, c. 1916/18
Oil on canvas, 180 × 90 cm
With permission of Galerie St Etienne, New York

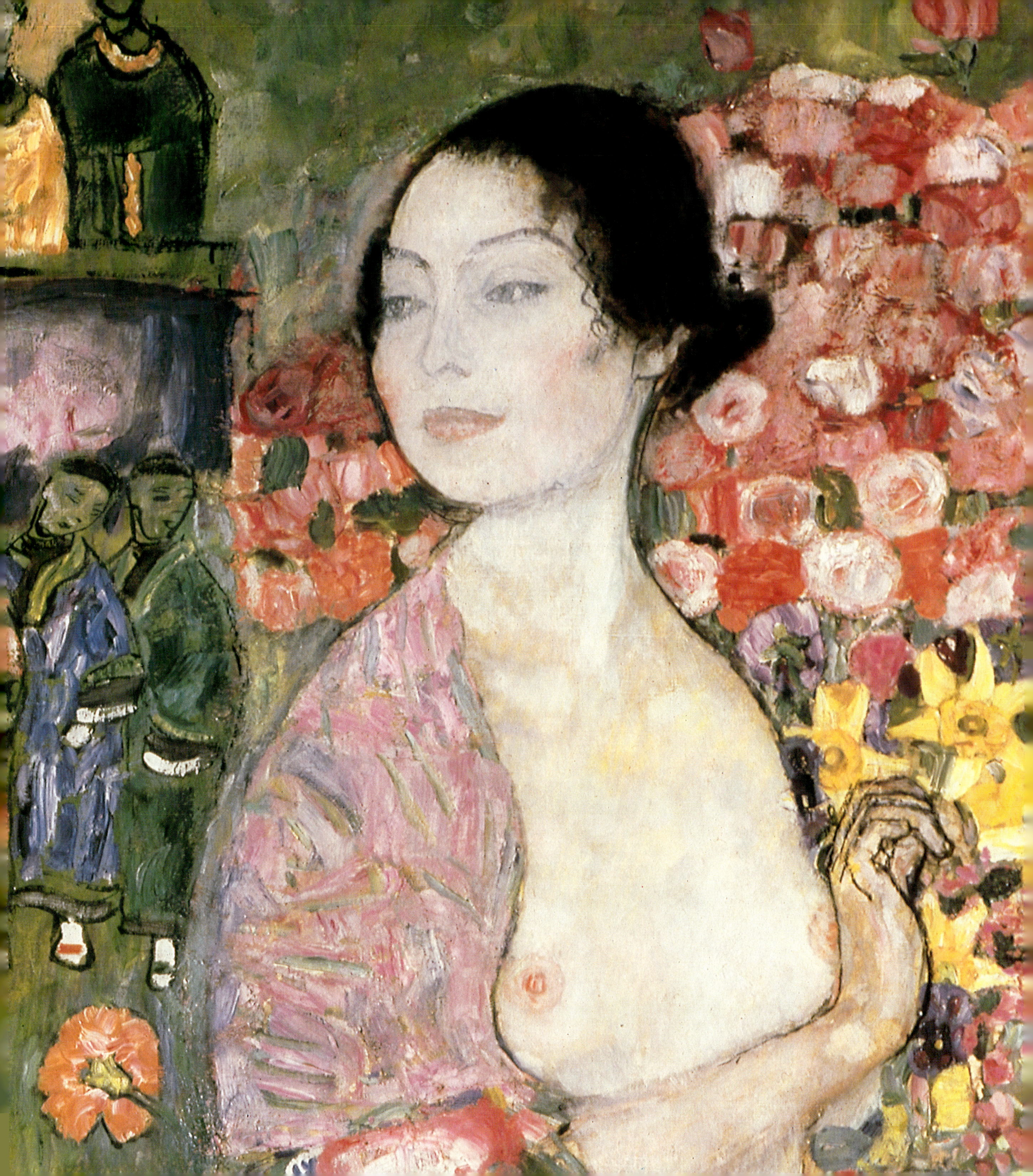

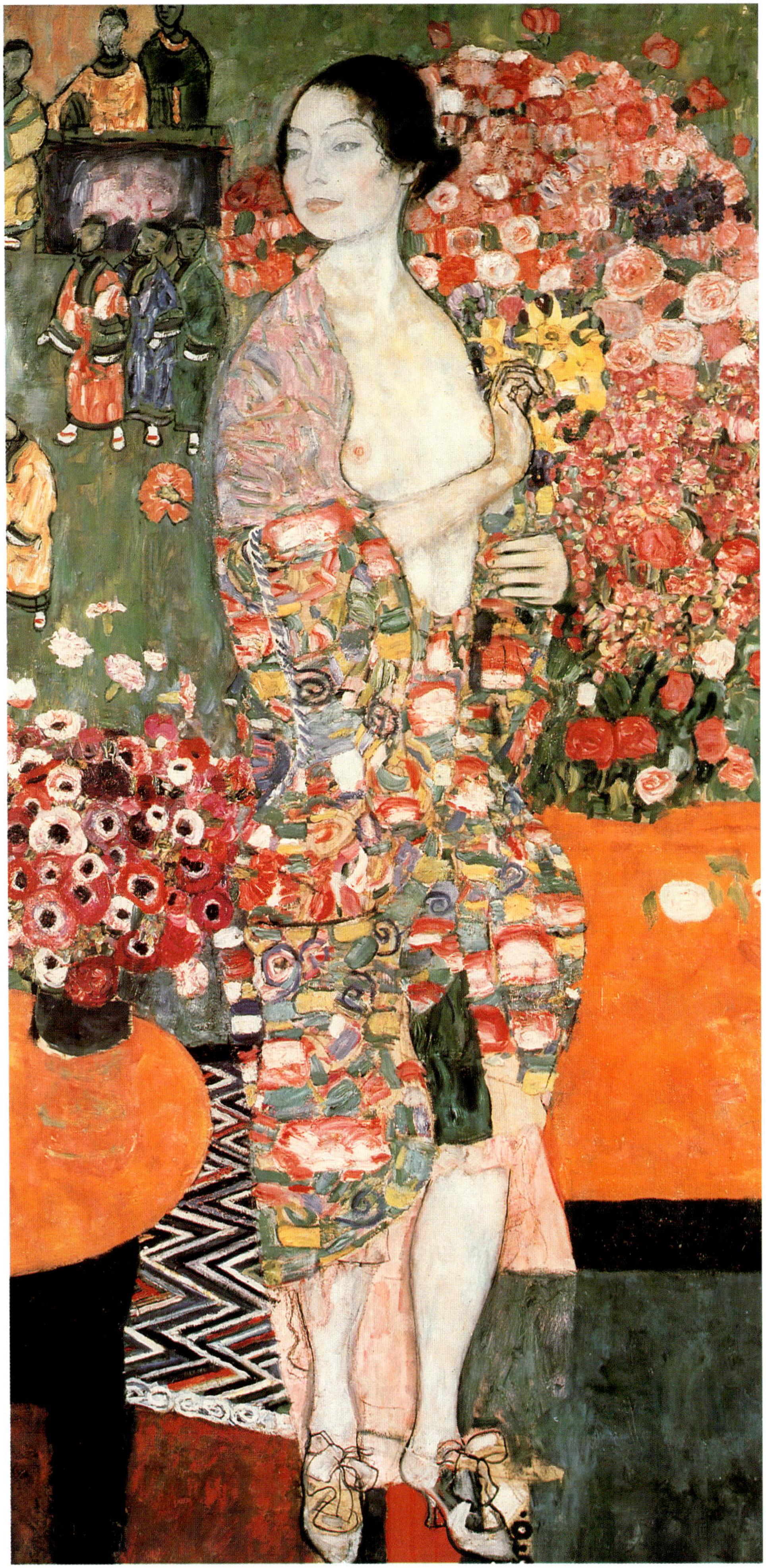

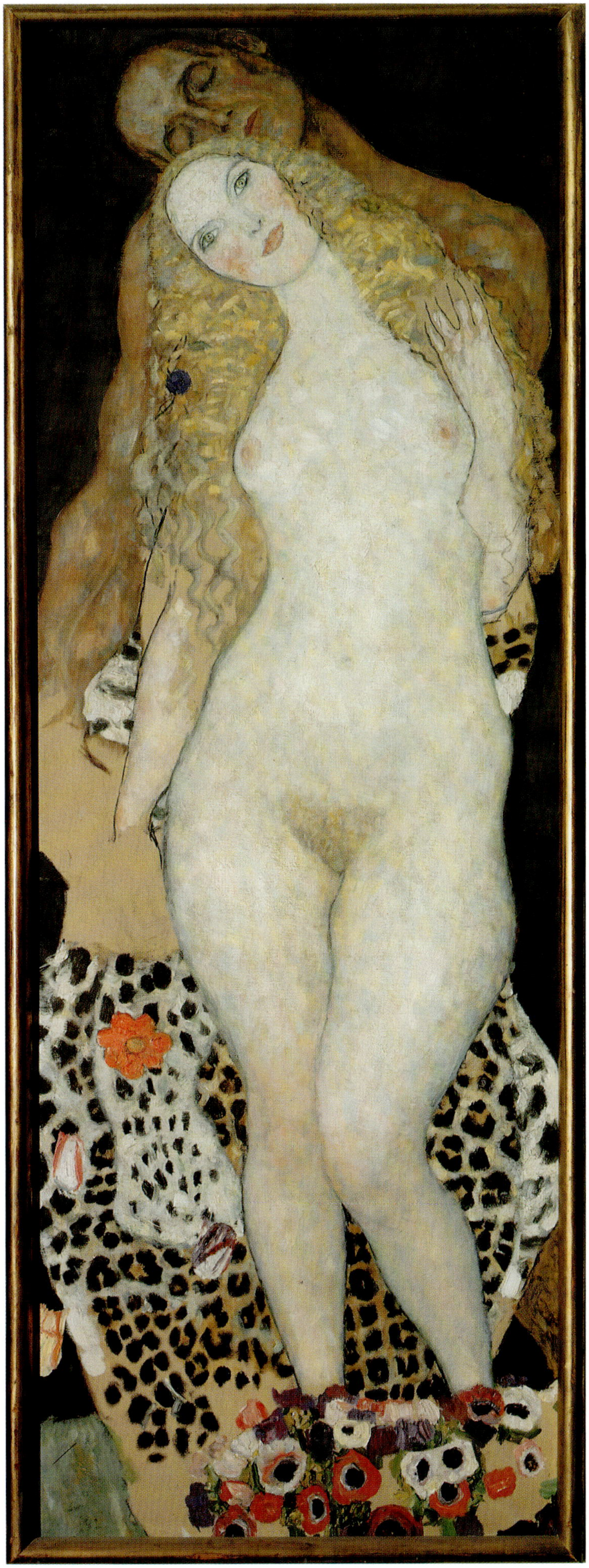

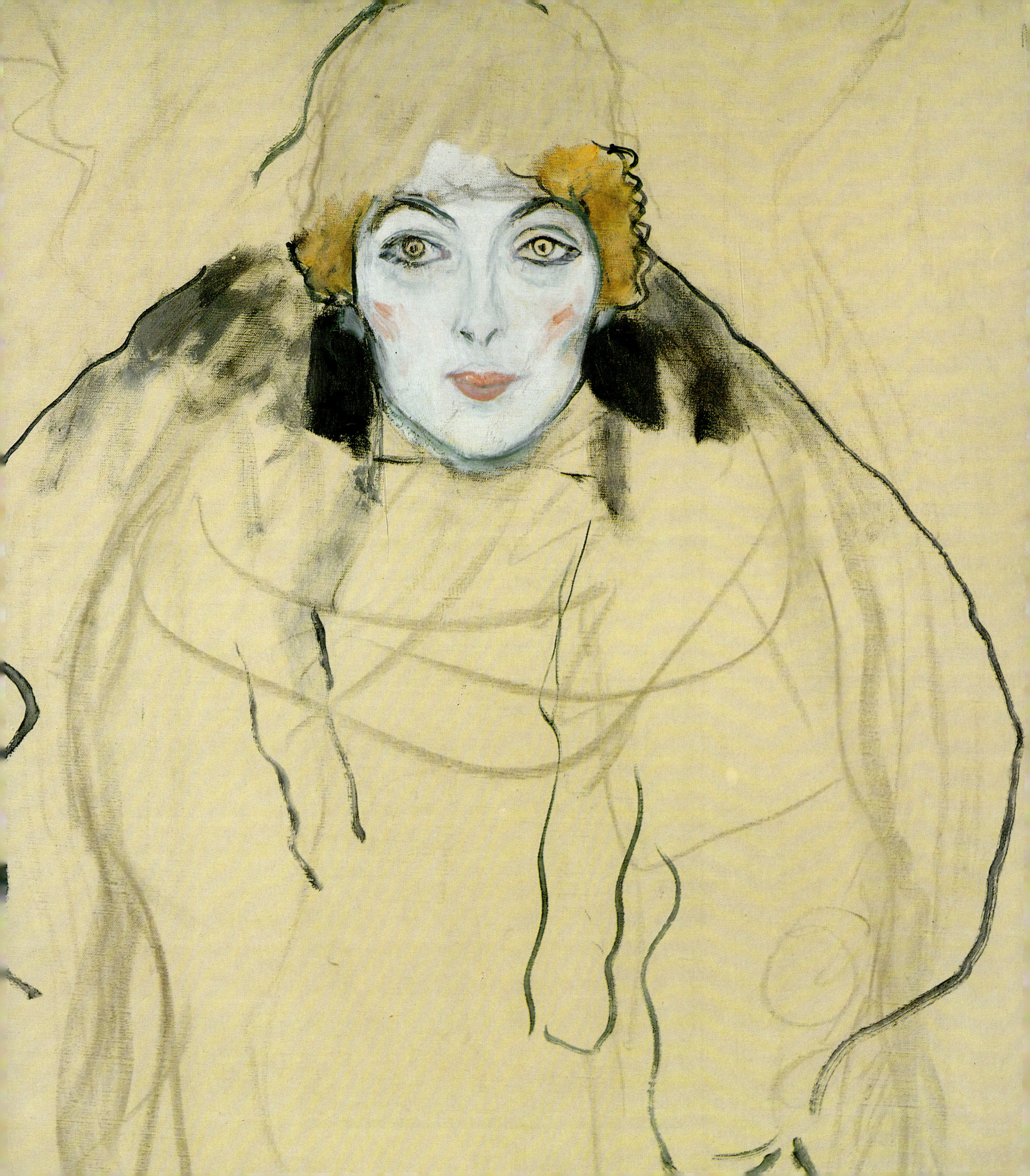

95 Adam and Eve, 1917/18 (unfinished)
Oil on canvas, 173 × 60 cm
Austrian Gallery, Vienna

96 Woman's Head, 1918 (unfinished)
Oil on canvas, 67 × 56 cm
New Gallery, Linz

have valued them once they had fulfilled their purpose, as is attested by a further eye-witness account: "I myself saw in Klimt's studio a pile of loose-leaf studies higher than a man, dozens of them on the same motif, a hand, an arm-pit, a rump... Klimt valued this abundant evidence of his industrious and penetrating study of nature only as means to an end, and he destroyed thousands of these leaves when they had fulfilled their purpose, or if they failed to combine maximum expressiveness with the application of a minimum of technique. On one occasion when I was sitting with Klimt, leafing through a heap of five hundred or so, surrounded by eight or nine cats meowing or purring, which chased each other around so the rustling leaves flew through the air, I asked him in astonishment why he let them carry on like that, spoiling hundreds of the best drawings." Klimt answered: "No matter if they crumple or tear a few of the leaves – they piss on the others and that's the best fixative!"[135]

Apart from its anecdotal value, this account shows not only that Klimt did not attach much importance to his drawings, but also that he himself destroyed some of them.

Until 1905 he drew exclusively on wrapping paper, using pencil, charcoal or crayon. Only rarely did he use several colours. Water colours and drawings in Indian ink become less and less common. Later he drew on imitation Japanese vellum, the scale became larger, and there are some studies not directly related to a completed painting. "In these... Klimt gave of his best. It is a pity that the best of them can neither be exhibited nor reproduced, being too free."[136] This cryptic remark refers to the nudes which have been discussed above (see p. 263–266).

Drawings by Klimt were used to illustrate a new edition of the 'Dialogues of the Courtesans' by Lucian (A. D. ca. 120–180), published in Leipzig in 1907. The drawings were not specially done for this purpose but were selected from the huge quantity of existing leaves.

Klimt regarded drawing as a means of working, not as a medium in its own right. For this reason he did not sell his drawings, though he might give them away. When he did part with them, he signed them. When August Lederer purchased the Beethoven Frieze from Carl Reininghaus in 1915 Klimt gave him 148 relevant sketches and studies.

After his death his heirs put a stamp on each of the leaves in their inheritance. Today most of the drawings are privately owned, some can no longer be located. Only a fraction can be viewed in museums, in Vienna more than elsewhere, but this fraction alone constitutes a large number.

The surviving drawings have been reproduced and made available in the three-volume inventory of Klimt's works, with excellent commentary, which appeared between 1980 and 1984; a supplementary volume is to follow. This material brought to light many new facts about Klimt, and it has been of the greatest assistance in the preparation of this book.

When today the drawings are exhibited as autonomous works of art it is important to bear in mind that for Klimt most of them were preliminary studies, and that during the decisive years he did not accord them any independent importance. As has already been mentioned, this had not always been the case. Up to 1898 he was still creating coloured drawings, such as the fair copy for the Secession's first exhibition. After the turn of the century transfer sketches for his paintings seem to have been made only for the faculty pictures. Otherwise he drew details of a figure, anatomical sketches, movements. Often the extremities of the figures are cut off, most frequently the head. In later years his style of drawing became more painterly, and it was the late drawings that gave rise, shortly after his death, to the tributes paid, mostly by art historians, to his draughtsmanship.

Epilogue – Death and Tribute

"Gustav Klimt died on Wednesday 6 February at 6 a. m., after a short, grave illness. Unrecognised by many, loved and respected all the more by his friends, he trod the lonely and mysterious path of great creators. Rigorous work and a pure mind were his companions. His restless ascent could be checked only by death. Art has suffered a great loss, mankind an even greater one... Union of Austrian Artists".[137]

On 11 January 1918 Gustav Klimt suffered a stroke. Half paralysed, he was moved from his home to a sanatorium. On 3 February he had to be moved to the General Hospital. He died there on 6 February as a result of pneumonia. Four days later he was buried in the cemetery in Hietzing, where his grave can still be seen today. The tomb of honour which the City of Vienna wanted to erect was rejected by the family. His death mask shows a face which seems most strange, since his beard had been shaved during the last days of his life. It was this alien face that Schiele drew in the hospital mortuary.

The funeral was attended by family and friends but also by representatives of the ministry of education, directors of the various museums in Vienna, and Viennese artists. Numerous members of the Secession were there. Press notices of his death were few, even fewer the tributes to his art. That was partly because of the date of his death. The papers were filled with reports of peace negotiations with the Ukraine and Russia, raising hopes that the war might soon be over. There was little space for artists' obituaries.

Klimt's friends were devastated and made no attempt to conceal the bitterness they felt over the scant recognition accorded to him during his lifetime. Otto Wagner, who had sustained a fictitious correspondence with his wife ever since her death, noted on 6 February: "I have to write to you again today, something dreadful has happened. Klimt is dead! If only this stupid world were to realise what it has lost today!"[138]

This bitterness was evident in one of the graveside speeches: "In Vienna, in what might be called the city of fundamental mis understandings, the artist Klimt was regarded in his lifetime as a Cagliostro, painter of hocus-pocus... which will of course, now that he is dead, not hinder the erection of a memorial – perhaps very soon. (He has already had a tomb of honour allotted to him!)"[139]

Egon Schiele, who died in the autumn of the same year, had the idea of preserving Klimt's studio for posterity: "His friends should buy the house in Hietzing, with garden and everything. Nothing should be removed – for the arrangement of Klimt's house is a whole, is itself a work of art, which should not be destroyed. The unfinished pictures, brushes, table and palette should remain untouched and be accessible to the few who enjoy art and love it."[140]

Whether other friends said the same, or whether the wish was ever put to the City of Vienna, is not known. The great shortage of accommodation after the war made it necessary for the studio to be turned into flats. If it had been preserved as Schiele suggested, more written material might have survived which would have given later generations some insight into the artist's personality. On the other hand, 'museums' of this sort tend to encourage a personality cult running counter to the individual artist's wishes; multiplying myths distort the artist's image in ways that usually fail to do him justice.

Apart from the uncompleted paintings in Klimt's studio, there were many drawings, which were divided up between Klimt's siblings and Emilie Flöge. All these leaves bear a stamp of the estate or a handwritten ascription. Many of them were sold. Although Klimt had been earning a lot of money with his pictures for a long time, he left nothing; any money that he received, he immediately spent. His sisters, who had continued to live with him after their mother's death and were supported by him, were obliged to sell their part of the inheritance.

Apart from the pictures and drawings, which say a great deal about the artist and his ideas when they are analysed with proper regard to the circumstances at the time, there are also some descriptions of Klimt, and there is a short text that he wrote himself, of unknown date:

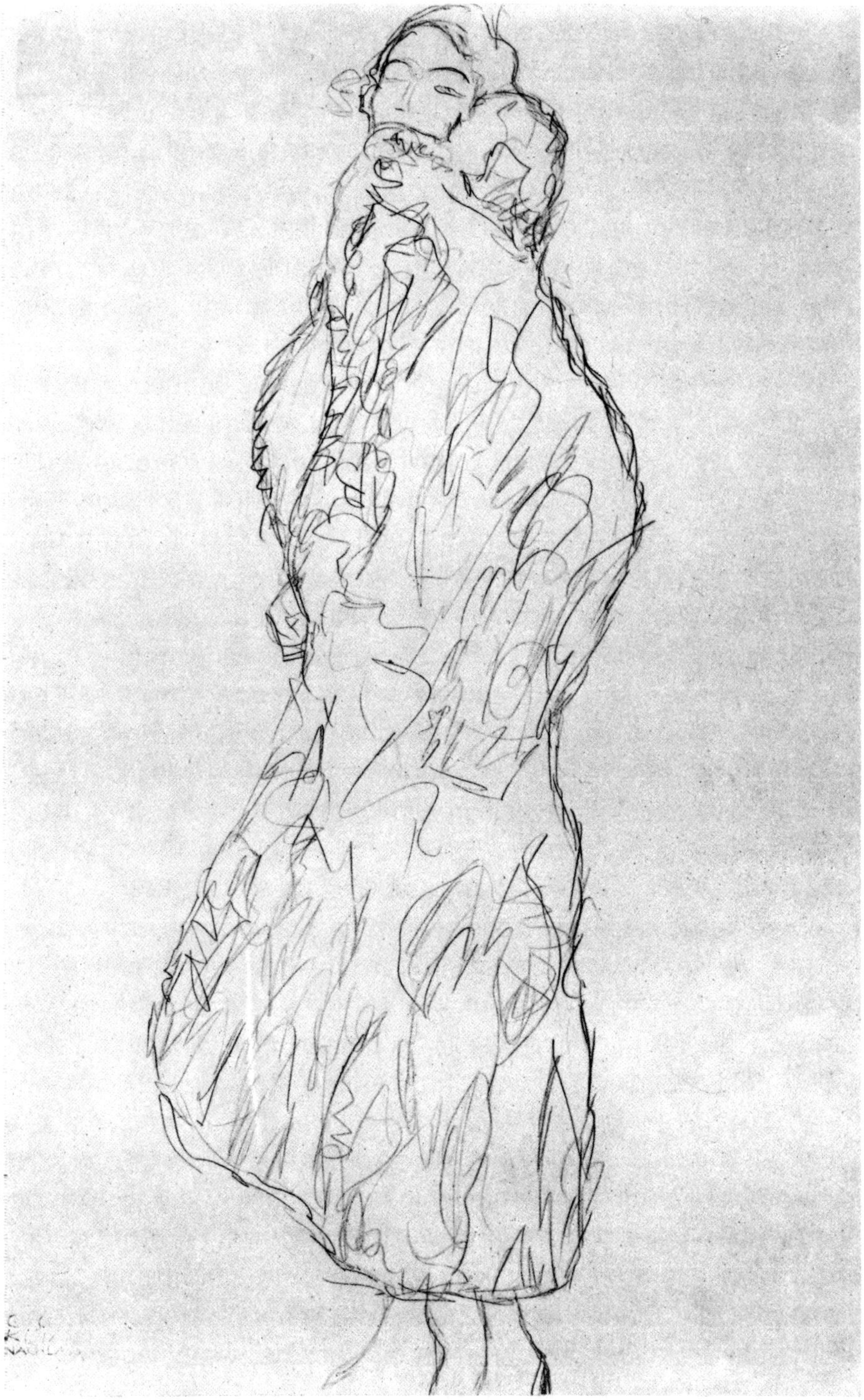

Woman in fur coat, 1916
Pencil, 50.2 × 32.5 cm

"Commentary on a non-existent self-portrait: I can paint and draw. I believe that myself and some other people say they believe it. But I am not entirely certain that it is true. Certain are two things only:

1. There is no self-portrait of me. I am not interested in myself as 'material for a picture', rather in other people, especially women, even more in other phenomena. I am convinced that as a person I am not specially interesting. There's nothing remarkable to be seen in me. I am a painter, one who paints every day from morning till evening. Figures, landscapes, occasionally portraits.

2. Words, spoken or written, do not come easily to me, especially not when I'm supposed to be saying something about myself or my work. If I have to write a simple letter I get just as scared as if I was going to be sea-sick. So people will have to do without an artistic or literary self-portrait. Which is just as well. Anyone who wants to find out about me – as artist, that's all that's of interest – should look at my pictures attentively and seek to discover from them what I am, and what I want."[141]

It is not easy to meet Klimt's challenge. So many anecdotes, stories and myths have crept up around him, which in turn are invoked in the interpretation of his pictures, that it does seem important to try to grasp something, at least, of what he was like as a person. His friend Carl Moll, who founded the Secession with Klimt and others and left at the same time as the nucleus of the 'artists of style', has described the daily routine which Klimt imposed on himself:

"Klimt liked to get up early and he needed exercise, early in the morning he walked the whole way from the Westbahnstraße, where he lived with his mother and sisters – for whom he was responsible – all the way to Meidling, to Café Tivoli, decorated in the Old Vienna style which most appealed to him, the New Artist, just next to Schönbrunn. As an illustrious 'regular' he was cosseted and cherished; a lavish breakfast, of which lashings of whipped cream were the vital part, had to give him strength for the rest of the day. That's where his friends used to call on him too . . . once he got to the studio he shut himself in. The way back to the studio took him through Schönbrunn Park, first to the Josefstädter Straße, later to Unter-St Veit. Having exercised his legs and reached his studio, he did arm exercises. Then work started: there were always several models available, and if he did not need them for work on his paintings, he drew them, but always the drawing was related in some way to the pictures. . . . He did not stop at midday. Fruit and sweets were enough for him until the evening meal, which had to be all the more lavish."[142]

So his daily routine in the city was very regular, just as it was during the summer months spent by the Attersee (see p. 280/81). The correspondence with Emilie Flöge shows that he often went to the theatre in the evenings, but also met friends in cafés and bars. He seems to have been very concerned about his health, and the weather was important to him. If Emilie was not in Vienna or he was away, he commented every day on the weather, and on the slightest catarrh.

There is general agreement that Klimt was not a talkative man, that he warmed up only in the company of his close friends, but that he then showed a distinctive sense of humour. His wit is evident in one of his pictures when its background is known:

In 1902 Klimt completed the picture known as 'Goldfish'. In it are several nude female figures, who must be swimming in water since they are joined by a golden fish. The figure crouching at the lower edge of the picture not only has her back turned towards the public, but also her large backside. She has turned her head too, and looks out of the picture with an ironic smile.

This picture was painted at a time when the dispute about the faculty pictures was at its height. Only the advice of good friends prevented Klimt from giving the picture the title that he had originally intended for it, namely, 'To My Critics'. It was understood even without the title, as is evident from contemporary comment:

"When the storm broke over his university pictures he painted a blunt reply to all his abusers: a work that presents to the beholder the amply rounded 'other side'. He named this rebus 'Goldfish'. He could more honestly have called it 'Götz von Berlichingen' (Goethe's Götz invited his enemies to lick his arse, transl.). But they understood any-way . . ."[143]

Another commentator spoke of the violently attacked 'Goldfish' as "a powerful joke, but one executed with the most delicate artistic means, with which the artist takes his revenge on the malignity and lack of understanding shown by public and critics . . ."[144].

In spite of the deep seriousness inherent in most of his paintings, he was capable of displaying humour even in this medium.

Klimt's sparse use of words may have had something to do with a certain diffidence, even dependence. His lack of independence was certainly the reason why he remained all his life with his mother and sisters and let them look after him. It was noticeable also when he travelled.

Many years passed before Klimt left Vienna for the first time. Although he started earning relatively early, he could not to begin with afford long journeys, since he and his brother Ernst were the family's chief breadwinners, supporting both their parents and their sisters. After the award of the Emperor's Prize in 1890 he was in a position to move more freely. Up to that time he had only travelled within Austria, usually to the places where the 'Company of Artists' was employed to decorate theatres.

He was not at ease on his travels, as is recorded by travelling companions. He knew no foreign language and soon became homesick for Vienna. Nevertheless, two of his journeys were very important for the development of his style. He first encountered Jugendstil art in Munich in 1890, and it quickly affected his pictures.

In 1903 Klimt set off with a friend for Ravenna, where he first saw the mosaics which had survived largely from the sixth century. He was so deeply impressed by the mosaics – the ornament, the figures, the gold ground – that covered the vaulted ceiling of the church that he went back there in the winter of the same year. These mosaics caused him to use gold more and more strongly in his pictures and to design the Stoclet Frieze as he did.

His timidity abroad, his inability to move at all in alien surroundings, is shown by his friend Carl Moll's account of a journey to Italy. In 1897 Klimt followed Moll and his family, who had been travelling in Italy for several months, to Florence, with a view to travelling further in their company. In his memoir of Klimt Moll described the planning of the journey and the artist's arrival in Florence: "... so the most helpless of men only needed ... to reach the rail compartment – to which his people could accompany him – and in Florence I would meet him at the door of the same compartment ... When I received news by telegram of his impending arrival I hurried to the station and waited . . . at the outer barrier. The newly arrived passengers flooded out - but no Klimt was among them. . . . I looked up and down the platform in vain and was leaving the station, instinctively wandering through all the waiting rooms. There, indeed, on a bench in one of them sat a sad Gustav Klimt with his little suitcase." In answer to Moll's inquiry as to why he had not come out, Klimt answered: "Because no-one was there and I don't know my way." When Moll inquired further what he would have done if he, Moll, had not come to the station but waited in the hotel, Klimt replied that he would have waited for the next train and gone home again.[145]

Even if there is some exaggeration in this account, in essence it seems to be true. Klimt probably acquired more confidence abroad later on, but he travelled with friends.

Further journeys to Berlin, Brussels, London, Munich and Prague in the years that followed were usually prompted by exhibitions at which his work was displayed, or they were connected with the mosaic frieze in Palais Stoclet.

In 1909 Klimt and Carl Moll undertook a long journey to Paris and Spain, but this did not encourage him to spend more time abroad. He seems to have preferred the regular summers spent by the Attersee. His roots were in Vienna, which led to the charge of provincialism, but today that does not seem justified.

His development as an artist was unusual. Success came early, to be followed by years of struggle, whereas the reverse is more common. The pattern is demonstrated by the honours accorded him. As a young man he was rewarded for his work by the emperor, with the other members of the 'Company of Artists'; at the age of 26 he obtained the Gold Order of Merit, two years later the Emperor's Prize. But he had to wait a long time before his native city was prepared to honour him again. After he had distanced himself from the Ring painters and founded the Secession with friends, he received more prizes and honorary membership of artists' associations, but only abroad. Not until 1917 was he made an honorary member of the Academy of Fine Arts in Vienna. It is understandable that the family refused a grave of honour.

In having to win recognition abroad before he could be recognised in his own city of Vienna, Klimt suffered what may be regarded as a typically Austrian fate. "There is a distinctively Austrian way of treating intellectual and artistic eminence, which often enough is sent into exile before it can be appreciated at home. This detour is almost a law, a law still valid today."[146] The most recent instance of this phenomenon is the writer Thomas Bernhard, who died in 1989.

During his lifetime Klimt was recognised only by a relatively small section of Viennese society, namely the Jewish haute bourgeoisie. They were his patrons, the ladies had their portraits painted by him. After his early success as one of the Ring painters he was never short of money. After his death a number of books were written about him, but it was not until the mid-1950s that true scholarly research began.

Since the establishment in 1968 of a Klimt archive in Vienna, numerous documents have appeared which shed light on the artist's life and work. His fame is growing, not only in Vienna, as is attested by the large exhibitions in Vienna, Paris and New York, and by the numerous exhibitions of his drawings, which have even been seen in Tokyo.

Certainly the last word has not yet been spoken. The articles on problems of detail which have appeared over the last years will be followed by many more. The writer Peter Altenberg, Klimt's friend, who described him as modern philosopher and poet, took leave of him in a brief poem in which he tried to paint a truthful picture:

Gustav Klimt, to the ideals of nature you,
in fact almost without knowing, came closer, and even your
simple, in fact noble farmhouse gardens with sunflowers
and weeds contained a breath of the poetry of the
creator! Gradually you came to hold yourself aloof from
the people, who had no kind of understanding!
Gustav Klimt, you were a man!"[147]

Appendix

Biographical Table

1862 Gustav Klimt born 14 July in Baumgarten (today XIVth District of Vienna), second of seven children of the gold-engraver Ernst Klimt from Bohemia and Anna née Finster of Vienna.

1868 Enters city school in VIIth District of Vienna.

1873 Great exhibition in Vienna precipitates economic crisis which affects Klimt family.

1876 Klimt leaves school with 'very good' certificate. Obtains 2-year scholarship to study at new School of Arts and Crafts attached to Austrian Museum of Art and Industry, under Rieser, Minnigerode and Hrachowina. Brother Ernst Klimt joins him there in 1877. Klimt brothers and Franz Matsch transfer to Ferdinand Laufberger's painting class in 1878.

1879 Klimt brothers and Franz Matsch commissioned by Laufberger to execute sgraffiti in Vienna's Art History Museum. They take part in preparations for Makart's pageant in honour of the Emperor's Silver Wedding Jubilee.

1880 Klimt brothers and Matsch paint 4 ceiling pictures for Palais Sturany in Vienna and receive first commission from theatre architects Fellner and Helmer, for ceiling picture for Spa Rooms in Karlsbad.

1881 Death of Laufberger. Further studies with Julius Victor Berger. Klimt brothers and Matsch set up joint 'Company of Artists' and are commissioned to contribute to 'Allegory and Emblem'.

1883 After completion of studies, Company moves to own studio. Klimt works principally for 'Allegory and Emblem'.

1885 Company commissioned to execute Makart's sketches for Villa Hermes in Lainz, and to work on theatres in Fiume and Bucharest.

1886 Klimt paints 2 ceiling pictures in Karlsbad theatre, paints curtains jointly with Ernst Klimt and Matsch. Work begins on ceiling and lunette paintings for the 2 stairways in the new Burg Theatre.

1888 Emperor's highest award, Golden Order of Merit, granted to Company for work on Burg Theatre. Klimt paints 'Auditorium in Old Burg Theatre'.

1890 Klimt receives Emperor's Prize with 400 guilders for Burg Theatre painting. Company begins work on 40 spandrel and intercolumnar paintings for stairway of Vienna Art History Museum.

1891 Membership of Vienna Association of Visual Artists.

1892 Work for Art History Museum puts Company in the running for paintings for great hall of new university of Vienna. Company moves to new studio. Death of Ernst Klimt on 9 December.

1894 Gustav Klimt and Franz Matsch begin to move apart but receive commissions to submit sketches for university paintings.

1895 Klimt begins work for 'Allegory. New Series', Vol. 3 of 'Allegory and Emblem'. Change in his style, discernible long before, becomes more evident.

1896 Klimt commissioned to paint 3 faculty pictures for university hall ceiling – 'Philosophy', 'Medicine' and 'Jurisprudence' – and 10 spandrel pictures on related themes. Matsch takes over the other pictures.

1897 Klimt and some 20 other artists leave the Association of Visual Artists and found the Secession, with Klimt as president. First landscapes.

1898 Klimt designs poster for Secession's first exhibition. Preliminary compositions for faculty pictures criticized and only conditionally accepted.

1899 Decoration of Palais Dumba music room completed.

1900 Unfinished faculty picture 'Philosophy' shown at VIIth Secession exhibition. Petition of 87 professors against its being positioned on university hall ceiling. With this picture Klimt wins the gold medal for foreign artists at autumn exhibition in Paris.

1901 'Medicine' exhibited at Xth Secession exhibition. Violent protest in press and parliament.

1902 'Beethoven Frieze' exhibited at XIVth Secession exhibition built round Max Klinger's Beethoven statue. Klimt's frieze still exists, all other murals were destroyed after the exhibition.

1903 Klimt impressed by visit to Ravenna. Josef Hoffmann and Koloman Moser found Vienna Workshops, much influenced by Klimt. 80 of Klimt's works exhibited by the Secession, including the three faculty pictures. Art commission considers hanging faculty pictures in Modern Gallery.

1904 Klimt commissioned to design dining-room frieze for Palais Stoclet in Brussels to be built by Vienna Workshops.

1905 Klimt terminates contract for faculty pictures and repays advance in full. Klimt and friends leave the Secession.

1906 Travels to Brussels and London in connection with Stoclet Frieze. First square portrait of 'golden period'.

1907 Faculty pictures finally completed, exhibited in final form. Height of 'golden period'.

1908 Klimt organizes exhibition of so-called 'Klimt Group', the 'Artists of Style' who had left the Secession. 'The Kiss', one of 16 Klimt pictures exhibited, is bought by Austrian State Gallery.

1909 End of 'golden period'. Klimt organises exhibition for last time. Travels in autumn to Paris and Spain.

1910 Participates in Venice Biennale. Designs for Stoclet Frieze completed, to be realised by Vienna Workshops.

1911 Participates in international exhibition in Rome, awarded 1st prize for 'Death and Life'. Moves into new studio; Company's original studio due to be demolished.

1912 Participates in Dresden exhibition. Long article on Klimt by A. Weixelgärtner in Graphische Künste.

1914 Sees Stoclet Frieze in place in Brussels.

1917 Honorary membership of Academy of Fine Arts in Vienna and Munich.

1918 Klimt suffers a stroke on 11 January and dies on 6 February leaving numerous paintings unfinished.

Further Reading

Bahr, H., Secession. Vienna 1900
Bahr, H., Gegen Klimt. Vienna-Leipzig 1903
Bäumer, A., Gustav Klimt. Frauen. Salzburg 1985
Benesch, O., 'Hodler, Klimt und Munch als Monumentalmaler', Wallraf-Richartz-Jahrbuch, XIV, 1962
Bisanz-Prakken, M., 'Zum Gemälde Pallas Athene', Alte und moderne Kunst 147, Vienna 1976
Bisanz-Prakken, M., 'Gustav Klimt und die Stilkunst Jan Toorops', Klimt-Studien, 1978–79
Bisanz-Prakken, M., Der Beethovenfries. Geschichte, Funktion und Bedeutung, Munich 1980
Bouillon, J.-P., Klimt: Beethoven, Geneva 1988
Breicha, O.(ed.), Gustav Klimt: Die goldene Pforte – Werk, Wesen, Wirkung. Bilder und Schriften zu Leben und Werk, Salzburg 1978
Casteels, M. , The New Style. Architecture and Decorative Design, London 1931
Comini, A., Gustav Klimt, London 1975
Crane, W., William Morris to Whistler, London 1911
Dobai, J., 'Zu Gustav Klimts Gemälde "Der Kuß"', Mitteilungen der Österreichischen Galerie, XII, 56 1968
Dobai, J., 'Gustav Klimt's "Hope I", Bulletin of the National Gallery of Canada, 17, Ottawa 1971
Dobai, J., Gustav Klimt: Die Landschaften, Salzburg 1983
DREAM AND REALITY. Vienna 1870–1930 (Exhibition Catalogue, 'Traum und Wirklichkeit. Wien 1870-1930', Vienna 1985)
Fischer, W. G., Gustav Klimt und Emilie Flöge. Genie und Talent, Freundschaft und Besessenheit, Vienna 1987
Fleischmann, B., Gustav Klimt. Eine Nachlese, Vienna 1946
Fliedl, G., 'Das Weib macht keine Kunst aber den Künstler. Zur Klimt-Rezeption', R. Berger & D. Hammer-Tugendhat (eds.), Der Garten der Lüste, Cologne 1985
Frodl, G., 'Begegnungen im Theater: Hans Makart und Gustav Klimt', Klimt-Studien, 1978–79
Giese, H., 'Matsch und die Brüder Klimt. Regesten zum Frühwerk Gustav Klimts', Klimt-Studien, 1978–79
Hevesi, L., Acht Jahre Secession, Vienna 1906, reprinted Klagenfurt 1984
Hofmann, H. Chr., Die Theaterbauten von Fellner und Helmer, Munich 1966
Hofmann, W., Gustav Klimt und die Wiener Jahrhundertwende, Salzburg 1970
Hofstätter, H. H., Geschichte der europäischen Jugendstilmalerei, Cologne 1977
Hofstätter, H. H., Gustav Klimt. Erotische Zeichnungen, Cologne 1979
Howarth, T., Charles Rennie Mackintosh and the Modern Movement, London 1952
Kallir, J., Gustav Klimt. 25 Meisterwerke, New York/Salzburg 1985
Klimt-Studien, Mitteilungen der Österreichischen Galerie, Vienna
Loos, A., 'Ornament und Verbrechen', Trotzdem, 1900–1930, Vienna 1982
Madsen, S. T., Art Nouveau, Oslo 1967
Madsen, S. T., Sources of Art Nouveau, New York 1976
Nebehay, C. M. (ed.), Gustav Klimt Dokumentation, Vienna 1969
Nebehay, C. M. Ver Sacrum 1898–1903, New York 1977
Nebehay, C. M. Gustav Klimt: Sein Leben nach zeitgenössischen Berichten und Quellen, Munich 1979
Nebehay, C. M., Das Skizzenbuch aus dem Besitz von Sonja Knips, Vienna 1987
Nebehay, C. M., Gustav Klimt, Egon Schiele und die Familie Lederer, Bern 1987

Novotny, F., 'Zu Gustav Klimts "Schubert am Klavier"', Mitteilungen der Österreichischen Galerie 7, 51 1963
Novotny, F. & Dobai, J., Gustav Klimt, Salzburg 1967
Pevsner, N., Pioneers of the Modern Movement from William Morris to Walter Gropius, London 1936
Pevsner, N., Pioneers of Modern Design. From William Morris to Walter Gropius, New York 1949
Pevsner, N., Charles Rennie Mackintosh, Milan 1950
Pirchan, E., Gustav Klimt. Ein Künstler aus Wien, Vienna-Leipzig 1942
Sabarsky, S., Gustav Klimt. Drawings, Milan 1983
Schweiger, Werner M., Wiener Werkstätte. Kunst und Handwerk 1903–1932, Vienna 1983
Sekler, E. F., 'Mackintosh and Vienna', J. M. Richard & N. Pevsner (eds.), The Anti-Rationalists, Wisbech 1973
Strobl, A., 'Zu den Fakultätsbildern von Gustav Klimt', Albertina Studien 4, 1964
Strobl, A., Gustav Klimt. Die Zeichnungen Vols. I–III, Salzburg 1980–1984
Strobl, A., 'Hanswurst auf der Stegreifbühne zu Rothenburg', Kunst um 1800 und die Folgen. Werner Hofmann zu Ehren, Munich 1988
TRAUM UND WIRKLICHKEIT. Wien 1870–1930, exhibition catalogue, Vienna 1985
Varnedoe, K., Wien 1900, Kunst, Architektur und Design, Cologne 1987
VER SACRUM, Journal of the Vienna Secession 1898–1903
Vergo, P., 'Gustav Klimts "Philosophie" und das Programm der Universitätsgemälde', Klimt-Studien 1978–79
Waissenberger, R., Die Wiener Secession, Vienna 1971
Zaunschirm, T., 'Wien und die Anfänge der Abstraktion', Orient und Okzident im Spiegel der Kunst. Festschrift für H. G. Franz, Graz 1986
Zaunschirm, T., Gustav Klimt. Margarethe Stonborough-Wittgenstein. Ein Österreichisches Schicksal, Frankfurt 1987

Colour Plates

chronological list

The Fable, 1883 19
The Idyll, 1884 20
Sappho, 1888/90 29
Allegory of Sculpture, 1889 1
Josef Pembaur, 1890 41
Poster Design, 1892 30
Music I, 1895 31
Love, 1895 (with detail) 51/52
Joseph Lewinsky as Carlos, 1895 (with detail) 53/54
Moving Water, 1898 32
Sonja Knips, 1898 (with detail) 63/64
Pallas Athene, 1898 65
Nuda Veritas, 1899 42
Water Sprites, 1899 66
After the Rain, 1899 99
Farmhouse with Birch Trees, 1900 100
Cows in Stall, 1900/01 136
Judith I, 1901 75
Island in the Attersee, c. 1901 78
Goldfish, 1901/02 76
Emilie Flöge, 1902 (with detail) 89/90
Beech Forest I, 1902 101
Beethoven Frieze, 1902 169–180
Birch Forest, 1903 102
Hope I, 1903 (with detail) 113/114
Hermine Gallia, 1903/04 87/88
Water Serpents I, 1904/07 77
Margarethe Stonborough-Wittgenstein, 1905 (with detail) 111/112
Three Ages of Woman, 1905 (with detail) 147/148
Farm Garden with Sunflowers, c. 1905/06 135

Fritza Riedler, 1906 123/124
Poppy Field, 1907 159
Adele Bloch-Bauer I, 1907 (with detail) 211/212
The Kiss, 1907/08 (with detail) 125/126
Danae, 1907/08 (with detail) 149/150
Schloss Kammer on the Attersee I, c. 1908 137
Judith II, 1909 (with detail) 247/248
Woman with Hat and Feather Boa, 1909 2
Drawings for Stoclet Frieze, 1905–10 189/190, 199–202
Schloss Kammer on the Attersee III, 1910 138
The Black Feather Hat, 1910 (with detail) 223/224
Upper Austrian Farmhouse, 1911/12 160
Adele Bloch-Bauer II, 1912 (with detail) 213/214
Mäda Primavesi, c. 1912 (with detail) 225/226
Avenue in Schloss Kammer Park, 1912 235
Apple Tree I, 1912 236
The Virgin, 1913 (with detail) 271/272
Unterach on the Attersee, 1915 238
Apple Tree II, c. 1916 237
Portrait of a Lady, c. 1916/17 (with detail) 259/260
Dancer, c. 1916/18 (with detail) 293/294
Portrait of a Lady in White, 1917/18 (with detail) 249/250
Portrait of a Lady, 1917/18 (with detail) 261/262
Baby, 1917/18 (with detail) 273/274
Johanna Staude, 1917/18 (with detail) 283/284
Adam and Eve, 1917/18 (with detail) 295
Woman's Head, 1918 296

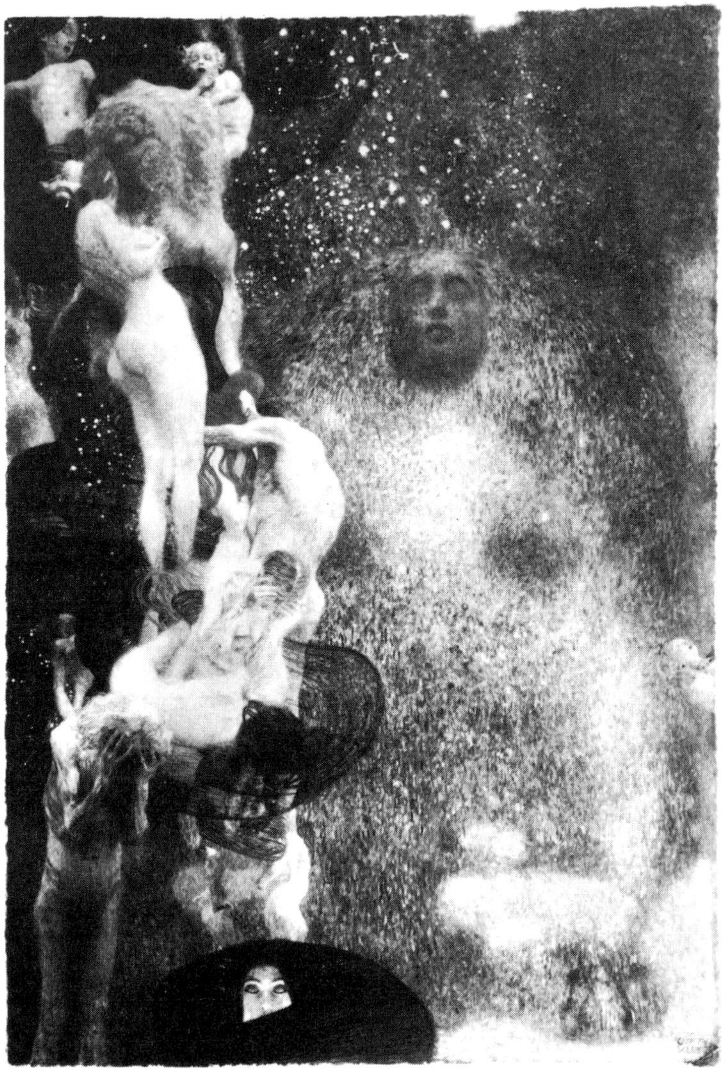

Philosophy, 1899/1907
Ceiling panel for the Great Hall
of Vienna University
Oil on canvas, 430 × 300 cm
1945 Burnt in Schloss Immendorf
(see p. 108–140)

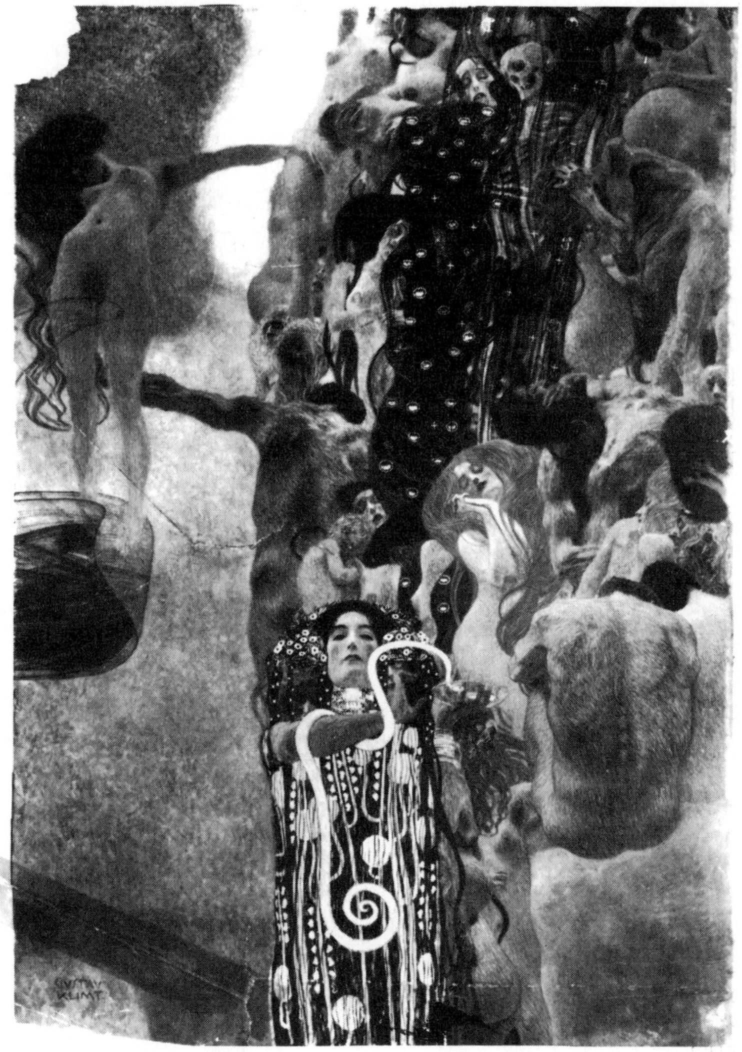

Medicine, 1900/07
Ceiling panel for the Great Hall
of Vienna University
Oil on canvas, 430 × 300 cm
1945 Burnt in Schloss Immendorf

(see p. 108–140)

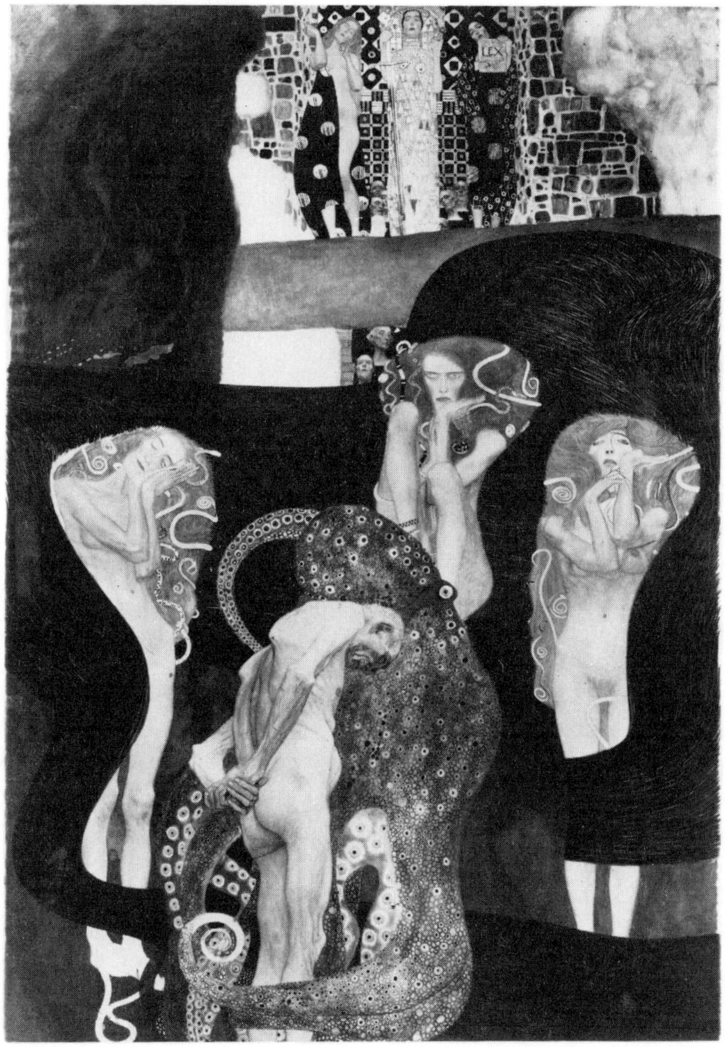

Jurisprudence, 1903/07
Ceiling panel for the Great Hall
of Vienna University
Oil on canvas, 430 × 300 cm
1945 Burnt in Schloss Immendorf

(see p. 108–140)

Index of names

Alt, Rudolf 239
Altenberg, Peter 206, 215, 306
Andri, Ferdinand 146, 151
Ashbee, Charles Robert 27, 194
Auchentaller, Josef Maria 146, 151
Bahr, Hermann 16ff, 22, 84, 94, 98, 131f, 206
Beardsley, Aubrey 27
Beethoven, Ludwig van 143–146, 151, 157f
Bellini, Giovanni 73
Berg, Alban 18
Berger, Julius Victor 47, 57, 60
Bernard, Emile 33ff, 130
Bernhard, Thomas 306
Bloch, Ferdinand 242
Bloch-Bauer, Adele 242, 244, 245
Böcklin, Arnold 95
Böhm, Adolf 146
Botticelli, Sandro 73
Brahms, Johannes 143, 239
Charles V 49
Cizek, Franz 210
Crane, Walter 27, 95
Dante 32, 134
Donner, Helene (née. Klimt) 163, 166f, 232
Dumba, Nikolaus 82ff
Eitelberger von Edelberg, Rudolf 44f, 47, 60ff
Elisabeth, Empress of Austria 12, 49, 60, 79
Engelhart, Josef 91, 107
Feldegg, Ferdinand von 130
Felix, Eugen 92
Fellner, Ferdinand 47, 57, 60, 208
Ferdinand I. 43
Feuerbach, Anselm 60
Fliedl, Gottfried 263, 276
Flöge, Barbara 166
Flöge, Emilie 163, 165ff, 182f, 185f, 188, 191f, 204, 220, 227, 234, 240, 244, 264, 275f, 279f, 288, 300
Flöge, Helene 163, 165ff, 183, 197, 204, 232
Flöge, Hermann (sen.) 163, 165
Flöge, Hermann (jun.) 163, 165
Flöge, Pauline 163, 165ff, 167, 197, 204
Forstner, Leopold 220, 227
Franz Joseph I. 7, 9, 11, 13f, 44f, 68f, 208f
Freud, Sigmund 22
Friedell, Egon 206
Gauguin, Paul 33, 34, 82, 107
Gerstl, Richard 18
Goethe, Johann Wolfgang von 132, 157
Gogh, Vincent van 97, 107
Goya, Francisco de 37, 107
Groß, Otto 188, 191
Hanfstaengl, Franz 84
Hartel, Wilhelm Ritter von 117f, 122, 127, 254
Hasenauer, Karl Freiherr von 61f, 67, 95
Helmer, Hermann 47, 57, 60, 208

Herzl, Theodor 10
Hevesi, Ludwig 48, 92, 95, 96, 98, 131, 141, 194, 207, 208f, 215, 251, 256, 267, 281
Hitler, Adolf 10
Hodler, Ferdinand 145
Hoermann, Theodor von 86, 91, 239
Hoffmann, Josef 16, 94, 106f, 166, 193f, 196f, 203f, 215f, 218ff, 222, 240
Hofmannsthal, Hugo von 18, 98
Hohenlohe-Schillingfürst, Marie, Princess 72
Ilg, Albert 55, 72
Kalbeck, Max 18
Kandinsky, Wassily 188
Khnopff, Fernand 80ff, 84, 96, 98
Klee, Paul 210
Klimt, Anna, née Finster (mother of Gustav) 44
Klimt, Anna (sister of Gustav) 44
Klimt, Ernst (father of Gustav) 44
Klimt, Ernst, (brother of Gustav) 44f, 47f, 50, 55, 58f, 62, 67f, 69, 74, 82, 109, 163, 183, 232, 304
Klimt, Georg 44, 67, 83, 96
Klimt, Hermine 44, 63
Klimt, Johanna 44
Klimt, Klara 44, 58, 230
Klinger, Max 55, 95, 142f
Knips, Sonja 167, 230ff, 291f
Kokoschka, Oskar 206ff, 216, 245
Kraus, Karl 22f, 85, 115
Kubin, Alfred 36
Kühn, Paul 145
Kupelwieser, Leopold 84
Laufberger, Ferdinand 45ff, 47, 50, 55
Lederer, August 84, 127, 151, 233, 298
Lederer, Serena 84f, 232
Liebermann, Max 95
Loos, Adolf 16, 22, 98, 198
Lorenzo Magnifico (de' Medici) 49
Lueger, Karl 10, 94
Macdonald, Margaret 27, 97, 194, 242
Mackintosh, Charles Rennie 97, 194, 197, 242
Maeterlinck, Maurice 80, 98
Mahler, Gustav 17f
Makart, Hans 11f, 47–50, 57, 60ff, 72, 82, 84, 208, 267
Maria Theresia 108
Marx, Karl 26
Matsch, Franz von 45, 46f, 50, 55, 58f, 60f, 68ff, 73f, 79, 82, 109f, 120ff, 127, 139
Michelangelo 59
Moll, Carl 91, 94, 107, 218, 302, 304
Monet, Claude 28
Morris, William 26f, 38, 194, 198
Moser, Koloman 103, 105, 127, 166, 193f, 196f, 203f, 207, 215, 222, 230, 240
Mozart, Wolfgang Amadeus 17
Munch, Edvard 145
Munkácsy, Mihály von 72
Münter, Gabriele 188
Myrbach, Felician von 194
Nebehay, Christian M. 166
Nietzsche, Friedrich 130, 146
Olbrich, Josef Maria 95
Pausanias 145
Pembaur, Josef 68, 72
Petrarch 131
Phidias 145
Piloty, Karl Theodor von 48
Pötzl, Eduard 115
Pollitzer, Adam 47
Primavesi, Mäda 167
Primavesi, Otto 203
Puvis de Chavannes, Pierre 95
Rainer, Archduke 69
Reininghaus, Carl 297
Rieser, Michael 45, 291
Rilke, Rainer Maria 98
Ringel, Erwin 22
Roda Roda 206
Rodin, Auguste 95, 130
Roller, Alfred 17f, 146
Rössler, Arthur 256
Roth, Joseph 9
Rudolf, Crown Prince of Austria 13f
Runge, Philipp Otto 37
Ruskin, John 26, 194
Salten, Felix 18
Scheffler, Karl 37, 198
Schiele, Egon 74, 215, 245, 299f
Schiller, Friedrich v. 104f, 156
Schnitzler, Arthur 18, 227
Schönberg, Arnold 18
Schopenhauer, Arthur 34, 130ff, 134
Schubert, Franz 84
Segantini, Giovanni 95, 97, 98
Seguin, Arman 33
Semper, Gottfried 26
Stirner, Max 25
Stoclet, Adolphe 198, 204f, 218ff, 228
Stonborough-Wittgenstein, Margarethe 204, 239ff, 264
Stranitzky, Josef Anton 67
Stuck, Franz von 55, 96f
Thoma, Ludwig 95
Titian 48, 58f
Toroop, Jan 145
Toulouse-Lautrec, Henri de 38
Uhde, Fritz von 95
Uhland, Ludwig 98
Varnedoe, Kirk 254
Velde, Henry van de 37, 191
Waerndorfer, Fritz 105, 193f, 196, 203, 221, 254
Wagner, Otto 16, 95, 299f
Wagner, Richard 48, 130f, 142ff, 146, 151, 156ff
Webern, Anton von 18
Weininger, Otto 244, 264, 275
Willbrand, Adolf von 62
Wittgenstein, Karl 204, 239f
Wittgenstein, Ludwig 18f
Wolter, Charlotte 79
Zaunschirm, Thomas 288
Zimmermann, Mizzi 186, 280f
Zuckerkandl, Berta 204, 207, 218

Notes on the text

1 Traum und Wirklichkeit, 1985, 40
2 Traum und Wirklichkeit, 1985, 40
3 Traum und Wirklichkeit, 1985, 43ff
4 Bahr 1900, 109
5 Loos 1982, 78–88
6 from Hilde Spiel, Glanz und Untergang. Wien 1866–1938, Vienna 1987, 55ff
7 E. Ringel, 'Über den Todestrieb', Vienna 1870–1930, 1984, 121
8 from W. Hofmann, Grundlagen der modernen Kunst, Stuttgart 1978, 349
9 W. Morris, Collected Works, London 1914, XXII, 26
10 J. W. Mackail, The Life of William Morris, London 1899, 186
11 W. Morris, Collected Works, London 1914, XXII, 75
12 from Hofstätter 1972, 64
13 from Hofstätter 1972, 65
14 from Hofstätter 1972, 72ff
15 from Hofstätter 1972, 51
16 H. H. Hofstätter, 'Die Bildwelt der symbolistischen Malerei', Symbolismus in Europa, exhibition catalogue Baden-Baden 1976, 14
17 from Hofstätter 1972, 24
18 from Hofstätter 1972, 24
19 from Hofstätter 1972, 29ff
20 from Nebehay 1969, 12
21 from Giese 1978, 60
22 from Giese 1978, 60
23 from W. Kitlitschka, 'Die Malerei der Wiener Ringstraße', Wagner-Rieger Vol. 10, 1981, 166
24 from Hofmann 1981, 10
25 Nebehay 1969, 120 n. 1
26 from Giese 1978–79, 65
27 Bahr 1900, 122
28 from Strobl 1980–1984 Vol. 1, 101
29 Hevesi 1906, 82
30 Hevesi 1906, 8
31 from Nebehay 1969, 148
32 from Strobl 1964, 142
33 from Strobl 1964, 142
34 from Strobl 1964, 144
35 from Nebehay 1969, 224
36 from Nebehay 1969, 225
37 from Strobl 1964, 152ff
38 from Strobl 1964, 152ff
39 from Novotny/Dobai 1967, 386
40 from Novotny/Dobai 1967, 386
41 from Novotny/Dobai 1967, 386
42 from Strobl 1964, 160
43 facsimile in Strobl 1964, 162
44 from Strobl 1964, 161ff
45 from Strobl 1980–84, Vol. 1, 151
46 from M. Bisanz-Prakken, 'Programmatik und subjektive Aussage im Werk von Gustav Klimt', Wien 1870–1930, 1984, 112ff
47 from M. Bisanz-Prakken, 'Programmatik und subjektive Aussage im Werk von Gustav Klimt', Wien 1870–1930, 1984, 113
48 from P. Vergo, 'Gustav Klimts "Philosophie" und das Programm der Universitätsgemälde', Klimt-Studien, 1978/79, 95
49 from Bisanz-Prakken 1980, 208
50 from Bisanz-Prakken 1980, 208
51 from Hevesi 1906, 392
52 from Hevesi 1906, 14
53 from Hevesi 1906, 22
54 see also Nebehay 1969, 283
55 F. Schiller, 'Ode to Joy'
56 from Bisanz-Prakken 1980, 49
57 from Bisanz-Prakken 1980, 49
58 from Bisanz-Prakken 1980, 50
59 from Bisanz-Prakken 1980, 50
60 see also Nebehay 1969, 266
61 from Fischer 1987, 195
62 A. Muthesius, 'Das Eigenkleid der Frau', Anziehungskräfte, Munich 1986, 452
63 from Nebehay 1969, 267
64 Nebehay 1969, 268
65 Nebehay 1969, 268 and 274
66 Fischer 1987, 170
67 Fischer 1987, 172
68 Fischer 1987, 176
69 Fischer 1987, 177
70 Fischer 1987, 178
71 Fischer 1987, 128
72 Fischer 1987, 23
73 A. Völker, 'Kleiderkunst und Reformmode im Wien der Jahrhundertwende', Anziehungskräfte, Munich 1986, 293
74 Schweiger 1982, 20
75 from Nebehay 1969, 237, n. 3
76 from Nebehay 1969, 237, n. 3
77 printed in Schweiger 1982, 42ff
78 from Schweiger 1982, 90
79 from Schweiger 1982, 90
80 from Schweiger 1982, 141
81 from Schweiger 1982, 60
82 A. Fridmann, 'Secessionistische Tafelfreuden', from Schweiger 1982, 60
83 Hevesi 1906, 311ff
84 from Nebehay 1969, 394

85 from Expressionisten. Avantgarde in Deutschland 1905–1920, Berlin 1986, 78
86 from Nebehay 1969, 423ff
87 from Schweiger 1982, 56ff
88 Fischer 1987, 181
89 from Schweiger 1982, 59
90 from Schweiger 1982, 52ff
91 from Nebehay 1969, 391
92 from Nebehay 1969, 391
93 from Fischer 1987, 184
94 from Fischer 1987, 173
95 Hermine Wittgenstein, unpublished family memories, from Zaunschirm 1987, 54
96 Hermine Wittgenstein, unpublished family memories, from Zaunschirm 1987, 77
97 Hofmann 1970, 18
98 K. Hauer, 'Weib und Kultur', 1978, from Zaunschirm 1987, 71ff
99 K. Hauer, 'Weib und Kultur', 1978, from Zaunschirm 1987, 72
100 K. Hauer, 'Weib und Kultur', 1978, from Zaunschirm 1987, 73ff
101 Fliedl 1985, 109
102 Fliedl 1985, 109
103 Varnedoe 1987, 161
104 Hevesi 1906, from Nebehay 1969, 428
105 A. Roessler, 'Klimt und seine Modelle', 1953, from Nebehay 1969, 428
106 from Nebehay 1969, 430
107 from Nebehay 1969, 430
108 Dobai 1971, 7
109 Fliedl 1985, 118
110 from Nebehay 1969, 428
111 from Nebehay 1969, 430
112 H. H. Hofstätter, Symbolismus und die Kunst der Jahrhundertwende, Cologne 1965, 216
113 Hofstätter 1979, 19
114 Fliedl 1985, 93ff
115 Fliedl 1985, 111
116 Fliedl 1985, 111ff
117 Fliedl 1985, 116ff
118 Nebehay 1969, 424
119 Nebehay 1969, 424
120 Fliedl 1985, 89
121 Pirchan 1942, 84
122 Varnedoe 1987, 159
123 Fliedl 1985, 123
124 Fischer 1987, 172
125 C. M. Nebehay, 'Gustav Klimt schreibt an eine Liebe', Klimt-Studien 1978–79, 109ff
126 C. M. Nebehay, 'Gustav Klimt schreibt an eine Liebe', Klimt-Studien 1978–79, 108ff
127 Hevesi 1906, 451
128 Dobai 1981, 13
129 C. M. Nebehay, 'Gustav Klimt schreibt an eine Liebe', Klimt-Studien 1978–79, 108
130 C. M. Nebehay, 'Gustav Klimt schreibt an eine Liebe', Klimt-Studien 1978–79, 19
131 C. M. Nebehay, 'Gustav Klimt schreibt an eine Liebe', Klimt-Studien 1978–79, 28
132 C. M. Nebehay, 'Gustav Klimt schreibt an eine Liebe', Klimt-Studien 1978–79, 35
133 Franz Servaes, from H. Bisanz 'Gustav Klimt-Zeichnungen und Vorstellungsbilder des Seelischen', in exhibition catalogue for 'Gustav Klimt, Zeichnungen', Vienna 1984, 11
134 from Nebehay 1969, 437
135 A. Roessler, 'In memoriam Gustav Klimt', Vienna 1926, from Nebehay 1969, 356
136 from Nebehay 1969, 359
137 from Nebehay 1969, 480
138 from Nebehay 1969, 488
139 from Nebehay 1969, 484
140 A. Roessler, 'Erinnerung an Egon Schiele', from Nebehay 1969, 461
141 from Nebehay 1969, 32
142 from Nebehay 1969, 54
143 Salten 1903, 12, from Nebehay 1969, 264
144 from Nebehay 1969, 263
145 from Nebehay 1969, 507
146 Zaunschirm 1987, 10
147 from Novotny/Dobai 1967, 392

The publisher is grateful to all the museums,
picture archives, galleries and private owners
for kind permission to reproduce the paintings
of Gustav Klimt.
Particular thanks go to Serge Sabarsky,
New York, for permission to reproduce the
drawings in this volume.
Finally the publisher gratefully
acknowledges the help and advice of
Gerbert Frodl of the Austrian Gallery
in Vienna.